DEVELOPING *the* THERAPEUTIC RELATIONSHIP

DEVELOPING *the* THERAPEUTIC RELATIONSHIP

Integrating Case Studies, Research, and Practice

Edited by
Orya Tishby and **Hadas Wiseman**

AMERICAN PSYCHOLOGICAL ASSOCIATION
Washington, DC

Published by
American Psychological Association
750 First Street, NE
Washington, DC 20002
www.apa.org

APA Order Department
P.O. Box 92984
Washington, DC 20090-2984
Phone: (800) 374-2721; Direct: (202) 336-5510
Fax: (202) 336-5502; TDD/TTY: (202) 336-6123
Online: http://www.apa.org/pubs/books
E-mail: order@apa.org

In the U.K., Europe, Africa, and the Middle East, copies may be ordered from
Eurospan Group
c/o Turpin Distribution
Pegasus Drive
Stratton Business Park
Biggleswade, Bedfordshire
SG18 8TQ United Kingdom
Phone: +44 (0) 1767 604972
Fax: +44 (0) 1767 601640
Online: https://www.eurospanbookstore.com/apa
E-mail: eurospan@turpin-distribution.com

Typeset in Goudy by Circle Graphics, Inc., Columbia, MD

Printer: Sheridan Books, Chelsea, MI
Cover Designer: Nicci Falcone, Gaithersburg, MD

Library of Congress Cataloging-in-Publication Data

Names: Tishby, Orya, editor. | Wiseman, Hadas, 1956- editor. | American Psychological Association, issuing body.
Title: Developing the therapeutic relationship : integrating case studies, research, and practice / [edited by] Orya Tishby, Hadas Wiseman.
Description: First edition. | Washington, DC : American Psychological Association, [2018] | Includes bibliographical references and index.
Identifiers: LCCN 2018000039 | ISBN 9781433829222 | ISBN 1433829223
Subjects: | MESH: Psychotherapy | Professional-Patient Relations | Case Reports
Classification: LCC RA440.6 | NLM WM 420 | DDC 616.89/14—dc23
LC record available at https://lccn.loc.gov/2018000039

British Library Cataloguing-in-Publication Data
A CIP record is available from the British Library.

Printed in the United States of America
First Edition

http://dx.doi.org/10.1037/0000093-000

10 9 8 7 6 5 4 3 2 1

To Tali, Avner, Ido, Noa, and Yael
—*Orya Tishby*

To Itzik, Adi, and Uri
—*Hadas Wiseman*

CONTENTS

Contributors .... *xi*

Introduction 3
Orya Tishby and Hadas Wiseman

Chapter 1. The Psychotherapy Relationship: Where Does the Alliance Fit? 15
Adam O. Horvath

I. The Case Studies: Integrating Research and Practice 29

Chapter 2. You Can't Cross the Same River Twice: A Case Study of Alliance Rupture and Repair 31
Laura Kohberger, Jeremy D. Safran, and J. Christopher Muran

Chapter 3. Patient and Therapist Relational Patterns: Implicit Negotiations 61
Emanuel Schattner and Orya Tishby

Chapter 4. Closeness and Distance Dynamics in the Therapeutic Relationship 81
Hadas Wiseman and Dana Atzil-Slonim

Chapter 5. Facilitating the Sense of Feeling Understood in Patients With Maladaptive Relationships 105
Sigal Zilcha-Mano and Jacques P. Barber

Chapter 6. Clinical Choice Points and Professional Ethics in Psychoanalysis 133
Gaby Shefler

Chapter 7. The Therapeutic Relationship: A Warm, Important, and Potentially Mutative Factor in Cognitive–Behavioral Therapy 157
Louis G. Castonguay, Soo Jeong Youn, Henry Xiao, and Andrew A. McAleavey

Chapter 8. Negotiating Multiple Roles and Stances in Cognitive–Behavioral Therapy 181
Yoni Elizur and Jonathan D. Huppert

Chapter 9. Affirming the Case for Positive Regard 211
Barry A. Farber and Jessica Y. Suzuki

Chapter 10. Empathy and Responsiveness in Emotion-Focused Therapy...235
Jeanne C. Watson

Chapter 11. Where the Alliance and Systems Theory Meet in Brief Family Therapy 257
Laurie Heatherington, Valentín Escudero, and Myrna L. Friedlander

Chapter 12. The Use of Immediacy in Supervisory Relationships...... 289
Clara E. Hill and Shudarshana Gupta

II. Mapping Models and Conclusions **315**

Chapter 13. Mapping Models of the Therapeutic Relationship: Implications for Integrative Practice 317
Stanley B. Messer and Daniel B. Fishman

Chapter 14. Conclusions: The Tapestry of the Therapeutic Relationship and Recommendations for Clinicians and Researchers.......341
Orya Tishby and Hadas Wiseman

Index....... 349

About the Editors....... 361

CONTRIBUTORS

Dana Atzil-Slonim, PhD, Lecturer, and Director, Clinical Training Program, Department of Psychology, Bar-Ilan University, Ramat Gan, Israel

Jacques P. Barber, PhD, Professor and Dean, Gordon F. Derner School of Psychology, Adelphi University, Garden City, NY

Louis G. Castonguay, PhD, Professor of Psychology, Department of Psychology, Pennsylvania State University, University Park

Yoni Elizur, Doctoral Candidate, Hebrew University of Jerusalem, Israel

Valentín Escudero, PhD, Professor, Department of Psychology, Universidade da Coruña, Spain

Barry A. Farber, PhD, Professor of Psychology and Education, Clinical Psychology Program, Teachers College, Columbia University, New York, NY

Daniel B. Fishman, PhD, Professor, Graduate School of Applied and Professional Psychology, Rutgers University, New Brunswick, NJ

Myrna L. Friedlander, PhD, Professor, Department of Educational and Counseling Psychology, University at Albany, State University of New York

Shudarshana Gupta, PhD, Diversity Coordinator and Staff Clinician, Counseling Center, Towson University, Towson, MD

Laurie Heatherington, PhD, Edward Dorr Griffin Professor of Psychology, Department of Psychology, Williams College, Williamstown, MA

Clara E. Hill, PhD, Professor, Department of Psychology, University of Maryland, College Park

Adam O. Horvath, EdD, Professor Emeritus, Faculty of Education, Simon Fraser University, Burnaby, British Columbia, Canada

Jonathan D. Huppert, PhD, Professor, Department of Psychology, Hebrew University of Jerusalem, Israel

Laura Kohberger, PhD, Supervising Clinical Psychologist, Herald Square Psychology Group, New York, NY

Andrew A. McAleavey, PhD, Instructor of Psychology in Psychiatry, Weill Cornell Medicine, New York, NY

Stanley B. Messer, PhD, Distinguished Professor, Graduate School of Applied and Professional Psychology, Rutgers University, New Brunswick, NJ

J. Christopher Muran, PhD, Professor and Associate Dean, Gordon F. Derner School of Psychology, Adelphi University, Garden City, NY; and Director, Mount Sinai Beth Israel Psychotherapy Research Program, Mount Sinai School of Medicine, New York, NY

Jeremy D. Safran, PhD, Professor of Psychology, New School for Social Research, New York, NY

Emanuel Schattner, PhD, Clinical Psychologist, private practice; and Supervisor of Mental Health Clinics, Herzog Hospital, Jerusalem, Israel

Gaby Shefler, PhD, Professor and Head, Freud Center for Psychoanalytical Research, Hebrew University of Jerusalem, Israel

Jessica Y. Suzuki, MPhil, Doctoral Candidate, Teachers College, Columbia University, New York, NY; and psychology intern, Mount Sinai Beth Israel Hospital, New York, NY

Orya Tishby, PsyD, Associate Professor in Clinical Psychology and Clinical Social Work, Hebrew University of Jerusalem, Israel

Jeanne C. Watson, PhD, C Psych, Professor and Program Chair, Counseling and Clinical Psychology Program, Department of Applied Psychology and Human Development, University of Toronto, Ontario, Canada

Hadas Wiseman, PhD, Professor, Counseling and Human Development, University of Haifa, Israel

Henry Xiao, MS, Graduate Assistant, Castonguay Lab, Pennsylvania State University, University Park
Soo Jeong Youn, PhD, Clinical Fellow, Department of Psychiatry, Massachusetts General Hospital, Harvard Medical School, Boston
Sigal Zilcha-Mano, PhD, Associate Professor, Department of Psychology, University of Haifa, Israel

DEVELOPING *the* THERAPEUTIC RELATIONSHIP

INTRODUCTION

ORYA TISHBY AND HADAS WISEMAN

During the last 2 decades, remarkable progress has been made in psychotherapy research, specifically in the development of evidence-based treatments for a range of disorders (e.g., Barlow, 2014; Lambert, 2013; Nathan & Gorman, 2002; Norcross & Wampold, 2011; Weisz & Kazdin, 2010). However, the mechanisms through which these therapies influence outcome are generally not yet well understood (Barber, Muran, McCarthy, & Keefe, 2013; Barber & Sharpless, 2015; Kazdin, 2011) and, furthermore, the strategy of matching research-based treatments to specific disorders is not always effective (Wampold & Imel, 2015). Attempts to delineate the active ingredients in the different treatments have pitted treatment methods against relationship variables, or *specific* versus *common* factors, as core mechanisms of change in the therapy process (Castonguay, 2011; Norcross & Lambert, 2011). However, years of research have shown that studying technique and relationship variables as separate entities yields inconsistent results, suggesting

http://dx.doi.org/10.1037/0000093-001
Developing the Therapeutic Relationship: Integrating Case Studies, Research, and Practice, O. Tishby and H. Wiseman (Editors)

that different change mechanisms play different roles with different clients (e.g., Webb, DeRubeis, & Barber, 2010; Webb et al., 2012).

In light of this, researchers have shifted the focus to how relationship variables and techniques interact with one another and affect outcome in different treatment modalities, and how technique is applied in the context of a particular relationship (Castonguay & Beutler, 2005; Goldfried & Davila, 2005; Hill, 2005; Horvath, Del Re, Flückiger, & Symonds, 2011). One of the conclusions of the second APA task force on the therapeutic relationship (Norcross & Wampold, 2011) was that "the relationship acts in concert with treatment methods, patient characteristics and practitioner qualities in determining effectiveness; a comprehensive understanding of effective (and ineffective) psychotherapy will consider all these determinants and their optimal combination" (p. 423).

In the reality of clinical practice, technique and relationship are intertwined and cannot be neatly separated—the therapy process consists of a synergy between technique and relationship. Applying a specific technique may strengthen the bond, whereas a strong bond may support the use of techniques that move clients out of their comfort zone. In our quest to gain a deeper understanding of what facilitates or hinders therapeutic process, we need to find new ways of conceptualizing and studying the complexity inherent in such interrelated processes during the unfolding of therapeutic relationships in practice.

ORIGINS OF THE BOOK

This book originated from a research workshop held in Jerusalem called "Multiple Lenses on the Therapeutic Relationship." As an extension of our collaboration in the Jerusalem–Haifa psychodynamic psychotherapy study (see Chapters 3 and 4), we invited leading psychotherapy researchers and clinicians to take part in the 3-day workshop. The key speakers addressed theoretical underpinnings, client–therapist relationship processes and experiences, client and therapist variables, techniques versus the relationship and outcome, and implications for training therapists (Wiseman & Tishby, 2014). On the last day of the workshop, we gathered for a closed meeting (without an audience) to watch videos of clinical cases in order to discuss "hands on" how to translate the presented contributions into practice. The focus on moment-to-moment process in specific cases treated by leading therapists who took part as speakers led to challenging "how" questions, including: How does the relationship work? How does the therapist make decisions on how to intervene? and, How similar or different are therapists of different orientations?

For example, in a video that Robert DeRubeis showed of himself conducting therapy with a patient who was extremely depressed, we were all struck by the centrality of his empathic reflection and affirming positive regard that went way beyond cognitive–behavioral therapy (CBT). In fact, if we had to guess the orientation of this therapist, we would probably not have easily recognized it as CBT. The lively clinical discussions highlighted the usefulness of intensive study of clinical cases in gaining a deeper understanding of therapeutic process and its relation to outcome. The choice to study clinical cases resonated with Stanley Messer's presentation to the group of his formulation with Dan Fishman of the methodology for pragmatic cases studies.

One product of the conference was a special issue of *Psychotherapy Research* called The Therapeutic Relationship: Innovative Investigations. The articles presented an array of empirical studies in which the contributors offered innovative ways of studying various relationship mechanisms as they relate to change processes and outcomes (Wiseman & Tishby, 2014). While the special issue, which was later published as a book (Wiseman & Tishby, 2015), fulfilled our intention of contributing to innovative research, the present book integrates theory, research, and practice in the form of case studies and has the potential to contribute more fully to practitioners, trainees, and supervisors. In other words, the culmination of our work together is our desire to build bridges between practitioners and researchers. We also believe that such bridges will contribute to the professional development of graduate students who can be trained as clinical researchers without having to choose one over the other.

OUR PURPOSE AND RATIONALE

This book examines the development of the therapeutic relationship through different "lenses" based on theory, research, and practice. Research on the therapeutic alliance shows that its contribution to outcome cuts across theoretical orientations (Flückiger, Del Re, Wampold, Symonds, & Horvath, 2012); however, we believe that this process develops in different ways in various types of therapies. Our contention is that the methodology of case studies (Chapter 13) is highly suited for examining in-depth links between relationship process and technique that enhance therapy process, leading to beneficial outcome. The authors of the chapters are clinicians who are also psychotherapy researchers; they faced the challenge of integrating their case studies with research and practice. In each chapter, they present a relationship conceptualization that guided them (involving *both* patient and therapist) and demonstrate through the case study how it contributes, together with technique, to successful outcome. Emphasis is on the unfolding of the client–therapist interaction and the development of the therapeutic relationship in their case study, rather than on discrete relationship variables (e.g., empathy, alliance, self-disclosure) or on schools of psychotherapy.

In examining the process of change in the case studies, the authors of each chapter outline their theoretical basis for the case (which may represent one or more models of psychotherapy) and describe the course of therapy.[1] In addition to the detailed case analysis in each chapter, the authors' relevant research supporting these relational concepts and their connections to process and outcome are presented. The contribution of their research to their clinical understanding and practice and to training is highlighted, as well as the contribution of practice to their research. Thus, we aim to demonstrate the mutual influence of research and practice, leading to strengthening the connections and dialogue between these two fields.

OVERVIEW OF THE CHAPTERS: INTEGRATING CASE STUDIES, THEORY, RESEARCH, AND PRACTICE

The book begins with an overview of the therapeutic relationship, and its centrality to the therapeutic process (Chapter 1). The chapter presents four main theoretical "threads," delineating different functions of the client–therapist relationship and how they facilitate therapy process. The chapter emphasizes the need to discover which parts of the therapy relationship are shared among different kinds of treatments, and which parts are unique. It also recommends examining specific ways in which the interactive nature of psychotherapy is differently manifested and utilized in a variety of contexts.

Eleven clinical case studies (Chapters 2–12) follow, describing a variety of relationship aspects and how they are manifested in different therapies. As volume editors, we were faced with a dilemma: to give the contributors as much freedom as they needed to present their ideas and case studies or to ask them to adhere to guidelines in order to provide a common framework. We resolved this by providing them the essential guidelines for the chapters, while accepting that some chapters would follow them more closely than others. We presented authors with the following overarching guideline:

Describe an aspect of the client–therapist relationship that you will be focusing on. The description should clearly depict a relational process between patient and therapist. This will be the "lens" through which you will analyze the case. Use the following five areas to discuss the case:

[1]Note: Case examples have been disguised to protect client confidentiality.

1. *A theoretical/conceptual basis for this relational process.* The conceptual basis can be drawn from any theoretical model of therapy, an integration of theories, or it can be transtheoretical.
2. *The clinical case study:*
   - Presenting problem and patient description.
   - Formal assessment and any quantitative measures that measure level of patient distress and outcome (e.g., standardized self-report questionnaires, clinician-rated instruments like the Structured Clinical Interview for *DSM–IV*).
   - Provide measures of relationship (e.g., alliance or Early Experience of Close Relationships or transference) and measures of technique (e.g., Multitheoretical List of Interventions, Comparative Psychotherapy Process Scale) if they were used in this case.
   - Initial interviews and case formulation.
   - Course of treatment: Focus on relationship concepts and how they interact with technique, clinical choice points, and relevant feedback leading to adaptations or changes in process and significant moments in therapy that moved the process along.
   - Outcome and prognosis: Include results from relevant quantitative measures.

   All identifying data should be changed, so that the patients cannot be recognized.
3. *Summary of the mechanisms of change* involving both relationship and/or technique factors and their interaction described in both qualitative and, when possible, quantitative terms.
4. *Research to practice and back:* Quantitative and qualitative measures used in research that are relevant to your concept and can be applied to practice and training.
5. *Practice implications and recommendations for clinicians and supervisors.*

It may come as no surprise that there is a built-in tension between these specific guidelines and the variations required to keep the clinical richness of the cases and to capitalize on the clinically and empirically informed insights and visions of our contributors.

ORGANIZATION OF THE BOOK

As indicated above, our goal was to present the development of the therapeutic relationship through different "lenses" based on theory, practice, and research. Although our emphasis is on microtheories of change (Cunha et al., 2012; Stiles, Hill, & Elliott, 2015) rather than on broad-based schools of psychotherapy, the contributors of the clinical cases formulated their conceptual lenses in the broader context of specific schools. Some adhere more closely to a specific school than others, but what is common to all is going beyond the boundaries of a specific major school of psychotherapy and breaking new ground for understanding what takes place between the client and therapist.

Schools of Psychotherapy

The chapters herein are organized under four broad schools of psychotherapy.

Psychodynamic and Psychoanalytic

Five chapters represent various modes of psychodynamic therapy and psychoanalysis, in which the therapeutic relationship is a key mechanism of change. These therapies examine the relationship on both conscious and unconscious levels, and from both the therapist's and the client's perspective. In psychodynamic therapy, the relationship as a means serves not only of creating a safe environment but also of reflecting various aspects of the client's inner world and interpersonal patterns that are a focus for change. Each of the five chapters thus focuses on a different relational aspect.

Kohberger, Safran, and Muran (Chapter 2) examine ruptures and repairs in the alliance in two successive courses of brief relational therapy with the same client. The process of identifying ruptures and attempting repairs helps clients gain a deeper understanding of their relationship patterns and creates an opportunity to experience new relationship patterns with the therapist. In this chapter, the authors examine how ruptures were addressed by each of the two therapists, and the relation of rupture and repair work to the outcome of the two treatments. Schattner and Tishby (Chapter 3) look at patterns of transference and countertransference in a successful case of psychodynamic therapy. Using the core conflictual relationship theme method, they identify core relational patterns of therapist and patient, and how these patterns play out in the therapy relationship. Wiseman and Atzil-Slonim (Chapter 4) rely on a conceptual combination of attachment theory and contemporary relational thinking about the mutual impact client and therapist have on each other in the process of change as the lens for the development of the therapeutic relationship. They address the issue of the subjective sense of closeness and distance in the relationship during the course of therapy as depicted in relational narratives and how it relates to therapist's and patient's attachment styles. Zilcha-Mano and Barber (Chapter 5) focus on patients' experience of feeling understood in treatment. They present two case studies to examine how patients' interpersonal patterns influence their ability to feel understood in treatment, whether the therapist actively deploys strategies to make the patient feel understood, and whether the patient indeed feels understood as a result of these efforts, which is the result not only of the patient's traitlike tendencies but also of the actual interactions between the therapist and the patient in the therapy room. The final chapter among the psychodynamic chapters is by Shefler (Chapter 6), who describes the dilemma of adhering to the classical psychoanalytic setting even when there is a risk of straining the alliance. He presents two clinical vignettes that show that maintaining professional boundaries can at times turn against the therapy process, and that the therapist has to make difficult choices regarding whether to break those boundaries in order to maintain the alliance.

The supervisory relationship provides the template for developing the therapy relationship. Thus, by focusing on the processing of the relationship in supervision, supervisees can incorporate these supervisor–supervisee experiences into their clinical work. Hill and Gupta (Chapter 12) apply the concept of "immediacy" (talking about the here and now in the relationship), which they have studied in the therapeutic relationship to the supervisory process. They present several vignettes that show how the use of immediacy helped resolve problems or tensions in supervision, which in turn helped supervisees in their work with clients.

Cognitive and Cognitive–Behavioral Therapy

Traditionally, the relationship in cognitive and CBT is a necessary but not a sufficient condition for successful therapy. In the two chapters in this section, the authors demonstrate the ways in which the therapeutic relationship becomes part of the process, although in ways that differ from psychodynamic therapy. Castonguay, Youn, Xiao, and McAleavey (Chapter 7) integrate relational concepts from other therapy models, such as addressing ruptures and repairs, in order to improve the efficacy of CBT. In their case example, they describe how the client missed several sessions, saying that he had felt judged in therapy. The therapist, instead of working on cognitive biases, focused on the rupture and even used some self-disclosure in order to repair the rupture and set the therapy back on track. Elizur and Huppert (Chapter 8) describe the different roles that the CBT therapist plays in the relationship, including that of expert, salesperson, ally against avoidance, and coach. These roles are described in detail in the treatment of a woman with social anxiety disorder.

Humanistic Psychotherapy, Emotion-Focused Therapy, and Experiential Therapy

Farber and Suzuki (Chapter 9) present the case for positive regard, demonstrating the impact of positive regard in the therapy of a young woman who had been abused as a child. The authors describe positive regard as "most effectively conveyed through multiple and ever-changing expressions of both verbal and nonverbal communication" (p. 212). Watson (Chapter 10) focuses on the central role of therapist empathy and responsiveness in emotion-focused therapy. She focuses on listening to clients closely and responding to their emotional needs in the moment and emphasizes attunement, acceptance, congruence, and warmth, and how these qualities contribute to changes in clients' self-structures.

Family Systems Therapy

Heatherington, Escudero, and Friedlander (Chapter 11) demonstrate the importance of engaging with each family member and with the family as a whole, in order to foster a sense of safety to facilitate family work. The relationship is not processed, and it is not in itself a mechanism of change. However, different creative interventions, attuned to each family member, are employed in order to build strong alliances.

Understanding the Therapeutic Relationship Framework

Chapter 13, by Messer and Fishman, offers a general framework for organizing these chapters (2–12) according to the different foci and lenses on the therapeutic relationship. This framework maps each chapter along two major dimensions: (a) The therapist's goal in establishing a relationship vis-à-vis therapeutic change: Is the relationship a necessary but insufficient component, or is it the central focus of therapy? (b) How directly does the technique address the therapeutic relationship versus techniques that impact the relationship, although they do not address it directly? These two dimensions form a two-by-two grid with four cells, and the cases are placed in their respective cells. Thus, readers can get an overall grasp of the similarities and differences between the different therapies in terms of the centrality of the relationship and its function in each treatment.

WHAT CAN TRAINERS AND SUPERVISORS GAIN FROM THE CASES?

This book can be used in a number of ways for training and supervision for both beginning and advanced trainees. The debate on how to teach psychotherapy (e.g., Castonguay, Eubanks, Goldfried, Muran, & Lutz, 2015;

Romano, Orlinsky, Wiseman, & Rønnestad, 2010), whether through separate courses on each major school of therapy or through common principles (e.g., insight, corrective experience) is also relevant to the way trainers can use the cases in this book. For beginning therapists, it would be helpful to focus on several individual chapters, defining and illustrating the relational concept that is at the heart of the chapter and how it plays out in the clinical case. It would probably be helpful to start with some didactic knowledge of basic concepts in a given model so that beginners could follow more closely the unfolding therapy process. For instance, to learn from the chapter on how family systems and alliance meet, some basic understanding of systems theory needs to be acquired and then be followed by reading and reflecting on the alliance as it plays out with different family members. More advanced trainees would be better equipped to compare and contrast the relationship themes presented in each chapter and think about how they could be used in therapy in different ways. For those, the Messer and Fishman grid (Chapter 13) would serve as a fruitful and broader prism to appreciate the breadth and complexity of the relationship. We propose that the chapters in this book can actually constitute an outline for a course syllabus on the therapeutic relationship. In addition to reading chapters, course instructors could accompany the chapters with demonstration video recordings to identify and observe these relationship processes, as well as to generate exercises to practice them.

One central theme that emerges from these clinical cases is the importance of monitoring the relationship throughout treatment. The supervisor can pick which process in the relationship he or she views the trainee as ready to apply, and can focus on guiding the trainee to attend to it and choose the relevant techniques to facilitate the process. As trainees gain experience and confidence, the supervisor can broaden their relational perspective by focusing on additional concepts the trainees can learn to recognize and monitor. A case in point is the use of types of immediacy, which requires some level of confidence before the supervisee can implement it with their clients. As Hill and Gupta suggest, the use of immediacy in supervision is a good way to experientially teach supervisees its application in the therapies they conduct. Such extensions for creative applications in supervision could be used with other relational themes and layers that are described in the chapters.

We hope that by integrating relationship and technique in innovative ways our book will appeal to clinicians from diverse orientations who will be able to draw on the relational concepts presented in the cases. In presenting research linked to clinical practice, we also hope to pique the interest of clinicians to conduct research, with the goal of improving the therapy we offer our clients.

REFERENCES

Barber, J. P., Muran, C. J., McCarthy, K. S., & Keefe, J. R. (2013). Research on dynamic therapies. In M. J. Lambert (Ed.), *Bergin and Garfield's handbook of psychotherapy and behavior change* (6th ed., pp. 443–494). New York, NY: Wiley.

Barber, J. P., & Sharpless, B. A. (2015). On the future of psychodynamic therapy research. *Psychotherapy Research, 25*, 309–320. http://dx.doi.org/10.1080/10503307.2014.996624

Barlow, D. (Ed.). (2014). *Clinical handbook of psychological disorders* (5th ed.). New York, NY: Guilford Press.

Castonguay, L. G. (2011). Psychotherapy, psychopathology, research and practice: Pathways of connections and integration. *Psychotherapy Research, 21*, 125–140. http://dx.doi.org/10.1080/10503307.2011.563250

Castonguay, L. G., & Beutler, L. E. (2005). *Principles of therapeutic change that work.* New York, NY: Oxford University Press.

Castonguay, L. G., Eubanks, C. F., Goldfried, M. R., Muran, J. C., & Lutz, W. (2015). Research on psychotherapy integration: Building on the past, looking to the future. *Psychotherapy Research, 25*, 365–82. http://dx.doi.org/10.1080/10503307.2015.1014010

Cunha, C., Gonçalves, M. M., Hill, C. E., Mendes, I., Ribeiro, A. P., Sousa, I., . . . Greenberg, L. S. (2012). Therapist interventions and client innovative moments in emotion-focused therapy for depression. *Psychotherapy, 49*, 536–548. http://dx.doi.org/10.1037/a0028259

Flückiger, C., Del Re, A. C., Wampold, B. E., Symonds, D., & Horvath, A. O. (2012). How central is the alliance in psychotherapy? A multilevel longitudinal meta-analysis. *Journal of Counseling Psychology, 59*, 10–17. http://dx.doi.org/10.1037/a0025749

Goldfried, M. R., & Davila, J. (2005). The role of relationship and technique in therapeutic change. *Psychotherapy, 42*, 421–430. http://dx.doi.org/10.1037/0033-3204.42.4.421

Hill, C. E. (2005). Therapist techniques, client involvement, and the therapeutic relationship: Inextricably intertwined in the therapy process. *Psychotherapy, 42*, 431–442. http://dx.doi.org/10.1037/0033-3204.42.4.431

Horvath, A. O., Del Re, A. C., Flückiger, C., & Symonds, D. (2011). Alliance in individual psychotherapy. *Psychotherapy, 48*, 9–16. http://dx.doi.org/10.1037/a0022186

Kazdin, A. E. (2011). Evidence-based treatment research: Advances, limitations, and next steps. *American Psychologist, 66*, 685–698. http://dx.doi.org/10.1037/a0024975

Lambert, M. (2013). Introduction and historical overview. In M. Lambert (Ed.), *Bergin and Garfield's handbook of psychotherapy and behavior change* (6th ed., pp. 3–19). New York, NY: Wiley.

Nathan, P. E., & Gorman, J. M. (Eds.). (2002). *A guide to treatments that work* (2nd ed.). New York, NY: Oxford University Press.

Norcross, J. C., & Lambert, M. J. (2011). Psychotherapy relationships that work II. *Psychotherapy, 48*, 4–8. http://dx.doi.org/10.1037/a0022180

Norcross, J. C., & Wampold, B. E. (2011). Evidence-based therapy relationships: Research conclusions and clinical practices. *Psychotherapy, 48*, 98–102. http://dx.doi.org/10.1037/a0022161

Romano, V., Orlinsky, D. E., Wiseman, H., & Rønnestad, M. H. (2010, June). *Theoretical breadth early in the psychotherapist's career: Help or hindrance*. Paper presented in the international meeting of the Society for Psychotherapy Research. Asilomar, CA.

Stiles, W. B., Hill, C. E., & Elliott, R. (2015). Looking both ways. *Psychotherapy Research, 25*, 282–293. http://dx.doi.org/10.1080/10503307.2014.981681

Wampold, B. E., & Imel, Z. E. (2015). *The great psychotherapy debate: The evidence for what makes psychotherapy work* (2nd ed.). New York, NY: Routledge.

Webb, C. A., DeRubeis, R. J., & Barber, J. P. (2010). Therapist adherence/competence and treatment outcome: A meta-analytic review. *Journal of Consulting and Clinical Psychology, 78*, 200–211. http://dx.doi.org/10.1037/a0018912

Webb, C. A., DeRubeis, R. J., Dimidjian, S., Hollon, S. D., Amsterdam, J. D., & Shelton, R. C. (2012). Predictors of patient cognitive therapy skills and symptom change in two randomized clinical trials: The role of therapist adherence and the therapeutic alliance. *Journal of Consulting and Clinical Psychology, 80*, 373–381.

Weisz, J. R., & Kazdin, A. E. (Eds.). (2010). *Evidence-based psychotherapies for children and adolescents*. New York, NY: Guilford Press.

Wiseman, H., & Tishby, O. (2014). The therapeutic relationship: Multiple lenses and innovations. Introduction to the special section. *Psychotherapy Research, 24*, 251–256. http://dx.doi.org/10.1080/10503307.2014.892648

Wiseman, H., & Tishby, O. (Eds.). (2015). *The therapeutic relationship: Innovative investigations*. New York, NY: Routledge.

1

THE PSYCHOTHERAPY RELATIONSHIP: WHERE DOES THE ALLIANCE FIT?

ADAM O. HORVATH

THE RELATIONSHIPS IN PSYCHOTHERAPY

In the most fundamental sense, psychotherapy is about relationships: Clients seek therapy to help them to come to terms with personal relations that are broken or painful, to restore dissonant relations with their inner selves, and for healing difficult connections between "me and the world." Indeed, it can be argued that psychotherapy achieved the status of a profession rooted in science when Freud discarded Charcot and his colleagues' method based on suggestibility (hypnosis) and invented "talk therapy" rooted in the idea of the power of intimate conversation. He proposed a relational framework both for the origin of psychological problems and also for their cure. In essence, his innovative insight was that a very special kind of relationship can be forged between doctor and patient, and in such an interpersonal context

http://dx.doi.org/10.1037/0000093-002
Developing the Therapeutic Relationship: Integrating Case Studies, Research, and Practice, O. Tishby and H. Wiseman (Editors)

the client's past traumas would be reexperienced dynamically and thus be made amenable to change.

A century has passed since these propositions were first published, and the practice of psychotherapy has developed in many different directions. By some counts, there are in excess of 500 named therapies today. While this count may be debated, and many items in such lists overlap, clearly we have witnessed the evolution of a number of distinct and efficacious ways of providing talk therapy to clients. But the unique thread that links these different kinds of treatment modalities—the common denominator—is the special connection between the helper and the person or persons seeking relief.

Therapy relationships have unique qualities; in many respects, they are unlike other social connections: Therapists and clients get together for a purpose, which is the improvement of the client's psychological condition the duration of the relationship (as a *therapy* relationship) is transient and comes to end when these goals are accomplished. The benefits to each party in the relationship are asymmetrical, and there are special formalities and ethical conditions that constrain what is permissible in these relationships. Helper and helpee connectedness can be framed as a contractual, temporary "partnership" forged only to achieve a common purpose.

Yet, on another level, therapists and clients are present for each other as "themselves," unique individuals with personalities, "character," and idiosyncratic presence. In this sense, they encounter each other in the context of therapy in ways similar to other close relationships. These layers and elements of the therapy relationship interact with the range of theoretical and practical features embedded in each kind of therapy praxis. The result is a wide range of "ideal" relational matrices, in which different features or elements of the relationship play different parts, of more or lesser importance. And, taken together, the therapist–client relation, the *therapy relationship* as such, plays different roles in facilitating client change. A detailed review of the full range of the ways the role of relationship in therapy is conceptualized is beyond the scope of this contribution. However, I will argue that there are four main, more or less interwoven "threads" or perspectives that have evolved on this topic.

Perhaps the oldest thread is based on the premise that the client's relationship with the therapist functions as a mirror or projection of past and present relationships. This concept can be traced back to Freud (1913). Arguably his greatest intellectual achievement was his work on the concept of transference, the idea that seminal past relationships—unresolved conflicts—are unconsciously projected onto and reenacted with the therapist. He proposed that the nonreactive, "abstinent" therapist serves as a blank screen, providing the client with the opportunity to reexperience and rework these unresolved relational crises. He also clearly identified the therapeutic opportunities such experiences offered: "The whole series of psychological experiences are relived, not as belonging to the past, but applying to the person of the physician *at the present moment* [emphasis added]" (Freud, 1963, p. 24). And going further: "It [transference] is a universal phenomenon of the human mind, it decides the success of all medical influence, and in fact dominates the whole of each person's relations to his human environment" (Freud & Strachey, 1963, p. 26).

Rogers (1951), influenced by existential perspectives on the nature of genuine human relationships (e.g., Buber & Agassi, 1999), also conceptualized the helper–helpee relationship as an active component of therapy and an essential source of change. Instead of proposing an unconscious process as the key mechanism in the therapeutic relationship, he argued that if the therapist is able to offer the client a positive, honest, accepting, and empathetic interpersonal relationship, such an interpersonal context would provide the client with a sense of safety, acceptance, and a feeling of being valued as the person they genuinely experience themselves to be. Rogers's framework generalizes to the proposition that such a relationship with a significant other generates unique opportunities for clients to explore all aspects of their self, including parts that have been repressed or denied, as well as parts that may be shameful or feared. Under these special circumstances, false selves can be discarded; disowned aspects of the genuine personality can be rediscovered, reabsorbed, and accommodated; and growth and healing will occur (Elliott, Bohart, Watson, & Greenberg, 2011; Rogers, Gendlin, Kiesler, & Truax, 1967; Stiles, Honos-Webb, & Surko, 1998).

The third thread is based on the idea that a positive relationship between therapist and client generates confidence in the therapist and reinforces faith in the therapy process (Goldfried, 1980). Confidence and trust in the therapist and belief that the resources made available by the particular treatment offered are efficacious are thought to have a positive impact on the client's acceptance of the therapist's recommendations and to promote compliance with therapeutic tasks such as homework and record keeping and the like. This framing of the role of the relationship as facilitative, but not in and of itself an active ingredient of change, is particularly compatible with treatments based on the cognitive behavior—learning-based theories of treatment and has been explicitly or tacitly adopted by CBT oriented clinicians.

The fourth major framework for the role of the relationship is based on the idea that the relationship within therapy provides the clients an opportunity to experiment with and try out new, healthier relational patterns (Castonguay, 2000). The safe confines of the therapy sessions offer clients a chance to experiment with new relational schemas, and they offer safe opportunities to take risks, expose vulnerabilities, and experience novel modalities "being with another" (Huang, Hill, Strauss, Heyman, & Hussain, 2016).

These four notions of the role of the relationship in therapy have been utilized and emphasized to different degrees in the traditional comprehensive theories of therapy (e.g., psychodynamic, behavioral–cognitive, systems, Rogerian/person-centered). Each of these theories has provided a fairly clear and cohesive framework for the role and function of the relationship in treatment. The psychodynamic and person-centered models put the relation between the client and the therapist at the core of the treatment agenda: The therapist utilizes and "leverages" the relationship with the client to achieve the goals of therapy. The relationship is construed as an active ingredient of treatment. Learning theory–based/behavioral models are more likely to position different aspects of the relationship as parts of the facilitative context that enhances the effectiveness of the prescriptive elements of treatment (DeRubeis & Feeley, 1991).

The brief summary presented so far describes the status of theorizing about the roles of the therapy relationship up to approximately the end of the 1970s. Toward the later part of the decade, a number of seminal quantitative research syntheses contrasting the effectiveness of psychological treatments based on different theories were published (e.g., Luborsky, Singer, & Luborsky, 1975; Smith & Glass, 1977; Stiles, Shapiro, & Elliot, 1986). Each of these analyses (and their subsequent replications) reached similar conclusions. Psychotherapy, in general, is effective in reducing symptoms of and/or shortening the length of suffering for clients. But, across the full spectrum of psychological and psychiatric treatments, therapies based on what previously were perceived as incompatible theories of treatment yielded roughly equivalent results (Wampold, 2001). A popular interpretation of these findings became known as the Dodo Bird verdict, referencing a quote from Lewis Carroll's (1865) whimsical novel *Alice's Adventures in Wonderland*, "Everybody has won and all must have prizes." Discovering no compelling links between specific theories and treatment effectiveness was frequently interpreted as an indication that therapies based on diverse theoretical premises must share some common underlying ingredients. The idea that some factors/ingredients common to different treatments are responsible for making psychotherapy "work" was not new. Rosenzweig (1936) and Frank (1961) put forward similar ideas decades before. But the studies on which the "Dodo bird verdict" was built provided strong empirical support for the common factor model, and raised questions about the long-standing assumption that treatments were effective because they implemented the "specific active ingredients" proposed by the theory they were based on (Ahn & Wampold, 2001). While the Dodo Bird interpretation of these meta-analytic results did not go uncontested (e.g., Chambless, 2002; DeRubeis & Feeley, 1991), the logic pointing to the presence of important common factors was compelling, and the hypothesis that there were "hardwired" connections between effective treatment modalities and theories of psychopathology became suspect. One of the significant consequences of the meta-analyses responsible for the Dodo Bird conclusion was a strong reawakening of interest in discovering common threads, shared effective ingredients, present in all forms of treatments. The client–therapist relationship is one of the obvious candidates of such a common factor (Horvath, 2011a). These developments formed the important historical–intellectual context in which the alliance made its reemergence as a significant theoretical, research, and clinical concept.

BRIEF HISTORY OF THE IDEA OF THE THERAPEUTIC ALLIANCE: THE PHOENIX RISES

The history of the alliance concept and theorizing on the nature, role, and function of a conscious or "ego-based" aspect of the therapist–client relationship begins with Freud. While he considered the influence of the unconscious superimposition of past relationships (transference) on each and every significant encounter to be ubiquitous, as a clinician he was clearly aware of the importance of the positive attachments of analyst and client: ". . . even the most brilliant results were liable to be suddenly wiped away if my personal relation with the patient was disturbed. . . . the personal emotional relation between doctor and patient was after all stronger than the whole cathartic process" (Freud & Strachey, 1963, p. 27). He speculated that these relational bonds make it possible to surmount the challenges and the occasional pain of the journey of self-discovery (Freud, 1913). Freud was, however, evidently wary of providing a "bypass" around the role of the unconscious in therapeutic relationships, and he used somewhat ambiguous terminology to describe these relational dynamics, such as "unobjectionable transference." He evidently thought that the client's projection of benevolent qualities onto the analyst was useful, and he cautiously suggested that friendly affection (toward the client) contributed to the success of psychoanalysis (Freud, 1913).

Within Freud's lifetime some of his students and colleagues (e.g., Adler, Ferenczi, & Sullivan) started to explore the nontransferential aspect of the therapeutic relationship more deeply. The role of the ego (i.e., the conscious) in therapy and in the relationship between analyst and client, in particular, remained a lively and somewhat controversial topic in psychoanalytic literature well into the 1960s (Meissner, 2006; Winnicott, 1993). Sterba (1934), Zetzel (1956), and Greenson (1965, 1967) have made significant contributions identifying and amplifying the role and importance of what Freud referred to as the therapeutic "pact"—now formally referred to as the alliance—while others in the analytic community expressed strong concerns that the alliance concept distorted the focus of analytic treatments

(Abend, 2000). However, the concept of the alliance was of relatively minor interest in the research world, and the theoretical conversation on the topic was contained largely within the psychodynamically oriented community up to the later parts of the 1970s.

As noted earlier, one of the consequences of the seminal meta-analyses appearing in the 1970s was refocused interest on the common essential elements actively contributing to successful therapies based on different theoretical premises. Relational concepts, therefore, emerged as an obvious focus of the quest for common factors responsible for treatment effects in talk therapy (Frank & Frank, 1991). In this quest, two features of the potential "generic factors" appeared critical: compatibility with each of the available theoretical frameworks and fit with the trend and preference for conceptualizations that were amenable to research.

The most viable candidate for the role of a common factor was provided by Bordin (1975, 1979) and Luborsky (1976). They promoted the alliance as a ubiquitous and universal concept standing for the conscious, collaborative aspect of the client–therapist relationship. In many ways their conceptualization was closely aligned with Freud's original "therapeutic pact" (both Bordin and Luborsky were psychodynamically trained), but this reinvented, "new" version of the alliance stood on its own, without reference to the unconscious elements or historical relational artifacts that were interactive partner components of the alliance concept in its earlier, psychodynamic formulations (Greenson, 1965). Bordin, in particular, was careful to position the alliance as a self-contained variable, a relational dynamic present in all forms of psychotherapy irrespective of the theoretical assumptions undergirding a specific treatment, and not dependent on transference as a complimentary relationship construct (Bordin, 1975).[1] However, he also believed (like Freud) that clients recreated their pathogenic relational issues in therapy (Bordin, 1994). This reformulation of the alliance concept emphasizing the collaborative aspects (bonds and tasks) and shared understandings (goals) provided a very attractive relational variable for researchers across the theoretical spectrum. Bordin's open-ended description of the concept suggested that different types of treatment would require alliances that varied in particulars of substance—the kinds of tasks, for example—but would focus on the same collaborative and consensual issues involving the goals of treatment, the therapeutic tasks (whatever these may be) and personal attachments or bonds. This reformulation of the alliance construct rapidly gained a following in the research world: from fewer than 200 publications with "alliance" as a keyword in the years between 1940 and 1950, to over 13,000 items by 2015 (Horvath et al., 2014).

[1]This reconceptualization of the alliance also bridged the previous distinctions made between "working alliance" and "therapeutic alliance" (Greenson, 1965).

The alliance became the "quintessential" common factor variable (Wolfe & Goldfried, 1988, p. 449).

In hindsight, two aspects of Bordin's pioneering work in laying the theoretical foundation for the "new" alliance concept seem to have had significant consequences for subsequent research. First, the open-ended ambiguity of his description of the concept. He emphasized agreements and collaboration and the focus on goals and therapeutic tasks, but he did not elaborate how these agreements come about, the kinds of personal qualities or contributions that may nourish the formation or maintain the alliance and, significantly, made no comments on the boundaries of the concept: *what the alliance is not.* Thus, the concept could be augmented, adopted, and absorbed into all kinds of overarching conceptualizations of the structure, role, and functions of the therapeutic relationship. Second, in proposing the alliance as a ubiquitous feature of all helping relationships, he abstained from commenting on the question of what other elements may be necessary or complementary components of the therapeutic relationship.

This omission has had both positive and challenging consequences. On the plus side, not tying the alliance to other concepts involved in the relational dynamics avoided the introduction of elements that may have been incompatible with some theoretical frameworks. But, on the other hand, Bordin's "silence" created an obvious vacuum, a blank space in the conversation, about the possibility of additional important common features of the therapeutic relationships. It seems evident that there is more to the therapeutic relationship than collaboration, such as agreements on tasks and goals combined with personal bonds. In some sense this gap, not having an overarching framework to help organize what is universal in therapeutic relationships, was felt as "the presence of the absence." This felt need, combined with the semiotic ambiguity of the alliance concept, seems at least partly responsible for the development of an unusually large number and variety of alliance instruments in use currently.[2]

Alliance measures, in practice, provide an implicit definition of what the alliance "is," at least for the purpose of the investigation. Since the post Dodo Bird conversations about the alliance have not directly engaged with, much less agreed on, the question of what the alliance "is not," most instrument constructors have inherited the freedom to incorporate additional features or elements (beyond tasks, bonds and goals)[3] of the therapy relationship

[2]Elvins and Green identified over 60 measures in 2008, while Horvath, Del Re, Flückiger, and Symonds (2011) identified over 35 in their meta-analysis of alliance and outcome; the best current estimate is over 80 in research use (Horvath, 2016).
[3]Less frequently, in the name of expedience or speed of application, removing some of the originally proposed dimensions.

they consider relevant to assess—for example, safety, working capacity, commitment, mutual affirmation, understanding and involvement, openness, empowering, confidence, and so on (Horvath, 2016). There are certainly some core notions common among these measures (e.g., collaboration, agreements, some kinds of personal attachments), but past these commonalities, a preliminary examination of the most frequently used alliance measures came up with an estimate of less than 50% of shared variance across the most frequently used measures using the same source of assessment, that is, different measures of clients' self-report or therapists' assessments (Horvath, 2011b). And the overlap is even thinner when the shared variance is estimated using measures based on different sources—for example, observation-based versus self-report instruments (Cecero, Fenton, Frankforter, Nich, & Carroll, 2001).

In effect, the diversity of measures has partly "solved" the challenge of capturing a more comprehensive image of the therapy relationship. In addition, including in an alliance assessment items sampling other important elements in the relationship improves the correlation between such measures and therapy outcome. But the use of such diversity of instrumentation in research has had some significant costs as well. A somewhat unique version of the alliance is implicit in each measure, but this implicit definition of the construct is not transparent to those reading the results of the investigation. As a result, the alliance measured with one instrument or assessment procedure is somewhat different from results using a different instrument, and a significant portion of the research on the alliance is vulnerable to an "inverse tower of Babel" effect: using the same sign (word) to point to different "objects" (semiotic dysphoria).

Another potential cost of adopting and extending the definition of the alliance is that the important distinctions between the alliance and the broader concept of the therapy relationship are in danger of being obscured (Horvath, 2016). Our central task, core mission, as therapy researchers, is to better understand what makes therapy work. To reach this goal we need to pull apart the fabric and make careful distinctions to gain insights about what works with whom in which circumstances. One of the greatest contributions research on the alliance has made is to focus on and document the value of the client's active and enthusiastic collaboration in therapy irrespective of the method of treatment and in addition to incremental gains (Duncan, Miller, Wampold, & Hubble, 2010; Horvath, 2011b). But the alliance does not stand by itself; patients do not get better simply because they are allied with the therapist and enthusiastically involved in treatment. Combining diverse relational concepts together under the umbrella label of "alliance" risks obscuring the unique contributions of the alliance and could end up masking the complexity of the relationship between client and therapists.

Notwithstanding these challenges, the work and energies of researchers invested in studying the alliance have led to some outstanding achievements. Perhaps the most visible accomplishment is the evidence of a modest but very reliable and statistically significant connection between alliance and therapy outcome (Horvath, Del Re, Flückiger, & Symonds, 2011). This link (approximately 6%–9% of the outcome variance) appears to be consistent, irrespective of the types of treatment or design variables like type of outcome, randomization, allegiance of the researcher, or theoretical orientation (Flückiger, Del Re, Wampold, Symonds, & Horvath, 2012). Moreover, the relationship between alliance and outcome is evident early in treatment (by the third to fifth session) and cannot be accounted for by prior therapeutic gains (Horvath & Bedi, 2002). The possibility of detecting early signs of progress (or lack of it) has contributed to the development of practical feedback strategies that have shown great promise of increasing treatment effectiveness (Lambert, 2013). There have been exciting developments involving conceptual and empirical work to better understand the ways collaboration is fostered and repaired in the therapy process (e.g., Muntigl & Horvath, 2016; Ribeiro, Ribeiro, Gonçalves, Horvath, & Stiles, 2013; Safran & Kraus, 2014), and in exploring ways the management or negotiation of the alliance can play a significant role in some therapies (Safran & Muran, 2001). Work on the alliance has led to important advances in therapist training, as well.

The above list is incomplete and meant only to indicate the significant breadth of contributions work on the alliance has made to our deeper understanding of the ways therapy can help clients change as well as to clinical practice. Examining the impact of the concept from a broader perspective, it seems evident that the alliance as a common factor variable has usefully refocused attention on the therapist–client relation as a vital and evidence-supported aspect of psychotherapy, and provided an important balance to the claim that the effects of therapy should be more narrowly attributed to techniques and strategies (Chambless, 2002; Lambert & Ogles, 2004; Wampold, 2001). The renewed interest in the alliance has also provided the base for development of a number of clinical innovations (Eubanks-Carter, Muran, & Safran, 2015; Muran & Barber, 2010).

However, as useful as these contributions were and are, there appears to be a significant risk that the fluidity of the limits of the construct and lack of clarity about its nexus to other relational concepts are beginning to obscure the distinction between the alliance and the broader concept of the therapy relationship (Horvath, 2017). The alliance, however broadly it is construed, cannot account for all of the aspects or elements in the relationship between therapist and client that matter. The lack of a consensually endorsed framework that speaks to the relations among evidentially important elements in the therapeutic relationship (e.g., empathy, genuineness, positive regard, alliance) and also takes account of the contributions of past relational experiences (e.g., transference, attachment style), has created a significant conceptual gap. The current reference volume on the empirical status of research on psychotherapy relationship uses "relationships" in the plural in the title in referring to the various elements, but does not offer a structure or framework addressing the issue of how these different elements that evidentially contribute to success in therapy complement, overlap, or fit together (Norcross, 2002; Norcross & Lambert, 2011). Although there were and are efforts to develop such a structure of the "generic" therapy relationship (e.g., Gelso, 2014; Grawe, 2004; Orlinsky & Howard, 1987; Safran & Kraus, 2014), so far these models have had limited consensual support in the research literature (Horvath, 2017).

Taking the above assessment into account, how shall one respond to the question posed in the title of this chapter: "Where does the alliance fit?" Clearly, the place of the alliance needs to be considered in a full context of how relationship elements that *matter* and are *common* to most forms of therapy fit together. Words such as *alliance*, *empathy*, and *congruence* are pointing to aspects of the therapy relationship that clinicians and researchers find useful to distinguish for purposes such as improving praxis and understanding what makes therapy work, but these semiotic signs exist without an a priori, concrete, external object to anchor or define them. As such, they are fluid and their meaning and the relations among them are determined by use. The usefulness of these concepts depends on the user's engagement in an ongoing process of clarification and refinement. Past experience indicates that consensus on concepts referencing common factors is the product of extended conversations among members of the cognate scientific community. Such a bottom-up process includes formal exchanges focusing on specific issues, such as the special section hosted by the journal *Psychotherapy* in 2006 and, equally important, volumes such as this one.

Contributions in this volume also illustrate the generativity of the concept of the therapeutic relationship and its potential to help us discover not only what parts of the therapy relationship are shared among different kinds of treatments, but also the unique ways in which the interactive nature of psychotherapy is differently manifested and utilized in a variety of contexts.

REFERENCES

Abend, S. (2000). The problem of therapeutic alliance. In S. T. Levy (Ed.), *The therapeutic alliance* (pp. 1–16). Madison, CT: International Universities Press.

Ahn, H., & Wampold, B. E. (2001). Where oh where are the specific ingredients? A meta-analysis of component studies in counseling and psychology. *Journal of Counseling Psychology*, 48, 251–257. http://dx.doi.org/10.1037/0022-0167.48.3.251

Bordin, E. S. (1975, September). *The working alliance: Basis for a general theory of psychotherapy*. Paper presented at the Society for Psychotherapy Research, Washington, DC.

Bordin, E. S. (1979). The generalizability of the psychoanalytic concept of the working alliance. *Psychotherapy, 16*, 252–260. http://dx.doi.org/10.1037/h0085885

Bordin, E. S. (1994). Theory and research on the therapeutic working alliance: New directions. In A. O. Horvath & L. S. Greenberg (Eds.), *The working alliance: Theory, research, and practice* (pp. 13–37). New York, NY: Wiley.

Buber, M., & Agassi, J. B. (1999). *Martin Buber on psychology and psychotherapy: Essays, letters, and dialogue*. Syracuse, NY: Syracuse University Press.

Carroll, L. (1865). *Alice's Adventures in Wonderland*. London, England: Macmillan.

Castonguay, L. G. (2000). A common factors approach to psychotherapy training. *Journal of Psychotherapy Integration, 10*, 263–282. http://dx.doi.org/10.1023/A:1009496929012

Cecero, J. J., Fenton, L. R., Frankforter, T. L., Nich, C., & Carroll, K. M. (2001). Focus on therapeutic alliance: The psychometric properties of six measures across three treatments. *Psychotherapy, 38*, 1–11. http://dx.doi.org/10.1037/0033-3204.38.1.1

Chambless, D. L. (2002). Beware the dodo bird: The dangers of overgeneralization. *Clinical Psychology: Science and Practice, 9*, 13–16. http://dx.doi.org/10.1093/clipsy.9.1.13

DeRubeis, R. J., & Feeley, M. (1991). Determinants of change in cognitive therapy for depression. *Cognitive Therapy and Research, 14*, 469–482. http://dx.doi.org/10.1007/BF01172968

Duncan, B. L., Miller, S. D., Wampold, B. E., & Hubble, M. A. (Eds.). (2010). *The heart and soul of change: Delivering what works in therapy* (2nd ed.). Washington, DC: American Psychological Association. http://dx.doi.org/10.1037/12075-000

Elliott, R., Bohart, A. C., Watson, J. C., & Greenberg, L. S. (2011). Empathy. *Psychotherapy, 48*, 43–49. http://dx.doi.org/10.1037/a0022187

Eubanks-Carter, C., Muran, J. C., & Safran, J. D. (2015). Alliance-focused training. *Psychotherapy, 52*, 169–173. http://dx.doi.org/10.1037/a0037596

Flückiger, C., Del Re, A. C., Wampold, B. E., Symonds, D., & Horvath, A. O. (2012). How central is the alliance in psychotherapy? A multilevel longitudinal meta-analysis. *Journal of Counseling Psychology, 59*, 10–17. http://dx.doi.org/10.1037/a0025749

Frank, J. D. (1961). *Persuasion and healing: A comparative study of psychotherapy*. Baltimore, MD: Johns Hopkins University Press.

Frank, J. D., & Frank, J. B. (1991). *Persuasion and healing: A comparative study of psychotherapy* (3rd ed.). Baltimore, MD: Johns Hopkins University Press.

Freud, S. (1913). On beginning of treatment: Further recommendations on the technique of psycho-analysis I. In J. Strachey (Ed., 1958), *Standard edition of the complete psychological works of Sigmund Freud* (Vol. 12, pp. 122–144). London, England: Hogarth Press.

Freud, S. (1963). *Dora: An analysis of a case of hysteria*. New York, NY: Collier Books/ Macmillan Publishing Co.

Freud, S., & Strachey, J. (1963). *An autobiographical study*. New York, NY: W. W. Norton.

Gelso, C. (2014). A tripartite model of the therapeutic relationship: Theory, research, and practice. *Psychotherapy Research, 24*, 117–131. http://dx.doi.org/10.1080/10503307.2013.845920

Goldfried, M. R. (1980). Toward the delineation of therapeutic change principles. *American Psychologist, 35*, 991–999. http://dx.doi.org/10.1037/0003-066X.35.11.991

Grawe, K. (2004). *Psychological therapy*. Ashland, OH: Hogrefe & Huber.

Greenson, R. R. (1965). The working alliance and the transference neurosis. *The Psychoanalytic Quarterly, 34*, 155–181. http://www.tandfonline.com/doi/abs/10.1080/21674086.1965.11926343

Greenson, R. R. (1967). *Technique and practice of psychoanalysis*. New York, NY: International University Press.

Horvath, A. O. (2011a). Alliance in common factor land: A view through the research lens. *Research in Psychotherapy, 14*, 121–135. http://dx.doi.org/10.4081/ripppo.2011.45

Horvath, A. O. (2011b, July). *The complex world of alliance assessments: Will the "real alliance" please stand up?* Paper presented at the Society for Psychotherapy Research, Bern, Switzerland.

Horvath, A. O. (2016). *The relationship puzzle: Where does the alliance fit?* Paper presented at the Society for Psychotherapy Research, Jerusalem, Israel.

Horvath, A. O. (2017). Research on the alliance: Knowledge in search of a theory. *Psychotherapy Research*, Advance online publication. http://dx.doi.org/10.1080/10503307.2017.1373204

Horvath, A. O., & Bedi, R. P. (2002). The alliance. In J. C. Norcross (Ed.), *Psychotherapy relationships that work: Therapist contributions responsiveness to patients* (pp. 37–70). New York, NY: Oxford University Press.

Horvath, A. O., Del Re, A. C., Flückiger, C., & Symonds, D. (2011). Alliance in individual psychotherapy. *Psychotherapy*, 48, 9–16. http://dx.doi.org/10.1037/a0022186

Horvath, A. O., Flückiger, C., Symonds, D., Lee, E., Jafari, H., & Del Re, A. C. (2014). *The relationship between helper and client: Looking beyond psychotherapy*. Paper presented at the Society for Psychotherapy Research Conference. Copenhagen, Denmark.

Huang, T. C., Hill, C. E., Strauss, N., Heyman, M., & Hussain, M. (2016). Corrective relational experiences in psychodynamic–interpersonal psychotherapy: Antecedents, types, and consequences. *Journal of Counseling Psychology*, 63, 183–197. http://dx.doi.org/10.1037/cou0000132

Lambert, M. J. (2013). The efficacy and effectiveness of psychotherapy. In M. J. Lambert (Ed.), *Bergin and Garfield's handbook of psychotherapy and behavior change* (6th ed., pp. 169–218). New York, NY: Wiley.

Lambert, M. J., & Ogles, B. M. (2004). The efficacy and effectiveness of psychotherapy. In M. J. Lambert (Ed.), *Bergin and Garfield's handbook of psychotherapy and behavior change* (5th ed., pp. 139–193). New York, NY: Wiley.

Luborsky, L. (1976). *Helping alliances in psychotherapy: The groundwork for a study of their relationship to its outcome*. Paper presented at the Texas Research Institute of Mental Sciences, Houston, Texas.

Luborsky, L., Singer, B., & Luborsky, L. (1975). Comparative studies of psychotherapies. Is it true that "everyone has won and all must have prizes"? *Archives of General Psychiatry, 32*, 995–1008. http://dx.doi.org/10.1001/archpsyc.1975.01760260059004

Meissner, W. W. (2006). The therapeutic alliance—a proteus in disguise. *Psychotherapy, 43*, 264–270. http://dx.doi.org/10.1037/0033-3204.43.3.264

Muntigl, P., & Horvath, A. O. (2016). A conversation analytic study of building and repairing the alliance in family therapy. *Journal of Family Therapy, 38*, 102–119. http://dx.doi.org/10.1111/1467-6427.12109

Muran, J. C., & Barber, J. P. (2010). *The therapeutic alliance: An evidence-based guide to practice*. New York, NY: Guilford Press.

Norcross, J. C. (Ed.). (2002). *Psychotherapy relationships that work: Therapist contributions and responsiveness to patients*. New York, NY: Oxford University Press.

Norcross, J. C., & Lambert, M. J. (2011). Evidence-based therapy relationships. In J. C. Norcross (Ed.), *Psychotherapy relationships that work: Evidence-based responsiveness* (2nd ed., pp. 3–21). New York, NY: Oxford University Press. http://dx.doi.org/10.1093/acprof:oso/9780199737208.003.0001

Orlinsky, D. E., & Howard, K. I. (1987). A generic model of psychotherapy. *Journal of Integrative and Eclectic Psychotherapy, 6*, 6–27.

Ribeiro, E., Ribeiro, A. P., Gonçalves, M. M., Horvath, A. O., & Stiles, W. B. (2013). How collaboration in therapy becomes therapeutic: The therapeutic collaboration coding system. *Psychotherapy Research: Theory, Research, and Practice, 86*, 294–314. http://dx.doi.org/10.1111/j.2044-8341.2012.02066.x

Rogers, C. R. (1951). *Client centered therapy*. Cambridge, MA: Riverside.

Rogers, C. R., Gendlin, G. T., Kiesler, D. V., & Truax, L. B. (1967). *The therapeutic relationship and its impact: A study of psychotherapy with schizophrenics*. Madison: University of Wisconsin Press.

Rosenzweig, S. (1936). Some implicit common factors in diverse methods of psychotherapy. *American Journal of Orthopsychiatry, 6*, 412–415. http://dx.doi.org/10.1111/j.1939-0025.1936.tb05248.x

Safran, J. D., & Kraus, J. (2014). Alliance ruptures, impasses, and enactments: A relational perspective. *Psychotherapy, 51*, 381–387. http://dx.doi.org/10.1037/a0036815

Safran, J. D., & Muran, J. C. (2001). The therapeutic alliance as a process of intersubjective negotiation. In J. C. Muran (Ed.), *Self-relations in the psychotherapy process* (pp. 165–186). Washington, DC: American Psychological Association.

Smith, M. L., & Glass, G. V. (1977). Meta-analysis of psychotherapy outcome studies. *American Psychologist, 32*, 752–760. http://dx.doi.org/10.1037/0003-066X.32.9.752

Sterba, R. F. (1934). The fate of the ego in analytic therapy. *The International Journal of Psychoanalysis, 115*, 117–126.

Stiles, W. B., Honos-Webb, L., & Surko, M. (1998). Responsiveness in psychotherapy. *Clinical Psychology: Science and Practice, 5*, 439–458. http://dx.doi.org/10.1111/j.1468-2850.1998.tb00166.x

Stiles, W. B., Shapiro, D., & Elliot, R. (1986). Are all psychotherapies equivalent? *American Psychologist, 41*, 165–180.

Wampold, B. E. (2001). *The great psychotherapy debate*. Mahwah, NJ: Erlbaum.

Winnicott, D. W. (1993). The value of the therapeutic consultation. In D. Goldman & D. Goldman (Eds.), *In one's bones: The clinical genius of Winnicott* (pp. 95–100). Lanham, MD: Jason Aronson.

Wolfe, B. E., & Goldfried, M. R. (1988). Research on psychotherapy integration: Recommendations and conclusions from an NIMH workshop. *Journal of Consulting and Clinical Psychology*, 56, 448–451.

Zetzel, E. R. (1956). Current concepts of transference. *International Journal of Psychoanalysis, 37*, 369–376.

I

THE CASE STUDIES: INTEGRATING RESEARCH AND PRACTICE

2

YOU CAN'T CROSS THE SAME RIVER TWICE: A CASE STUDY OF ALLIANCE RUPTURE AND REPAIR

LAURA KOHBERGER, JEREMY D. SAFRAN,
AND J. CHRISTOPHER MURAN

One of the primary objectives of psychotherapy research has been to determine how people change over the course of therapy and to identify specific elements that contribute to therapeutic changes. With psychotherapy research increasingly supporting the quality of the therapeutic alliance as the strongest predictor of outcome (Horvath, Del Re, Flückiger, & Symonds, 2011; Horvath & Symonds, 1991; Martin, Garske, & Davis, 2000), many researchers are advocating for measures of therapeutic process that assess changes in therapists' ability to negotiate negative interpersonal process and ruptures in the therapeutic alliance (Doran, Safran, & Muran, 2016; Safran, Muran, & Eubanks-Carter, 2011). Research has supported the hypothesis that working through problems in the alliance can lead to positive change; this generation of alliance research has attempted to better understand the factors that lead to ongoing changes in the alliance and processes involved in repairing alliance ruptures (Safran et al., 2014; Safran, Muran, & Eubanks-Carter, 2011; Safran, Muran, Samstag, & Stevens, 2002).

http://dx.doi.org/10.1037/0000093-003
Developing the Therapeutic Relationship: Integrating Case Studies, Research, and Practice, O. Tishby and H. Wiseman (Editors)

Safran and Muran (1996, 2000) have suggested that the alliance is an "ongoing process of intersubjective negotiation" between the needs of both participants, which becomes most salient during moments of rupture or breakdown in the collaborative process between the client and therapist. The process of navigating these difficult moments can offer unique and powerful opportunities for change. They are often experienced as a kind of tension within the therapeutic relationship, which can range from subtle (e.g., a client's passively complying with the therapist) to explicit (e.g., a client's aggressively disagreeing with the purpose of a task). According to Safran and Muran (1996), clients come into therapy with "relational" schemas, which are based on early attempts for finding relatedness that become maladaptive in adulthood. These schemas become enacted in the therapeutic relationship; the therapist's goal is to attend to these schemas and disconfirm the expectations underlying them. A key ingredient in resolving ruptures is helping clients to recognize that they can express their needs without destroying the relationship. Resolving ruptures can empower clients to confront conflicts in their lives, acknowledge parts of themselves that they have disowned, and negotiate their needs for relatedness and agency in a more effective way (Safran & Muran, 2000; Sommerfeld, Orbach, Zim, & Mikulincer, 2008).

Brief Relational Therapy

Safran and Muran (2000) developed a relationally and experientially informed brief relational therapy (BRT), which has been empirically tested through a number of studies (Safran & Muran, 1996, 2000; Safran, Muran, Samstag, & Winston, 2005) and is based on their therapeutic alliance rupture resolution work. The model is based on a two-person psychology and a constructivist epistemology. There is a present-focused dimension to the approach that emphasizes the value of approaching each session with a beginner's mind in order to track subtle processes as they occur in the here and now (Safran & Muran, 1996, 2000). One important principle in BRT consists of therapeutic metacommunication, that is, engaging the client in a collaborative process that explores how both client and therapist contribute to repetitive relational scenarios (Eubanks-Carter, Muran, Safran, & Hayes, 2010).

Emergence of a Two-Person Psychology

The relational turn in American psychoanalysis has emphasized the construct of a two-person psychology that began to challenge the idea that it is possible for a therapist to stand outside of the therapeutic process in which he or she is participating. This shift has inspired analysts to extend their interest beyond the client's intrapsychic life to include all facets of the therapeutic relationship (Aron, 1990; Ghent, 1989; Mitchell, 1988; Safran, 2012; Safran & Muran, 2000).

ONE CLIENT, THREE THERAPISTS

Although systematic case studies have been used to investigate the same therapist working with different clients (Silberschatz & Curtis, 1993; Strupp, 1980), limited research (Castonguay et al., 2012) has investigated mechanisms of therapeutic change for the same client being treated by different therapists. At the Brief Psychotherapy Research Program at Beth Israel Medical Center, over the years a phenomenon has emerged in which clients who have completed short-term psychotherapy have returned to the program for additional treatment. This occurrence has permitted us unique opportunities to explore the ways in which therapeutic process and outcome may differ for the same client working with different therapists and in different therapeutic modalities. Treatments are 30 sessions in length. Clients wishing to return for treatment in the program are told that they can only do so after a mandatory waiting period. They are also told that if they do return, they will be randomly assigned to the treatment modality (i.e., BRT or cognitive–behavioral therapy [CBT]). Considering that ruptures can provide powerful opportunities for change, an understanding of alliance ruptures and their resolution is essential. This chapter intensively investigates a single case in which two separate treatment modalities were conducted by three different therapists, in order to explore similarities and differences between the ways in which alliance ruptures emerged and were addressed and to explore similarities and differences in the types of changes that took place over the courses of these two treatments.

To this end, we employed a discovery-oriented approach in which the moment-to-moment processes of rupture and resolution were observed and described in a fine-grained manner. The investigation consisted of a mixed-method case study design utilizing both quantitative and qualitative measures in examining videotaped therapy sessions and client interviews. A qualitative descriptive analysis of the sessions and interviews was conducted by the primary investigators to provide an in-depth understanding of the therapeutic process and how it relates to treatment outcome. In adopting a method of data triangulation, the study used an analysis of data that captured the client's subjective understanding of rupture events in addition to the primary researchers' analysis of sessions containing ruptures.

Rupture and Repair Processes

Important questions guiding the current case study included the following:

- How did ruptures events differ in the client's treatments?
- How did different therapists attempt to repair ruptures with the same client?
- What were the particular challenges in the repair process?
- Did ruptures occur around certain themes for the client?
- What was the context in which ruptures occurred?
- How did rupture events influence the course of treatment?
- Did the way in which ruptures occurred and were then attended to in the separate treatments influence the kinds of therapeutic gains that the client experienced?
- Could variations in the therapists' styles and interventions be other critical factors in contributing to differences in treatment outcome?

Identification and Exploration of Rupture Events

The client participated in an additional follow-up interview for the purpose of this study. The interview was recorded and the researcher used a modified version of interpersonal process recall (Elliott, 1986). As the client was not willing to watch her own therapy, transcriptions from segments of the sessions were read to her. Prior to the interview, the primary researchers collected and watched therapy sessions that the client had previously identified as rupture sessions on the Post Session Questionnaire (PSQ; Muran, Safran, Samstag, & Winston, 2002). The interviewer first read back descriptions that the client had provided in reporting a rupture event and then read transcriptions from segments of the session that correlated with her description. The client was asked a series of questions about her understanding of these rupture events and their resolution.

Client Background and Characteristics

The client was a 31-year-old Caucasian woman. She had been married for 4 years and did not have any children. The client was raised Christian but described being influenced by Buddhism as an adult. For the past 4 years, she had been working part-time as a paralegal. The client had a history of diverse work experiences but was unable to finish college due to needing to work full-time after being kicked out of her house at 18 years old. The client was born and raised in New York and had one younger sister. Both of her parents were still alive, although her father was being treated for leukemia at the time of therapy.

Describing her childhood, the client painted a picture of a strict, chaotic, and enmeshed family. She described her parents as overly controlling and said that the household was governed by strict rules (e.g., she and her sister were not allowed to lock their doors and had to constantly ask for permission). She described one incident at the age of 10 in which was scolded after pouring herself some water without permission. During childhood she was accommodating and did not question her parents' controlling tendencies. However, during her adolescence, the atmosphere of control within the household was exacerbated when her mother became involved with a "born again" church. The client described rebelling against her parents during the ensuing years, which led to ongoing conflicts. The tension between the client and her parents, initiated by her desire to assert her individuality, eventually led to her being kicked out of the house at the age of 18. Her contact with her parents has been limited in the many subsequent years.

Treatment Measures

The client completed both standardized process and outcome measures. Outcome measures were completed at intake, termination, and at a 6-month follow-up. Two outcome measures were examined: the Symptom Checklist-90–Revised (SCL-90–R; Derogatis, 1983), which is a self-report inventory developed to assess general psychiatric symptoms, and the Inventory of Interpersonal Problems (IIP; Horowitz, Alden, Wiggins, & Pincus, 2000), a 64-item self-report inventory designed to assess interpersonal difficulties.

Criteria for Case Selection

The client was selected from a larger data set of repeater cases that had completed at least two rounds of short-term psychotherapy at the Brief Psychotherapy Research Program.[1] This client completed two rounds of BRT treatment. Eight months after finishing her first BRT treatment, which consisted of 30 sessions, she underwent the assessment process and was randomly assigned to CBT. However, after six sessions the client requested to be reassigned due to dissatisfaction with the treatment. The client then completed another course of BRT treatment with a different therapist. Thus, the case was of interest since the six sessions of CBT also allowed us to examine rupture episodes for the client in the context of an unsuccessful treatment episode. Because the study was to extensively investigate how therapeutic process is related to outcome, the case needed to have adequate

[1]Details of this case example have been altered to protect confidentiality.

outcome and process data and sufficient video data. In addition, the case allowed researchers to detect mechanisms of change that contributed to good outcome.

Presenting Problems and Therapeutic Outcome During the First Course of Treatment

At the start of her first treatment, the client was interviewed with Structured Clinical Interviews for *Diagnostic and Statistical Manual of Mental Disorders* (*DSM*; First, Spitzer, Gibbon, & Williams, 1995), and met criteria for an Axis I diagnosis of Major Depressive Disorder. She sought treatment because she wanted to learn how to cope better with stress, and she indicated a pattern of isolation and turning to food. She reported poor self-care and a lack of satisfaction with her job; she was unable to finish college due to having to work full time to support herself. In identifying treatment goals, the client's first target complaint was a lack of confidence, mostly at her job, in which she reported feeling upset when she did not receive approval from others. She reported sensitivity, particularly during episodes of depression, and a constant need for acknowledgment since childhood. She identified her second target complaint as episodes of overeating in response to feelings of sadness and anger. In addition, her father had recently been diagnosed with cancer, which was a cause of concern.

Treatment outcome was determined by the overall mean scores on the SCL-90–R and IIP. The study assessed clinical significance, or the extent to which the client's change over the treatment revealed a shift to normal functioning. In determining cutoff scores, Jacobson and Truax (1991) suggest that the client is considered to have achieved clinically significant change when her level of functioning following therapy places her closer to the mean of the functional population than the mean of the dysfunctional population. Reliable Change Indexes (RCIs; Jacobson & Truax, 1991) were calculated to establish statistically reliable criteria accounting for measurement error in indicating how much change occurred. The RC coefficient equals the difference between two scores divided by the standard error of difference between the scores.

The client experienced positive therapeutic change over the course of her two BRT treatments. For her first treatment, from intake to termination, the client experienced significant clinical change on the SCL-90–R but not on the IIP. Similarly, from intake to 6-month follow-up the client experienced both reliable change and clinically significant change on the SCL-90–R but not on the IIP. While there was a decline in her overall symptom severity at termination and at 6-month follow-up, there was no significant change in her report of interpersonal difficulties.

Presenting Problems and Therapeutic Outcome During the Second Course of Treatment

In returning for a second course of treatment, the client underwent the assessment process once again and was randomly assigned to CBT. After completing six sessions of CBT treatment, the client dropped from the treatment and was immediately randomly reassigned to another BRT treatment. She met *DSM* criteria for Major Depressive Disorder and Anxiety Disorder Not Otherwise Specified. She reported still struggling with turning to food when she was feeling emotionally stressed. The client had also been told by her doctor that she needed to lose weight in attempting to conceive. She reported experiencing more stress since starting college. The client identified her first target complaint as feeling sad and depressed with low levels of energy. She reported insomnia and oversleeping, which she related to stress and poor self-care. Her second target complaint was feeling isolated, as her life had recently been disrupted when close friends moved out of state. Her third target complaint was a lack of balance in her life and spacing out in feeling either "100% on or 100% off."

When the client returned to treatment, there was no significant increase in her symptoms on the SCL-90–R, suggesting that she was able to hold on to the gains from her first treatment. By the end of her second BRT treatment, the client experienced both reliable and clinically significant change on the IIP but not on the SCL-90–R. Since she had already begun treatment with reduced symptoms, it appeared that she was able to maintain those gains while experiencing new ones. Although she was considered a good outcome case in both treatments, change occurred on different dimensions: first through a reduction in her symptoms and then through a decrease in her interpersonal difficulties.

Qualitative Analysis of Therapy Sessions

All of the videotaped therapy sessions were available, including 30 sessions from the client's first time in BRT, six sessions from her second time in CBT, and 30 sessions from her second time in BRT. All of the sessions were transcribed and closely examined. Using a discovery-oriented approach, qualitative descriptive analyses were performed by the primary investigators. The researchers adopted methods from comprehensive process analysis (CPA; Elliott, 1994; Elliott et al., 1994), which allows for an understanding of therapeutic events that are critical to the change process. Qualitative methods were adapted from CPA to allow for a microanalysis of rupture moments in exploring the immediate and preceding contexts in which ruptures occurred, salient themes, and the subsequent clinical significance of the event.

The PSQ that the client completed after each session was utilized in order to identify rupture sessions. The PSQ is a self-report measure that assesses various dimensions of the therapeutic relationship. This particular scale on the PSQ included six questions that were designed to capture a global assessment of alliance ruptures and resolutions during the course of the session. These questions assess (a) whether the client experienced any tension, problems, misunderstandings, or conflicts with the therapist; (b) to what extent there was a perception of "smoothing over" or "holding back" on the part of the client or therapist; (c) a description of the problem; (d) the extent to which the problem was addressed; (e) the degree to which the problem was resolved; and (f) a description of what contributed to the resolution. The questions are responded to along a 5-point Likert Scale, from 1 (*Not at all*) to 5 (*Constantly*).

For this particular chapter, we were interested in better understanding the rupture and resolution process from the client's perspective, so although the therapists also completed the PSQ, we focused on the ruptures that the client identified. Sessions were identified as rupture sessions if the client responded with a score of at least 2 or higher on question (a) or (b) and/or an intensity score of 2 or higher for how tense the client experienced the rupture event as being. For her first treatment, the client identified rupture events in 11 of the 30 sessions. For the CBT condition, rupture events were identified in two out of six sessions, and for her second BRT treatment, the client identified rupture events in five out of 30 sessions.

THREE COURSES OF TREATMENT

An overview of the different courses of treatment is provided in this section. Included are results from the analyses of sessions involving episodes of ruptures and repairs, thematic analyses of the rupture sessions, as well as preceding sessions and subsequent sessions.

Course of Therapy for First Time in Brief Relational Therapy Treatment

The client's first course of therapy lasted 30 sessions. All of the therapists in the Brief Psychotherapy Research Program were affiliated with Beth Israel Medical Center. The first BRT therapist was a 26-year-old single Caucasian woman. She was a psychology doctoral intern and reported 3 years of prior clinical experience. She reported clinical training in psychodynamic, interpersonal/experiential, and integrative orientations. Eleven sessions were identified as rupture sessions, with a score of 2 or higher on the PSQ specifying that the client "experienced any tension, problems, misunderstandings or conflicts with the therapist" or "there was a perception of smoothing over or holding back on the part of the client or therapist." For the purposes of this chapter, three of the rupture sessions are discussed in depth to illustrate the findings. The sessions were chosen since they indicated the highest degree of rupture and/or were sessions that the client was able to adequately discuss during her interview.

Sessions 1 Through 4: Early Session Rupture Reports

In the first four sessions, the client reported initial awkwardness. The therapist focused on the client's past and was active in making interpretations. While the therapist was emotionally present, the client remained descriptive and detached. She tentatively discussed her marriage difficulties, with her tone of voice reflecting defensiveness in expressing negative feelings towards her husband. When the client began to express conflict related to her wish to return to college, the therapist was directive in helping her to validate her own needs. In subsequent sessions, the client revealed excitement about deciding to return to college, and the therapist was supportive of her decision.

Session 6 Rupture: Is Therapy Another Project?

The client began the session by discussing a pattern of overcommitting herself to projects. She expressed difficulty in being present due to her need to please people. On the PSQ for Session 6, the client reported moderate tension or conflict (score of 3). She wrote, "I felt uncomfortable talking about trust because I don't want to have to question our relationship. I guess I'm more comfortable with blind faith than examined truth." During the follow-up interview, the client revealed feeling like the session was unproductive. She shared frustration in "humoring" the therapist, because she felt uncomfortable expressing any negative feelings.

Significant Event (Analysis of Rupture Experience). The client began to share how she turns to food when she is feeling overwhelmed and is unable to express her feelings to others. The therapist explored whether what was occurring in the therapy was connected to the client's larger interpersonal patterns.

Therapist: Do you feel like this is another project?

Client: Yes, sorry [laughs].

Therapist: So if this is a project, are we a team?

Client: Yes, I trust you.

Therapist: So, I'm playing devil's advocate a bit, but how come you trust me?

Client: Because I don't have a choice, honestly.

Therapist: Well I'm glad you're being honest.

Client: And also I don't gain anything if I don't trust you.

Within-Session and Postsession Effects. During the follow-up interview, the client reported that a rupture had occurred in response to the therapist questioning whether therapy was just another task. In focusing on the therapeutic relationship, the client confronted some of her discomfort in questioning her trust in the therapist. The therapist continued to explore whether the client's difficulty in expressing her feelings, a theme that was pervasive in her life, was also present in the therapeutic relationship. The client appeared uncomfortable but addressed her discomfort. Although the discomfort was addressed, the rupture was not fully resolved, with the client indicating it as "somewhat" resolved on the questionnaire. The client then proceeded to discuss her reluctance to assert her needs with coworkers and her belief that emotional expression must serve a purpose.

In subsequent sessions the client continued to focus on her familial relationships and her coping by turning to food. She shared how in a recent argument with her parents, she had been able to confront them after feeling invalidated. The therapist was validating and active in making interpretations. The client experienced the external change in her life of being accepted into college. She reported feeling more excitement and an emergence of a sense of self-esteem in setting boundaries with her family.

Session 10: Just What Are the Expectations?

The session opened with the client offering the therapist a scarf when the latter felt cold. The therapist affectionately reflected back the client's desire to take care of people. The therapist initiated a two-chair technique to help the client access her feelings towards her mother, but she quickly shifted tasks in response to the client's discomfort. The client shared a sense of progress in not colluding with her family but acknowledged continuing to struggle in expressing her feelings.

The client shared memories of being physically abused by her mother. She stated, "She would hit me with a spatula and my nails would be bruised. I would be crying and would head to the bathroom in school to clean myself up." The client moved away from her feelings in dismissing the impact of the abuse. When the therapist redirected attention to feelings, the client revealed an urgency to label her feelings quickly in order to move on. The therapist interpreted the client's pattern of putting feelings into action, and the client acknowledged fears of being overwhelmed by her emotions.

On Session 10's PSQ, the client reported some tension or conflict (score of 2) and high accommodation or holding back (score of 4). She wrote, "I was worried about how she would react or feel about something that we talked about, I addressed it with her." The client reported a high rupture resolution (score of 5). When asked what contributed to the resolution, she wrote, "Naming the problem and hearing my therapist say she wants me to be happy and doesn't have specific expectations." During the follow-up interview, the client revealed not wanting to burden the therapist by talking about her family again. She shared, "It was a turning point. I started to feel more comfortable in talking about things especially family stuff because I have this feeling that people are judgmental and so I hate telling the story over and over again."

Significant Event (Analysis of Rupture Experience).

Therapist: Is there a sad feeling or bad feeling in this room?

Client: No, I don't know. Maybe a little bit today, it's hard. I think my therapist is going to be mad that I am talking about my parents again [laughs]. I know you're not mad, but that's me worrying about what you're thinking.

Therapist: The wonderful part is that you have a great desire to know where other people are coming from and an ability to approximate what is going on for them emotionally and intellectually. It's like the shoemaker who has no boots, the hairdresser with an ugly hair style, the person who is so good at anticipating other people's needs is like "My needs first—how does that work again?"

Client: Yeah.

Therapist: You said that you're worried about what I'm thinking. Even if I had expectations for you, I wouldn't want you to put my needs first.

Postsession Effects. In subsequent sessions, the alliance seemed stronger, indicated by increased warmth and attunement. The client experienced the external life changes of informing her job of her departure and starting classes. She began to discuss how the inconsistency in her childhood has contributed to her trust difficulties. Further exploration of the therapy relationship emerged, in which the client expressed trust in the therapist but also discomfort in needing help. In subsequent sessions, there continued to be a cycle of the therapist probing for the client's emotions and the client experiencing difficulty in expressing feelings. In Session 12 (a rupture session), the client started to cry when discussing the lack of safe spaces in her life to express her feelings.

Session 15: Confronting Emotions

At the start of the session, the client discussed feeling unacknowledged on her last day at work. While the therapist probed for her feelings, the client remained disconnected in providing irrelevant details. The therapist continuously attempted to help her connect to painful feelings. In exploring what happens to the client's anger and sadness, the client expressed embarrassment about using food to cope with feelings. She revealed discomfort in confronting her coworkers, but the therapist encouraged her to practice asserting her feelings in the moment.

On the PSQ for Session 15, the client reported high tension or conflict (score of 4) and high accommodation or holding back (score of 3). She wrote, "It was tense and intense. The therapist was confrontational, which made me uncomfortable. I think she was doing it on purpose to get me to acknowledge my feelings. I didn't want to bring it up, which is my own pattern."

During the interview, the client shared how her therapist's confrontational style made her feel "on the spot," stating, "She wanted me to stand up to people, and I wasn't necessarily sure I wanted to. She was trying to give a solution to what I was proposing, but what she was saying was intimidating so that felt awkward."

Significant Event (Analysis of Rupture Experience). The therapist confronted whether the client allowed herself to experience emotions.

> *Therapist:* I'm wondering, when you say I don't want to be too upset or I don't want to tell other people what shitty coworkers I have because then they will get upset, and I don't want to upset you or your husband or whoever, I wonder to what extent that is an excuse basically.
>
> *Client:* Uh, for what?
>
> *Therapist:* Not an excuse in that you don't care about others but a way of saying let's not bother anyone, let's not unearth this thing that's difficult or messy.
>
> *Client:* Yeah, because it's easier not to, so yeah I guess so.

Within-Session and Postsession Effects. The wording of this interpretation was not well received, as the client's tone of voice and facial expression revealed discomfort. The client did not address her discomfort but defended her position in expressing fear of being overwhelmed by her emotions. The therapist provided a rationale for the task, stating, "It's not for the person hearing it but for you the person saying it to relieve that burdensome bitterness feeling." The session ended with a sense of residual disconnect between the client and therapist.

In the following session, the therapist continued to connect the client's relationship with food to the lack of agency in her childhood. The client indicated another rupture in this session, which occurred when the therapist tracked how the client moved away from sad feelings. The therapist intervened more carefully, which allowed the client to remain more present. When the client dismissed her own emotional experience, the therapist validated her defensive position.

Final Portion of the First Brief Relational Therapy Treatment

Themes continued to center on the client's difficulty with asserting herself and accessing her emotions. The client expressed increasing awareness of maladaptive patterns that led her to feeling overwhelmed. She more readily shared painful feelings about her family and was less guarded in discussing her marriage difficulties. The therapist was active in interpreting the client's inner experience and helping to foster self-esteem. Although the client still struggled in anticipating the needs of others, she experienced increased self-worth and excitement at school. Ruptures occurred in Sessions 22 and 23 in response to the therapist exploring the client's emotional avoidance. These ruptures were not adequately addressed. In Session 23, the therapist confronted the client on how her choices contributed to her unhappiness, and the client was self-critical of her difficulty in saying no to others. The therapist validated this, saying, "Well, that instinctual saying yes, that knee-jerk reaction, it doesn't have to do with thinking something through, but it comes from some place deeper that takes a lot longer to understand."

In final sessions, the client was more in touch with the unhappy aspects of her marriage. She was more emotional in session and acknowledged how avoiding her feelings has impacted her relationships. Sessions were often characterized by the client turning to the therapist for guidance. She was also better able to express when things upset her, even when there was no immediate answer. She attributed the changes in her life—quitting her job and returning to school—to the work in therapy. In ending, she was tearful and expressed warm feelings of appreciation towards her therapist.

Course of Therapy for Second Time in Cognitive–Behavioral Therapy Treatment: Drop Condition

Approximately 8 months after completing treatment, the client returned to seek a second course of treatment. This time, she was randomly assigned to the CBT treatment condition. The second therapist from the CBT condition was a 27-year-old single Caucasian woman, a psychology doctoral extern, who reported 2 years of previous clinical experience. She reported clinical training in psychodynamic, cognitive–behavioral, and integrative orientations. Although all treatments are 30 sessions in length, the client asked to be reassigned to a different therapist after only six sessions. She reported not benefiting from the treatment and not feeling comfortable with the therapist. She was subsequently reassigned to the BRT treatment modality. We will discuss the course of treatment with her second BRT therapist shortly. But first, we examine what occurred in two of the six CBT sessions that the client identified as rupture sessions.

Session 2: Keeping Things Surface

The therapist began the session by setting an agenda and using a thought record to help the client identify thoughts connected to procrastination. The client revealed self-critical thoughts. The therapist attempted to problem solve with the client. On the PSQ of Session 2, the client reported some accommodation or holding back (score of 2). She wrote, "I felt like I wanted to be more honest and go into things deeper, but my therapist is only concerned about her own agenda. This will probably get easier as we learn to work together." During the follow-up interview, the client shared, "Focusing on little things made me feel more reticent to open up about deeper issues."

Significant Event (Analysis of Rupture Experience).

Therapist: Could you have looked up the information online?

Client: I guess I could have.

Therapist: Is that something?

Client: Not really. In this class we are specifically not supposed to do that.

Within-Session and Postsession Effects. The therapist offered an additional suggestion, which the client again rejected. The misattunement on tasks continued to occur, with the therapist responding by providing a rationale. At times, the therapist appeared anxious, as indicated by nervous smiling. Early in the treatment both participants focused on goals related to body image. Although the client appeared uncomfortable in sharing her body image concerns, the therapist was not attentive in checking in with the client's feelings.

Session 6: Therapy Mismatch

On the PSQ for Session 6, the client reported high tension or conflict (score of 4) and modest accommodation (score of 3). She wrote, "I told her that I didn't think this therapy is right for me. It was very awkward. The therapist is young and I was worried about her feelings."

During the follow-up interview, the client stated,

> Yeah, it was just awkward, and my feeling is that she was trying to turn me into a thought robot. You could talk about thoughts and feelings, but you can't talk about anything that is actually going on in your life.

She also discussed doubting the therapist's competence.

Significant Event (Analysis of Rupture Experience).

Client: Well, it's awkward to bring this up, but I don't know if we are a really good fit. I feel like our personalities are a bit different. The Center told me I should come to session and bring it here.

Therapist: Well, why don't you tell me a little more about your thoughts.

Client: Sure. I'm sure you're not taking it personal, so I'm not going to worry. It's not that I need you to be my friend or anything, the last therapist was not super warm or fuzzy either. but I guess I just don't really feel comfortable.

Therapist: Do you think it might be the type of therapy at all? I guess that I'm just trying to understand. Maybe you can take me through your thought process.

Client: Well, I was thinking about what brought me back into therapy again. I guess I'm thinking of some of the bigger picture things that have been causing my depression, and our focus is on all of the little things. When bigger things have come up, you have said, well, we will do those some other time.

Therapist: We can definitely change the focus. I have been talking about it more in supervision, that we can focus more on self-view and self-esteem. I'm not sure if you would want to see if we can work on the bigger things.

Client: Well, sometimes, no offense, but I feel like you look at me like I'm an alien.

Within-Session and Postsession Effect. When the client expressed feeling judged, the therapist defended how she often intervened in order to understand her. The client discussed how this therapy had not been helpful for her current problems. The therapist proceeded to problem solve in discussing new goals for treatment. The client described feeling inferior in comparing herself with others and not having a clear sense of identity. The therapist foreclosed this exploration by problem-solving, which led the client again to express dissatisfaction. The client questioned whether the therapist would be more flexible, and the therapist indicated that she would talk with her supervisor. The client subsequently dropped from treatment. She was immediately randomly reassigned to a different BRT treatment.

Course of Therapy for Second Time in Treatment: Reassignment to Brief Relational Therapy Condition

The second BRT treatment lasted 30 sessions. The third therapist was a 27-year-old married Caucasian man of Middle Eastern descent. He was a psychology doctoral extern who reported 3 years of previous clinical experience. He reported clinical training in integrative, psychodynamic, and cognitive–behavioral orientations. Five of the sessions were identified as rupture sessions, with a score of 2 or higher on the PSQ. Three of the sessions are discussed in detail here. These sessions were selected because they suggested the highest degree of rupture and/or were sessions that the client spoke about in depth during her interview.

Prerupture Session Context

In initial sessions the therapist was tentative; he often refrained from making interpretations, allowing the client to be the arbiter of her own experience. The client discussed wanting to know herself better and having a desire for greater community. She also revealed ongoing difficulties with saying no to others. Although the client was able to share difficult aspects of her past, she remained more protective when discussing her marriage. She demonstrated more emotional accessibility but still struggled to remain present with painful feelings. The therapist was experiential in drawing attention to the process and helping the client become aware of her feelings. He often engaged in a cocreative process with the client, in which they would both work together to identify words and feelings that best captured her unique experience.

Session 6: Post Session Questionnaire "This Is Silly"

The client discussed marital difficulties in expressing her feelings to her husband. The therapist explored whether this difficulty was also present in their relationship, but the client moved away from this exploration, expressing isolation in having to repress her feelings in anticipating her husband's needs. Shortly after, the therapist asked the client to engage in a two-chair exercise to access feelings towards her husband. On the PSQ, the client reported moderate tension or conflict (score of 3) and some accommodation (score of 2). She wrote, "An exercise he wanted me to do (talking to chair) seemed kind of pointless but we talked about it." When asked what was helpful, she wrote, "Being honest and able to trust that it was okay to doubt the process. The therapist didn't take it personally." During the follow-up interview, the client shared her discomfort in discussing anger toward her husband. However, she was able to express her discomfort to the therapist, and the therapist was open to exploring the issue. She stated, "How he handled the conflict in the process showed me that it was okay to disagree and it was not the end of the world."

Significant Event (Analysis of Rupture Experience).

Client: Wait, can I ask you a question first? When I started thinking about this I got really angry. I'm feeling pretty angry about it, but I can't say that to him. So am I supposed to say what I want to say or say what I would actually say?

Therapist: Just to see where it goes. What's the hesitancy in feeling very angry?

Client: Well, it's a chair, so that's silly. I don't know what the point of bringing it up is, if I can't say or do anything about it.

Therapist: So this activity is a little silly and there might not be a point to it.

Client: Not just the activity. I mean, whether it's a conversation with you or with the chair, I feel kind of wrong for getting angry. I feel like he's in this vulnerable, lost place, and I don't want to kick him because that feels like the wrong thing.

Therapist: Part of the reason that I wanted to do this exercise is because I get the sense that you're feeling a lot of anger but there is a reluctance to talk about him. It is as if by talking about your anger you are actually kicking him. It's as if feelings in general are something to feel guilty about. Even if we are doing it in this silly hypothetical way, there is this twinge of guilt that won't allow you to really express how you are feeling. Even in here, you had to pause before oscillating to the chair. Tell me about that.

Within-Session and Postsession Effects. The client was able to address her discomfort with the task and the therapist was open in wanting to understand the client's experience. When the therapist focused on the client's difficulty with expressing anger, the client shared her fear of losing control of her feelings. She was also able to express fear of disappointing the therapist. The therapist metacommunicated his experience of the client as open and engaged.

In subsequent sessions, the client became more emotionally present and tearful. She was able to acknowledge unhappiness in her marriage and fears of confronting her husband. The client linked her difficulty in expressing emotions in session to her fears of coping with the aftermath of her feelings. Although she demonstrated more awareness of her feelings, she continued to struggle with asserting them.

Session 13: Post Session Questionnaire "Cocreation"

The client began by reflecting on a previous session and feeling that the therapist was suggesting that she contributed to all of her problems. The therapist invited the client's feelings, but she moved away to discuss feeling tired. The therapist questioned the client's marriage.

When she moved away, the therapist again refocused, and the client was able to express feeling unacknowledged by her husband. The therapist inquired whether there was a word other than tired that could capture her experience, but the client appeared unreceptive to this exploration. Upon further prompting by the therapist, she revealed embarrassment in not having the right word to describe her experience. The therapist refrained from interpretation, allowing the client to elaborate. The latter expressed isolation and sadness in needing to hide her pain.

On Session 13's PSQ, the client reported moderate tension or conflict (score of 3) and accommodation (score of 3). She wrote, "He used the word *depressed*. I didn't like it and had to confront him, which was uncomfortable. However, it was helpful in talking about why I dislike the word." During the interview, the client shared how being labeled depressed left her feeling that she couldn't get better. She addressed the issue, describing this process as a turning point in being able to take a risk by expressing her feelings in the moment. She also described a sense of cocreating their experience: "It was empowering to think that I'm an individual with my own experience of the world right now."

Significant Event (Analysis of Rupture Experience). There is difficulty for the client in directly expressing hurt feelings towards the therapist. The client stated, "Well I guess that contributes to my 'tired' feeling." She elaborated, "Well, it's the wrong word, you know what I mean." When the therapist questioned whether the client felt criticized, she expressed a sense of incompetence. The therapist suggested that they could collaboratively build a vocabulary to identify the client's inner experience, and the therapist tentatively used the word *depressed* to reflect the client's experience. The client shared feeling inauthentic. She initially seemed complacent in using the word depressed but the therapist attempted to foster her opinion.

Therapist: Well, really you could best tell me if that describes it for you.

Client: Yeah, I don't know. I just feel too tired to figure out who I am. I'm just like what do you want me to do, fine I'll do this. It's like everything right now is making me depressed or tired. *Depressed* is like this catch-all word, we can use that word if it is the right word. I just feel like it is a life sentence or that I should be on medication or something. It makes me uncomfortable.

Therapist: So when I said *depressed*, it felt a bit damning.

Client: Yeah, I don't know, it's dismissive. I guess because I have felt depressed before and it didn't make it any better to call it that. It was like I'm depressed so that's what's wrong, but it didn't really mean anything. It's kind of the stupidest word ever because it's different for everybody. You called it an umbrella word. I guess it's an okay umbrella word but I don't think people should use it.

Therapist: So we will chuck that word then.

Within-Session and Postsession Effects. The client was able to address the rupture by expressing disagreement with the therapist in a genuine way. The therapist validated her feelings, which allowed her to be more honest. The therapist connected the client's inauthentic feeling to not expressing herself with others. In subsequent sessions, the client reported communicating more openly in relationships. The therapist helped the client to become aware of what happens for her experientially when she asserts herself. The client shared how feeling dismissed by her husband leads to intense anger. She also introduced concerns related to her weight and expressed shame in discussing her body, as well as fears of the therapist judging her.

In Session 21, the client reported a rupture of feeling more tension in session. In discussing her weight concerns, the therapist began to probe for information, and the client revealed discomfort in talking about her weight. She became tearful when discussing these body struggles. On the PSQ, she reported that it felt like they both were less present and more self-conscious. The rupture was not addressed, and the client did not report a resolution. In the following sessions, they continued to focus on the client's fear of bringing up negative emotions when she feels happy. The therapist frequently invited an exploration of the therapy relationship. The client was more present and shared how she had been communicating more with her husband rather than allowing her feelings to build up.

Session 27: "Wrapping It Up"

The client began the session by discussing a recent argument with her mother, in which she was able to stand up for herself. The therapist was supportive of the client's effort to communicate her feelings in the moment. On the PSQ, the client reported some accommodation or holding back (score of 2) and moderate conflict (score of 3). She wrote, "My therapist suggested I was holding back, and I felt defensive and put on the spot. It was uncomfortable even though it was probably necessary. I didn't consider whether it upset me until after." In the interview, the client shared how it was difficult to share painful feelings in session and then feel abandoned in leaving the therapy and lacking the space to process those feelings.

Significant Event (Analysis of Rupture Experience). The therapist tentatively questioned the client's need to report something positive in therapy and questioned whether she was holding back.

Therapist: Maybe you are holding back from the negative.

Client: I don't think that I'm holding stuff back. I think I have a sense that we are wrapping up soon, but I don't think I'm holding stuff back. Not on purpose.

Therapist: So tell me about wrapping up soon.

Client: I don't know. How many sessions do we have left, three? So I'm aware of that. I think it's kind of nice to reflect on the things that went well rather than, you know, walking out and thinking of all of the things that are still wrong, I guess. I don't think it's on purpose, I think I've tried to notice the good things more.

Within-Session and Postsession Effects. The therapist continued to explore whether the client might be avoiding talking about unresolved difficulties. The therapist was attentive to the patient's discomfort and became more tentative and exploratory in stance. This appears to have helped the client to subsequently express her negative feelings. In the following session, the client addressed the rupture in expressing how she had felt criticized. The therapist expressed accountability for pushing the client to focus on negative feelings. The client acknowledged her desire to be a good patient.

As the sessions proceeded, the client became tearful when discussing awareness of her desire to feel more connected in her relationships. She described feeling more capable of confronting her husband. In final sessions, she expressed sadness in ending but revealed feeling lighter and less angry in knowing that she can continue to work on asserting herself.

WHAT WAS THE NATURE OF RUPTURE EVENTS AND RESOLUTION ATTEMPTS?

This chapter investigates how rupture events differed throughout the various treatment conditions and the ways in which the different therapists attempted to repair ruptures with the same client. How did rupture events appear to influence the treatment course, and how did the ways in which ruptures were attended to and resolved affect the types of therapeutic changes that the client experienced?

First Brief Relational Therapy Treatment: Type of Rupture Events

In her first treatment, the client experienced a greater number of rupture events. She reported minor ruptures in experiencing awkwardness with the therapist in initial sessions. Ruptures occurred around the client experiencing difficulty with expressing her emotions, and themes of mistrust and fear of how the therapist was perceiving her, seemingly related to the invalidation that she experienced during childhood.

Therapist Interventions and Attempts at Resolution During the First Brief Relational Therapy Treatment

Rupture events typically occurred in response to the therapist focusing on the therapeutic relationship or drawing attention to the client's avoidance of emotions and her difficulty in asserting herself. Although the therapist adhered to the BRT modality and often explored the therapeutic relationship or helped the client access painful feelings, the therapist was also active in focusing on the client's past and making interpretations in linking her defenses to past experiences. When rupture events occurred, the client usually would not address her discomfort with the therapist or the task. The client's emotional avoidance potentially impacted her ability to directly share how she felt about the rupture. She perhaps felt more comfortable sharing her reaction nonverbally or changing the topic. At times the therapist also exhibited subtle avoidance by not staying in the here and now, instead making more general interpretations.

First Brief Relational Therapy Treatment: Therapist Style and the Therapeutic Relationship

The therapist would often use humor in session. Her style was supportive and empathetic, which appeared to facilitate the client's engagement in treatment and her ability to be vulnerable in sharing painful aspects of her past and current relationships. The therapist was normalizing and validating, which appeared corrective given the client's history of feeling invalidated and criticized by her parents. At times the therapist was confrontational, particularly around the client's reluctance to assert her feelings in outside relationships. In ruptures where the therapist was more confrontational, the client appeared less willing to assert her discomfort. The therapist's lack of flexibility in attending to the client's fears appeared to stunt the exploration around the rupture event, not allowing it to unfold and be meaningfully resolved. It is possible that it was difficult for the client to address her feelings or any anger towards the therapist if she believed that asserting herself would be a threat to the relationship.

Cognitive–Behavioral Therapy Drop Condition: Type of Rupture Events

Differences emerged with regard to the type of ruptures that occurred, with ruptures occurring in response to disagreement on tasks and therapist behavior that was more controlling and directive. Ruptures also occurred around themes of mistrust and fears of being judged by the therapist. The therapist's inflexibility also contributed to the client's reluctance to engage in tasks. The client's sensitivity to feeling controlled by others potentially interacted with the therapist's style and the directness of the modality.

Cognitive–Behavioral Therapy Drop Condition: Therapist Interventions and Attempts at Resolution

In line with the cognitive model, the therapist would often intervene by focusing on the client's distorted thoughts and providing psychoeducation. When rupture events occurred around disagreement with tasks, the therapist appeared to intensify the use of cognitive interventions in a somewhat rigid fashion. This appears to have exacerbated the client's experience of not feeling heard. The client responded with reluctance and would shift topics to talk about distressing life events. The therapist would redirect attention to the task, not attending to the client's discomfort or issues unfolding in their relationship. By the time the client addressed her discomfort, the therapist attempted to better understand, but the client was less willing to repair issues in the relationship. In response to the rupture, the therapist again gravitated towards problem-solving, which further worsened the client's frustration. Rather than remaining with the intimacy of the therapeutic relationship and engaging in a more open dialogue with the client, the session ended with the therapist indicating that she would speak with her supervisor. The client did not return and was reassigned to another therapist and course of treatment.

Cognitive–Behavioral Therapy Drop Condition: Therapist Style and the Therapeutic Relationship

The therapist's style was directive and active. She was less responsive in reflecting back feelings and was more focused on the client's cognitions and behavioral interventions. The client shared that she did not experience the therapist as warm, which left her feeling judged. Given that the client struggled with fears of being judged by others, it appeared that the therapist's detached stance impacted the client's ability to be more vulnerable in session. At times the therapist seemed anxious with the client, as evidenced by nervous smiling and referring to her supervisor in session. The therapist's mention of her supervisor appeared to create a further barrier in the therapeutic relationship. Although the particular form the ruptures took may have been influenced by the directive and psychoeducational style of the therapeutic modality, the therapist's failure to directly engage with and negotiate the emerging ruptures appears to have contributed in important ways to the client's dropping out of the treatment.

Second Brief Relational Therapy Treatment: Type of Rupture Events

While in the first treatment minor ruptures occurred in initial sessions, in the second BRT treatment a rupture was not reported until Session 6. Although differences emerged in how rupture events manifested, ruptures occurred around similar themes of the client fearing judgment, relational difficulties with expressing her emotions and a need to perform with others. However, there was a more active focus on the client's difficulty in expressing emotions in her relationship with her husband.

Second Brief Relational Therapy Treatment: Therapist Interventions and Attempts at Resolution

Rupture events would typically occur in response to the therapist's tentatively exploring whether the client was holding back from sharing negative feelings, or when the therapist tried to help the client to access painful emotions through experiential exercises. However, the client was better able to address her discomfort or assert disagreement with the therapist during the rupture events. When she was unable to do so in the immediate context, she addressed her concerns in subsequent sessions. During the ruptures, the therapist did not push the client to continue with the task and did not immediately validate the client by shifting focus. Instead, the therapist would refrain from providing interpretations and would invite an exploration of what was occurring for the client, which facilitated the client's agency in helping her to elaborate on her experience. This process appeared to play a pivotal role in allowing the client to find her own voice and verbalize any threatening feelings that she was experiencing. The therapist also metacommunicated his own feelings and was willing to acknowledge responsibility.

Second Brief Relational Therapy Treatment: Therapist Style and the Therapeutic Relationship

The therapist's style was calm and tentative, which seemed to permit the client more agency in the room. Overall, the therapist was less active and directive than the other therapists. He was very adherent to the BRT model, less interpretive in focusing on the client's past, and more attuned to the process in tracking what occurred for the client experientially. The therapist was collaborative in cocreating an understanding of the client's experience, often by working together to find words to best capture the client's experience. He demonstrated a high level of competency and comfort in staying in the rupture moment, while validating the client's feelings and still encouraging her to elaborate with curiosity on her intrapsychic and interpersonal experience with him.

WHAT WERE THE CONSEQUENCES OF RUPTURE EVENTS ON TREATMENT OUTCOME?

First Course of Brief Relational Therapy Treatment

In completing her first treatment, the client experienced a significant reduction in her symptoms. She also experienced important life changes, including leaving her job and beginning college, a long-term wish that she had been unable to act upon previously. As these decisions were initiated after treatment began, it is likely that treatment helped her to gain more clarity in making them. The client began treatment to better understand how her feelings contributed to maladaptive coping and to address issues related to her self-worth. She reported experiencing increased self-worth and excitement at school.

Although rupture events occurred more often during her first treatment, they were less frequently addressed. However, the strength of the relationship appeared to permit the client and therapist to experience moments of rupture without the relationship being adversely affected. The therapist's validation might have been particularly therapeutic given the client's experience of her own mother as critical, dismissive, and unsupportive. This process seemed to help facilitate insight and awareness for the client and to lessen her depressive symptoms and increase her self-worth. In addition, there appeared to be less of an experiential focus on negative feelings, which might have been more in sync with the client's level of readiness in first beginning therapy.

Second Course of Brief Relational Therapy Treatment

In her second treatment, the client was able to maintain treatment gains while experiencing additional interpersonal changes. Ruptures appeared to play a pivotal role in helping the client to address her discomfort and express her feelings with the therapist. In asserting herself with the therapist, the client was able to better express herself in outside relationships. The therapist was experientially focused which allowed the client more agency in the room. These findings fit with Safran and Muran's (1996) assertion that effectively resolving ruptures can be powerful opportunities for therapeutic change. By encouraging clients to explore ruptures, clients can acquire new relational schemas. During a follow-up interview, the client shared, "I'm not carrying as much anger around, because I'm not thinking about stuff that bothers me as much. I either try to let it go or address it right in the moment, and that's a pretty big shift."

Mechanisms of Change and Differences Between the Two Brief Relational Therapy Treatments

In understanding the mechanisms of change that contributed to good outcome, the examination of the two different courses of treatment highlighted several common factors that may have contributed to this client's therapeutic outcome. Common relationship factors noted during both treatments included a strong therapeutic bond, as well as relative agreement on therapeutic tasks and goals. As evident in both the sessions and the client interview, both BRT therapists demonstrated a high level of competence and skill, empathy, warmth, and flexibility. Both therapists were very emotionally present and attuned to the client and persistently engaged in an exploration of the client's emotions to help her become more aware of her emotional and interpersonal needs. Both treatments similarly focused on the client's relational difficulties of asserting herself with others, by exploring the here and now of the therapy relationship, utilizing therapeutic metacommunication, two-chair experiential exercises, and facilitating an awareness of the client's maladaptive patterns. In addition, both treatments appeared to instill a sense of mastery and hope in the client.

There were also significant differences, in the client behaviors, styles and techniques of the therapists, and ways in which the therapists attended to rupture events. During the first treatment, the therapist was more directive and active, and there emerged more of a pattern of the client turning to the therapist for explicit guidance. The therapist often focused on the client's past, providing interpretations that linked the client's defenses to childhood experiences. The therapist was very supportive, which appeared to facilitate the client's ability to implement major life decisions during treatment. During the interview, the client stated,

> With my first therapist, there were a lot of outer changes. I mean there were inner changes too, but that's where I saw most of it, but with my second therapist we worked on the nitty gritty things, and he was helpful in suggesting to do role play to help me recognize my feelings.

In the second treatment, the therapist was less active and more tentative, which appeared to allow more space for the client and a more facilitative environment for self-exploration. The therapist focused closely on what was occurring experientially for the client. The client was better able to express her feelings both with the therapist and in outside relationships. The therapist's experiential focus on the here and now of the therapy relationship appeared to help the client to express her feelings in the therapy in a way that she struggled to do in her outside life. Yet as the treatment continued, this appeared to translate to the client's outside life in helping to decrease her interpersonal difficulties and allowing her to better access her feelings and assert herself with others.

During the CBT drop interval, there were differences in how ruptures manifested, with ruptures occurring predominantly in response to disagreement with therapy tasks and therapist behavior that was more directive and controlling. When rupture events occurred around disagreement with tasks, the therapist would increase her cognitive interventions. This is in line with research that has demonstrated that rigid adherence to interventions during ruptures has resulted in poorer outcome (Castonguay, Goldfried, Wiser, Raue, & Hayes, 1996). The therapist's lack of flexibility seemed to make the client feel less comfortable to engage in the therapy tasks. Given the client's controlling childhood, it appears that her schemas of being controlled by others interacted with the directiveness of the modality and the style of the therapist. When the client appeared dissatisfied with the task or aspects of the therapeutic relationship, the therapist did not attend to discomfort or issues that were unfolding in their relationships.

PRACTICE IMPLICATIONS AND RECOMMENDATIONS FOR CLINICIANS AND SUPERVISION

In using this case study, we proposed to contribute to the discourse on therapeutic ruptures and repairs, and their impact on process and outcome. Although there are limitations to utilizing a case-study design, systematic case studies can provide critical opportunities to comprehensively investigate the theories that inform treatment. Given the opportunity to examine the same client with separate therapists, we were interested in exploring how the intersection of unique therapeutic relationships and the use of specific interventions may have contributed to different types of changes. Safran and Muran (1996) suggested that the negotiation of alliance ruptures is at the heart of the change process.

During the first BRT treatment, the therapist's active presence helped the client to feel safe and validated and to implement major life decisions.

Therapy was a safe place where the client benefited from validation and insight, which helped to increase her self-worth and lessen her symptoms of depression. There was a greater occurrence of ruptures, although the ruptures were less frequently addressed and resolved.

In the second BRT treatment, the therapist was more experientially focused. He was less active in making interpretations and was more tentative, which appeared to allow the client to better access and express her feelings. Ruptures appeared to play a significant role in helping the client to address any disagreement and express her feelings. Rupture events were more sufficiently addressed in session by both the client and the therapist, and there were more frequent resolutions of ruptures. In addition, the therapist more closely followed Safran and Muran's (1996) stage process model of rupture resolution. The therapist's experiential focus on the here and now of the therapy relationship appeared to help the client express her feelings in a way that she struggled to do in her outside life. As the treatment continued, this process translated to the client's outside life in lessening her interpersonal difficulties, allowing her to better access her feelings and assert herself with others.

This chapter highlights the importance of attending to ruptures and fostering favorable conditions to allow for their understanding and resolution. Future research would benefit from replicating these findings with multiple clients and exploring the relationship between rupture events and therapeutic change in poor outcome cases.

REFERENCES

Aron, L. (1990). One person and two person psychologies and the method of psychoanalysis. *Psychoanalytic Psychology*, *7*, 475–485. http://dx.doi.org/10.1037/0736-9735.7.4.475

Castonguay, L. G., Goldfried, M. R., Wiser, S., Raue, P. J., & Hayes, A. M. (1996). Predicting the effect of cognitive therapy for depression: A study of unique and common factors. *Journal of Consulting and Clinical Psychology*, *64*, 497–504. http://dx.doi.org/10.1037/0022-006X.64.3.497

Castonguay, L. G., Nelson, D. L., Boswell, J. F., Nordberg, S., McAleavey, A., Newman, M., & Borkovec, T. (2012). Corrective experiences in cognitive behavioral and interpersonal–emotional processing therapies: A qualitative analysis of a single case. In L. G. Castonguay & C. E. Hill (Eds.), *Transformation in psychotherapy: Corrective experiences across cognitive behavioral, humanistic, and psychodynamic approaches* (pp. 245–279). Washington, DC: American Psychological Association. http://dx.doi.org/10.1037/13747-013

Derogatis, L. R. (1983). *SCL-90–R: Administration, scoring, and procedures manual II.* Baltimore, MD: Clinical Psychometric Research.

Doran, J. M., Safran, J. D., & Muran, J. C. (2016). The alliance negotiation scale: A psychometric investigation. *Psychological Assessment, 28*, 885–897. http://dx.doi.org/10.1037/pas0000222

Elliott, R. (1986). Interpersonal process recall (IPR) for psychotherapy process research. In L. Greenberg & W. Pinsof (Eds.), *Handbook of psychotherapy process research* (pp. 503–527). New York, NY: Guilford Press.

Elliott, R. (1994). *Understanding the change process in psychotherapy: Comprehensive process analysis.* Unpublished manual, Toledo, OH.

Elliott, R., Shapiro, D. A., Firth-Cozens, J., Stiles, W. B., Hardy, G. E., Llewelyn, S. P., & Margison, F. (1994). Comprehensive process analysis of insight events in cognitive–behavioral and psychodynamic–interpersonal psychotherapies. *Journal of Counseling Psychology, 41*, 449–463. http://dx.doi.org/10.1037/0022-0167.41.4.449

Eubanks-Carter, C., Muran, J. C., Safran, J. D., & Hayes, J. A. (2010). Interpersonal interventions for maintaining an alliance. In L. M. H. S. Strack (Ed.), *Handbook of interpersonal psychology: Theory, research, assessment, and therapeutic interventions* (pp. 684–702). Hoboken, NJ: Wiley.

First, M. B., Spitzer, R. L., Gibbon, M., & Williams, J. B. (1995). *Structured clinical interview for DSM–IV Axis I disorders: Patient edition* (SCID-I/P, Version 2.0). New York, NY: Biometrics Research Department.

Ghent, E. (1989). Credo: The dialectics of one-person and two-person psychologies. *Contemporary Psychoanalysis, 25*, 169–211. http://dx.doi.org/10.1080/00107530.1989.10746289

Horowitz, L. M., Alden, L. E., Wiggins, J. S., & Pincus, A. L. (2000). *Inventory of Interpersonal Problems manual.* Odessa, FL: The Psychological Corporation.

Horvath, A. O., Del Re, A. C., Flückiger, C., & Symonds, D. (2011). Alliance in individual psychotherapy. *Psychotherapy, 48*, 9–16. http://dx.doi.org/10.1037/a0022186

Horvath, A. O., & Symonds, B. (1991). Relation between working alliance and outcome in psychotherapy: A meta-analysis. *Journal of Counseling Psychology, 38*, 139–149. http://dx.doi.org/10.1037/0022-0167.38.2.139

Jacobson, N. S., & Truax, P. (1991). Clinical significance: A statistical approach to defining meaningful change in psychotherapy research. *Journal of Consulting and Clinical Psychology, 59*, 12–19. http://dx.doi.org/10.1037/0022-006X.59.1.12

Martin, D. J., Garske, J. P., & Davis, M. K. (2000). Relation of the therapeutic alliance with outcome and other variables: A meta-analytic review. *Journal of Consulting and Clinical Psychology, 68*, 438–450. http://dx.doi.org/10.1037/0022-006X.68.3.438

Mitchell, S. A. (1988). *Relational concepts in psychoanalysis: An integration.* Cambridge, MA: Harvard University Press.

Muran, J. C., Safran, J. D., Samstag, L. W., & Winston, A. (2002). *Patient and therapist postsession questionnaires*, Version 2002, Beth Israel Medical Center, New York, NY.

Safran, J. D. (2012). *Psychoanalysis and psychoanalytic therapies*. Washington, DC: American Psychological Association.

Safran, J. D., & Muran, J. C. (1996). The resolution of ruptures in the therapeutic alliance. *Journal of Consulting and Clinical Psychology, 64*, 447–458. http://dx.doi.org/10.1037/0022-006X.64.3.447

Safran, J. D., & Muran, J. C. (2000). Resolving therapeutic alliance ruptures: Diversity and integration. *Journal of Clinical Psychology, 56*, 233–243. http://dx.doi.org/10.1002/(SICI)1097-4679(200002)56:2<233::AID-JCLP9>3.0.CO;2-3

Safran, J. D., Muran, J. C., Demaria, A., Boutwell, C., Eubanks-Carter, C., & Winston, A. (2014). Investigating the impact of alliance-focused training on interpersonal process and therapists' capacity for experiential reflection. *Psychotherapy Research, 24*, 269–285. http://dx.doi.org/10.1080/10503307.2013.874054

Safran, J. D., Muran, J. C., & Eubanks-Carter, C. (2011). Repairing alliance ruptures. *Psychotherapy, 48*, 80–87. http://dx.doi.org/10.1037/a0022140

Safran, J. D., Muran, J. C., Samstag, L. W., & Stevens, C. (2002). Repairing alliance ruptures. In J. C. Norcross (Ed.), *Psychotherapy relationships that work* (pp. 235–254). New York, NY: Oxford University Press.

Safran, J. D., Muran, J. C., Samstag, L. W., & Winston, A. (2005). Evaluating alliance-focused intervention for potential treatment failures: A feasibility study and descriptive analysis. *Psychotherapy, 42*, 512–531. http://dx.doi.org/10.1037/0033-3204.42.4.512

Silberschatz, G., & Curtis, J. T. (1993). Measuring the therapist's impact on the patient's therapeutic progress. *Journal of Consulting and Clinical Psychology, 61*, 403–411. http://dx.doi.org/10.1037/0022-006X.61.3.403

Sommerfeld, E., Orbach, I., Zim, S., & Mikulincer, M. (2008). An in-session exploration of ruptures in working alliance and their associations with clients' core conflictual relationship themes, alliance-related discourse, and clients' post-session evaluations. *Psychotherapy Research, 18*, 377–388. http://dx.doi.org/10.1080/10503300701675873

Strupp, H. H. (1980). Success and failure in time-limited psychotherapy: Further evidence (Comparison 4). *Archives of General Psychiatry, 37*, 947–954. http://dx.doi.org/10.1001/archpsyc.1980.01780210105011

3

PATIENT AND THERAPIST RELATIONAL PATTERNS: IMPLICIT NEGOTIATIONS

EMANUEL SCHATTNER AND ORYA TISHBY

In this chapter we examine the implicit negotiation of therapist and patient interpersonal patterns that we consider to be inherent to any therapy encounter. Alongside the negotiation of the therapy goals and tasks, which are made explicit in the therapeutic dialogue, there is also a less visible aspect, which often remains unconscious and unspoken: the meeting of two sets of wishes, expectations, and needs regarding self and others (Pizer, 1998). We refer to these embedded sets as *relational patterns*, as they seem to profoundly affect the way that therapist and patient relate to one another and work together.

Our focus in this chapter is on understanding how these relational patterns contribute to the development of the therapeutic relationship and to outcome. We chose to study this question by looking at a successful case, examining how the meeting of two minds plays out explicitly and implicitly in psychodynamic psychotherapy. From a sample of 70 cases of psychodynamic

http://dx.doi.org/10.1037/0000093-004
Developing the Therapeutic Relationship: Integrating Case Studies, Research, and Practice, O. Tishby and H. Wiseman (Editors)

psychotherapy (Wiseman & Tishby, 2011), we chose the therapeutic dyad in which patient outcome showed the most improvement. We then proceeded to examine qualitative and quantitative data depicting the unique, subjective meaning given to the therapeutic relationship by both participants and linking it to outcome. Methodologically, a systematic single case study may grant a closer look at the workings of change mechanisms than what is provided by process-outcome data from large samples. Such an in-depth analysis of cases with the broad aim of extrapolation to all therapeutic encounters, is indebted to the tradition pioneered by Hans Strupp (e.g., 1980, 1993; Hilliard, Henry, & Strupp, 2000). In recent years there have been calls to renew systematic case studies alongside large randomized controlled trials (RCTs). Stiles (2009) claimed that therapist's responsiveness to the patient's needs in psychotherapy plays a key role in psychotherapy process and can only be studied through case analyses. Similarly, Fishman (2013) advocated for a bottom-up approach, adding qualitative analysis to quantitative data in order to create "thick descriptions that include the detail, complexity, context, subjectivity and multifaceted nature of human knowledge" (p. 406). Stiles, Hill, and Elliott (2015), in a review of the past and a look to the future of psychotherapy research, recommended using mixed methodology or sophisticated quantitative methods in the systematic investigation of a small number of cases to learn about process at the micro level. They pointed out that qualitative methodology adds to quantitative data by allowing researchers to "investigate phenomena that occur infrequently (e.g., intense weeping), that are very complex and contextually dependent (e.g., insight), or that reflect inner experiences not reliably observable to external judges" (p. 284).

THEORETICAL AND CONCEPTUAL BASIS

In our analysis of cases we are guided by relational psychoanalysis, which views the evolving therapeutic relationship as the core of the therapy process. The relational paradigm describes the unique meeting of two subjectivities, patient and therapist, which try to know and make themselves known to one another (Aron, 1996). Jay Greenberg (1995) captured the mutuality in the therapy process in his concept of the interactive matrix: "The interactive matrix is shaped from moment to moment, in every treatment, by the personal characteristics of the analysand and of the analyst . . . It is only within the context of the interactive matrix that the events of an analysis acquire their meaning" (p. 1). Therapy, according to the relational view, is a process of cocreation of meaning, often focusing on patient–therapist enactments, where the patient's dynamics come to life, as they touch on or trigger emotions and cognitions within the therapist that, in turn, evoke their own characteristic interpersonal pattern. Patient and therapist can each get stuck in old familiar patterns, which at times are also dysfunctional patterns. However, working through these enactments provides an opportunity for productive in-session exploration (Safran & Kraus, 2014) as the unconscious worlds of both parties is called upon.

In the process of working through ruptures and enactments, both patient and therapist take risks, as they move away from the old, secure relational patterns, allowing different, sometimes unfamiliar dimensions of themselves to emerge and to be discussed (Davies, 2004; Safran & Muran, 2000). In this process both therapist and patient relinquish certain self–other perceptions and responses, so that there is a real change in the interaction of the dyad, leading to new possibilities and new internalizations in the patient.

The dyadic process of negotiation of needs between patient and therapist parallels mother–infant patterns of synchrony and coordination. Ham and Tronick (2009) pointed out that these interactions are not ideal, but rather "messy," involving "mismatches of affective states, miscoordination of responses, and misapprehensions of relational intentions" (p. 620). They emphasized the importance of reparation, which facilitates the development of shared meaning. In addition,

> Through reparation, the infant and the caregiver come to implicitly know that the negative experience of mismatch can be transformed into a positive affective match, that the partner can consequently be trusted, and that the infant (and caregiver) can act effectively in the world. (Ham & Tronick, 2009, p. 620)

Another consequence of reparative processes is the development of new implicit ways of being together (Tronick, 2003).

Research on the therapy relationship has initially focused on the therapeutic alliance and its contribution to outcome (see Chapter 1). Going beyond alliance as a predictor of outcome, and capturing relational processes, Safran and Muran (2000) focused on alliance ruptures and repairs as entailing "an important mechanism of change in and of itself since it affords patients the experience of constructively negotiating the competing needs of self and other" (Safran & Kraus, 2014, p. 382). The repair of alliance ruptures has been found to be significantly related to patient outcome (Safran, Muran, & Eubanks-Carter, 2011; see also Chapter 2, this volume).

Another way of capturing interpersonal process is by focusing on *therapeutic immediacy*, defined as the processing of the therapeutic relationship, and processing interactions that occur in the here and now (Hill & Knox, 2009; see also Chapter 13, this volume). In a study of immediacy events in one psychodynamic therapy, these events were found to be initiated mostly by the therapists, leading to patients' expressing feelings, opening up, and gaining insight. In addition, patients indicated in posttherapy interviews that they remembered and profited from immediacy (Hill et al., 2014).

A key concept that is related to our focus on the meeting of therapist and relational patterns is the study of countertransference (Gelso & Hayes, 2007; Hayes, 2004). Ligiéro and Gelso (2002) showed that both positive and negative countertransference appeared to be associated with weaker alliances. Furthermore, patients' specific personality pathologies were associated with consistent therapists' emotional responses, suggesting that clinicians can make diagnostic and therapeutic use of their responses to patients (Colli, Tanzilli, Dimaggio, & Lingiardi, 2014).

Looking at therapists' relational patterns and how they play out in therapy, Tishby and Wiseman (2014) applied the core conflictual relationship theme (CCRT) method (Luborsky, 1998) to study countertransference. The CCRT is a method to identify consistent interpersonal patterns extracted out of narratives about interactions with significant others. The CCRT consists of three components: (a) Wish Towards the Other, (b) the Response of the Other, and (c) the Response of Self. To study countertransference by applying the CCRT method, therapists' interpersonal patterns with their parents are identified, and the repetition of these patterns in their narratives about their patients is examined (Tishby & Vered, 2011; Tishby & Wiseman, 2014). Developing a typology of types of countertransference, five types were identified corresponding to different CCRT components from therapists' relationships with their parents that also appeared in their CCRTs with patients. The five types were

- wish from parent transferred to the patient,
- projecting the Parent Response of Other on the patient (i.e., perceiving the patient as similar to the parent),
- repetition of the Response of Self (responding to the patient as they had responded to their parents),
- repeating the negative or positive parent Response of Other as the Response of Self (responding to the patient as their parents had responded to them), and
- repairing the negative parent Response of the Other as the Response of Self (responding to the patient in a manner opposite to their parents' response to them).

The analysis of countertransference types was applied to two cases, selected from a larger sample of patients in psychodynamic therapy in a university counseling center. One patient had a positive outcome and showed an increase in the alliance throughout therapy, whereas the second patient showed a decrease in alliance and little improvement, leading to dropout. It was found that in the less successful case, the therapist's countertransference dynamics dominated the relationship and did not become more flexible in the course of therapy. One such dominant type was "Repair of the parents' response," in which the therapist tried to relate and intervene in a manner that was *opposite* of what she had experienced with her parents, and which was not attuned to the patient's needs. Another countertransference type that recurred throughout therapy was "Wish from the parent transferred to the patient." In the successful case, the therapist was able to gradually "let go" of countertransference patterns, and shift his response to fit the patient's needs. This therapist seems to have managed his countertransference better than the therapist in the less successful case (Tishby & Wiseman, 2014). Indeed, a meta-analysis of studies on the effects of countertransference management (Hayes, Gelso, & Hummel, 2011) showed that managing countertransference successfully was related to better patient outcome.

To summarize, relational psychoanalysis provides us with the lens through which to view this process. In the following case the analysis focuses on the dyadic relationship at three time points in therapy and looks at the contributions of both therapist and patient to the process—moving from near dropout to a therapeutic success.

STUDYING THE THERAPEUTIC RELATIONSHIP METHOD

We analyzed a successful case of psychodynamic psychotherapy, taken from a larger sample of 27 therapists and 70 patients who participated in a study conducted at a university counseling center (Wiseman & Tishby, 2011, 2014). All patients were seen once a week for psychodynamic therapy. Outcome measures used were the Outcome Questionnaire—45 (OQ–45; Lambert et al., 1996), and the Target Complaints Scale (TCS; Battle et al., 1966), in which patients describe the three main problems for which they seek therapy, listing them in descending order. Therapeutic alliance was measured using the Working Alliance Inventory (WAI; Horvath & Greenberg, 1989). The Patient and Therapist Post Session Questionnaire (PSQ; Muran, Safran, Samstag, & Winston, 1991) was used to assess the therapeutic relationship in a particular therapy session, as well as rupture and repair of the alliance.

Patient and therapist relational patterns were identified using the Relationship Anecdote Paradigm Interview (RAP; Luborsky, 1998). The RAP interview was developed to identify patients' relational patterns before they begin therapy (Barber, Luborsky, Crits-Christoph, & Diguer, 1998). In this study both patients and therapists underwent RAP interviews at three time points during the course of therapy, at which they were asked to recount three relational narratives about their parents and about each other (patient about therapist and therapist about patient). Thus, on the basis of the RAP interviews we were able to identify the relational patterns with parents that were repeated in the therapeutic relationship, and how the therapy relationship changed in the course of a year of psychodynamic psychotherapy. At intake, the patients completed the OQ–45 and the TCS. Patient and therapist underwent RAP interviews and completed the WAI and the PSQ after Sessions 5, 15, and 28. The OQ–45 was completed at intake and following Sessions 5, 15, 28, and 32, and the TCS was completed at intake and following Session 32. Residual gains were computed for the OQ–45 and the WAI. Thus, change scores were adjusted for pretreatment differences between participants.

To capture the complexity of the relational themes, the RAP interviews of the therapist and patient were also analyzed using qualitative methodology by adapting steps from consensual qualitative research (CQR; Hill, 2011; Hill et al., 2005). The primary team members who judged the data included one postdoctoral and one senior researcher with an external and senior auditor reviewing the work. To minimize bias, in Step 1 both judges formed an account of the therapeutic process over time based solely on the self-reported quantitative data. This account pointed out corollaries in the self-report data (e.g., higher tension in sessions [on PSQ] or absence of symptom improvement seemed linked to a decreasing alliance). Only then, in Step 2, were the RAP interviews read and analyzed, the product being a characterization of the relational patterns with significant others of the therapist and patient. This was eventually condensed into a description (e.g., mother is warm, supportive, and weak; therapist is distant, dependable, and critical). As before, this step of the analysis also attempted to account for changes over time. Finally, Step 3 consisted of a consensual process to gather the multiple data and perspectives into an integrated account of the therapeutic process.

CLINICAL CASE STUDY

Amanda was a 23-year-old undergraduate student who sought treatment for her difficulties in interpersonal relationships.[1] She was single, lived away from home, and was involved in an on-and-off romantic relationship that she considered "unhealthy." Her parents were married but emotionally estranged from each other, with a history of marital infidelity on the mother's part, which Amanda had a role in uncovering. Her background included difficulties in forming intimate relationships, including past experiences of sexual harassment, and coping with a learning disability. Several years before, she had been in a psychotherapy that was supportive and directive, which

[1]Details of this case example have been altered to protect confidentiality.

she had experienced as helpful. Amanda reported feeling satisfied with her academic studies in humanities.

The case was chosen for having the highest gain on the OQ–45 relative to the entire sample. The gain between the intake and Time 4 was −1.47, with the second-highest gain in this sample a relatively distant −1.32 (the minus sign denotes improvement). In addition, there was a substantial and mutual increase in alliance between Time 1 and Time 3 (therapist's gain was .36, and Amanda's gain was .89), and a significant decrease in Target Complaints (dealing with sexual harassment dropped from 12 to 7 on a 13-point scale, and dealing with a learning disability dropped from a rating of 10 to 6).

Case Formulation and Description of Patient and Therapist

Amanda's experience of her parents was split between that of an idealized, pitied father and a devalued, critical mother. In her own words, her father was "an incredible person, whom I love very much and value more than anyone on earth" (all quotation marks in this study denote verbatim quotes from the RAP interviews). Amanda perceived him as protective of her, compassionate, but also as helpless, naïve, and imperceptive. His weakness was underlined for her by his unwillingness to divorce her mother, who had been unfaithful to him, a fact Amanda herself had discovered and made known a few years earlier. In addition, Amanda felt that he did not set any limits and would give her whatever she asked for, whereas at times she needed him to stand up to her and direct her. In their conversations, Amanda often made a conscious effort to unburden herself to him, only to realize that for all his sympathy he could offer her little more than to direct her to seek professional help. She often wished that he would share some of his own issues with her, but he never did. In contrast, Amanda perceived her mother as "treacherous, childish . . . needlessly provocative." Much of this was tied to the above-mentioned infidelity, but the mother was also criticized for her alleged lack of insight, egocentricity, and superficiality. Amanda felt that her mother needed her mainly as a narcissistic extension of herself and was not really interested in her life and her academic studies. Amanda reflected that she was often upset and offended by her mother, though she could readily forgive her father for saying similar things. Based on her narratives of her parents, Amanda's CCRT formulation was: *She wished to open up, to be cared for and helped. Others are perceived as helping but also as distant and not caring, and in response she opens up sometimes, but at other times she feels misunderstood and disappointed.*

Amanda's initial OQ–45 score was 49, which was not in the clinical range because she did not suffer any specific symptoms. However, based on the initial interview, she was clearly experiencing difficulties in forming trusting, intimate relationships with both men and women and was still in the process of consolidating her identity. She depended on others to mirror her feelings and needs, and she did not trust her own intuition and feelings, which led to difficulties in decision making. The goals of therapy were as follows: (a) to create a safe and supporting environment where Amanda could get in touch with the deep pain and longing for love and care; (b) for Amanda to experience a close and positive relationship in therapy, in which her interpersonal conflicts would be enacted and worked through, enabling her to develop satisfying relationships; and (c) to help her find her own "voice" in terms of wishes, needs, and choices, so as to develop a consolidated identity. In light of these goals, one long-term psychodynamic therapy was recommended. Therapy lasted for 2 years.

The therapist was a 38-year-old female clinical psychologist, married, who had 3 years of previous clinical experience. The treatment was based on principles of contemporary psychodynamic psychotherapy (e.g., Summers & Barber, 2010), object relations (Winnicott, 1971), and relational psychotherapy (Aron, 1996). She received weekly supervision from a licensed psychologist. In her RAP interview she described her father as a "powerful, protective figure." However, she then recounted two relational narratives that seemed to convey her sense of being left to cope alone with danger, unshielded. Though benign, the father "just wasn't there in the moments that count . . . he didn't want to see, didn't even look." In one narrative she recounted how, as a child, she skated down the road as her father watched from the sidewalk. All of a sudden she saw a car coming towards her, and she froze, terribly frightened. She then caught a glimpse of her father covering his eyes in terror, also freezing. Within a minute the car passed her, and she was not harmed. In describing this event, she said that at the moment when she most needed him, her father was unavailable. The therapist's mother was described as "a strong type . . . stable and happy"; however, she was constantly trying to set limits to her as a child, provoking angry outbursts and a pervading sense of being unloved. In retrospect, however, "Dad was excessively devoted (i.e., a sucker), while Mom, poor thing, tried to educate me, but didn't love me." In another narrative, the therapist describes how her mother, who was always strong and practical, suffered a crisis once she quit a long-term job. She lay in bed for hours, and the therapist cared for her and encouraged her. She described mixed emotions of concern and anxiety, on the one hand, and pride in her caretaking ability on the other hand. She was relieved when her mother was back on her feet again. The therapist's accounts of parents and spouse were complex and highly perceptive, and the interviews as a whole portrayed her as resilient, an achiever, and someone who enjoyed her role as a caregiver both within the family and professionally. Simultaneously, in some narratives she expressed a strong yearning, perhaps disavowed, to lean on someone. When she felt weak or in distress, she felt "abandoned," and she experienced the significant other as often incapable of reassuring her. Her CCRT formulation was *She wishes to be liked, helped, and cared for, whereas others are often perceived as anxious and not helping, leading to mixed feelings of liking the other but also feeling hurt, anxious, and disappointed.*

COURSE OF TREATMENT

Early Phase

Soon after the beginning of the treatment, following the second session, the therapist managed to rescue the treatment from an almost certain dropout. She received a call from the clinical coordinator at the clinic, informing her that Amanda had requested to switch therapists, and was advised to bring this up in their next session. The therapist was taken aback and was conscious of feeling somewhat rejected. She had thought that "everything had been OK . . . (Amanda) is growing closer, and that she built a relationship, and trust." However, she was able to react nondefensively and decided to broach the subject with Amanda in their next session. When they met, Amanda said that she felt that talking to the therapist was "like talking to a friend," and she "needed someone more directive to 'manage' her," like her previous psychotherapist. The therapist responded that she was glad Amanda had been able to speak her mind, but considered her wish to be an indication of the problem: "I'm not willing to take that role. You're looking for someone to tell you what to do, but *that's just what we're going to tackle in therapy*. The solution isn't for me to tell you what to do in your life." Amanda listened and returned for the next session saying she was "very happy" with the previous session, and that the therapist's interventions made a strong impact. Specifically, she understood that her need to be directed, to be "managed" by a strong other, was the problem and not the solution. She reasoned in her interview that the previous therapist's directive, limit-setting style of "do's and don'ts" was suited to the boundary-crossing phase her life was in at the time, but that the present therapist's goal was also her own, as she indicated in her RAP interview: "I'm not seeking her approval. I want that approval to come from myself. That's what we're trying to build." Amanda mentioned that rather than saying anything that might discredit the previous therapist, the current therapist emphasized that "she believed in the previous therapist," but also thought that at this point in time, the goal was for Amanda to become more independent. The therapist felt they had overcome the initial obstacle, although she perceived herself as actually quite directive in telling the patient that her need for direction is what they had to work on in therapy. Clearly, from the beginning, the conflict of dependence–independence, providing direct help versus helping the patient find her own path, was a dominant theme in this treatment. Amanda expressed a need to be cared for by a strong figure, which neither her father (perceived as caring but weak) nor her mother (perceived as distant and not caring) provided. This is the relational pattern behind her request from the therapist to "manage her" and lead her. The therapist's CCRT shows similar needs for caring, which have not been fulfilled, and so the patient's request may have touched on these feelings, leading to a countertransference response of strong objection. In addition, the therapist experienced her mother's educational directives and limit setting as emotionally distant, which may have contributed to her refusal to provide those same interventions. Although the therapist's stance was in accordance with the psychodynamic model, she may have not been empathetic to the client's requests, and was quick to reject them with little inquiry. The patient may have picked up on the therapist's emotions, and this may be one explanation for her wish to switch therapists. Once the therapist was able to acknowledge Amanda's needs, explain the rationale of the treatment and begin an implicit negotiation on responding to these needs, the patient accepted those terms and felt helped.

An examination of the quantitative data shows that neither patient nor therapist reported a rupture at this point, which supports the possibility that the discrepancies in perceptions of the therapy process and therapy goals between Amanda and her therapist were probably beginning to be negotiated (by the fifth session). However, there was still a gap between the patient and therapist alliance ratings, with Amanda rating the alliance as quite high WAI = 5.83 and the therapist WAI = 4.81. Perhaps the therapist was still cautious, having been taken aback by Amanda's wish to leave treatment, and was not quite sure that their collaboration was strong. Her CCRT with Amanda at this point reflected a wish transferred from the relationship with her parents: "to be liked and to be understood," and a wish "to achieve and be good"—meaning a wish to be successful as a therapist, and to be accurate in her interventions. She perceived Amanda as strong and understanding, which was partly accurate (Amanda's narrative reflects her acceptance of therapy process and goals), but she missed Amanda's characteristic feelings of being hurt and feeling misunderstood. She thus projected the parent RO (her mother) on the patient, seeing both as somewhat more resilient than they actually were. Her Response of Self was liking the patient and feeling that she was helping, but also feeling anxious and hurt, repeating the Response of Self from the relationship with her parents, but managing those feelings successfully.

Middle Phase

As therapy continued, so did the negotiation between Amanda and the therapist about the main issue raised earlier. Even as she was progressing, Amanda continued to refer ambivalently to incidents in which she perceived the therapist as warm and close, and therefore, in her experience, as too much of "a friend" to be able to protect and to set limits effectively. The adjectives Amanda used to describe the therapist reflect this basic ambivalence: the therapist was "good, kind," "charming," "perceptive," "reinforcing," "identifies with me," but was also "just like a friend, not a therapist." At this midtherapy phase, Amanda described a session in which she told the therapist she was planning to visit an ex-boyfriend in a different city, supposedly for a project that she was working on. The therapist conveyed her trust in Amanda's judgment and encouraged her to carry out her plan. Amanda then protested in the interview, stating firmly

> My dad and the previous therapist, who was far better, would never have allowed me to do that. I keep asking (the therapist) to be more aggressive with me, because I need someone to give me a cold shower. She doesn't; she doesn't set me the limits I need.

She further described how a good friend of hers persuaded her not to go, and even the boyfriend called and asked her not to come. In the end, she changed the project and decided not to go, which is actually a sign of maturation and independence; however, she still believed that the therapist was wrong in not stopping her. In a second narrative, she took the opposite stance, commenting on the therapist's perception and sensitivity in appreciating an art project that reflected themes pertaining to an issue she was struggling with. Amanda brought the project to the session and the therapist immediately commented on what she saw, which some of the art teachers had missed. In this narrative, Amanda claimed that regardless of what she had said before, her therapist is a very good therapist. Interestingly, in this incident the therapist was unwittingly responding to her wish that someone would help and care for her. Although the therapist did not actually tell Amanda what to do, she was quite direct and accurate in mirroring the themes that were present in the project, verbalizing the issues and emotions that she perceived. From the therapist's perspective, the mid-phase narratives reflected a good therapeutic alliance. She reported a newfound confidence in the relationship, which allowed her to take more risks when interpreting: "It was quite hard for me, frustrating (Amanda's) wish to be told what to do . . . but I feel that things are starting to move along" and that the theme of "telling her she can stand on her own two feet, that she'll be OK" was sinking in. However, she commented, there were also times of despair when confronted with the "big hole in (Amanda's) sense of self, which I keep trying to refill, but there's no solution." These mixed feelings were also reflected in her CCRT—the main wish was "to achieve and to be good"—focusing on helping Amanda and trying to become more accurate in her perceptions and interpretations. The former wish of being loved and understood was not present anymore in this phase, so she was able to overcome this repetition. She continued to perceive Amanda as strong and open, trusting the relationship more. Her Response of Self was a mix of feeling helpful and feeling helpless, at times understanding and at times not understanding. Her rating of the alliance increased from 4.81 to 5.36, so that perhaps she was feeling they were working together as well as becoming more accepting of the fact that she could not always help. Her countertransference on the one hand was not to lead the patient too much, yet on the other hand it was *very important* for her to feel that she was helping and that she was accurate in her interpretations. She described a session during which Amanda told her that she had relationships with several guys at the same time, and there was an old boyfriend that she could always go back to. From the therapist's perspective, it seemed that Amanda was concerned about the morality of her behavior, once again expecting the therapist to set limits. The therapist described how, as she was listening to Amanda, she realized that the issue was not morality but Amanda's fear of being alone, and her need to keep someone at bay, at all times. Amanda was surprised but acknowledged there was some truth in the interpretation. The therapist was working hard to be accurate, and in doing so she was "Repairing the parent RO," but adapting this countertransference type to Amanda's needs. Amanda's rating of the alliance remained quite high, WAI = 5.44. Therapist and patient did not report any ruptures.

Late Phase

At this time, Amanda described how she was gradually making her own choices and gaining a wider and clearer perspective on various events and relationships. She attributed these developments to the therapy process, and she was able to recognize how she had grown in therapy. She no longer criticized the therapist but spoke about "the good interpretations that the therapist provides." She stated that she wished the therapist would say more, because her input is important and makes her want to share more and more of her life with her. She was beginning to feel that her therapist values her and encourages her independence: "She really values me, she thinks about me all the time, she says so. She's very impressed by how I deal with things." Notwithstanding her sense that "the treatment is really moving forward," Amanda also voiced her concern that the therapist would be able to look after her own well-being, such as by being able to keep work and private life separate. She explicitly contrasted the therapist with her mother: "It's amazing how (the therapist) related to that and how my mom did . . . (the therapist) is really sensitive . . . I love sharing with her." She felt that she "had a place in the therapist's heart." In one of the narratives she described how, with the help of therapy, she reached a decision not to return to a former workplace, where she was at risk of becoming romantically involved with an older man to whom she had been attracted in the past. In her description of the process, it was clear that when she initially presented the idea of working with this man, whom she really liked, the therapist did not raise any objections but helped her look more deeply into her plan. The more they discussed it, the more she realized that she may be tempted to begin a relationship that would not be good for her. When she finally decided to give up the idea of returning to this job, the therapist agreed that this was a good choice for her, which made Amanda very happy. Although the decision was hers, Amanda realized that she still needed the therapist's approval, and would have to work further on relinquishing this need.

At this time, Amanda developed a strong and positive transference, expressed through guesswork regarding the therapist's education of her children or her marital fidelity. Regarding her own mother, Amanda noted she had become more forgiving towards her: "I don't have the same anger towards her that I used to . . . my mom has good intentions, no ulterior motives."

The therapist's narratives in this phase reveal a great deal about the process that she had gone through in this therapy and shed light on the evolving nature of the therapeutic relationship. The therapist described an encounter in which Amanda expressed her concern that the therapist may be overburdened from listening to people's troubles all day long and thinking about them between sessions. She was happy that the therapist was thinking about her, but worried that it might impact the therapist's private life. The therapist interpreted Amanda's concern that she may not be able to "hold" her (a maternal transference), but she also felt that Amanda saw her as a separate person, for the first time. She felt that alongside the transferential concerns, there was also a newly developed recognition of her own subjectivity, which indicated progress. Regarding countertransference, this relationship episode reflects the therapist's wish to be loved and understood, which was very prominent at the early phase of therapy. However, at this time, she saw the patient's ability to "see her" and other people in her life as progress achieved through therapy. Thus, the therapist's own countertransference need to be recognized was partially fulfilled in a manner that facilitated therapy progress. Parallel to Amanda's developing a wider perspective on her relationships, the therapist's perceptions of Amanda became increasingly more complex. In the narratives, the Response of the Other is not only strong and open but also anxious and hurt. Perhaps it has become less threatening to get in touch with her pain, and perhaps this is what made it possible for the therapist to reflect more often on her avoidance of setting limits or her objections to being somewhat more directive at times. For example, in one of the narratives the therapist described Amanda's casual sexual flings, wondering whether she was overly encouraging, supporting Amanda's pleasure in being attractive to men. She wondered whether she should have spoken about the risks entailed in careless sexual behavior. In this and the other narratives, her Responses of Self consisted of feelings of helplessness and ambivalence, alongside feelings of being helpful. Thus, the therapist was gradually able to let go of her need to feel strong and successful—feelings she may have learned to rely on as a child.

The working alliance in this phase was high, with an increase in Amanda's ratings from 5.36 to 6.44 (higher than the sample mean for this phase, WAI = 5.35) and the therapist remaining constant at WAI = 5.31, slightly above the sample mean for therapists. Interestingly, Amanda indicated a rupture in this phase, the intensity of which was 4 on a scale of 5. The rupture occurred in a session where Amanda confronted the therapist about her position that fidelity among couples was possible, whereas Amanda experienced many incidents where she was approached by married men or single men in long-term relationships. She described that instead of getting into an argument, the therapist acknowledged her fears and perceptions, stemming from her mother's infidelity, and encouraged her to reflect on why she focused solely on these experiences and sometime even encouraged them unconsciously. Amanda felt that they were able to discuss and look at the rupture together (assigning a rating of 5 on a scale of 5—to the extent they were able to talk about the rupture), and a resolution rating of 4 on a 5-point scale.

In the last narrative, the therapist described an incident in which Amanda called her to consult about renting an apartment that she really liked; her friends had tried to persuade her against renting it, since it was in a noisy neighborhood. The therapist reflected on the situation and thought about possible responses. She emphasized that she felt more free expressing herself than before, when "I had an agenda of not letting her remain dependent . . . I was hysterically against that. Now, I felt that I could speak my mind." Instead of denying Amanda that guidance, the therapist helped her define the pros and cons and then told her to trust her own intuition about the apartment. Thus, although she did not tell Amanda what to choose, the therapist was direct in supporting Amanda in her own choices. This may seem a somewhat trivial therapeutic intervention, but in the course of this particular treatment its significance was not lost by either participant. This episode reflects the therapist's and patient's ability to move towards each other and renegotiate the relationship—with Amanda becoming more independent and relying on her therapist to strengthen her own choices, and the therapist moving away from a rigid position of refraining from any type of guidance.

OUTCOME

As mentioned earlier, Amanda's gain on the OQ–45 was an outstanding −1.47. Her ratings dropped gradually from 49 at intake to 40 at Time 3, then fell sharply to 15 at follow-up. Although her OQ–45 score was not in the clinical range at intake, the decrease is still impressive. In the Target Complaints, Amanda listed eating problems as the initial problem, rating it 11 on a 13-point scale, followed by sexual harassment with a rating of 12, and a learning disability, rated 10. After the 28th session, the same problems were rated by her 5, 7, and 6 consecutively. Based on the self-report data, Amanda achieved a significant improvement in the problems that brought her to therapy. The alliance also increased for both therapist and patient in the course of therapy. Amanda reported satisfaction with the way tensions in the therapeutic relationship were resolved in the late phase of treatment. Thus, in this case the bond and collaboration that developed contributed to sustaining the intensity of the therapeutic work.

SUMMARY AND MECHANISM OF CHANGE

A bird's eye view of Amanda's treatment suggests that the improvements in outcome and alliance were the result of a continuous and implicit negotiation between patient and the therapist regarding the therapeutic goals and tasks. The main theme of this negotiation was the contrast between what Amanda wished the therapist to be for her, and the therapist's idea of Amanda's needs and her perception of her own role in therapy. Using a psychodynamic conceptualization, our understanding of the case is that Amanda presented with a strong wish that her therapist constitute an authoritative, protective object for her, a wish drawing on her previous experience with a directive therapist but also on her psychological background. She experienced herself as dangerously "without limits" and in need of someone to fill the role neither of her parents could (for different reasons). From the start, this wish of Amanda's clashed with the therapist's conviction that what Amanda, in fact, needed was a supportive and reflective object, and that granting her wish would leave Amanda in an infantile, dependent position and would ultimately backfire. What may have strengthened this perception of Amanda is a certain similarity in the relational patterns of both participants in this therapeutic encounter. Both Amanda and, to some extent, the therapist, had weak but benign fathers, and both felt the need to be taken care of—although the therapist was more ambivalent about this need. The first scene of this negotiation, which we can trace with the available data, is when the therapist successfully prevented Amanda's dropout in the early phase. Amanda's move stemmed directly from the main theme of the negotiation: frustration with the "passivity" of her therapist and worry that she was "just a friend" and would fail in telling her what to do. In response, the therapist did three things: (a) she kept her own boundaries as a psychodynamic therapist by avoiding telling Amanda what to do, (b) she avoided a split with the previous therapist by refraining from criticizing her and reframing the difference between the two therapists as a difference in Amanda's own needs then and now, and (c) she delivered clearly and convincingly the treatment goal of empowering Amanda and fostering her autonomy. In terms of the implicit negotiation, the therapist thus conveyed to Amanda that though she was reluctant to comply with her wish, she was nevertheless neither weak (like Amanda's father) nor controlling and egotistic (like her mother), but worked towards achieving the developmental goals of young adulthood. Amanda responded to these explicit and implicit messages with an about-turn, now feeling safe, understood, and hopeful. The therapist did not consciously plan to deliver the complex messages described above. Rather, they flowed naturally from a self-disciplined application of her training and, in our interpretation, from the interaction of the two's relational patterns.

The basic relational patterns of the participants were different. While the therapist had two strong, supportive parents, Amanda did not. Both had to idealize and be idealized, but Amanda was more narcissistically sensitive. Amanda's mother was experienced as a "friend": confusing, childish, and lacking in authority, which is why she wished for a therapist who would be "mature": strong, guiding, and consistent. The therapist's aversion to filling that role may stem not only from the psychodynamic principle of neutrality but also from her experience of her own mother as too strict, "educational," and not warm or loving enough. The therapist was a far more autonomous person than Amanda, dealing differently with her own needs for dependence. Therefore, though she felt surprised and to some extent "abandoned" by Amanda's wish to terminate, she was not tempted to placate the patient or criticize her, but responded firmly and empathically. By reframing instead of confronting, she made it possible for Amanda to identify with the therapeutic goal of gaining autonomy and make it her own. She also modeled how setting boundaries for oneself and the other was compatible with a warm, caring relationship. As the therapy progressed, Amanda reported feeling warmly supported, even idealized (in the Kohutian sense of the word) by the therapist, without being intruded upon. Looking at the entire process, it becomes apparent to us that change was mutual, as Amanda and her therapist edged nearer to each other. Amanda took the therapist's emphasis on autonomy and made it her own, while the therapist learned to allow Amanda to lean on her for direction, without feeling she was relinquishing an interpersonal stance that was valuable to her. In summary, the treatment may be seen as an example of a successful implicit negotiation of the therapeutic goals (autonomy) and means (how to interpret, how much empathy, how much shielding). This negotiation is continuous until the late phase. The very fact that the negotiation took place is in itself a success, in this context.

FROM RESEARCH TO PRACTICE AND BACK

The methodology of the systematic case study, as advocated by experienced researchers (e.g., Fishman, 2013; Stiles et al., 2015) and employed in this study, is a promising direction for future research into the therapeutic process. Further research is needed, with more therapist–patient dyads—preferably using session transcripts—in order to look at how therapists' relational patterns affect the choice and impact of specific interventions that they use. In this study, we used the CCRT method to examine therapist and patient interpersonal patterns and how they interact in treatment. The CCRT method can be used quantitatively and qualitatively, thus providing very rich data for psychotherapy research. In studying this case, we began with quantitative outcome data, eager to learn what made this treatment so successful. Of course, there were many factors that operated in this treatment, but our focus was on the meeting and negotiation of relational patterns. The coding of the CCRT categories made it easy to identify the patient's and therapist's main relational themes and gain an understanding of the differences they had to overcome in the treatment. The relationship episodes provided us with rich data on how each member of the dyad perceived the other, which is something we usually do not know much about in the course of psychotherapy. The results of this and similar studies alert us to the importance of monitoring the therapeutic relationship and to paying attention to countertransference early on in treatment. These results support relational theory, which views each dyad as unique and thus each treatment as the product of the meeting of two minds.

IMPLICATIONS FOR PRACTICE AND TRAINING

This study underlines the need for therapists' routine self-observation of relational patterns and their impact on therapy—not only when the relationship reaches a rupture or impasse. Questions such as "What happened in today's session that was emotionally meaningful to me?" "Why? To what familiar patterns does this connect?" and "How could this have affected my own clinical choices in the session and the patient's reactions?" may be explored in supervision. Attending to one's relational patterns and the discrepancies with the patient's needs can help prevent pitfalls and assist in managing countertransference.

REFERENCES

Aron, L. (1996). *A meeting of minds: Mutuality in psychoanalysis*. Hillsdale, NJ: Analytic Press.

Barber, J. P., Luborsky, L., Crits-Christoph, P., & Diguer, L. (1998). Stability of the CCRT from before psychotherapy starts to early sessions. In L. Luborsky & P. Crits-Christoph (Eds.), *Understanding transference: The core conflictual relationship theme method* (2nd ed., pp. 253–260). Washington, DC: American Psychological Association. http://dx.doi.org/10.1037/10250-017

Battle, C. C., Imber, S. D., Hoehn-Saric, R., Nash, E. R., & Frank, J. D. (1966). Target complaints as criteria of improvement. *The American Journal of Psychotherapy, 20*, 184–192.

Colli, A., Tanzilli, A., Dimaggio, G., & Lingiardi, V. (2014). Patient personality and therapist response: An empirical investigation. *The American Journal of Psychiatry, 171*, 102–108. http://dx.doi.org/10.1176/appi.ajp.2013.13020224

Davies, J. D. (2004). Whose bad objects are we anyway? Repetition and our elusive love affair with evil. *Psychoanalytic Dialogues, 14*, 711–732. http://dx.doi.org/10.1080/10481881409348802

Fishman, D. B. (2013). The pragmatic case study method for creating rigorous and systematic, practitioner-friendly research. *Pragmatic Case Studies in Psychotherapy*, 9, 403–425. http://dx.doi.org/10.14713/pcsp.v9i4.1833

Gelso, C. J., & Hayes, J. A. (2007). *Countertransference and the therapist's inner experience: Perils and possibilities*. New York, NY: Psychology Press.

Greenberg, J. (1995). Psychoanalytic technique and the interactive matrix. *The Psychoanalytic Quarterly, 64*, 1–22.

Ham, J., & Tronick, E. (2009). Relational psychophysiology: Lessons from mother–infant physiology research on dyadically expanded states of consciousness. *Psychotherapy Research, 19*, 619–632. http://dx.doi.org/10.1080/10503300802609672

Hayes, J. A. (2004). The inner world of the psychotherapist: A program of research on countertransference. *Psychotherapy Research, 14*, 21–36. http://dx.doi.org/10.1093/ptr/kph002

Hayes, J. A., Gelso, C. J., & Hummel, A. M. (2011). Managing countertransference. *Psychotherapy*, 48, 88–97. http://dx.doi.org/10.1037/a0022182

Hill, C. E. (Ed.). (2011). *Consensual qualitative research: A practical resource for investigating social science phenomena.* Washington, DC: American Psychological Association.

Hill, C. E., Gelso, C. J., Chui, H., Spangler, P. T., Hummel, A., Huang, T., . . . Miles, J. R. (2014). To be or not to be immediate with clients: The use and perceived effects of immediacy in psychodynamic/interpersonal psychotherapy. *Psychotherapy Research, 24,* 299–315. http://dx.doi.org/10.1080/10503307.2013.812262

Hill, C. E., & Knox, S. (2009). Processing the therapeutic relationship. *Psychotherapy Research, 19,* 13–29. http://dx.doi.org/10.1080/10503300802621206

Hill, C. E., Knox, S., Thompson, B. J., Williams, E. N., Hess, S. A., & Ladany, N. (2005). Consensual qualitative research: An update. *Journal of Counseling Psychology, 52,* 196–205. http://dx.doi.org/10.1037/0022-0167.52.2.196

Hilliard, R. B., Henry, W. P., & Strupp, H. H. (2000). An interpersonal model of psychotherapy: Linking patient and therapist developmental history, therapeutic process, and types of outcome. *Journal of Consulting and Clinical Psychology, 68,* 125–133. http://dx.doi.org/10.1037/0022-006X.68.1.125

Horvath, A. O., & Greenberg, L. S. (1989). Development and validation of the Working Alliance Inventory. *Journal of Counseling Psychology, 36,* 223–233. http://dx.doi.org/10.1037/0022-0167.36.2.223

Lambert, M. J., Burlingame, G. M., Umphress, V., Hansen, N. B., Vermeersch, D. A., Clouse, G. C., & Yanchar, S. C. (1996). The reliability and validity of the Outcome Questionnaire. *Clinical Psychology & Psychotherapy, 3,* 249–258. http://dx.doi.org/10.1002/(SICI)1099-0879(199612)3:4<249::AID-CPP106>3.0.CO;2-S

Ligiéro, D. P., & Gelso, C. J. (2002). Countertransference, attachment, and the working alliance: The therapist's contribution. *Psychotherapy, 39,* 3–11. http://dx.doi.org/10.1037/0033-3204.39.1.3

Luborsky, L. (1998). The Relationship Anecdotes Paradigm (RAP) interview as a versatile source of narratives. In L. Luborsky & P. Crits-Christoph (Eds.), *Understanding transference: The core conflictual relationship theme method* (2nd ed., pp. 109–120). Washington, DC: American Psychological Association. http://dx.doi.org/10.1037/10250-007

Muran, J. C., Safran, J. D., Samstag, L. W., & Winston, A. (1991). *[Patient and therapist post-session questionnaires].* Unpublished instruments. New York, NY: Beth Israel Medical Center.

Pizer, S. A. (1998). *Building bridges: The negotiation of paradox in psychoanalysis.* Hillsdale, NJ: Analytic.

Safran, J. D., & Kraus, J. (2014). Alliance ruptures, impasses, and enactments: A relational perspective. *Psychotherapy, 51,* 381–387. http://dx.doi.org/10.1037/a0036815

Safran, J. D., & Muran, J. C. (2000). *Negotiating the therapeutic alliance: A relational treatment guide.* New York, NY: Guilford Press.

Safran, J. D., Muran, J. C., & Eubanks-Carter, C. (2011). Repairing alliance ruptures. *Psychotherapy, 48*, 80–87. http://dx.doi.org/10.1037/a0022140

Stiles, W. B. (2009). Responsiveness as an obstacle for psychotherapy outcome research: It's worse than you think. *Clinical Psychology: Science and Practice, 16*, 86–91. http://dx.doi.org/10.1111/j.1468-2850.2009.01148.x

Stiles, W. B., Hill, C. E., & Elliott, R. (2015). Looking both ways. *Psychotherapy Research, 25*, 282–293. http://dx.doi.org/10.1080/10503307.2014.981681

Strupp, H. H. (1980). Success and failure in time-limited psychotherapy: A systematic comparison of two cases: Comparison 2. *Archives of General Psychiatry, 37*, 708–716. http://dx.doi.org/10.1001/archpsyc.1980.01780190106013

Strupp, H. H. (1993). The Vanderbilt psychotherapy studies: Synopsis. *Journal of Consulting and Clinical Psychology, 61*, 431–433. http://dx.doi.org/10.1037/0022-006X.61.3.431

Summers, R. F., & Barber, J. P. (2010). *Psychodynamic therapy: A guide to evidence-based practice*. New York, NY: Guilford Press.

Tishby, O., & Vered, M. (2011). Countertransference in the treatment of adolescents and its manifestation in the therapist–patient relationship. *Psychotherapy Research, 21*, 621–630. http://dx.doi.org/10.1080/10503307.2011.598579

Tishby, O., & Wiseman, H. (2014). Types of countertransference dynamics: An exploration of their impact on the client–therapist relationship. *Psychotherapy Research, 24*, 360–375. http://dx.doi.org/10.1080/10503307.2014.893068

Tronick, E. Z. (2003). "Of course all relationships are unique": How co-creative processes generate unique mother–infant and patient–therapist relationships and change other relationships. *Psychoanalytic Inquiry, 23*, 473–491. http://dx.doi.org/10.1080/07351692309349044

Winnicott, D. W. (1971). *Playing and reality*. London, England: Tavistock.

Wiseman, H., & Tishby, O. (2011). *The patient–therapist 'dance': Interplay of patient and therapist interpersonal patterns, working alliance and psychotherapy outcome* (Grant No. 187/07, 2007–2011). Final Scientific Research Report: Israel Science Foundation.

Wiseman, H., & Tishby, O. (2014). Client attachment, attachment to the therapist and client-therapist attachment match: How do they relate to change in psychodynamic psychotherapy? *Psychotherapy Research, 24*, 392–406. http://dx.doi.org/10.1080/10503307.2014.892646

4

CLOSENESS AND DISTANCE DYNAMICS IN THE THERAPEUTIC RELATIONSHIP

HADAS WISEMAN AND DANA ATZIL-SLONIM

> . . . unless a therapist can enable his patient to feel some measure of security, therapy cannot even begin.
>
> —Bowlby, 1988, p. 140

> To discover truth about the patient is always discovering it with him and for him as well for ourselves and about ourselves.
>
> —Loewald, 1980, pp. 297–298

The major conceptualization of the development of the therapeutic relationship at the heart of our chapter relies on attachment theory and on contemporary relational thinking about the mutual impact client and therapist have on each other in the process of change.

ATTACHMENT-INFORMED CONCEPTUALIZATION

Bowlby's attachment theory provides a powerful lens to examine the therapeutic relationship in ways that are both empirically supported and clinically relevant (Eagle & Wolitzky, 2009; Farber & Metzger, 2009; Mallinckrodt, 2010). Bowlby (1969/1982) posited that individuals form internal working models of the self and others in close relationships based on their early experiences with caregivers. The therapeutic relationship is likely

http://dx.doi.org/10.1037/0000093-005
Developing the Therapeutic Relationship: Integrating Case Studies, Research, and Practice, O. Tishby and H. Wiseman (Editors)

to reactivate the client's long-standing expectations about the availability and responsiveness of others (Bowlby, 1988). Specifically in considering the application of attachment theory to the therapeutic process, Bowlby (1988) saw the therapist's role as providing "the conditions in which his patient can explore his representational models of himself and his attachment figures with a view to reappraising and restructuring them in light of the new understanding he acquires and the new experiences he has in the therapeutic relationship" (p. 138). Using the concept of *secure base* that Ainsworth introduced in her seminal work on infant–mother/caretaker attachment (Ainsworth, Blehar, Waters, & Wall, 1978), according to Bowlby, the therapist's first task is to provide the patient a secure base for exploration of his or her thoughts and feelings that is analogous to the mother providing her child a secure base from which to explore the world. As Bowlby noted, the concept of secure base is similar to Winnicott's (1971) "holding" and Bion's (1962) "containing." However, going beyond providing empathy and sensitivity (Rogerian-like conditions) and encouraging explorations, the therapist needs to respectfully challenge the client's internal working models of self and others (Dozier & Tyrrell, 1998; Farber & Metzger, 2009). This is where the therapist's own attachment history may also play in, contributing to the way he or she relates to the client and affecting the therapeutic relationship between them in the here and now (Bowlby, 1988).

Given that the client's working models dictate his or her expectations from the therapist, individual differences in attachment style will lead to different manifestations and dynamics in the relationship that will develop between the client and therapist. An individual's location in the two-dimensional space defined by attachment avoidance and attachment anxiety reflects both the person's sense of attachment security and the ways in which he or she deals with threats and distress. Individuals who score low on these dimensions are generally *secure* and tend to employ constructive and effective affect-regulation strategies. Those who score high on either the anxiety or the avoidant dimension (or both) suffer from attachment insecurities and tend to rely on *secondary attachment strategies*. To cope with threats when individuals feel their efforts to meet their emotional needs through a secure relationship have failed, they shift to one of two secondary attachment strategies (Mikulincer & Shaver, 2007). Individuals who rely on hyperactivating strategies intensify dependency needs and closeness in their relations with attachment figures, whereas those who rely on deactivating strategies increase distance so as not to get hurt. These diverse attachment strategies require therapists to conceive how clients with different secondary attachment strategies may work through their insecurities to establish a secure relationship with their therapist and build a working alliance that enables a collaboration on the goals and tasks in therapy (Mikulincer, Shaver, & Berant, 2013).

Daly and Mallinckrodt (2009) suggested that to foster a secure attachment in the psychotherapy relationship, it is important that the therapist regulate the *therapeutic distance* to enable clients to experience a corrective emotional experience. On the basis of qualitative interviews with experienced interpersonal therapists, they defined therapeutic distance as "the level of transparency and disclosure in the psychotherapy relationship from both client and therapist, together with the immediacy, intimacy, and emotional intensity of a session" (p. 559). Therapists distinguished between an initial *engagement phase* in which they largely acceded to a client's desired (but ultimately maladaptive) level of therapeutic distance, followed by a *working phase* in which therapists gradually attempted to steer the relationship toward a more optimal level of therapeutic distance. The therapeutic distance that is optimal for each phase is regulated by the therapist and depends on the client's hyperactivating versus deactivating strategies. With hyperactivating clients (high in anxiety), the therapist agrees to reduce levels of therapeutic distance in the engagement phase, and then after progress markers are reached, gradually increases distance as clients enter the working phase, thereby fostering autonomy. In contrast, with deactivating clients (high in avoidance), the therapist agrees to high levels of therapeutic distance in the engagement phase, and then after progress markers are reached, gradually lessens distance as clients enter the working phase, thereby fostering engagement. Thus, a corrective emotional experience is fostered not by one attachment relationship offered by the therapist, but rather by many relationships tailored to meet the client's needs through the changing phases of therapy (Mallinckrodt, 2010).

Attachment patterns in the therapeutic relationship are nearly always in a state of dynamic change rather than in static equilibrium. Either the client or the therapist, and more often both simultaneously, work actively to change the attachment dynamics (Mallinckrodt, 2010). In fact, the similarity or dissimilarity in attachment style of client and therapist will affect these dynamics (Wiseman & Tishby, 2014). In this sense, it has been suggested from both the perspective of interpersonal theory and attachment theory that "contrasting" (dissimilar) interpersonal orientations of the client and therapist are optimal for the process and outcome of psychotherapy (Bernier & Dozier, 2002).

CONTEMPORARY RELATIONAL PSYCHOTHERAPY CONCEPTS

These ideas fit with contemporary relational psychotherapy models that take a two-person psychology perspective assuming "that both therapist and client are always contributing to everything that takes place in the therapeutic relationship" (Safran, 2012, p. 196). From this perspective, theorists such as Benjamin (2004) and Aron (2006) have contended that client and therapist may revive the wounds in the other related to the relational experiences that each internalized in interactions with early caregivers in a way that often leads to getting stuck in complementary relations. This complementarity is characterized by a split in which one side takes a position complementary to the other: If one person is experienced as "the doer," then the other becomes "the done to." The more each member of the dyad locks into a singular position, the more rigidly the other is locked into the opposing, complementary position. In the complementary structure, the dynamics are such that conflicts cannot be processed, observed, held, mediated, or played with. Instead, each partner feels that her perspective on how this is happening is the only right one, or at least that the two are irreconcilable. This structure may involve polarizations such as those between attachment and separation, autonomy and dependency, closeness and distance. Conceptualizing the dynamics of polarization in this way captures the mutual experience of the client and the therapist of deep, generally unconscious needs and vulnerabilities that are being revived in the therapeutic relationship. Thus, in this relational perspective (Mitchell, 1993), in order to facilitate the gradual transformation from relations of complementarity to relations of mutuality, it is important that therapists deeply accept their own contribution to enactments in the therapeutic relationship. This enables both the client and the therapist to open up the psychic space for self-reflection and mentalization.

In this chapter, we draw on attachment theory and contemporary relational psychoanalytic concepts in order to shed light on the dynamics of closeness versus distance in the development of the therapeutic relationship in psychodynamic psychotherapy. In the clinical case that we analyze, we focus on the encounter between a client and her therapist, in which at the beginning of treatment, when one party tended to use deactivating strategies, the other party tended to use hyperactivating strategies, without being aware of the opposite pole within herself. We examine the interplay between the relational processes of the client and the therapist and shifts in closeness and distance as key for the development of a therapeutic relationship.

ASSESSMENT

Assessment included two types of measures: (a) interpersonal patterns of clients and therapists in close relationships and in the therapeutic relationship were assessed with RAP interviews during the course of psychotherapy, and the CCRT method was applied to these interviews (Wiseman & Tishby,

2017); and (b) self-report measures of attachment, client attachment to the therapist, working alliance, and outcome.

RAP and CCRT

The Relationship Anecdote Paradigm interview (RAP; Luborsky & Crits-Christoph, 1998) was employed to obtain clients' and therapists' relationship narratives in close relationships and with each other (see Chapter 3, this volume, for the method). The underlying premise is that the client–therapist narratives serve as a window into clients' and therapists' unique relational experiences with each other during the sessions.

The Core Conflictual Relationship Theme (CCRT) method (Luborsky & Crits-Christoph, 1998) was applied to the relational narratives to assess client and therapist relational patterns (see Chapter 3 for a definition). Our CCRT approach to analyzing the narratives combines applying the standard categories (and clusters) and conducting in-depth qualitative analysis of the client-therapist narratives within dyads (Wiseman, 2017; see also Chapter 3, this volume).

Self-Report Questionnaires

The Experiences in Close Relationships Scale (ECRS; Brennan, Clark, & Shaver, 1998) was used to assess attachment of both client and therapist. The ERC is a widely used 36-item self-report measure of adult attachment that consists of two scales: Anxiety (18 items; e.g., "I worry about being abandoned") and Avoidance (18 items; e.g., "I prefer not to show a partner how I feel deep down").

The Client Attachment to Therapist Scale (CATS; Mallinckrodt, Gantt, & Coble, 1995) was used to assess the therapeutic relationship within the perspective of attachment theory. The CATS is a 36-item measure that includes three subscales: Secure (14 items; e.g., "My counselor is sensitive to my needs"), Avoidant–Fearful (12 items; e.g., "Talking over my problems with my counselor makes me feel ashamed or foolish"), and Preoccupied–Merger (10 items; e.g., "I wish my counselor could be with me on a daily basis"). For a recent meta-analysis of the CATS, see Mallinckrodt and Jeong (2015).

The working alliance of client and therapist were measured using the Working Alliance Inventory (WAI; Horvath & Greenberg, 1989). Outcome was assessed using the Outcome Questionnaire—45 (OQ–45; Lambert et al., 1996) that yields a total distress score that has been found to be sensitive to change; and the Target Complaints Scale (TCS; Battle, Imber, Hoehn-Saric, Nash, & Frank, 1966), referring to three main problems for which the client sought therapy, indicating severity of each complaint on a scale ranging from 1 (*not at all*) to 13 (*couldn't be worse*).

CLINICAL CASE STUDY

This case was chosen for intensive analysis from Wiseman and Tishby's research program on client–therapist relationship patterns in psychodynamic psychotherapy (see Chapter 3). We chose this case for four reasons (on the basis of the assessment on the above measures):

- Both partners of the dyad were characterized by having an insecure attachment style as measured on the ECRS.
- CCRT themes of closeness and distance were dominant in both the client's and the therapist's relational narratives and these themes evolved through the three measurement points of the study (after Sessions 5, 15, and 28).
- The client's attachment to the therapist on the CATS showed change from low CATS security and high avoidance in the early phase (Session 5), to an increase in CATS secure attachment to the therapist and decrease in avoidance by the later phase (Session 28).
- The client reported improvement on her main complaint (on Target Complaints) and some improvement in her overall symptom distress (on the OQ–45).

Client Description and Presenting Problems

Hannah was a 25-year-old undergraduate student.[1] She was single and lived in a rented apartment off campus. She sought treatment because of feelings of depression and anxiety that had worsened recently when she had to take exams during her first undergraduate year in a prestigious program. Hannah said she continuously felt stressed and inferior compared with others and that it clearly affected her performance on all tasks and challenges in her life. She also described a pattern in which she usually avoided developing intimate relationships because she had difficulty trusting people and was afraid of being rejected or hurt. On the few occasions on which she actually began to date someone, she constantly felt anxious about being rejected, and this fear was usually confirmed in that the partner initiated a breakup at a relatively early stage of the relationship.

[1]Details of this case example have been altered to protect confidentiality.

Family Background

Hannah was the youngest of four children from an educated mid/upper class family. She described a general atmosphere of stress and extreme criticism in her childhood home. Her mother worked part-time and was described as intrusive and controlling; her father, who was busy with his career, was described as distant and rejecting. The parents' relationship was stormy and often included fights and outbursts of verbal violence. The sibling relationship was also a source of distress, as her older siblings were abusive toward her. When she turned to her mother for help, the mother dismissed her complaints. Hannah recalled that as a young child, she felt she had nowhere to escape the turmoil and shouting that were the norm at home; but as an adolescent, when the fighting started, she used to run outside and walk the streets until things calmed down a bit.

Diagnosis, Case Formulation, and Therapy Goals

Diagnosis. Based on the fifth edition of the *Diagnostic and Statistical Manual of Mental Disorders* (American Psychiatric Association, 2013) and the ICD–10 *Classification of Mental and Behavioural Disorders* (World Health Organization, 1993), Hannah was diagnosed with generalized anxiety disorder. Her anxieties specifically concerned her academic performance and feeling alarmed upon hearing loud noises or in the dark, as well as continuously experiencing excessive worries about various life challenges. In addition, she described some avoidant traits manifested in unwillingness to get involved with people because of fear of disapproval or rejection.

Case Formulation. Hannah grew up in a family in which negative emotions were not managed or regulated. Her parents did not handle their own anxieties, feelings of anger and aggressiveness, nor did they acknowledge Hannah's difficult feelings or assist her in coping with them. Thus, Hannah did not internalize capacities to tolerate and regulate her negative emotions. She felt alone in the face of intense and overwhelming negative emotional experiences. Hannah's caregivers failed to protect her from her brothers' aggressiveness or meet her emotional needs through a secure, accepting, and responsive relationship. Throughout her childhood, Hannah experienced both her parents as critical toward her: Her mother was perceived mainly as controlling and intrusive, and her father as rejecting and distant. Therefore, both closeness and distance in relationships evoked fears of being hurt. She was left with an injured sense of self, and though she was yearning for comfort, support, and recognition, she felt she had to protect herself from being hurt again. On the basis of her early experiences she tended to minimize her expectations from close relationships, expected them to be either too invasive or disappointing and therefore tended to avoid them.

Goals. The main goals of therapy were (a) to create a safe and supporting environment where Hannah could start exploring her actual and internalized relationships so as to open up new ways of experiencing self and others, (b) to help Hannah tolerate and regulate negative and stressful emotions, and (c) to help Hannah face developmental academic and interpersonal challenges with greater flexibility and freedom.

Client's Interpersonal Patterns

Hannah's CCRT patterns with her parents, as revealed by the first RAP interview (after the fifth session), were consistent with the above case formulation. The first narrative that she told about a meaningful interaction with her mother was the following:

> I talked with my mom about something, she wanted to know what was going on in my sessions. I told her that . . . I didn't want to tell her it's none of her business . . . I just said I don't want to talk about it. She started to get angry right away. She yelled and accused me of only wanting her money but not sharing my inner world with her. She said she would not pay for my treatment if she cannot know what is going on there. I tried to explain to her that this is private, this is my stuff, and I can't talk about it with her, I don't want to. We were both yelling at this point. She said I don't share anything with her and that I don't care about her. I just wanted her to go away and leave me alone. I also hated myself for being so unpleasant to her. All this just made me more distant than before. She cannot realize what is going on inside me and how stressed I am. I wish she could see what I really feel and take responsibility for her contribution to my state.

In this narrative Hannah described an encounter in which her mother tried to get close to her in a way that was experienced as inappropriate and intrusive. In response, Hannah pushed her mother away and distanced herself from her even more. At the same time, she expressed the wish that her mother could recognize how distressed she was and understand her situation. She felt bad because needing her mother evoked anxieties of being controlled by the mother, but she was also self-critical because she felt that her reaction toward her mother was offensive.

Hannah's first relationship narrative about a meaningful interaction with her father was from a memorable event from childhood:

> I think I was about 10; I needed help with my homework. I usually didn't turn to him for help, but this time I did. Then, after a very short while, he started to explain things beyond the task that was asked by the teacher.

> He said he wanted to enrich my knowledge. I was afraid that this would confuse me. It was not what I needed. I said I don't want to learn new things at that time. I just needed him to help me with my homework. He insisted and he got angry and critical toward me. I just waited for him to stop shouting and I went away. He let me go. I regretted that I asked for his help to begin with.

A second relationship episode about a more current interaction with her father revealed a similar lack of responsiveness.

In the narratives, Hannah described situations in which she asked her father for help and support, but in his reactions he did not see her and the kind of age-appropriate help that she needed, or he failed to attend and respond appropriately to her seeking his help (proximity seeking). In both cases this made her regret turning to him for help to begin with.

Hannah's CCRT pattern with her parents consisted of two opposing wishes (Ws), the first one more apparent than the other. On the one hand, she expressed *a need to be distant so as not to feel intrusiveness and feel controlled or rejected by the other.* She repeatedly perceived the other (response of other [RO]) as reacting in a way that was not congruent with her needs either by imposing his or her own needs and way of thinking or by rejecting her. On the other hand, a more hidden primary wish, was the wish *to get close to the other and be helped in a manner suited to her needs.* Her response of self (RS) in reaction to the other was to feel hurt, angry, and withdrawn. Thus, although she wished for help and closeness, through repeated frustration of this wish she had very low expectations that her wish to be helped and close could be fulfilled. In turn this contributed to her dominant tendency to avoid closeness and to keep her distance from the other so as not to be hurt.

A similar pattern was described in her relationship with her friends. All three narratives about friends described interactions in which Hannah had very low expectations that she could get help or sympathy from or establish closeness with her friends. These negative expectations were confirmed in her interactions with friends, as she experienced the other as rejecting, leading her to feel disappointed, hurt, and distant.

The Therapist

The therapist was a woman in her early 30s and married. She was a clinical psychology intern with 3 years of post–master's degree clinical experience. She received ongoing individual and group supervision as part of her internship. She also reported that she had had previous personal therapy, as well as current personal therapy.

Therapist's Interpersonal Patterns

The therapist also participated in a RAP interview relating to interactions with her own parents (and spouse/romantic relationship). The narrative the therapist told about her mother was as follows:

> I was about six years old. I really wanted to learn to play piano but I was terribly afraid to go to the first class on my own. I worried how it would be . . . on the one hand I guess I really wanted to please my mother and to behave in a mature way. On the other hand I was afraid I would not be able to please her. We got there . . . the teacher was scary: white hair tied back and a rigid look on her face. I was very scared to enter the class on my own and wanted my mother to go in with me. She didn't know what to do with me. She was very angry and impatient, and she said I was acting like a little girl. I was hurt, and I guess I was disappointed in myself.

The narrative the therapist told about her father was as follows:

> I was 5 years old, and my parents dressed me up as Peter Pan for a costume party in kindergarten. I really didn't want to wear that costume. I objected and I cried. My father took me to preschool with the costume, and he sort of pushed me in forcefully . . . and I continued to object. He was probably stressed about getting to work on time. It was unpleasant. He wanted to get it over with, wanted me to stop crying and go inside. I felt angry and helpless. You can't really decide anything when you are 5 years old. (See also Tishby & Wiseman, 2014, p. 367.)

The therapist's CCRT with her parents showed that her primary wishes were *to be close and not to be abandoned.* She also wished to let her voice be heard, not to be forced, and at the same time to please the other. She perceived her parents as misunderstanding her, angry and controlling, and also helpless (RO). Her response of self (RS) with them was to feel helpless, angry, disappointed, and somewhat guilty.

Client and Therapist Matching in Attachment and CCRT

As is the case for any therapeutic dyad, Hannah's and her therapist's encounter was unique and included its baggage of hopes, fears, and internalized object representations that each brought to the relationship. Considering similarities and dissimilarities in relational patterns between Hannah and her therapist showed some prominent similarities in attachment style and interpersonal themes. The fearful attachment style that characterized Hannah—high on both avoidance (5.67, 98th percentile of clients in the larger sample) and anxiety subscales (4.22, 67th percentile)—also characterized her therapist, though to a lesser extent. The therapist's scores on the ECRS avoidance (3.89, 99th percentile of therapists in the larger sample) and anxiety (4.83,

77th percentile) subscales were high compared with the other therapists in the larger sample (Wiseman & Tishby, 2014). Thus, the therapist can also be classified as "fearful attachment" relative to the therapists in the study. However, the therapist's avoidance was considerably lower than Hannah's. In fact, while Hannah was higher on avoidance than anxiety, the opposite was true of her therapist, that is, she was higher in anxiety than in avoidance.

In examining the narratives that the therapist recounted regarding meaningful interactions with her parents, it can be seen that while there are differences between her and the client (as could be expected between different individuals, and given that one is the client and the other is the therapist), there are also significant similarities. It appears that both the client and the therapist tend to avoid closeness so as not to be hurt, as they experience the other as controlling and/or rejecting. It should be noted that in terms of form, the therapist's narratives about childhood experiences were relatively coherent and organized, possibly due to her working on these issues in her personal therapy.

Course of Treatment: Closeness and Distance in the Therapeutic Relationship

We describe the course of psychotherapy through the relational narratives the client and therapist told about meaningful interactions during psychotherapy at the three time points of assessment: early (fifth session), middle (15th session) late (28th session; Wiseman & Tishby, 2017). In addition, for this dyad we conducted a qualitative narrative analysis that was applied to the three narratives that each told about the other at the three assessment points (a total of 18 narratives). This analysis shed light on the pushes and pulls of the closeness versus distance "dance" in this dyad as therapist and client attempted to negotiate distance and closeness between them over the course of psychotherapy. In what follows, for each phase we provide excerpts from the narratives revealing their experiences with each other from the client's and therapist's perspectives followed by our CCRT and qualitative understanding, as well as quantitative data on self-report measures (WAI and CATS).

Early Phase of Therapy

The inner drama of each member of the dyad is clearly captured in their narratives, which show that both client and therapist did not have an easy start. Hannah recounted her difficulty opening up and trusting her therapist:

> She kept telling me that I should share things with her. She said I am always alone with what I feel and that I should give her access to what I feel. I wanted her to stop pushing me to open up to her. This is the

> way I am, I can't share, I don't trust people. She was making all kinds of gestures so I would trust her and she repeated the same mantra again and again telling me that I shouldn't stay alone with what I feel. I backed off. I felt very hesitant to share things with her. My instincts told me slow down, back off.

Hannah's CCRT toward her therapist at the beginning point of treatment conveyed the wish to be distant and to avoid close contact with the therapist. She perceived her therapist's repeated invitations to open up as invasive and as a rigid technique imposed on her. Her response of the self was to close up and feel even more distant.

The therapist's perspective is depicted by the following narrative:

> Throughout the session there was some sense that there is something we did not manage to touch. I tried to reach out to her and help her open up and share what was going on inside her, but she wouldn't let me. And then finally, just before the end of the hour, she became more in touch with her emotions and she looked sad and upset. I wanted to stay with her in that moment and I felt it was very hard for her that we had to stop. I felt helpless to have to send her away like that and that I couldn't stay with her. There was a very heavy atmosphere.

The therapist's CCRT toward her client included the wishes to get close, to help, and not to hurt Hannah. She perceived her as distant and unreachable as well as needy and vulnerable. Her responses of the self were to try hard to get close to Hannah but also to feel guilty, as though she were abandoning or rejecting her.

The client and the therapist appeared to be caught in complementary positions. Hannah mainly experienced closeness as a threat that included coercion and imposition of the will of the other; thus, she was mainly in touch with her wish *to avoid closeness with the therapist*. In contrast, the therapist mainly experienced distance as abandonment and was mainly in touch with her wish *to get close to Hannah and to help her open up*. It seems that the more the therapist tried to get close, the more Hannah pulled away and avoided the therapist. Both Hannah and the therapist described these contradictory positions without being in touch with the opposite experience within them. That is, Hannah did not identify with the therapist's wish to get close and the therapist seemed not to identify the parts in herself that are hesitant and anxious about getting close.

CATS and WAI Self-Report Measures. Hannah's scores on the CATS reflect her difficulty to feel secure with the therapist and to trust her. On the CATS secure subscale she is rather low in Secure (4.18) and high in Avoidant (3.08), and moderate on Preoccupied (2.30) (compared with the sample from Mallinckrodt, Choi, & Daly, 2015). Surprisingly, unlike the CATS, her Alliance score on the WAI after Session 5 does not depict difficulty in building a strong alliance, with a score of 5.38. The therapist's WAI was 5.42, similar to Hannah's rating.

Middle Phase of Therapy

At midtherapy, the narratives that Hannah told about interactions with her therapist continue to show her struggles to open up and her difficulty feeling safe enough to explore. However, at the same time the narratives are more elaborate and she appears more aware of her approach–avoidance conflicts—not wanting to be left alone but also not being able to open up.

> She asked what goes on in my head. I told her I feel like everything is confused, and I didn't know how to find words to express it. She said it was okay, that we have time and that things will come out slowly. But it just made me more stressed and nervous and I just wanted her to leave me alone. I get into a kind of loop and inability to communicate. I tried to explain to her that on the one hand I don't want to be left alone, but on the other hand, this is the way I am. I am always suspicious about people's intention. I wish I could trust more.

Another narrative that she recounted at this time point was

> In the last meeting I was in a good mood after having made a successful presentation in class. She simply asked questions and she looked interested. We just sat and talked, you know, and I guess I was a bit less closed than usual. I was still excited because of the presentation I gave, and it was nice I could share it with her. But I also wondered whether her interest in me was genuine, or that she was putting on the face of the interested psychologist and that she was just doing her job. Anyway, I kept talking about myself and it felt OK.

Hannah's CCRT included her ongoing avoidance but also a wish to open up and to trust the therapist. In the first narrative, although indicating again her difficulty in accepting the therapist's invitation to disclose her thoughts, she appears more aware of her conflict between wanting not to "stay alone" and being able to trust. In the second narrative, while she begins to describe herself as a bit more open (sharing an experience of success), she still questions the possibility that the therapist was really interested in listening to her, but then ends by indicating feeling good about herself.

The therapist told again a narrative about the end of session:

> It was toward the end of a session and she only started talking about her difficulty to open up toward the end of the session. She said she felt as though she was in a closed room and could not find the key to get out. I could feel her pain and helplessness. I felt it was an important image and I wanted to explore it further with her, but it was the end of the

> session. I felt conflicted. On the one hand, I felt so desperate that these moments are so rare with her and always occur at the end of an hour. I felt exhausted and I wanted the hour to end. But on the other hand I felt I didn't want to give up trying and I could feel that she was trying, too.

In another narrative, the therapist refers to the time that Hannah came to the session in a good mood:

> She came in a good mood; it's not typical for her. She was happy about some presentation she did in class. On the one hand, I felt happy that I had the opportunity to be with her in a moment of contentment. She was also much less inhibited than usual. It made me feel close to her, but I also felt I had to be so cautious, because everything is so fraught and fragile with her. I wanted to get closer, but I felt too afraid to tread heavily. I felt I was being careful, approaching slowly.

The therapist's CCRT was similar to the earlier time point: She wished that Hannah would open up, to get close to her and not to hurt her, but here the opposite wish for distance is also present. She perceived Hannah as distant, avoiding contact, and vulnerable but also as struggling to get close and as slightly more open in sharing a positive experience. The therapist's RS was trying to get close, and at the same time being cautious and hesitating to get close.

At this time point, Hannah began to be able to speak of her relationship with the therapist in a more reflective and emotionally connected way. Although she still questioned her therapist's sincerity, she was able to reflect on her contribution to this experience and instead of warding the therapist off as she automatically tended to do, she was able to begin to try to disclose more to her therapist in the session. The therapist showed a greater awareness of the complexity of the emotions between them and the conflicted voices within herself. Although the therapist's main voice aimed to get close and Hannah's main voice was to fear closeness, these two voices were no longer isolated. Though still whispering, the opposite of the main voice was expressed by both parties. The therapist was more in touch with her own ambivalence regarding getting close to Hannah, and at the same time her caution seemed necessary, leading to more gentle steps toward Hannah instead of the direct invitation to get close that characterized their initial encounter. The therapist's awareness of her own ambivalence regarding getting close evolves at the same time as Hannah's increased awareness of her own yearning to get close. The therapist does not give up trying to find the right way to get close to Hannah, and this appears to enable Hannah to develop more trust in the therapist.

CATS and WAI Self-Report Measures. On the CATS, Hannah's scores showed somewhat higher secure attachment to the therapist (4.50 compared with 4.18), and the Preoccupied score decreases somewhat (2.00). However, her avoidant attachment also increased (3.27). Consistent with this high avoidance, Hannah's WAI in midpoint was somewhat lower (from 5.38 to 4.89). The therapist's WAI was also lower at this point (from 5.42 to 4.64), perhaps related to the sense that progress was slow to develop given the time that had passed (about 4 months).

Late Phase of Therapy

In the RAP interview, Hannah and her therapist chose to recount the same moment in therapy. From the client's perspective:

> One time I came and I didn't want to sit in the chair, and I looked for a corner of the room where I could sit down. In the end I sat on the carpet. She asked: "Do you want me to sit with you on the carpet?" I answered, "No, I just feel comfortable sitting on the floor, it calms me down. I don't want you to sit on the floor, if it is not comfortable for you." I didn't want her to do something that she didn't want to do. And she sat with me and we sat together, and it calmed me down and also I guess it drew us closer. I felt I could trust her, that she was trying to get close to me. She was trying to adapt herself to me. It gave me a sense of security, it was like reaching out. I felt a bit uncomfortable that maybe I was making her do something she didn't really want to do, but then she probably wouldn't have done it. It gives me a good feeling when someone is really trying. It feels close when you sit with someone on the same eye level. I would like her to be the responsible one who I look up to (from the floor), but also want to talk on the same eye level.

From the therapist's perspective:

> I deliberated with myself as to where I should sit, so I asked her, "Where do you want me to sit?" She said: "It is up to you, I won't tell you where to sit." I felt uncomfortable, embarrassed, as it was not clear what was appropriate. So I decided I would sit with her on the floor, on the carpet. We sat on the carpet and it opened up a new kind of relationship between us. She told me more things, and talked about her problems in relationships and with men. We both sat on the carpet and there was feeling of closeness, pleasantness, it was a good session, where we could talk, and get connected, and look together, and ask questions and explore, something that isn't always possible with her . . . I wanted to be with her. . . . (See also Wiseman, 2017.)

In this interaction the possibility of being wrong while trying to get closer was taken into account by both parties. However, the risk of making a mistake while trying to get closer was less anxiety-evoking than it had been earlier in their relationship, and thus they both dared to cautiously take the step toward one another. This led to a more mutual and collaborative encounter in which they felt safer to get close and to explore new experiences together.

Hannah began therapy with especially high attachment avoidance (and relatively high anxiety). When the therapist, with her high anxiety (and high avoidance relative to the therapist sample), insisted upon engaging, Hannah experienced it as a repetition of her object relations and resisted the therapist's attempts to get close. However, gradually, when the therapist became more attuned to Hannah's needs and accepted her request to get close at her own pace, a more secure attachment was developed. As the therapeutic relationship slowly developed to a point where both partners trusted each other, they were able to survive the other's feelings and tolerate their own and each other's "mistakes," because with a more secure attachment there is always another chance. As treatment progressed Hannah's internal representations of self and other developed (Atzil-Slonim, Wiseman, & Tishby, 2016).

CATS and WAI Self-Report Measures. Hannah's scores on the CATS reflected the greater security (from 4.5 in Session 15 to 5.5 in Session 28) and the reduced avoidance with the therapist (from 3.27 to 1.70), while some moderate preoccupation remained (2.22). The drop in avoidance was especially impressive and was also reflected in the higher alliance scores of both Hannah and her therapist (5.81 and 5.44, respectively). It appeared that after 28 sessions, Hannah and her therapist had established a collaborative relationship.

Interpersonal Patterns in Close Relationships at the Late Phase. The narratives from the RAP interview with Hannah about her relationships with her parents and friends at this later phase of treatment show some positive change. Hannah recounted this narrative about an interaction with her mother:

> We talked on the phone. She asked how I am and I usually don't tell her too much, but this time I tried to talk with her. I tried to explain to her why I am not sharing things with her. I didn't want to throw the blame on her, just wanted to explain my point of view. I wanted her to understand that on the one hand I want to be close to her and share things with her, she is really important to me, but on the other hand, when she makes demands to know things and imposes her opinion on me I find myself distancing. It makes me sad that this is how things have been between us for so many years. I wish she could understand, but she didn't, she was very defensive and we both felt frustrated. I guess she was sad too because she is also trying to make things better between us and it's not easy.

Hannah also recounted a narrative about her father:

> He is constantly looking for someone to listen to him and I have no patience for that. He seems so helpless and needy. He called me a few days ago and he wanted to tell me something that had happened to him at work. I didn't have any patience to listen to him. I just wanted him to leave me alone. I told him "make it shorter." He got upset and offended. I just didn't have the energy to listen to him.

Hannah's CCRT with her parents at the later phase of treatment included the wish to be understood, to be close and to be distant; the RO was angry, not understanding, sad and needy; and the RS was frustrated, feeling not understood, sad and distant. Although the interaction with her mother included similar themes to those described in the initial interview, in the later narrative Hannah not only avoided her mother's intrusive attempts to get close to her but also experienced and reflected on the contradictory wishes of both parties. With the father, however, the split was reversed without significantly changing the structure of the complementarity—the needy one and the one who rejects were reversed, but the experience remained one-dimensional.

In her relationships with friends, Hannah also exhibited a greater repertoire of thoughts and feelings and a greater ability to reflect on her wish to get close, which still continued to be accompanied by the fear of getting hurt. The differences between the change processes in the relationship in different close relationships (mother, father, friend, and the therapist) demonstrate that emotional and cognitive changes do not necessarily occur in a symmetrical way within all relationships. In Hannah's case, there was more expansion and growth in the relationship with the therapist, her mother, and friends, but not much change with her father.

ASSESSMENT OF PROGRESS AND OUTCOME

The last research evaluation in the study was conducted after 32 sessions. Hannah's scores on the OQ-45 decreased by 16 points (from 101 to 85) and showed a clinically significant change, although she remained in the clinical range. On the Target Complaints, her three main complaints—anxiety, sadness, and low self-esteem—decreased on a scale (from 13 to 1) from a mean of 12 to 5. Compared with published data (Paivio, Jarry, Chagigiorgis, Hall, & Ralston, 2010) using an effect size analysis (d = the difference between scores of this case and the mean of published data divided by the standard deviation of the published data) showed that at pretreatment she was more distressed on the TCS ($d = 1.05$) than clients in published data, and after the 32nd session she was similar to clients in published data ($d = .09$), suggesting her distress alleviated more than clients in the published data. Hannah continued treatment for another 50 sessions for a total length of 2 years of treatment. Termination was set by mutual agreement at the therapist's completion of her internship. Overall, there was marked improvement in Hannah's ability to regulate her anxious and depressed emotions, as well as improvement in different domains in her life (academic functioning and being involved in a supportive romantic relationship).

Our analysis of Hannah's case echoes recent findings regarding the importance of therapists' attunement to their clients' changing experience as it fluctuates from session to session throughout therapy (e.g., Atzil-Slonim et al., 2015; Zilcha-Mano et al., 2015). Future studies may benefit from examining whether therapists who are more congruent with their clients' changing needs for closeness and distance gain better therapy outcome.

Recent findings on attachment style representations indicate that it is informative to be aware of clients' specific attachment styles as they relate to specific representational themes of their therapist and therapy (Geller & Farber, 2015). Many of the challenges that therapists face in treating insecurely attached individuals arise with these clients'

> two-fold difficulties: on the one hand, they become painfully disappointed when their needs (whether unconscious or disavowed) for caring and affection are frustrated; on the other hand, they have great difficulty accepting the caring concern and affection of their therapists. (Geller & Farber, 2015, p. 466)

We contend that clients who oscillate between the two kinds of difficulties pose the most challenge for therapists, who need to be aware of their own attachment style and to monitor their own reactions to the conflicting representational patterns of the clients as well as to the conflicting patterns within themselves.

Alliance-focused training (AFT), designed to enhance therapists' ability to work constructively with negative therapeutic process or problematic transference–countertransference enactments (Muran, Safran, & Eubanks-Carter, 2010; Safran & Muran, 2000; see Chapter 2, this volume), can be especially beneficial to therapists in facing such challenges. Although Hannah's therapist did not receive formal AFT, it is possible that through the supervision she received, she was more able to recognize her own needs for reassurance that were frustrated by Hannah's difficulty in trusting her, and this enabled her to push Hannah less and later adjust herself to Hannah by providing a more optimal emotional distance that facilitated her engagement in therapy.

Mallinckrodt developed the Therapeutic Distance Scale (TDS) to assess the way clients perceive the therapist's responses to them in light of their attachment style in terms of distance and engagement. He showed that, as expected, client attachment avoidance (on the ECR) was significantly correlated with perception of therapists as *too close* (but not *too distant*). While, client attachment anxiety was significantly correlated with perception of therapists as *too distant* (but not *too close*) (Mallinckrodt et al., 2015). Egozi, Wiseman, Tishby, and Sharabany (2016) adapted Mallinckrodt's TDS self-report scale to an observer version (TDS–O) that includes client and therapist versions. This allows revelation of attachment dynamics that may not be evident from clients' self-reports and exploration of different trajectories of therapeutic distance in different styles of attachment insecurity in client–therapist dyads. Some preliminary findings suggest that clients' distance–closeness dynamics play out as a function of client attachment needs, therapist awareness of these needs, and the ability of therapists to monitor their own reactions and tailor their interventions accordingly.

Future research that includes more fine-grained analyses of these dynamics has the potential to inform clinicians and supervisors how to work with these dynamics in order to foster the needed corrective emotional experiences that will improve our clinical effectiveness.

IMPLICATIONS FOR CLINICAL PRACTICE AND SUPERVISION

A common dyadic pattern in psychotherapy is when client and therapist are locked in a complementary relation in which there appear to be only two choices: either submission or resistance to the other's demands. A common theme of this complementarity structure involves polarization between closeness and distance in the therapeutic relationship. Once therapists can deeply accept their own contribution to the impasse, and the fact of two-way participation becomes a vivid experience, it opens the space for negotiating differences, making it possible to connect. From the experience of communicating and restoring dialogue emerges a more advanced form of relatedness. When clinicians are caught in complementary interactions, instead of having to choose between closeness and distance, they may try to open up the space to explore the internal battle that is taking place within themselves as well as within their clients. Exploring the longing and dread of closeness and distance may lead to a greater ability to bear conflict in these painful matters and to allow new ways of being together.

Facilitating corrective emotional experiences is a highly complex process in general, and with fearful clients in particular. When encouraging clients to share their inner feelings and inviting them to immerse themselves in the relationship, therapists need to be cautious not to get caught up by their own lenses without enough awareness of how these meet the client's lenses. Focusing on closeness–distance dynamics in attachment-informed training and supervision may be beneficial for reducing dropout and improving outcome.

SUMMARY AND MECHANISMS OF CHANGE

In this chapter we explored the interpersonal dynamics played out in a client–therapist dyad that began therapy with a disharmonious dance characterized by the pushes and pulls of closeness and distance. Client and therapist, who were both characterized by insecure attachment, each enacted in the therapeutic encounter their affect-regulation strategies that appeared to clash within the therapeutic context. The therapist's attempts to get close to the client were experienced as intrusive and controlling, and the client reacted with avoidance and distance. The more the therapist tried to get closer, the more rigidly the client was locked in the avoidant position. The therapist was caught in a relational dilemma in which trying to get close to the client was experienced as intrusiveness and distance was experienced as abandonment and rejection. As therapy progressed, instead of the direct invitation to get close that characterized the therapist's stance in the initial encounters, the therapist became more attuned to Hannah and made more gentle steps toward her. The therapist's awareness of her own ambivalence regarding getting close evolved at the same time as Hannah's increased awareness of her own yearning to get close. Moreover, the therapist did not give up trying to find the optimal way to get close to Hannah, and this appears to have enabled the client to develop more trust in the therapist and to use her as a secure base to engage in exploration.

The experience of surviving breakdown into complementarity, and subsequently of communicating and restoring dialogue, is crucial to therapeutic action (Benjamin, 2004). The centrality of the dialogue to the therapeutic relationship is key to working with ruptures in the therapeutic relationship. Recognizing ruptures provides a unique opportunity to explore and rework them in the therapeutic relationship in order to develop new avenues for experiencing the self and the other (Mitchell, 1993; Muran, 2002). As we have demonstrated, successful negotiation of the optimal distance in the therapeutic relationship is a central change mechanism that is crucial for promoting client change.

REFERENCES

Ainsworth, M. D. S., Blehar, M. C., Waters, E., & Wall, S. (1978). *Patterns of attachment: Psychological study of the strange situation*. Hillsdale, NJ: Erlbaum.

American Psychiatric Association. (2013). *Diagnostic and statistical manual of mental disorders* (*DSM–5*). Washington, DC: American Psychiatric Association.

Aron, L. (2006). Analytic impasse and the third: Clinical implications of intersubjectivity theory. *The International Journal of Psychoanalysis*, *87*, 349–368. http://dx.doi.org/10.1516/15EL-284Y-7Y26-DHRK

Atzil-Slonim, D., Bar-Kalifa, E., Rafaeli, E., Lutz, W., Rubel, J., Schiefele, A.-K., & Peri, T. (2015). Therapeutic bond judgments: Congruence and incongruence. *Journal of Consulting and Clinical Psychology, 83*, 773–784. http://dx.doi.org/10.1037/ccp0000015

Atzil-Slonim, D., Wiseman, H., & Tishby, O. (2016). Relationship representations and change in adolescents and emerging adults during psychodynamic psychotherapy. *Psychotherapy Research, 26*, 279–296. http://dx.doi.org/10.1080/10503307.2015.1010627

Battle, C. C., Imber, S. D., Hoehn-Saric, R., Nash, E. R., & Frank, J. D. (1966). Target complaints as criteria of improvement. *The American Journal of Psychotherapy, 20*, 184–192.

Benjamin, J. (2004). Beyond doer and done to: An intersubjective view of thirdness. *The Psychoanalytic Quarterly, LXIII*, 5–46. http://dx.doi.org/10.1002/j.2167-4086.2004.tb00151.x

Bernier, A., & Dozier, M. (2002). The client–counselor match and the corrective emotional experience: Evidence from interpersonal and attachment research. *Psychotherapy, 39*, 32–43. http://dx.doi.org/10.1037/0033-3204.39.1.32

Bion, W. R. (1962). *Learning from experience*. New York, NY: Basic Books.

Bowlby, J. (1969/1982). *Attachment and loss: Attachment* (Vol. 1, 2nd ed.). New York, NY: Basic Books.

Bowlby, J. (1988). *A secure base: Clinical applications of attachment theory*. London, England: Routledge.

Brennan, K. A., Clark, C. L., & Shaver, P. R. (1998). Self-report measurement of adult attachment: An integrative overview. In J. A. Simpson & W. S. Rholes (Eds.), *Attachment theory and close relationships* (pp. 46–76). New York, NY: Guilford.

Daly, K. D., & Mallinckrodt, B. (2009). Experienced therapists' approach to psychotherapy for adults with attachment avoidance or attachment anxiety. *Journal of Counseling Psychology, 56*, 549–563. http://dx.doi.org/10.1037/a0016695

Dozier, M., & Tyrrell, C. (1998). The role of attachment in the therapeutic relationship. In J. A. Simpson & W. S. Rholes (Eds.), *Attachment theory and close relationships* (pp. 221–248). New York, NY: Guilford Press.

Eagle, M., & Wolitzky, D. L. (2009). Adult psychotherapy from the perspectives of attachment theory and psychoanalysis. In J. H. Obegi & E. Berant (Eds.), *Attachment theory and research in clinical work with adults* (pp. 379–409). New York, NY: Guilford Press.

Egozi, S., Wiseman, H., Tishby, O., & Sharabany, R. (2016, June). *Development of an observer version of the therapeutic distance scale (TDS–O): Associations with client attachment, attachment to therapist and outcome*. Paper presented at the International Annual Meeting of Society for Psychotherapy Research (SPR), Jerusalem, Israel.

Farber, B. A., & Metzger, J. A. (2009). The therapist as secure base. In J. H. Obegi & E. Berant (Eds.), *Attachment theory and research in clinical work with adults* (pp. 46–70). New York, NY: Guilford Press.

Geller, J. D., & Farber, B. A. (2015). Attachment style, representations of psychotherapy, and clinical interventions with insecurely attached clients. *Journal of Clinical Psychology, 71*, 457–468. http://dx.doi.org/10.1002/jclp.22182

Horvath, A. O., & Greenberg, L. S. (1989). Development and validation of the Working Alliance Inventory. *Journal of Counseling Psychology, 36*, 223–233. http://dx.doi.org/10.1037/0022-0167.36.2.223

Lambert, M. J., Burlingame, G. M., Umphress, V., Hansen, N. B., Vermeersch, D. A., Clouse, G. C., & Yanchar, S. C. (1996). The reliability and validity of the Outcome Questionnaire. *Clinical Psychology & Psychotherapy, 3*, 249–258. http://dx.doi.org/10.1002/(SICI)1099-0879(199612)3:4<249::AID-CPP106>3.0.CO;2-S

Loewald, H. W. (1980). *Papers on psychoanalysis*. New Haven, CT: Yale University Press.

Luborsky, L., & Crits-Christoph, P. (1998). *Understanding transference: The core conflictual relationship theme method* (2nd ed.). Washington, DC: American Psychological Association. http://dx.doi.org/10.1037/10250-000

Mallinckrodt, B. (2010). The psychotherapy relationship as attachment: Evidence and implications. *Journal of Social and Personal Relationships, 27*, 262–270. http://dx.doi.org/10.1177/0265407509360905

Mallinckrodt, B., Choi, G., & Daly, K. D. (2015). Pilot test of a measure to assess therapeutic distance and its association with client attachment and corrective experience in therapy. *Psychotherapy Research, 25*, 505–517. http://dx.doi.org/10.1080/10503307.2014.928755

Mallinckrodt, B., Gantt, D. L., & Coble, H. M. (1995). Attachment patterns in the psychotherapy relationship: Development of the Client Attachment to Therapist Scale. *Journal of Counseling Psychology, 42*, 307–317. http://dx.doi.org/10.1037/0022-0167.42.3.307

Mallinckrodt, B., & Jeong, J. (2015). Meta-analysis of client attachment to therapist: Associations with working alliance and client pretherapy attachment. *Psychotherapy, 52*, 134–139. http://dx.doi.org/10.1037/a0036890

Mikulincer, M., & Shaver, P. R. (2007). *Attachment in adulthood: Structure, dynamics, and change*. New York, NY: Guilford Press.

Mikulincer, M., Shaver, P. R., & Berant, E. (2013). An attachment perspective on therapeutic processes and outcomes. *Journal of Personality, 81*, 606–616. http://dx.doi.org/10.1111/j.1467-6494.2012.00806.x

Mitchell, S. A. (1993). *Hope and dread in psychoanalysis*. New York, NY: Basic Books.

Muran, J. C. (2002). A relational approach to understanding change. Plurality and contextualism in a psychotherapy research program. *Psychotherapy Research, 12*, 113–138. http://dx.doi.org/10.1080/713664276

Muran, J. C., Safran, J. D., & Eubanks-Carter, C. (2010). Developing therapist abilities to negotiate alliance ruptures. In J. C. Muran & J. P. Barber (Eds.), *The therapeutic alliance: An evidence-based guide to practice* (pp. 320–340). New York, NY: Guilford Press.

Paivio, S. C., Jarry, J. L., Chagigiorgis, H., Hall, I., & Ralston, M. (2010). Efficacy of two versions of emotion-focused therapy for resolving child abuse trauma. *Psychotherapy Research, 20*, 353–366. http://dx.doi.org/10.1080/10503300903505274

Safran, J. D. (2012). *Psychoanalysis and psychoanalytic therapies*. Washington, DC: American Psychological Association.

Safran, J. D., & Muran, J. C. (2000). *Negotiating the therapeutic alliance: A relational treatment guide*. New York, NY: Guilford Press.

Tishby, O., & Wiseman, H. (2014). Types of countertransference dynamics: An exploration of their impact on the client–therapist relationship. *Psychotherapy Research, 24*, 360–375. http://dx.doi.org/10.1080/10503307.2014.893068

Winnicott, D. W. (1971). *Playing and reality*. London, England: Tavistock.

Wiseman, H. (2017). The quest for connection in interpersonal and therapeutic relationships. *Psychotherapy Research, 27*, 469–487. http://dx.doi.org/10.1080/10503307.2015.1119327

Wiseman, H., & Tishby, O. (2014). Client attachment, attachment to the therapist and client–therapist attachment match: How do they relate to change in psychodynamic psychotherapy? *Psychotherapy Research, 24*, 392–406. http://dx.doi.org/10.1080/10503307.2014.892646

Wiseman, H., & Tishby, O. (2017). Applying relationship anecdotes paradigm interviews to study client–therapist relationship narratives: Core conflictual relationship theme analyses. *Psychotherapy Research, 27*, 283–299. http://dx.doi.org/10.1080/10503307.2016.1271958

World Health Organization. (1993). *ICD–10 classification of mental and behavioural disorders: Diagnostic criteria for research*. Geneva, Switzerland: Author.

Zilcha-Mano, S., Solomonov, N., Chui, H., McCarthy, K. S., Barrett, M. S., & Barber, J. P. (2015). Therapist-reported alliance: Is it really a predictor of outcome? *Journal of Counseling Psychology, 62*, 568–578. http://dx.doi.org/10.1037/cou0000106

5

FACILITATING THE SENSE OF FEELING UNDERSTOOD IN PATIENTS WITH MALADAPTIVE RELATIONSHIPS

SIGAL ZILCHA-MANO AND JACQUES P. BARBER

The association between therapeutic alliance and symptomatic change has gained increasing recognition in recent years. To further advance our ability to turn this association into helpful practical knowledge in treatment, it is worthwhile considering what the therapeutic elements of alliance are. In this chapter, we focus on the patient's feelings of being understood in treatment as such an element. By exploring this element, we study the intertwined relationship between (a) therapeutic techniques used in treatment, and (b) trait and state aspects of the alliance, as well as their ability to predict outcomes. We use two case studies of patients—both suffering from difficulties in their interpersonal relationships—who received psychodynamic treatment to demonstrate the importance of the process of building a feeling of being understood. The process of helping the patient feel understood may actualize an unmet interpersonal wish to feel understood, which in turn reduces the use of maladaptive patterns of responding to the other that may

http://dx.doi.org/10.1037/0000093-006
Developing the Therapeutic Relationship: Integrating Case Studies, Research, and Practice, O. Tishby and H. Wiseman (Editors)

have originally contributed to the patients not being understood by others (because of processes such as repetition compulsion). We conclude that active, collaborative therapeutic work on the patient's sense of being understood may trigger, at least to some extent, changes in the patient's patterns of relating to others. We end with a discussion of the implications of the study for clinical practice and research.

CONCEPTUAL BACKGROUND

One of the most consistent findings emerging from psychotherapy research is that the quality of therapeutic alliance is a predictor of outcome: Stronger alliance is associated with better therapeutic outcomes (e.g., Horvath, Del Re, Flückiger, & Symonds, 2011). It is therefore crucial to investigate which factors influence the quality of alliance (i.e., why the alliance is strong in one patient–therapist dyad and not in another), whether it changes over time, and if so, how such change occurs and which techniques are involved in the process. In this chapter, we explore these general questions while focusing on a specific aspect of alliance: the patient's sense of feeling understood by the therapist.

Most studies on the ability of alliance to predict outcome assessed the therapeutic relationship at a single point in time (usually at the beginning of treatment) or calculated an average of alliance scores over several treatment sessions (Horvath et al., 2011). Such studies demonstrate that patients who generally tend to form a strong alliance across treatment enjoy better therapeutic outcomes than those who form a weak alliance. Some researchers, however, have argued that a continuous strengthening of the alliance throughout treatment is not necessarily the predictor of the best outcome (Eubanks-Carter, Muran, & Safran, 2010). They have suggested an alternative perspective focusing on processes of rupture and repair that take place in the course of constructing the alliance. Such processes are signified by episodes of tension or breakdown in the collaborative relationship between patient and therapist, which can then be worked through and resolved (Safran, Muran, & Eubanks-Carter, 2011). Indeed, the literature demonstrates that many patients who complete treatment with beneficial outcomes show variability in the alliance over the treatment. Often, such progress begins with a high level of alliance followed by a low phase, in which patients often feel ambivalent about therapy, followed in turn by successful negotiation of this ambivalence, indicating that the ruptures have been worked through and resolved (Mann, 1973; Patton, Kivlighan, & Multon, 1997; for a review, see Safran et al., 2011).

It is possible to integrate the above two perspectives on alliance with the terms *trait* and *state* (Zilcha-Mano, 2017). The trait aspects of alliance refer to its general level and permanent characteristics as assessed in a single or aggregated measurement; they can also be conceptualized as differences in alliance level between patients. A general strong traitlike alliance is associated with better outcomes in treatment. The state aspects of alliance refer to changes that take place over the treatment; they can also be conceptualized as changes within the individual. Rupture and repair processes are one example of how the statelike aspects may develop over treatment. Although the two effects can be conceptualized as independent, the traitlike alliance also refers to a general tendency of a patient to show fluctuations in interpersonal interactions and to benefit from benevolent interactions (Zilcha-Mano, 2017). In this chapter, our focus is on therapist actions during the sessions and on patient characteristics.

Some patients come to treatment with better traitlike abilities to form satisfying relationships with others and tend to form strong, positive traitlike alliances with their therapists, as well. They are therefore likely to do better in treatment (Connolly Gibbons et al., 2003; DeRubeis, Brotman, & Gibbons, 2005; Garfield, 1994; Martin et al., 2000). A patient's pretreatment characteristics, such as interpersonal patterns, may determine the creation of a traitlike alliance. The statelike aspects of alliance, however, illustrate the changeability of alliance through the interactions with the therapist: the ways in which changes take place throughout treatment and predict improvement in symptoms. For example, a rupture weakens the alliance, impairs the momentary ability of the patient to benefit from treatment, and weakens symptom reduction, but a formative experience or resolution of this rupture can render the alliance even stronger than it had been before the rupture, reducing symptoms more drastically than if the rupture had not occurred. The use of effective techniques by the therapist, in a competent way, contributes statelike changes in alliance, which in turn contribute to outcome (Zilcha-Mano, 2017).

Although both traitlike and statelike aspects of alliance are important in predicting outcome, the statelike aspects fit more closely with the concept of alliance as an *active* ingredient in bringing about therapeutic change. Active collaborative work on alliance by patient and therapist is what makes it an active ingredient in bringing about therapeutic change (Zilcha-Mano, 2016). A corrective interpersonal experience with the therapist can trigger changes in interpersonal relationships outside the therapy room. Conversely, patients with maladaptive patterns of relating to others may reenact these patterns in the course of treatment, with no real change in alliance and no effective work being done to change them. In the absence of such work, the traitlike aspects of alliance dominate treatment. Alternatively, when real change takes place in alliance and effective work is done to change maladaptive patterns, the statelike aspects of alliance dominate treatment. Such real work is by definition not just the result of the patient's traitlike tendencies to show fluctuations in the alliance, but is the result of the unique interactions between the patient and the therapist in the therapy room. Specifically, based on Safran and Muran's (2000) seminal work on rupture resolution in therapeutic alliance, active work on negotiating alliance between the patient and the therapist may create formative experiences in the patient's life. As the result of such an active work, the state aspects of alliance dominate the treatment more beneficially.

Although we have described trait and state aspects of alliance independently from one another, it is important to note that they influence one another. The trait and state aspects are in constant interactions with the patient's interpersonal patterns outside the therapy room. One of our studies demonstrated how representations of significant others in the patient's life before the beginning of treatment predict the alliance formed between the patient and the therapist (Zilcha-Mano, McCarthy, Dinger, & Barber, 2014). Specifically, our findings showed that benevolent representations of others at intake were positively related to the alliance subsequently developed with the therapist, whereas malevolent representations of others were negatively related to this alliance. We also showed, however, that representations of others are not automatically projected onto alliance, and our findings suggest that such projections were also influenced by the real relationship with the therapist. In other words, alliance has a tendency to evolve into a collage of significant others in a process of assimilation that emerges during treatment, in which the most relevant representations of significant others are projected onto the alliance with the therapist (Zilcha-Mano, McCarthy, et al., 2014).

Feeling Understood in Treatment: Conceptualization and Examination

Many therapeutic schools conceptualize feeling understood in treatment using different terms. However, all seem to agree on its importance in the development of psychopathology and the promotion of therapeutic change. Using its own language, and based on its core assumptions, each theory stresses the importance of feeling understood by significant others in the course of one's development, and the adverse consequences of not feeling understood. Winnicott referred to the feeling of being seen as one really is and highlighted the ability of the infant to see oneself as one really is, in the mother's eyes. This feeling has been acknowledged as important for providing the infant with a stable sense of "going on being," which is crucial in the process of developing a true self (Winnicott, 1971). Feeling understood is also important in developing a sense of cohesiveness (Kohut, 1984). Through empathic listening (Rogers, 1975), the therapists may be able to facilitate change in treatment by helping the patient feel understood.

Using the terminology of the core conflictual relationship theme (CCRT) framework (Luborsky & Crits-Christoph, 1998), individuals wish to be understood by others. In some cases, individuals feel that this wish is not being fulfilled by others, and react to this interpersonal conflict of unmet need in various ways. Some of these reactions exacerbate the situation and further reduce the individual's chances of feeling understood (repetition compulsion; Freud, 1922). For example, an individual may wish to be understood by others but feels that the others fail to understand him or her, and as a result becomes hurt, avoids future interactions with others, begins to speak more softly, more briefly, perhaps begins to stutter, further lowering the chances of feeling understood.

In treatment, the patient and therapist may work through these tendencies, helping the patient gain insight into the maladaptive patterns and learn interpersonal skills and ways to negotiate interpersonal needs (Safran & Muran, 2000). The therapist may also facilitate the formation of a corrective experience in treatment, in which the patient's need to be understood is met. As a result of this work in the course of the treatment, patients learn to better communicate their interpersonal needs, which may contribute to their chances of feeling better understood in interpersonal relationships in the future. Patients may also experience the therapists' efforts to understand them as actualizing the unmet interpersonal need to feel understood. Meeting this need, in turn, may reduce the use of maladaptive patterns in responding to others, which may have contributed to the patients' not being understood in the first place.

A patient's sense of "feeling understood" by the therapist can be perceived as one important aspect of the alliance. It is related to what Bordin (1979) called "deeper bonds of trust and attachment" (p. 254). For some patients, these bonds may serve as a curative interpersonal experience and create an environment of mutual understanding where a patient's wish to be understood can be actualized. A result of such understanding of patients by the therapist, of their needs, and of the difficulties that caused them to seek treatment, may result in an increase in the agreement between patient and therapist on the goals and tasks of treatment.

The wish to be understood can be seen both as a trait aspect of alliance (whether the patient tends to feel understood or misunderstood and to show fluctuations in this tendency) and as a state aspect that evolves over treatment, so that the patient feels misunderstood when a rupture occurs and feels understood again if the therapist is able to resolve it. In this chapter, we resort to two case studies to examine how patients' interpersonal patterns influence their ability to feel understood in treatment, whether the therapist actively deploys strategies to make the patient feel understood, and whether the patient indeed feels understood as a result of these efforts, which is the result not only of the patient's traitlike tendencies but also of the actual interactions between the therapist and the patient in the therapy room. We describe how we measure the feeling of being understood in treatment and the effect that this element has on the outcome of treatment.

Many therapists view the patient's sense of feeling understood in treatment as an important aspect of alliance, but very few studies, if any, have quantified the effect of these feelings on outcome. To examine empirically the feeling of being understood in treatment, we developed the Feeling Understood in Treatment (FUT) coding system, which focuses on three related aspects: (a) the extent to which the therapist communicates, actively or passively, that he or she is trying to understand the patient; (b) the extent to which the patient seems to show feelings of being understood by the therapist; and (c) the extent to which patients seems to show during the session that they feel understood by significant others in their lives. A clear advantage of a rating system is that it does not depend on what the patient and therapist are interested or able to report, but a clear disadvantage is that it may not represent how the patients and therapists actually feel during the session.

In this chapter, we demonstrate the use of the FUT in two case studies, aiming to relate therapist techniques to patient signs of being understood in treatment. To the best of our knowledge, this is the first study to examine the development of the feeling of being understood in treatment and the effects of this feature on the course and outcome of treatment. To do so, we coded all sessions for two patients. A session-by-session focus enables us to examine both the trait aspect and the state aspects of the sense of feeling understood, as it evolved during treatment: its establishment, what may prevent it from developing, and how different patterns in its development are related to treatment outcome.

PRESENTING PROBLEM AND PATIENT DESCRIPTION

Patient Selection and Measures Used

The two participants in the present study were selected from a randomized controlled trial (RCT) involving supportive expressive therapy for depression (Barber, Barrett, Gallop, Rynn, & Rickels, 2012). The two patients were completers and had been treated by the same therapist: one with good and one with poor outcome. We chose patients with the greatest number of available sessions to maximize our ability to learn about the development of the sense of feeling understood during treatment. To protect the confidentiality of the patients and of the therapist described in the following clinical vignettes, we disguised their background details and asked for their written permission.

As part of the RCT, the patients completed several questionnaires and underwent clinical assessments at multiple time points in the course of treatment, as well as at 4 months after treatment (for more information, see Barber et al., 2012; Zilcha-Mano, Dinger, McCarthy, Barrett, & Barber, 2014). In this chapter, we refer to the following measures: the 12-item patient-rated version of the Working Alliance Inventory (WAI; Tracey & Kokotovic, 1989), the 21-item self-report Beck Depression Inventory (BDI; Beck, Steer, & Carbin, 1988), the 17-item version of the clinician-administered Hamilton Rating Scale for Depression (HRSD; Hamilton, 1967), the 64-item version of the Inventory of Interpersonal Problems (Horowitz et al., 2000), the Depressive Experiences Questionnaire (DEQ; Blatt, D'Afflitti, & Quinlan, 1976), and the 93-item Quality of Life Enjoyment and Satisfaction Questionnaire (QLESQ; Endicott, Nee, Harrison, & Blumenthal, 1993).

Patient Descriptions and Presenting Problems

Dan is a single, African American man in his early 40s, with two children from two women.[1] He has a partial college education, works full-time in the finance industry, and has an income in the 25% tax bracket. Dan explained that he had sought therapy to address his depression, which had been affecting him socially and professionally for the last 5 years. At intake, he was diagnosed by a clinician (not his therapist) with major depressive disorder (BDI: 31 and HRSD: 17, indicating moderate depression), and met the criteria for personality disorder not otherwise specified, with narcissistic and borderline tendencies. Dan did not have any comorbid anxiety disorders.

In the questionnaires he completed, Dan reported higher than average levels of interpersonal distress (as indicative by his Inventory of Interpersonal Problems [IIP–64; Horowitz, Rosenberg, Baer, Ureño, & Villaseñor, 1988] total, which was 0.80 points above the norm) and a tendency to be cold and distant in interpersonal interactions, with difficulty maintaining long-term connections. He reported a need to be in control in interpersonal interactions, and a dislike for situations in which he is given orders (angle: 173.38 on the Inventory of Interpersonal Problems–Circumplex [IIP–C; Alden, Wiggins, & Pincus, 1990]). Based on the DEQ questionnaire, Dan was characterized as having pathological depressive experiences with feelings of guilt, insecurity, and hopelessness (as indicated by self-criticism level of 2.09).

The second patient, Ben, is an African American man in his mid-40s. He is married, has one child, has less than a high school education, and was

[1]Details of case examples have been altered to protect confidentiality.

unemployed at the time of the sessions because of an accident in his former workplace, which happened 2 years before the beginning of treatment. His income from this job was in the 15% tax bracket. At his first session of treatment, Ben described having social and psychological difficulties since his accident. He felt he was withdrawing from his family and friends and was not contributing enough to his family and home (e.g., not taking part in cleaning the house, not shouldering other responsibilities). He sought to become more lively and social. At intake, he was diagnosed with major depressive disorder (with BDI: 33 and HRSD: 28, indicating severe depression) and met the criteria of the fourth edition of the *Diagnostic and Statistical Manual of Mental Disorders* (American Psychiatric Association, 1994) for accident-related posttraumatic stress disorder (PTSD). Ben did not have any comorbidity with Axis I anxiety disorders, and did not meet criteria for any personality disorders.

On the questionnaires he completed, Ben reported high levels of interpersonal distress (IIP–64 total: 1.26 points above the norms), had a cold and socially avoidant orientation (he reported being anxious in the presence of others and did not initiate social interactions), as well as lack of self-confidence (angle: 193.25 on the IIP–C). Ben was characterized as having pathological depressive experiences with feelings of guilt, insecurity, and hopelessness (as indicated by DEQ, self-criticism: 0.92). He showed no sense of inner strength or satisfaction with his accomplishments (DEQ, efficacy: –0.55).

Coding for Feeling Understood in Treatment

The development of the FUT is described at the end of this chapter. The final version of the FUT is coded based on videotaped sessions and includes six items rated on a 7-point Likert scale. The first two items refer to the extent to which the patient shows signs of feeling understood by the therapist, the next two refer to the extent to which the patient shows signs of feeling understood by significant others, and the final two refer to the extent to which the therapist communicates that he or she understands the patient. For each set of two items, one refers to feeling understood emotionally (e.g., the therapist actively asks questions that refer to the patient's feelings and acknowledges them; the therapist has no misconceptions about the patient's feelings) and one refers to feeling understood cognitively (i.e., the therapist actively asks questions about the ways the patient thinks and perceives events or about the stories the patient brings to treatment; the therapist actively shows good understanding of the cognitive aspects of the patient's experiences). The items are listed in Table 5.1. Examples for techniques used by the therapist to communicate that he or she understands the patient, includes

TABLE 5.1
Feeling Understood in Treatment (FUT) Items and General Scale

The FUT scale		
Items	a. The patient seems to feel understood by the therapist intellectually. b. The patient seems to feel understood by the therapist emotionally. c. The therapist shows the patient that she/he understands him/her intellectually. d. The therapist shows the patient that she/he understands him/her emotionally. e. The patient seems to feel understood by his/her significant others intellectually. f. The patient seems to feel understood by his/her significant others emotionally.	
Rating scale	1. No understanding	No understanding between therapist and patient or patient and significant other, or poor understanding by the therapist or significant other.
	2. Minimal understanding	Very limited evidence that the patient and therapist, or the patient and significant other, understand each other.
	3. Some understanding	Patient and therapist or patient and significant other occasionally show some passive signs of understanding.
	4. Passive understanding	Passive signs of understanding between therapist and patient, or the patient and significant other.
	5. Passive understanding with minimal active understanding	Patient and therapist or significant other passively show understanding, with occasional active signs of understanding.
	6. Some signs of active understanding	Evidence of both active and passive understanding between the patient and therapist or between patient and significant other.
	7. Active understanding	Many active signs of understanding between therapist and patient or between patient and significant other.

specific passive signs, such as nodding or making statements of passive acceptance, such as "mhmm," and/or specific active signs, such as actively and accurately mirroring the patient's story, thoughts and feelings ("That wasn't stupid, it was important for you. You felt like nobody really cares about you at that moment").

We coded a total of 34 treatment sessions (out of a total 20 sessions for each patient) using the FUT scale. Two external coders coded all the available sessions for each patient (session-by-session coding). Interrater reliability, as assessed by intraclass correlations (ICC [2,1]; Shrout & Fleiss, 1979), was excellent ($\rho I = .89$).

Dan

In the initial phase of treatment (the first seven sessions), Dan described himself as feeling misunderstood and mistreated by others. He said his mother had been neglectful of his needs as a child (e.g., leaving him in a public place as a little boy and forgetting to bring him back home). He reported similar feelings of being mistreated and misunderstood by other significant figures in his life. For example, he described his son's mother as mistreating him and being disrespectful to him (e.g., recounting how she had ignored him at a party). Together with feelings of invisibility to his son's mother, he expressed concern that she was neglecting his son's needs (e.g., neglecting to buy school supplies and help with school work). In these sessions, Dan described others in his life as doing little to try to understand him, and provided many examples of situations in which he felt misunderstood. In this phase of treatment, Dan viewed others outside of the therapy room as unhelpful and the relationships with them as unsatisfying (as can be seen in his low scores on the "patient's feelings of being understood by others" subscale of the FUT coding system, in Figure 5.1, Phase 1 of treatment).

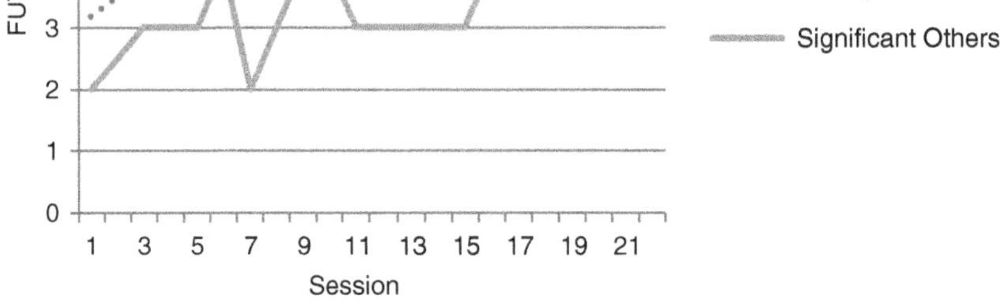

Figure 5.1. Dan's changes on the three Feeling Understood in Treatment (FUT) subscales over treatment. Patient = the extent to which the patient shows signs of being understood by the therapist. Therapist = the extent to which the therapist communicates actively or passively that she is trying to understand the patient. Significant Others = the extent to which, during the session, the patient shows signs of feeling understood by significant others in his life.

For external observers of this phase of treatment, it seemed like a monologue: Dan described in detail how he felt in his relationships with significant others, and the therapist listened carefully and asked few questions. From time to time, she provided brief interpretations. Her questions conveyed an interest in Dan's story and feelings, as indicated by the moderately high scores in the "therapist's use of strategies to facilitate feeling understood" on the FUT coding system subscale (see Figure 5.1). However, Dan showed only passive signs of feeling understood by the therapist, as described by the low-to-moderate scores on the "patient's feeling of being understood in treatment" subscale in the FUT coding system (Figure 5.1). In his self-report on alliance, after this initial phase of treatment, Dan reported a better alliance than what he had expected before meeting his therapist (as indicated by intake WAI = 4.58, and week 2 WAI = 5.41, scale range: 1–7).

In the second stage of the therapy (Sessions 8–15), Dan began to discuss his need for intimate relationships in which he would feel understood and respected, and his fears of being in a vulnerable position in which he could be mistreated and hurt by other people ("I try to put myself in the position where I don't trust anybody because I stay away from the outcome of their untrustworthiness so it doesn't affect me"). He gave examples of specific instances in which he wanted other people's closeness and felt disappointed by their negative reactions. For example, Dan described feeling upset when his son did not call him on Father's Day, and was angry at his son's mother for not reminding him to call. At the same time, Dan began to mention concerns with not being understood by his therapist. He explained that he was trying not to share too many intimate details about himself, because he did not want to place himself in a position in which she could mistreat him. Dan seemed to communicate both the fact that he did not trust the therapist and the hope that this would change gradually: "I have children and we haven't really discussed that yet, hopefully we can avoid that subject for a couple of months . . . but maybe we will be able to discuss it sometime." Session after session he conveyed his hope that he would be able to feel understood by the therapist: "I wish I had somebody, anybody in my corner . . . but maybe one day . . . maybe even here."

Serious ruptures started to occur in these sessions, as evidenced by both Dan's and the therapist's reports on alliance. Their scores showed a jagged pattern, both reporting their lowest level of alliance in the treatment during this phase (Dan's WAI = 4.15, the therapist's WAI = 3.85). Issues of power and trust arose. For example, on one occasion, Dan explained that the therapist's expectation of him to be the first to talk in the sessions put him in a disadvantaged position. He felt as though the sessions were a business meeting, in which the first to talk loses ("you [therapist] want me to talk first, and in sales this is a bad thing, the first person to talk loses"). The therapist reacted empathetically, as she did in the course of other ruptures that occurred during this phase of treatment. To resolve this rupture, the therapist explained the rationale for letting him talk first, saying "but we are not in sales; I keep quiet to see where you're coming from . . . I want to give you the space to decide."

This process of rupture resolution seemed to strengthen the relationship between Dan and the therapist. Dan started to communicate feeling understood by the therapist and began to bring examples of his experiences in vulnerable situations to be worked on in treatment (e.g., feeling offended after someone in whom he was romantically interested spurned his overtures). These narrative impressions are supported by the FUT coding: As can be seen in the diagrams of the FUT coding (Figure 5.1), Dan started to show more active signs of feeling understood in treatment while the therapist used active strategies to enhance his feeling of being understood. In addition, the outcome of the rupture resolution process can also be seen in Dan's reported WAI, at the end of this midperiod in treatment (WAI = 5.25), which was above his average. Finally, at this point in treatment, his responses on the self-report questionnaire indicated that he felt that his depressive symptoms were improving (BDI = 15).

The third phase of therapy consisted of the final eight sessions (16–23), when small ruptures arose in connection with the end of therapy and upcoming separation (e.g., Dan inquired whether the therapist was obligated to confidentiality after the end of treatment, and wondered whether he should be more careful with what he was sharing). Despite the small ruptures during this period, Dan also reported improvement on many levels. He recognized the work he did in therapy, as well as the commitment and intimacy that formed between him and the therapist ("I don't think I did anything that required a commitment before this one"). Dan reported improvement in his interpersonal relationships outside the therapy room. For example, he told the therapist that his son came to visit him for the summer, that their relationship grew stronger, and that they spent quality time together. This improvement was also evident in the decrease in Dan's reported levels of distress in interpersonal relationships (manifest in a decrease in his IIP, to a standardized score of 0.48). Dan stated that he was looking for more meaningful relationships in the future. As evidenced by the coding on the "patient's feelings of being understood in treatment" subscale of the FUT, during the third phase of treatment Dan showed high levels of feeling understood in treatment. He also reported an increase in feeling understood outside of treatment (Figure 5.1). The therapist's self-reported WAI increased from week 8 (WAI = 4.25) to the highest point at week 16 (WAI = 5.12). Based on the FUT ratings, it appears that the therapist's use of techniques to help the patient feel understood in treatment were effective. The patient responded well, felt better understood, first in the relationship with the therapist and later also outside of treatment. For example, Dan appreciated being asked about his feelings and thoughts and acknowledging his difficulties and unmet needs.

Ben

In the initial phase of treatment (Sessions 1–5) Ben described in detail how he saw his life before and after his work accident. He seemed to idealize his life before it, describing himself as an energetic and vital person, who was close to friends and family, who took on rewarding jobs, and earned the respect of his colleagues. In contrast, he portrayed himself after the accident as depressed, unable to sleep, and unmotivated to interact with others ("I have been avoiding people for a long time, haven't been socializing at all"). Nevertheless, Ben said that he maintained strong relationships with his wife and children even after the accident. However, at the same time, he explained to the therapist that he tried to hide his feelings of depression and worthlessness from them for fear of "letting them down." He said that he did not want his daughter to find out about his depression because he felt he was disappointing to her as a father, neglecting to play or spend time with her. Similarly, he related that he did not want to attend a family party so as not to draw attention to his problem: "I haven't even told my own people." Ben hoped that hiding his depression would convince others he was fine, but this tendency seemed to contribute to his current state of unemployment. For example, he was called in for a job but was afraid to take it, so as not to let the boss down if he could not complete it in a satisfactory way. It was also causing difficulties in his relationship with his wife (e.g., he related having problems with sexual arousal, because he was afraid that he would not be able to satisfy her).

Similar patterns seemed to emerge in his relationship with the therapist. Ben asked for reassurances that he was doing a good job in treatment, and tried to avoid speaking about occasions in which he was not making adequate progress. For example, his scores on the Q–LES–Q after one of the sessions at the end of the initial period of treatment reflected lack of improvement in quality of life. At that session, the therapist asked him directly about quality of life, but Ben tried to avoid the question by changing the topic of the conversation, then responded that he felt better. The patient's self-reported WAI scores were high in these sessions at the initial phase of treatment (WAI = 6.75).

During the first phase of treatment, the therapist showed some signs of trying to passively understand Ben (nodding or making statements of passive acceptance, such as "mhmm"), and Ben occasionally showed passive signs that he felt understood cognitively and emotionally by also nodding or saying "mhmm" from time to time (Figure 5.2). Specifically, Ben often seemed indifferent to the therapist's suggestions, responding with statements

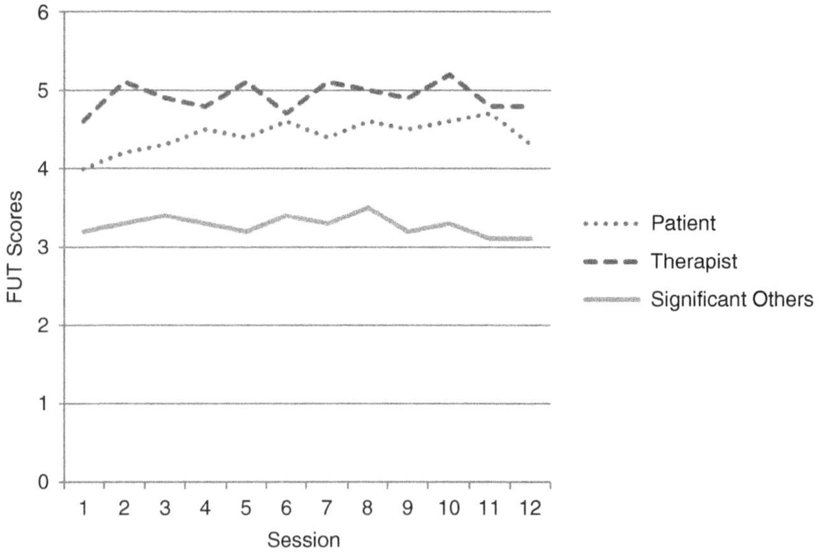

Figure 5.2. Ben's changes on the three Feeling Understood in Treatment (FUT) subscales over treatment. Patient = the extent to which the patient shows signs of feeling understood by the therapist. Therapist = the extent to which the therapist communicates actively or passively that she is trying to understand the patient. Significant Others = the extent to which, during the session, the patient shows signs of feeling understood by significant others in his life.

of passive agreement ("yeah . . . I know . . . I guess") in a manner that seemed devoid of emotion. Ruptures were not apparent on the surface in the therapy sessions, but beneath the surface the interactions could be characterized by withdrawal ruptures, as described below. Ben reported to the therapist that the treatment was helpful, but on the self-report questionnaires, which he was told were not revealed to the therapist, he reported no improvement in his depressive symptoms (BDI = 28).

In the middle stage of treatment, which consisted of the next five sessions (6–10), it became apparent that Ben was not acting on the advice given to him by the therapist, although he seemed to agree with her during the session. For example, when the therapist suggested that he should see a neurologist for his headaches, Ben agreed but did not make an appointment. When the therapist suggested that he should take protein drinks to improve his appetite, Ben agreed but did not make an attempt to change his dietary habits. Similar patterns were also apparent in his relationship with his wife: although he promised to accompany her to church, he did not do so. Whether suggestions for action came from the therapist, from Ben's wife, or from others, Ben's reaction appeared to suggest that he was merely attempting to please. To us, he appeared highly motivated to please others, as opposed to agreeing with their suggestions but not acting because of lack of energy or inability.

In this middle phase of the treatment, almost no confrontational ruptures were apparent, but withdrawal ruptures seemed to take place, especially in deferential ways. Several times, Ben implicitly raised issues about his ability to feel understood by the therapist, but these were instantly resolved, without the therapist and Ben investing much work in their resolution. For example, Ben raised the question of whether the therapist could really understand the complexities of his relationship with his daughter ("I'm not sure if it even makes sense to somebody all that stuff"). The therapist replied that she had children, and in response Ben quickly said, "It makes me happy to know you have kids," and immediately changed the topic of conversation. In this way, it was not possible for active work on building a sense of feeling understood to take place.

The third phase of therapy consisted of the final four sessions (11–14), where the themes that surfaced in the second phase were continued. At the end of treatment, Ben agreed with the therapist's claims about how successful the treatment was and how much it had helped him feel less depressed. At the same time, on both the self-report questionnaires and the external clinician-based interview (the Hamilton), he reported no change in his depressive symptoms. Some clues about Ben's feelings of worthlessness arose in one of the last sessions, when he told the therapist that his wife did not think he could take his daughter on a school trip because of his depression. Eventually, Ben's wife asked his brother to serve as chaperone on the trip, which contributed to Ben's feelings of inadequacy. Other "old" patterns of relating to others were clearly apparent, and in the last session the themes of not wanting to disappoint others and of seeking the therapist's approval were dominant. In an especially telling moment, Ben admitted that he had not wanted to come to the session, but came anyway because he did not want to disappoint the therapist. Based on the FUT ratings, it appears that the therapist's use of techniques to help the patient feel understood in treatment was ineffective, based mainly on passive acts intended to communicate the therapist's effort to understand the patient (Figure 5.2). The patient communicated passively that he felt understood, which in turn precluded the therapist from moving on to more active communication. Had the patient used clear signs that he did not feel understood, or if the therapist could have interpreted the patient's passive communication to be inauthentic, reflecting withdrawal and efforts to please the therapist, more active communication may have ensued. For example, the therapist could actively ask the patient how he feels and thinks at specific moments in treatment, checking when the therapist truly understands how he feels and how he thinks, and negotiating how better understanding could be reached (e.g., "Now I understand that I didn't get correctly what you meant. It's very important for me to understand you. What can I do to be more attentive to what you want to say and how you feel?"). With the lack of such strategies, when both partners in the dyad did not actively communicate and discuss the patient's feeling of being understood in treatment and the passive–aggressive stance of the patient was not addressed, there was no genuine change in the patient's tendency to form interactions in which he could feel understood within or outside treatment.

Outcomes

The two cases were chosen based on their outcomes. In the course of treatment, Dan showed a gradual reduction in depressive symptoms, especially during the middle phase of treatment, whereas Ben did not show much change. Dan's depressive symptoms dropped 9 points on the HRSD measure and 16 points on the BDI, whereas Ben showed an increase of 2 points on the HRSD and 4 points on the BDI during the course of treatment. This pattern held true for other types of outcomes, such as quality of life, interpersonal distress, and mental health. Dan continued to show improvement in the 4 months of follow-up, whereas Ben did not show much change. Therefore, we refer to Dan's case as one of good outcomes and to Ben's as one of poor outcomes. Although this distinction is dichotomous and somewhat simplistic, it supports our efforts to identify mechanisms of change that may take place mainly in cases with good outcome and less often in those with poor outcome.

MECHANISMS OF CHANGE IN THE TREATMENTS

Although each case has its unique characteristics, both Dan and Ben arrived at treatment with maladaptive interpersonal relationships, which manifested as trait aspects of feeling misunderstood in the alliance. The first stages of the two treatments were similar in their state aspects as well: In both cases the therapist used passive and active strategies to enhance the patients' feeling of being understood. For example, the therapist did not limit herself to gestures such as nods and wordless reactions ("mhmm"), which are passive signs communicating that they are trying to understand the patient, but also used more explicit and active messages, such as mirroring the patient's feelings or suggesting insightful reflections (active signs of communication). In this phase, both patients still felt frequently misunderstood in their relationships outside the therapy room. Dan reported these feelings directly, whereas the stories that Ben told in treatment revealed such feelings covertly. However, the patient–therapist dynamics in the two cases diverged in the middle phase of therapy, as changes in the state aspects of Dan's alliance with the therapist began to take place. Dan directly communicated his concerns in treatment, at times testing the therapist's ability to provide him with experiences of feeling understood.

Such tests, or confrontation ruptures, were not apparent in the middle phase of Ben's treatment. Based on Ben's and his therapist's self-report WAI, no confrontational ruptures were evident. Indeed, the two were involved in negative interpersonal cycles, in which Ben enacted his previous patterns of trying to fend for himself, without revealing the deep concerns and the needs he had in connection with others. Ben's tendency to be compliant by withdrawing from the relationship whenever disagreement arose can be articulated as quiet or withdrawal ruptures, which may have interfered with the therapist's awareness of the issues at hand. As a result of the radically different dynamic between these patients and their therapist during the middle phase of therapy, the two also experienced radically different final phases of treatment. Whereas in Dan's case there emerged a genuine patient–therapist relationship, characterized by intimacy and warmth, in Ben's case the outcome was a "false alliance" (adopting Winnicott's, 1965, conceptualization of false self), in keeping with the first and second phases of treatment, as well as with Ben's interpersonal patterns outside the therapy room.

It is important to stress that the same therapist treated both patients, so that the traitlike characteristics of the therapist (level of experience, traitlike interpersonal characteristics) cannot account for the differences between the two cases. The dynamic between the patients and the therapist appears to have been influenced by the differences between the patients' pretreatment interpersonal characteristics, their hopes, and the fit between patient and therapist characteristics. Dan may have started therapy with more hope, and did not forfeit the chance of making a change in his traitlike tendency to feel misunderstood. By contrast, it seems that Ben had no hope that his general tendency to feel (mis)understood might change, and did not dare communicate not feeling understood because of his submissive interpersonal traitlike tendencies. Winnicott (1965) wrote about this hope in his classical work on the antisocial tendency, highlighting the hope in confrontational interactions. In this two-person story, the patient's abandonment of hope met with a therapist satisfying with passive techniques to communicate feeling understood, thus, resulting in no corrective experience in treatment.

DISCUSSION

This chapter described one way in which alliance may contribute to the success of treatment. We focused on the effect of collaborative work between patient and therapist (including active negotiation of patient's needs to feel understood and the way they manifest in the treatment through active signs of communications by both patients and therapists) on treatment outcome, and questioned whether the patient's improved sense of "feeling understood" is related to this outcome. We examined this question in the case of two patients who reported unsatisfying relationships outside the therapy room. In the good outcome case, the patient and the therapist worked together to enhance the patient's sense of feeling understood in treatment, and the therapist used active techniques to achieve this aim, resulting in an increase in alliance. In the poor outcome case, such work did not take place, and a false sense of positive alliance, which was based on pseudo-secure attachment (Mallinckrodt et al., 2017), was apparent over the entire course of treatment. Based on the FUT rating, it is possible to conclude that the therapist did not use active signs to communicate her effort to understand the patient (e.g., asking clarifying questions about his way of reacting in treatment, trying to confront the patient's withdrawal behavior), and she might not even have been aware of an enactment taking place in the here and now of the therapy room. It is difficult to determine the precise causes of the therapist's different behaviors and patient outcomes, because each patient has his own characteristics, comorbidities, and histories of relating to others. But it is important both clinically and empirically to discuss the suggested active ingredients in these cases that may have contributed to their ability to benefit from treatment.

Both patients declared that they had a traitlike tendency not to feel understood in close relationships, which manifested in unsatisfying relationships outside the therapy room, and in turn seemed to impair their ability to feel understood in their relationship with the therapist. Thus, in both cases the trait aspect of feeling understood appeared to have been impaired. The differences between the two cases lay in the changes that did or did not take place in the state aspects of this need. In the good outcome case, we identified a strong positive alliance built through a process of rupture and repair episodes, whereas in the poor outcome case a stable, positive (perhaps pseudo) alliance appeared to be in place from the beginning. Based on these two cases, it is possible to argue that active work on alliance made possible changes in one patient's patterns of relating to others, whereas a lack of similar work caused the other patient to report no significant change in these patterns. We suggest, therefore, that in the good outcome case the patient underwent corrective experiences with the therapist, which formed a genuine, intimate relationship, helping the patient feel truly understood. These corrective experiences were then generalized, and went on to contribute to changes outside the therapy room. According to the patient's account, the therapeutic relationship was the first intimate interpersonal relationship to which he felt committed, which fostered a hope in him for future fulfilling relationships. In Dan's case, changes occurred in the state aspects of alliance. By contrast, in the poor outcome case, trait aspects dominated the alliance, causing it to mimic the other unfruitful relationships experienced by the patient outside the therapy room. The therapist may not have been aware of this enactment, and therefore made no effort to actively communicate to the patient her attempts to understand him. The negative transference was not addressed and the ruptures were not acknowledged, therefore the treatment had no remarkable effect on other relationships in the patient's life. Whereas it was easier for the therapist to pick on the ruptures in the good outcome case given their confrontational nature (which may represent the patient's hope to feel understood), it is less clear which elements made it hard for the therapist to introspect on the enactment with the other. Although such investigation of the therapist's countertransference is outside of the scope of the present chapter, the take-home message seems clear: therapists need to use active techniques in the efforts to understand their patients who show general tendencies to feel misunderstood in interpersonal relationships, and to delve into self-introspection or supervision when they feel reluctant to do so.

FROM RESEARCH TO PRACTICE AND BACK

Two primary team members (undergraduate research assistants) and one auditor (the first author) followed the consensual qualitative research (CQR) method of Hill et al. (1997) to construct the FUT, based on sample data from 14 therapy sessions of a psychodynamic treatment for depression in a recent randomized trial (Barber et al., 2012; the sessions were not part of the therapies of the two patients described in the present chapter). Data analysis involved three central steps. First, based on a review of sessions, domains of "feeling understood" in treatment were developed from the data. Specifically, the team members independently segmented the data into domains, then worked to achieve consensus on several cases. Next, based on the domains, they developed core ideas or summaries of the data that capture the essence of what was said, using fewer words and achieving greater clarity. Finally, a cross-analysis produced common themes across participants: categories were developed to describe the common themes reflected in the core ideas in domains across cases.

The resulting coding system is based on videotaped sessions and includes six items. The first two items refer to the extent to which the patients show signs of feeling understood by the therapists, the next two refer to the extent to which the patients show signs of feeling understood by significant others, and the final two refer to the extent to which the therapists communicate to the patients that they understand them. For each set of two items, one refers to feeling understood emotionally (e.g., the therapist actively asks questions that refer to the patient's feelings and acknowledges them, the therapist does not hold misconceptions about the patient's feelings), the other to feeling understood cognitively (i.e., the therapist actively asks questions that refer to the ways in which the patient thinks and perceives events, or to the stories the patient brings to treatment; the therapist actively shows good understanding of the cognitive aspects of the patient's experiences). The items are presented in Table 5.1. Each item is coded on a 7-point Likert scale, with a higher score indicating better understanding (see Table 5.1 for response categories). Moderate scores (a mean score of 4) indicate passive understanding, and high scores (a mean score higher than 5) indicate active understanding. Specifically, passive understanding by the therapist can be expressed by limited gestures such as nods and wordless reactions ("mhmm"), whereas active understanding involves more explicit messages, such as mirroring the patient's feelings or accurate and insightful reflections. For the items that focus on the patient's expression of feeling understood, passive expressions are similar to those of the therapist (a nod or "mhmm"), whereas active expressions convey stronger statements of feeling understood such as "Yes, it's exactly like you said," "That's really true," and "I feel that it's important for you to understand how I feel." The FUT coding system is used with taped therapy sessions, so that the coder can take into account nonverbal communication such as eye contact, tone of voice, and so on. The items referring to the patient's significant others may refer to parents and other close relatives, friends, or romantic partners.

The present findings inspired further research in our labs using the FUT. In two trials of supportive–expressive treatment for depression conducted in the United States and Israel, several sessions of each patient were coded using the FUT. Two of the questions examined using this data included (a) Which patient and therapist characteristics (demographic, intrapersonal, and interpersonal) predict patient feelings of being understood in treatment and therapist actions in the course of treatment that facilitate feelings of being understood in treatment? and (b) What is the ability of the traitlike tendency of the patient to feel understood and of the statelike dynamic of feeling understood in treatment to predict treatment outcome?

IMPLICATIONS FOR PRACTICE

The literature on alliance would have predicted a more beneficial outcome for Ben's case because of the stronger alliance reported during the first sessions; the findings of the present study, however, show otherwise. A clear clinical implication therefore emerging from this study is the importance of active, collaborative work on building a relationship in which the patient can feel understood. Because the process of active collaborative work on building the alliance seems to be of great importance, the state aspects of alliance should be understood as having great significance for patients with maladaptive patterns of relating to others. The case that showed greater state changes in alliance, rather than better trait aspects, was the more beneficial one.

It is important to stress that both patient and therapist have important contributions to make in determining whether the treatment of a patient with traitlike tendencies not to feel understood will be effective. In the present case, given that the same therapist worked with both patients, it is important to understand which factors account for the state changes that occurred only in the good-outcome case. Several such factors may be suggested, some involving the therapist's interpersonal and intrapersonal characteristics, which may have led to different countertransference for each patient, others focusing on the dyad or on a possible variance in attachment orientations between the therapist and each of the patients. In this chapter, we have chosen to focus on two possible factors: (a) the patient's characteristics and (b) the therapist's use of active versus passive techniques in the effort to understand the patient. It is clear that the patients differed in the manner in which they expressed the fear of not being understood by the therapist. Dan showed a tendency for confrontational (albeit not hostile) ruptures, whereas Ben showed a tendency for withdrawal ruptures. Consistent with Bennett, Parry, and Ryle (2006), it seems that the explicit threat to alliance expressed by Dan enabled the therapist to more easily recognize and focus attention on most of the ruptures, whereas in Ben's case, the therapist usually failed to identify such threats. Like Ben, many patients cannot or find it difficult to reveal that they are uncomfortable or disagree with their therapist and choose to withdraw in such instances. Rennie (1994) found that such withdrawal from the therapist (also termed *deference*) plays a significant role in therapeutic interactions. He identified several factors associated with patient withdrawal, including fear of criticizing the therapist, the need to meet the therapist's perceived expectations, acceptance of the therapist's limitations, fear of threatening the therapist's self-esteem, and a sense of indebtedness to the therapist. It is therefore crucial for therapists to be able to pick up on cues of false alliance, also termed *pseudoalliance* (Mallinckrodt et al., 2017), in such cases.

The other factor contributing to state changes in the alliance, the therapist's actions, concerns the techniques used to promote the patient's feeling of being understood. Identifying the techniques that facilitate statelike changes in the patient's feeling of being understood is of great importance for clinical practice. Although the therapist was not offensive or critical toward either of the patients during the ruptures that occurred (as happens on occasion, especially in confrontational ruptures), she used more explicit and active techniques with Dan than she did with Ben to make the patient feel understood. She might have been more active in this area with Ben had she been as aware of the ruptures that occurred in his case, but as the empirical literature shows, even experienced therapists can have considerable difficulty recognizing such withdrawal ruptures in alliance (Hill, Nutt-Williams, Heaton, Thompson, & Rhodes, 1996; Hill, Thompson, Cogar, & Denman, 1993; Regan & Hill, 1992).

How can therapists become more aware of the withdrawal ruptures that debilitate the process of actively building a sense of feeling understood in treatment? One recommendation is to infer risks to alliance from the patients' tendencies in their existing relationships. Patients who tend to fear criticism in their interpersonal relationships and have a need to meet their significant others' perceived expectations may tend to behave similarly in their relationship with the therapist. Our research showed that patients' interpersonal patterns of relating to others strongly influence alliance (Zilcha-Mano, Dinger, et al., 2014). Ben, the poor-outcome case, had a tendency for withdrawal in his interpersonal relationships outside the therapy room.

Even therapists who are aware of their patients' tendencies still face the challenge of addressing ruptures constructively. In Dan's case, the therapist was attentive to the challenges and initiated a process of adapting to the patient's needs through the ruptures. It appears that some techniques are more effective than others in resolving challenges in alliance, and that patients are likely to vary in this regard. For example, it has been suggested that adhering rigidly to specific treatment models (Piper, Azim, Joyce, & McCallum, 1991; Piper et al., 1999) and responding defensively to ruptures (Henry et al., 1993) may weaken the alliance, impair the patient's sense of feeling understood in treatment, and increase the odds of patient dropout. Ben's case demonstrates that passively (rather than actively) communicating the therapist's efforts to understand the patient is not effective for patients with interpersonal problems. By contrast, when therapists and patients work directly and nondefensively on repairing ruptures in the alliance, it may result in both improved alliance and outcome (Foreman & Marmar, 1985; Lansford, 1986; Rhodes et al., 1994; Safran & Muran, 2000), as demonstrated in Dan's case. Therefore, it appears that some techniques may generally be more effective than others. Building on the literature on personalized treatment (Hamburg & Collins, 2010), it is also possible to go beyond general recommendations and delve into recommendations that are adjusted to the specific patient. Personalized treatment suggests that instead of trying to select the best treatment based on the characteristics of an average patient, it is important to consider the technique to use based on the patient's pretreatment interpersonal patterns of relating to others, because it may predict the ruptures that are likely to occur in alliance (e.g., Zilcha-Mano et al., 2015). Future research should examine which techniques are most effective for which patients.

Active work with patients to arouse a feeling of being understood by the therapist also has important implications for training and supervision. In training, therapists need to learn how to differentiate between patient's passive and active signs of feeling understood. Trainees should be taught to detect cases in which patients' pretreatment traitlike tendencies to feel misunderstood are maintained and even reinforced by their tendencies to please others in interpersonal relationships. Implementing methods such as the CCRT with regard to the relational experiences (relational episodes with significant others) described by the patient in treatment can help achieve this aim. Training should include role playing and videos of experienced therapists modeling the desirable techniques, expressing active efforts to understand the patient. The FUT should also be used in training and supervision to monitor the therapists' use of passive versus active techniques in trying to understand the patient.

Many questions remain open. For example, Ben's general tendency to suspect and mistrust others may be, to some extent, the result of his PTSD, a condition that may have interfered with active work on his feeling of being understood. It is also important to ascertain the ways in which patients' pretreatment interpersonal patterns contribute to different courses of treatment. In our case study, both patients were male minority group members, whereas their therapist was female and Caucasian, which may have affected the course of treatment. Future studies focusing on these questions should explore which techniques are most beneficial in addressing the different backgrounds of patient and therapist, and determining when these backgrounds (ethnic minority, socioeconomic status) contribute to the difficulty in making the patient feel understood in treatment. In this context, it can be suggested that therapists should explore cultural issues that may affect the therapeutic work and should be aware of their own and their clients' cultural background and explore the differences between them. Therapists should make an effort to become familiar with their client's cultural background, and distinguish between what is normal and what is perceived as impaired in the client's cultural context.

CONCLUSION

In this chapter, we focused on certain aspects of the presented cases from our own perspectives (and countertransferences) of the cases. It should be noted that additional examinations from other clinical orientations and points of view could have contributed to our understanding of the full complexity of these cases. This chapter has demonstrated the importance of the process of building a feeling of being understood in patients through collaborative work between patient and therapist. One example of such work is active therapist response to the patient's concerns about their relationship, validating the latter's need to feel understood, and actualizing this wish in the therapy room. Genuine alliance can be a result of such active work, in which the therapist helps the patient feel understood in the working alliance. Such alliance, which may be considered therapeutic in its own right, may in turn have important effects on the patient's interpersonal relationships outside the therapy room.

REFERENCES

Alden, L. E., Wiggins, J. S., & Pincus, A. L. (1990). Construction of circumplex scales for the Inventory of Interpersonal Problems. *Journal of Personality Assessment*, *55*, 521–536. http://dx.doi.org/10.1207/s15327752jpa5503&4_10

American Psychiatric Association. (1994). *Diagnostic and statistical manual of mental disorders* (4th ed.). Washington, DC: Author.

Barber, J. P., Barrett, M. S., Gallop, R., Rynn, M. A., & Rickels, K. (2012). Short-term dynamic psychotherapy versus pharmacotherapy for major depressive disorder: A randomized, placebo-controlled trial. *The Journal of Clinical Psychiatry*, *73*, 66–73. http://dx.doi.org/10.4088/JCP.11m06831

Beck, A. T., Steer, R. A., & Carbin, M. G. (1988). Psychometric properties of the Beck Depression Inventory: Twenty-five years of evaluation. *Clinical Psychology Review*, *8*, 77–100. http://dx.doi.org/10.1016/0272-7358(88)90050-5

Bennett, D., Parry, G., & Ryle, A. (2006). Resolving threats to the therapeutic alliance in cognitive analytic therapy of borderline personality disorder: A task analysis. *Psychology and Psychotherapy*, *79*, 395–418. http://dx.doi.org/10.1348/147608305X58355

Blatt, S. J., D'Afflitti, J. P., & Quinlan, D. M. (1976). Experiences of depression in normal young adults. *Journal of Abnormal Psychology*, *85*, 383–389. http://dx.doi.org/10.1037/0021-843X.85.4.383

Bordin, E. S. (1979). The generalizability of the psychoanalytic concept of the working alliance. *Psychotherapy*, *16*, 252–260. http://dx.doi.org/10.1037/h0085885

Connolly Gibbons, M. B., Crits-Christoph, P., de la Cruz, C., Barber, J. P., Siqueland, L., & Gladis, M. (2003). Pretreatment expectations, interpersonal functioning, and symptoms in the prediction of the therapeutic alliance across supportive–expressive psychotherapy and cognitive therapy. *Psychotherapy Research*, *13*, 59–76. doi: 10.1093/ptr/kpg007

DeRubeis, R. J., Brotman, M. A., & Gibbons, C. J. (2005). A conceptual and methodological analysis of the nonspecifics argument. *Clinical Psychology: Science and Practice, 12*, 174–183. http://dx.doi.org/10.1093/clipsy.bpi022

Endicott, J., Nee, J., Harrison, W., & Blumenthal, R. (1993). Quality of life enjoyment and satisfaction questionnaire: A new measure. *Psychopharmacology Bulletin, 29*, 321–326.

Eubanks-Carter, C., Muran, J. C., & Safran, J. D. (2010). Alliance ruptures and resolution. In J. C. Muran & J. P. Barber (Eds.), *The therapeutic alliance: An evidence-based guide to practice* (pp. 74–93). New York, NY: Guilford Press.

Foreman, S. A., & Marmar, C. R. (1985). Therapist actions that address initially poor therapeutic alliances in psychotherapy. *The American Journal of Psychiatry, 142*, 922–926. http://dx.doi.org/10.1176/ajp.142.8.922

Freud, S. (1922). *Beyond the pleasure principle*. London, England: International Psychoanalytical Press.

Garfield, S. L. (1994). Research on client variables in psychotherapy. In A. E. Bergin & S. L. Garfield (Eds.), *Handbook of psychotherapy and behavior change* (pp. 190–228). Oxford, England: John Wiley.

Hamburg, M. A., & Collins, F. S. (2010). The path to personalized medicine. *The New England Journal of Medicine, 363*, 301–304. http://dx.doi.org/10.1056/NEJMp1006304

Hamilton, M. (1967). Development of a rating scale for primary depressive illness. *British Journal of Clinical Psychology, 6*, 278–296. http://dx.doi.org/10.1111/j.2044-8260.1967.tb00530.x

Henry, W. P., Strupp, H. H., Butler, S. F., Schacht, T. E., & Binder, J. L. (1993). Effects of training in time-limited dynamic psychotherapy: Changes in therapist behavior. *Journal of Consulting and Clinical Psychology, 61*, 434–440. http://dx.doi.org/10.1037/0022-006X.61.3.434

Hill, C. E., Nutt-Williams, E., Heaton, K. J., Thompson, B. J., & Rhodes, R. H. (1996). Therapist retrospective recall of impasses in long-term psychotherapy: A qualitative analysis. *Journal of Counseling Psychology, 43*, 207–217. http://dx.doi.org/10.1037/0022-0167.43.2.207

Hill, C. E., Thompson, B. J., Cogar, M. C., & Denman, D. W. (1993). Beneath the surface of long-term therapy: Therapist and client report of their own and each other's covert processes. *Journal of Counseling Psychology, 40*, 278–287. http://dx.doi.org/10.1037/0022-0167.40.3.278

Hill, C. E., Thompson, B. J., & Williams, E. N. (1997). A guide to conducting consensual qualitative research. *The Counseling Psychologist, 25*, 517–572. http://dx.doi.org/10.1177/0011000097254001

Horowitz, L. M., Alden, L. E., Wiggins, J. S., & Pincus, A. L. (2000). *Manual for the Inventory of Interpersonal Problems*. Oxford, England: Harcourt Assessment/The Psychological Corporation.

Horowitz, L. M., Rosenberg, S. E., Baer, B. A., Ureño, G., & Villaseñor, V. S. (1988). Inventory of Interpersonal Problems: Psychometric properties and clinical applications. *Journal of Consulting and Clinical Psychology*, *56*, 885–892. http://dx.doi.org/10.1037/0022-006X.56.6.885

Horvath, A. O., Del Re, A. C., Flückiger, C., & Symonds, D. (2011). Alliance in individual psychotherapy. *Psychotherapy*, *48*, 9–16. http://dx.doi.org/10.1037/a0022186

Kohut, H. (1984). *How does analysis cure?* Chicago, IL: University of Chicago Press. http://dx.doi.org/10.7208/chicago/9780226006147.001.0001

Lansford, E. (1986). Weakenings and repairs of the working alliance in short-term psychotherapy. *Professional Psychology: Research and Practice*, *17*, 364–366. http://dx.doi.org/10.1037/0735-7028.17.4.364

Luborsky, L., & Crits-Christoph, P. (1998). *Understanding transference: The core conflictual relationship theme method* (2nd ed.). Washington, DC: American Psychological Association. http://dx.doi.org/10.1037/10250-000

Mallinckrodt, B., Anderson, M. Z., Choi, G., Levy, K. N., Petrowski, K., Sauer, E. M., & Wiseman, H. (2017). Pseudosecure vs. individuated–secure client attachment to therapist: Implications for therapy process and outcome. *Psychotherapy Research*, *27*, 677–691. http://dx.doi.org/10.1080/10503307.2016.1152411

Mann, J. (1973). *Time-limited psychotherapy*. Cambridge, MA: Harvard University Press.

Martin, D. J., Garske, J. P., & Davis, M. K. (2000). Relation of the therapeutic alliance with outcome and other variables: A meta-analytic review. *Journal of Consulting and Clinical Psychology*, *68*, 438–450. http://dx.doi.org/10.1037/0022-006X.68.3.438

Patton, M. J., Kivlighan, D. M., Jr., & Multon, K. D. (1997). The Missouri Psychoanalytic Counseling Research Project: Relation of changes in counseling process to client outcomes. *Journal of Counseling Psychology*, *44*, 189–208. http://dx.doi.org/10.1037/0022-0167.44.2.189

Piper, W. E., Azim, H. F., Joyce, A. S., & McCallum, M. (1991). Transference interpretations, therapeutic alliance, and outcome in short-term individual psychotherapy. *Archives of General Psychiatry*, *48*, 946–953. http://dx.doi.org/10.1001/archpsyc.1991.01810340078010

Piper, W. E., Ogrodniczuk, J. S., Joyce, A. S., McCallum, M., Rosie, J. S., O'Kelly, J. G., & Steinberg, P. I. (1999). Prediction of dropping out in time-limited, interpretive individual psychotherapy. *Psychotherapy: Theory, Research, Practice, Training*, *36*, 114–122. http://dx.doi.org/10.1037/h0087787

Regan, A. M., & Hill, C. E. (1992). Investigation of what clients and counselors do not say in brief therapy. *Journal of Counseling Psychology*, *39*, 168–174. http://dx.doi.org/10.1037/0022-0167.39.2.168

Rennie, D. L. (1994). Clients' deference in psychotherapy. *Journal of Counseling Psychology*, *41*, 427–437. http://dx.doi.org/10.1037/0022-0167.41.4.427

Rhodes, R., Hill, C., Thompson, B., & Elliott, R. (1994). Client retrospective recall of resolved and unresolved misunderstanding events. *Journal of Counseling Psychology*, *41*, 473–483. http://dx.doi.org/10.1037/0022-0167.41.4.473

Rogers, C. R. (1975). Empathic: An unappreciated way of being. *The Counseling Psychologist*, *5*, 2–10. http://dx.doi.org/10.1177/001100007500500202

Safran, J. D., & Muran, J. C. (2000). *Negotiating the therapeutic alliance: A relational treatment guide*. New York, NY: Guilford Press.

Safran, J. D., Muran, J. C., & Eubanks-Carter, C. (2011). Repairing alliance ruptures. *Psychotherapy*, *48*, 80–87. http://dx.doi.org/10.1037/a0022140

Shrout, P. E., & Fleiss, J. L. (1979). Intraclass correlations: Uses in assessing rater reliability. *Psychological Bulletin*, *86*, 420–428. http://dx.doi.org/10.1037/0033-2909.86.2.420

Tracey, T. J., & Kokotovic, A. M. (1989). Factor structure of the Working Alliance Inventory. *Psychological Assessment: A Journal of Consulting and Clinical Psychology*, *1*, 207–210. http://dx.doi.org/10.1037/1040-3590.1.3.207

Winnicott, D. W. (1965). *The maturational process and the facilitating environment: Studies in the theory of emotional development*. New York, NY: International Universities Press.

Winnicott, D. W. (1971). *Playing and Reality*. London, England: Tavistock.

Zilcha-Mano, S. (2016). New analytic strategies help answer the controversial question of whether alliance is therapeutic in itself. *World Psychiatry*, *15*, 84–85. http://dx.doi.org/10.1002/wps.20305

Zilcha-Mano, S. (2017). Is the alliance really therapeutic? Revisiting this question in light of recent methodological developments. *American Psychologist*, *72*, 311–325. http://dx.doi.org/10.1037/a0040435

Zilcha-Mano, S., Dinger, U., McCarthy, K. S., Barrett, M. S., & Barber, J. P. (2014). Changes in well-being and quality of life in a randomized trial comparing dynamic psychotherapy and pharmacotherapy for major depressive disorder. *Journal of Affective Disorders*, *152–154*, 538–542. http://dx.doi.org/10.1016/j.jad.2013.10.015

Zilcha-Mano, S., McCarthy, K. S., Dinger, U., & Barber, J. P. (2014). To what extent is alliance affected by transference? An empirical exploration. *Psychotherapy*, *51*, 424–433. http://dx.doi.org/10.1037/a0036566

Zilcha-Mano, S., McCarthy, K. S., Dinger, U., Chambless, D. L., Milrod, B. L., Kunik, L., & Barber, J. P. (2015). Are there subtypes of panic disorder? An interpersonal perspective. *Journal of Consulting and Clinical Psychology*, *83*, 938–950. http://dx.doi.org/10.1037/a0039373

6

CLINICAL CHOICE POINTS AND PROFESSIONAL ETHICS IN PSYCHOANALYSIS

GABY SHEFLER

Psychoanalysis and psychoanalytic therapy take place within clearly defined settings and boundaries. Maintaining the proper setting is a fundamental professional and ethical demand in any psychological and psychoanalytic treatment. There are different severity levels of ethical misconduct in the media and in professional literature, as reflected in the American Psychological Association's *Ethical Principles of Psychologists and Code of Conduct* (2017) and in the International Psychoanalytical Association's *Ethics Code* (2015). In this chapter, I refer to subtly defined ethical dilemmas in psychoanalytic praxis. The capacity to interpret transference is based on the solid construct of well-defined boundaries and settings. However, in exceptional situations, analysts may need to adjust these rules and boundaries to fit the patient's specific needs. Changes in setting or technique may be called for when the patient's sense of safety, continuity, and constancy are threatened and there is a risk of rupture in the alliance. These situations

http://dx.doi.org/10.1037/0000093-007
Developing the Therapeutic Relationship: Integrating Case Studies, Research, and Practice, O. Tishby and H. Wiseman (Editors)

pose an ethical dilemma: keeping the professional rules of best practice versus bending the rules to facilitate the therapeutic relationship (i.e., the alliance). This chapter focuses on the interrelations between the setting, clinical and situational considerations, and their possible influences on the therapeutic alliance.

THEORETICAL AND CONCEPTUAL BASIS

Psychodynamic psychotherapies in all their variations, including psychoanalysis itself, both as theory and clinical practice, have developed vastly since Freud's early versions of psychoanalysis from a method of treating severe histrionic cases to the utmost method of knowing one's self, introspection, and personal development. Beginning with Freud's ever-evolving thinking and model up to post-Freudian developments such as object relations theory and self-psychology, relational theories have defined different structures of psychic developments both in the healthy and the disturbed personality.

Despite the differences between theories and their practical implementation into methods of treatment, there are common principles in the praxis of psychoanalysis that differentiate it from psychotherapy:

- The use of the couch: The patient lies on a couch while the analyst is seated behind the patient's head (Freud, 1913) and with no direct eye contact, which enables both patient and analyst to feel more freedom to free associate (for the patient), think, and be in reverie, and free floating attention (for the analyst).
- The intensity of analysis: Typically three to six weekly scheduled sessions of 45 or 50 minutes in length (Freud, 1913) creates continuity for the patient and a significantly larger working space for patient and analyst, and so affects the working alliance.
- The duration of analysis: Long-term process from at least 2 years up to several years enables the patient to feel safe to start long-term processes of development and growth while regression occurs.
- Psychoanalysis is a nonfocal therapeutic method. The patient is guided to free associate, and the therapist is trained to listen with free-floating attention to the patient's association (Freud, 1919).
- In most psychoanalytic methods, interpretation of the transference relationship is the core of analysis (Freud, 1915). Interpretation of transferencial relationships shows they are almost opponents to maintaining therapeutic alliance, since in many occasions these interpersonal activities are nonrational and

sometimes may sound fantastic. It is the good working alliance created along the way—mainly in the opening phase of therapy—that enables these crucial ingredients to exist and maintain their central role and position during psychoanalysis.

- The analyst is a main agent in the maintenance of the working alliance (Gabbard & Lester, 1995) and should be aware of the working alliance, including the rising of resistances or instances where special acts should be taken by the analyst in order to foster the working alliance.
- It is very important for the analyst to distinguish clearly between fantasy and reality in the course of analysis (Gabbard & Lester, 1995), especially knowing and defining reality from fantasy in the patient's mental life.
- The importance of the realistic setting in psychoanalysis and transference relationships emphasizes the need for clear ethical codes and rules of conduct (Freud, 1915; Gabbard & Lester, 1995). Addressing realistic issues within analysis and the optional changes in setting may have a double meaning. On the one hand, changes in the setting are sometimes necessary to maintain the alliance and the analysis. On the other hand, in some instances changing the setting boundaries is a preamble to getting closer to the slippery slope of ethical misconduct. Sometimes, it is clearly done out of the analyst's bias towards his or her own needs, wishes or drives; and sometimes it may address the patient's unconscious needs to be fulfilled by the analyst.

Many of these points exist in many forms of dynamic psychotherapy as well, but the setting and its crucial importance is greater in psychoanalysis, and especially in classical psychoanalysis, due to the intensity of the treatment and the potential psychic regression that is immanent to it. The therapeutic role, the regression that is induced in the process, and the confusion between reality and fantasy put the analyst (and the therapist) in a position of power in relation to the patient. Ethical rules of conduct and codes are strongly needed to help the analyst to cope in this confusing arena.

Ethics and Professional Ethics

There is a difference between *ethics*—the philosophical study of moral values and virtues—and *professional ethics*, defined by Kasher (2005, 2007) as a set notion of the practical ideal for professional conduct. In his definition, *professional conduct* refers to the expected standard to which members of a given profession aspire. Anything that does not meet this standard is deemed professionally unethical. Arnold Goldberg (1999) related also to "the difficulties to distinguish between the definitions of the moral and the ethical" (p. 248). Goldberg held to the boundary concept and made the distinction between *boundary crossing*, which he found very often in many psychoanalysts' activities, and *boundary violations* (as put also by Gabbard and others) to describe unacceptable action of the analyst. Goldberg used these concepts to differentiate moral mistakes from the ethical aim, which is working towards the benefit of the patient. He emphasized the aim of the professional act taken by the analyst and concluded that as long as they are needed and temporary, these actions can be regarded as accepted boundary crossing. In a later article, Goldberg (2008) related to self-psychology and relational psychology, which demonstrate some limits of the boundaries concept. In these theories of practice, professional boundary crossing such as self-disclosure or fulfillment of a patient's need for reassurance from the analyst are essential to therapeutic results. Goldberg differentiated between moral mistake, to which the adjective *wrong* can be assigned, and rules or technical rules that the analyst needs to obey. Breaking the rules can be regarded as technical mistakes that may make one feel guilty or ashamed, and are often categorized as wrong, but these wrongs should not be considered as moral failures. These to my understanding are *ethical misconduct*. This point is strongly supported by Gabbard (2008) portraying Goldberg's ideas in the frame of a consensus of professionals regarding the professional rules (ethical codes) and leaving the mores as imperatives that regulate ethics.

Erikson (1964) stipulated that appropriate conduct for analytical work involved using ethical tools based on an ideal to which we aspire both professionally and clinically.

Clinical psychoanalysis is built upon the assumptions that the unconscious exists, that parataxic phenomena such as transference and countertransference are universal, and that transference is an appropriate professional tool. Other major basic concepts in the psychoanalytic clinic include process, setting, regression as a mental state during therapy, resistance, empathetic listening and its expressions, idealization and its role in analysis, patient self-exposure, and others as well. As mentioned above, often the very existence of these concepts, and certainly their significance, their definitions, and the proper way to use them as psychoanalytic tools, are matters of major dispute among us.

Etchegoyen (1991) stated that what is told in the session on the couch has to be first and foremost seen as analytic material, informing the analyst of the patient's inner functioning. If it appears to be informative of external reality, the questions are "Why now?" and "Could what appears informative only have an unconscious meaning as part of the sessions material?"

It is clear that the therapeutic relationship in psychoanalysis is based both on real perceptions of both participants, but also on fantastic surrealistic images and perceptions of each other. This creates a situation where each analysis is a unique creation of interpersonal relationship, leading to intrapsychic processes and changes, where strict, generalized rules will fail to cover most of the cases.

The analyst can use transference and countertransference for the patient's therapeutic benefit on the one hand, but he or she may possibly misuse this power for his or her own purposes on the other. According to Hannah Segal (1981), "Countertransference is the best of servants but the worst of masters" (p. 86). Betty Joseph (2003) referred to the analyst's obligation to enable the feelings of countertransference to emerge but also the attendant obligation to supervise these feelings as they develop so as to avoid the slippery slope into the realm of the unethical. So even at this point, we see psychoanalysis comprises a continuum of analytic acts of varying professional quality, ranging from the ethical at one end of the spectrum to the unethical at the other. Actually, in spite of the urgent need to define what is professionally ethical and what is not, still there is a wide range of variance, and in some instances it is very difficult to decide whether an act was ethical or not. Even members of ethics committees diverge in certain cases. These warnings have been written to help the analytic clinicians to be aware of these unconscious psychological pressures and to warn them of the danger of unintended behaviors, but if observed and taken into account, they can be a source of deep understanding of psychic forces. Professional steps taken by the analyst to tip the pendulum of potential conflicts of interest in his own direction (clearly *unethical*) must be distinguished from those that are not so motivated. The first group includes acts from which the therapist derives emotional profit, sexual satisfaction, narcissistic self-aggrandizement, or avoidance of abhorrent feelings, as well as more concrete benefits such as money, time, influence, or power. Often such situations also involve unethical actions as well. Let me put it very clearly: In my (and many others) opinion, these analysts are unfit to work in this field. The second group includes acts in which the analyst has no personal interest or motive, whether conscious or unconscious, in choosing one or the other or is at this point unaware of such interest or motive. For such cases, the question of ethics is of a different nature; since there is no conflict of interest between the needs of the patient and the motives of the therapist, moral issues do not necessarily arise. This is the focus of my paper. As noted clearly by Gabbard and Lester (1995), Gabbard (2003), Joseph (2003), Sandler and Godley (2004), and others, the analytic work is very difficult and in the course of treatment the need to check one's tendency to act and react to the projections and unconscious manipulations of the patient is of paramount importance. If we neglect this side of our work, we may inadvertently enact rather than analyze unconscious wishes and enactments of the patient, and that can cause sliding down the slippery slope into acting out and unethical behavior.

I believe the culmination of professional ethics involves observing and being attentive to all expressive and symbolic verbal dimensions as well as considering and analyzing each and every therapeutic situation at its particular time and place with its unique participants and singular circumstances. The analytic session sometimes involves verbal interchanges or enactments between analyst and patient, while at others it comprises both behavioral and verbal enactments. Under such circumstances, it is difficult or even impossible to determine what is "right" or "wrong."

The ultimate decision regarding which type of intervention to choose is a purely professional matter or, as Asa Kasher (2007) put it, a *definitively ethical–professional choice*. Similarly, Etchegoyen (1991) noted the obvious link between psychoanalytic technique and professional ethics:

> Just as there is a strict correlation between psychoanalytic theory and technique, and investigation, so the relation between ethics and technique also rises in singular manners in psychoanalysis. It can even be said that ethics are a part of technique. Ethics is integrated into the scientific theory of psychoanalysis not as a simple moral aspiration but as a necessity of its praxis. A failure of ethics in psychoanalysis leads inexorably to technical failure. (p. 11)

Betty Joseph (2003) wrote the following:

> When we think about the relation between technical errors and unethical behavior we are necessarily considering the analyst's aims, conscious and unconscious, his/her motivation—how much for example is he trying to influence the patient, however subtly, to think or act in a way he thinks desirable? (p. 149)

Michels (1976) warned and argued that human beings, including psychoanalysts, attempt to influence the behavior of others. This has led to legal processes through which the public ultimately imposes its values upon a particular profession (as, e.g., in Israel, with the 1996 Patient's Rights Law). In the best case, such processes motivate and obligate professionals toward ethical professional thinking, on the complexity of the human condition, resulting, among other things, in the development of professional ethical codes. The professional standards constitute the ethical criteria according to which such professionals must behave towards the general public.

Goldberg (2008) in revising his thoughts of boundaries summarized that "reexamination of the boundary concepts suggests that it is an amalgam of technical and moralistic standards" (p. 872). Some of these principles are gathered in the International Psychoanalytical Association's *Ethics Code* (revised 2015).

On Responsibility

The weighty personal and professional responsibility assumed by analysts derives from a number of sources. First, those engaging in psychoanalysis are required by law to act responsibly to their patients, their colleagues, and society. The level of an analyst's professional skills and abilities is guaranteed by the studies, training, and supervision required to become a licensed psychoanalyst. This professional license, along with the obligation to uphold the professional rules set out in the ethical code, have established a professional consensus. According to Kasher (2005), this consensus transcends standards for conduct to include more ambiguous matters.

Klimovsky, Dupetit, and Zysman (1995) discussed psychoanalysts' responsibility toward their therapeutic goals as well as their ethical obligations. In the authors' view, these ethical obligations include taking responsibility that the patient responds to the treatment, taking responsibility for any suffering involved in treatment, and the creation of the underlying meaning of these sufferings. If an analyst lacks solid groundwork for assuming the psychoanalytic process can help alleviate the patient's suffering, the decision to treat the patient or even to propose verbal or other therapeutic intervention is unethical and the treatment must stop.

Chetrit-Vatine (2003, 2004) and others adopted and considerably expanded the approach of Emanuel Levinas (1996), according to which responsibility for the other is the essence of ethics. The significance of such a definition for psychoanalysis is that the analyst, based upon his inner, personal, and professional insight, takes upon himself responsibility for the patient's progress during therapy, without any desire or interest in satisfying his own needs. Akhtar (1999) enumerated six basic human needs the analyst must meet: (a) the need for one's physical needs to be deemed legitimate; (b) the need for identity, recognition, and affirmation; (c) the need for interpersonal and intrapsychic boundaries; (d) the need for understanding the causes of events; (e) the need for optimal emotional availability of a love object; and (f) the need for a resilient responsiveness by one's love objects under special circumstances. As in a pregnancy, the analysand, in representing himself, is inside, and the analyst carries the analysand inside himself. When the analyst allows the other to enter his or her space, he or she assumes complete responsibility for the other. Hence, within the psychoanalytic space, ethical responsibility, like other psychoanalytic terms, assumes the status of an interactive and subjective concept.

In my view, the analyst must act according to his or her best professional judgment on the one hand and knowledge of the professional consensus on the other. A different view may consider the analyst's total devotion as an impediment to his or her freedom to proceed to the best of his ability for the benefit of the patient. On the other hand, this total devotion is not always in the best interest of the patient's development, and may reflect some of the analyst's needs to nurture, devote, and protect.

I believe that *responsibility* is an important conceptual crossroads, one where Levinas's (1996) concept of ethics as an expression of overall responsibility intersects with Kasher's (2007) and Goldberg's (1999, 2008) practical approach to professional ethics and the responsibility to be inferred from these ethics. These two concepts converge in the analyst's basic approach toward the patient, one that involves enabling, listening, observing, contemplating, thinking, obligating. In adopting this viewpoint, the analyst, *to the best of his understanding*, believes in the central importance and undisputed neediness of the patient. Hence, analysts limit and circumscribe their personal, narcissistic, and idiosyncratic needs and their own sexual desires during the patient–analyst encounter. This approach also comprises the professional obligation analysts (like any other professional) take upon themselves to act in accordance with the highest, indeed the ideal, standards of the profession.

This chapter focuses on everyday situations and on practical ethical dilemmas associated with the course of psychoanalytic therapy, including the setting and the therapeutic processes.

THERAPEUTIC SETTING

Winnicott (1955/1975) defined the *therapeutic setting* as the sum of all sequential details, and Bleger (1967) proposed relating to setting as to the analytic situation as a whole, that is, all the phenomena composing the therapeutic interaction between analyst and patient. According to Bleger, the analytic situation involves a process that is learned, investigated, analyzed, and interpreted, as well as a frame or nonprocess constituting the fixed conditions in which the process takes place. It is not surprising that a large percentage of ethical violations are related to the frame. Nevertheless, many ethical dilemmas involve the process and the use of various tools in the process. The setting is created to provide a casing, within which the imagination can blossom and realize the desires safeguarded in the setting frame.

Considerations with respect to changing the setting arise during the entire course of the analysis, and it is not clear whether the answer can be reduced to a simple yes or no. Such cases constitute ethical dilemmas, that is, problematic situations to which there is no single solution and certainly not a perfect solution. In a dilemma, every solution to the problem feels imperfect, deficient, short of the mark, even to some degree harmful. In spite of this, the professional work must progress while attempting to cope with the dilemma and taking a stand about it. Indeed, taking a stand is unavoidable and often involves saying,

> This is my best solution at the moment, this is my logical suggestion at the moment, this is the practical ideal for this moment, and I can also think about what is not good in this solution or this step.

Such situations are changeable, and it is possible that at some later time, or even when the decision is made, thoughts about the opposite side of the dilemma will crop up. This does not mean the solution is incorrect. Rather, this is the nature of a dilemma. Contemplation and indecision, sometimes during the therapy itself and certainly outside the therapy session, individually or as a team, during training and during individual analysis, constitute a fundamental ethical practice and an essential professional practice as well.

The two clinical examples will demonstrate the analyst's coping with settling the dilemma posed by strict setting demands necessary to the psychoanalytic process and the need to adjust and cope with obstacles threatening the working alliance. In both examples, the conscious goal of the psychoanalyst was to protect the analysis while suggesting or accepting major permanent changes in the basic setting (in the first example) or making an exception under unusual circumstances (in the second example). In my discussion, I choose to emphasize the impact of such circumstances on the analyst as well as on the patient. Thus, the two illustrative vignettes I have chosen represent both sides of the couch, the perspective of the patient and that of the analyst for, in fact, I play in them both roles. These vignettes illustrate situations in which the analyst deviated from the frame or made decisions that could potentially harm the analytic process. Such circumstances raise clear ethical considerations: What is the meaning and the impact of the act in the relationship, and does the analyst's response stem from motivation to help the patient and contribute to the analysis or from personal motives and gains? These are all relationship factors that should be considered by the analyst. Though they demand the analyst make a professional choice based on a professional opinion in a particular situation, they do not violate any moral rules whatsoever, nor do they imply that the analyst profits in any way.

The clinical examples are taken from two different analyses. The first one is from my first analysis, which took place long ago; in this example, I focus on how I, as a patient, interpreted what happened while attempting to surmise the analyst's possible insights and professional choices. The second example is from my experience as an analyst at a mental health clinic in north Jerusalem.[1]

First Example

The analysis took place in the living room of my analyst's apartment, with the living room couch doubling as the therapeutic couch. This couch had teakwood handles, as was the style back then.

During the first sessions I felt there wasn't enough room for me to lie comfortably on the couch. I was uncomfortable. The couch seemed too narrow and too short. When I told the analyst about my discomfort, his interpretation was, "You don't feel there is enough room for you here." Another time he said, "You're not comfortable with the analysis." Yet another time he asked, "Can you think of anything else that's difficult for you here? What else is not comfortable for you?" My take on this was the following: I'm a big guy, my legs dangle past the end of the couch and my shoulders are being cramped and squashed by the backrest cushions that take up a good deal of the couch's width. My preoccupation with these annoying physical sensations and the distress these feelings brought me irked me to the point of practically blocking any other thoughts. After a number of sessions and in response to the analyst's recurring interpretations of my complaints, I made concrete suggestions for several changes that would make things much more suitable and comfortable for me. The analyst's interpretation was, "You want to do as you wish. It's important to you that I accept your desires." I realized that even if he was right, and perhaps he was, what was *also and really* important to me was to be comfortable. Another time he said, "You want to adjust my couch to you," and I realized he was right. I really did want the couch to fit me. I wanted him to readjust his couch for me, because it was not good for me to lie there feeling cramped and squished. I really did not like feeling that way, and, mainly, I did not understand why I had to get used to feeling that way and why he could not accept my suggestions for change.

One morning, I arrived with a plan for action. As usual, together we went through a fixed routine at the opening of each session: I ring the doorbell, he opens the door and greets me with a smile, he closes the door, he stands by the entrance to the therapy room, I enter the room, he follows me, closes the door and pulls the heavy curtain over it, I stand waiting while he finds my pillow covering and arranges it over the pillow, he sits down in his armchair and I lie down on the couch. This time, instead of lying down, I said, "Don't be alarmed by what I'm about to do. This is a very simple solution to what I've been complaining to you about for such a long time." I removed the three backrest cushions and placed them in a pile at the foot of the couch. In

[1]Details of case examples have been altered to protect confidentiality.

one fell swoop, the couch got longer and wider. The analyst said nothing. He just stared. I lay down and said, "Ah, this I understand. Now I'm comfortable." He still did not respond. I quickly began talking about matters that concerned me, but I was also busy appraising his response, or, more accurately, his lack of response, to my suggestion–action. The truth is, I was hesitant to bring up many of my thoughts. My satisfaction from this act, my feelings of excitement and of calm all brought me back to more or less the same place. Again I was silent. I thought a bit and said aloud, "Now, even though the couch is very comfortable, I still find it very difficult to talk." More silence, and then, a minute or two before our hour was up, he said to me, "This will be the permanent arrangement when you're here." I remember thinking then that I "beat" him. I felt very pleased and appeased that he did not reject the solution (which indeed was a good solution). From then on and until the analysis came to an end, removing the cushions and piling them up at the foot of the couch was added to the session's opening routine performed by the analyst.

In analyzing the professional–ethical significance of this incident, I took into consideration the possible alternatives at the analyst's disposal. At first he was convinced, and as you can see with some degree of justification, that the patient was resistant to (as we used to say in the profession) or was having difficulty with (as we say today) the therapy. This resistance was expressed by recurring complaints about the unsuitability of the couch but also by silence and by difficulties in speaking and in expressing his thoughts and the products of his imagination. The patient was not conscious of his resistance, and even the analyst's initial attempts to interpret this resistance did not help. He was preoccupied with feelings that the couch was not suitable for his size. I believe the analyst's continued interpretations constituted appropriate professional–ethical conduct in that he behaved in accordance with the therapeutic model. From the analysand's perspective, the analyst was relating to his requests to change the couch as expressions of resistance and was not attentive to a more pressing need to be included and understood, nor to how difficult it was when this need was not met.

The patient felt that what he stated so clearly did not lead to any insight. Thus, he chose to act, presenting the analyst with a new situation constituting a change in the setting. What had been before is not what is now. Is this the way things will now be?

What were the analyst's possible insights in this situation? What did he take into consideration in choosing to act as he did? Most obviously, something extraordinary had happened. Something different. The patient said something in a determined and loud voice. By acting to change the setting, the patient was demanding to be heard, demanding that something be done. The patient was saying, "You haven't heard me up to now and you didn't realize that there is something that I really need. This isn't totally symbolic; it is a real need."

The analyst could have seen this as the patient acting out, choosing to do something rather than say something. What is the significance of acting out? Is it a behavioral expression of resistance? A desire to take apart the analyst's couch? To take apart and destroy the analyst? The patient demonstrating to the analyst: see how much power I have, what I am able to do if I so desire.

The analyst could have a different insight as well. The patient is definitely trying to tell me something. Is he saying my interpretations of the resistance are not valid? Not correct? Maybe he's trying to say that in addition to his resistance, his difficulty, I don't recognize how uncomfortable he actually is. Moreover, he seems to need to be understood in his own way. The analyst also sees how determined the patient is, how he has repeated his plea more than once: Let's change the couch, change the couch for me. This change involves a physical adjustment of the couch to the patient, but also a response to the patient's need to feel that here, in my clinic, he has a place, and he has an impact on this place, that he is taking part in creating his therapeutic setting. The analyst may also have been thinking: This acting out is not feasible. It must be interpreted, and the situation must be restored to what it was at the outset. Inside a frame.

What could the analyst do with each of these insights?

- He could interpret the motive for action.
- He could interpret the action and its significance.
- He must decide whether to respond to the action, to accept it, to reinforce it, or to reject it.

My analyst chose not to interpret either the motives for my action or the significance of the act itself. He chose to hear, to listen, and to accept the act as part of the therapeutic dialogue. Not delving into all these possibilities immediately after the act empowered me in a number of ways: (a) it made me feel accepted and able to exert influence; and (b) it helped me relax, so that, as I thought, I was able to connect more concretely with my resistance. That is, the analyst's acceptance of the change in the setting (at first, not by talking but rather by not responding to the change I had initiated) loosened me up, enabling me to contemplate and look inside myself, to face my difficulties in speaking, this time unconnected to my discomfort on the couch. (In fact, because I did feel more comfortable, it became clearer to me that I also had difficulty talking.) This act enabled me to experience anxiety that I was not conscious of before the event, anxiety that now took on counterphobic significance. Only after I acted did I understand how much I feared this act, and how I anxiously awaited the analyst's reactions.

When I think about this vignette today, I see an act that, while it cannot be interpreted, is professional and remarkably acceptable. It is part of the delicate balance involved in entering into the analytic process and creating a working alliance, a therapeutic covenant, a relationship with the patient. Clearly, changing the couch was not the therapist's idea. This incident makes me think about the type of uniformity we expect from all our patients. Beyond the unique interpersonal and other attributes of each and every patient, there is also something quite uniform in what we offer them. Moreover, it is clear to me that my analyst did not think the couch caused me so much discomfort. Today, I believe that at first he was predisposed to understand, but his insight, his ethical–professional mandate, and the overall responsibility dictated by this insight inclined him to interpret this as the most classic form of resistance. When I actually did something, he was faced with a dilemma, forced to mull over this unusual professional problem, and sort through his toolbox to find the most appropriate tool. He did not stick to the resistance interpretations he had adopted previously. Rather, he was able to look analytically at aspects unknown to him, to listen, to accept, and to adapt to what he understood were my needs. Based on my confidence in the good intention and professionalism of my analyst (i.e., the patient's perception of the therapeutic alliance), I relied on my analyst understanding and felt safe enough to suggest this radical change (which could be easily interpreted also as acting in or out the treatment or as an act of violation towards the couch and the analysis by taking it virtually apart). He accepted and assimilated my basic need into the fabric of our relationship. I added a component to this fixed relationship, on the basis of which he created and strengthened the therapeutic setting. Indeed, he totally accepted and internalized this component. This to my experience and understanding is what we mean by fostering the working alliance.

Second Example

The second vignette exemplifying the ethical issues involved in a change of setting, this time from the analyst's perspective, is taken from an analysis that began while I was still in training and continued for years afterward.

Shimon, an ultra-Orthodox man of Russian origin living in one of the communities in Judea and Samaria, began treatment to cope with outbursts of rage, particularly toward his young son. Despite Shimon's love for his son, he often lost control, hitting and insulting the boy. Shimon sought treatment because he feared he might endanger his son. He also strongly suspected that the authorities were likely to remove him from the home or distance him from his son. In the intake interview, a fascinating life story emerged of a man with tremendous inner resources on the one hand and extremely self-limiting, tormented, and hurtful behavior on the other. He is a complex, interesting, and creative man, speaks pleasantly, yet holds very extreme political and religious views and a missionary belief that he can have an impact on the entire world, including me. His distress is great, as is his enthusiasm for change. He is the younger of two sons. His father, an intellectual who died when Shimon was 6, was physically weak, emotionally lenient, and permissive; his mother is an aggressive, work weary, and opinionated woman whom he believed allied herself with his older brother. He was punished physically, humiliated, and belittled by both of them. The early relational experiences he had in his family were authoritative and arbitrary.

The technical arrangements for this analysis were not simple. Shimon came to Jerusalem only twice a week. The journey was dangerous, and he was afraid. We found 2 hours on the days he came to Jerusalem for a very part-time academic job, and he made two special trips for two additional sessions. His financial situation was so bad that I received special permission to charge him 10 shekels per session instead of the usual 25 I charged my other patients at the clinic. This arrangement was made after he explained that he could not afford both the bus fare and the payment for four weekly sessions. For Shimon, coming to the clinic was both expensive and dangerous; however, he did not miss even one therapy session.

In the third year, the analysis focused on Shimon's labile self-image and feelings of worthlessness. He felt that people took advantage of him and sought out his quirks in order to knock him down and then blame him. He would say,

> It's my fault. I always want people to believe me. And they don't. It's the hurt little boy inside me. Always. Even today, when I've become what I am, there's that hurt little boy, who's been rejected, who has to lash out, who doesn't believe he's wanted, who doesn't believe he's worthy. It's me against the world of the grownups. I'm not one of them. Surely my son thinks differently, but that's him, and as for me . . . I'm not convincing, I don't pass, I can't enter the world of the grownups. I don't belong. I can't find my place there.

All this was expressed by small and subtle feelings and sometimes by implosion: "I don't exist. There's no room. I've disappeared. I'm in the sewer. I'm flowing out to sea." In transference as well, he demonstrated extreme fluctuation, ranging from feelings of tremendous admiration and closeness toward me and the analytic method, to constant suspicion that I was not really getting close to him, that I was so different from him that I could not be genuinely interested in him, and that perhaps even I could not understand what he was feeling. "Other than me, only you understand about me: about how I'm rejected, unwanted, and unsure." And he was capable of violent attachment, of attacking me with words as he attacked his children with blows (which stopped close to when the analysis began). He said,

> In the zoo, the tigers are in a glass cage. You can put your nose two centimeters from the tiger's head, and though he sees you he can't touch you, can't do a thing. The tiger thinks, "Let's see how brave you'd be without the glass."

Shimon, considering himself rejected and dangerous, did not believe I was close to him, that I truly accepted him as he was without the barrier of the therapeutic setting. "You're in my life whether near or far. I'm only meaningful to you here. You're meaningful to me always, in the infinite space of my experience."

One day, as I was waiting for Shimon in the therapy room, the clinic secretary phoned me to tell me the guard would not let Shimon enter the building. I went downstairs and found Shimon in the midst of an argument with the guard stationed at the entrance to the clinic. Shimon had a license to carry a weapon. But since the murder of four mental health workers in a public mental health clinic 15 years before this event, no one was allowed to bring weapons into the clinic building. Because the guard was new, he did not have the key to the safe, and he was not willing to allow Shimon into the building with his weapon. On the other hand, Shimon was unwilling to leave the weapon with the guard but would only put it in the safe. Though I felt helpless, I still intervened. I said to the guard, "I've known this man for many years. It's OK." This didn't work. The situation was very frustrating and reached an impasse. When I remembered how much effort Shimon invested in coming to each session, the financial hardship and the physical endangerment, it was difficult for me to accept that there was no solution. On the one hand, I agreed completely with the guard about not entering the building with a weapon. On the other hand, the way Shimon experienced this situation was very arbitrary, authoritative, and from his perspective, unbearable.

I thought about what to do. There was no public place to sit anywhere near the clinic. I also felt Shimon would not even consider canceling the session. I made a suggestion to Shimon. "What do you think about sitting in my car?"

"Great idea," he answered. We got in the car. Shimon sat in the seat next to the driver's seat, and I sat in the back seat. After we got in, there was complete silence for quite a while. I thought, "This is both embarrassing and quite interesting. What's going to happen here?"

After a few minutes, I said, "It's hard to begin talking in a situation that's so different from usual."

Shimon said,

> It's very strange to me. I can't think about anything but how relieved and calm I feel. I've forgotten what I wanted to discuss when I arrived at therapy. I'm preoccupied with being here in the car with you, coping with powers greater than us, and succeeding. And when you succeed, it doesn't matter that you don't talk. You are very creative. I never would have thought of such a solution.

I said, "I understand you're reacting to the fact that I found a solution to a situation that endangered our session, thus enabling both of us to overcome a serious obstacle."

Then Shimon said,

> And you didn't get into an argument with the guard. I was afraid you'd yell at him, that you'd tell him you're the chief psychologist, you're in charge, you'd order him to let me in with the gun, and if he didn't comply you'd lose your cool and yell at him.

"Just like what happens with you with your son, when he doesn't capitulate to your authority."

> Yes, that's me. I need to learn from you how to control my emotions. Tell me the truth, didn't it irritate you that he didn't know who you are? That he didn't listen to you? That he stuck to his guns? That he determined the result even though you've been there for years and he just started working today? You are the chief psychologist, right, the boss?

> I wasn't worried about him. I was worried about you. I was thinking about how to make sure you didn't come here for nothing. How to go on with the therapy despite the hitch. The problem wasn't with him. He was doing his job properly.

Did I behave professionally? Ethically? Clearly this situation was outside the frame and represented a drastic change in setting. Shimon was barred from the therapeutic room. I suggested an alternative I knew was problematic. I moved the therapeutic space from the public clinic to my private car: a cramped space, on the street, open for anyone to see in. The analytic routine was disrupted, could not take place. In practice, I had four options: (a) not to hold the session, (b) to offer to take responsibility for the gun, (c) to ask Shimon what he thought should be done, or (d) to hold the session in an alternative location.

Not to hold the session was the obvious and simplest option. Despite the desire to view therapy as a stable, permanent process that cannot be disturbed, in fact, a situation arose that prevented holding the session in its usual form. What does accepting such a situation mean? Does it resemble coping with vacation, reserve duty, snow, or sick leave? Canceling a session does not put the treatment at risk, but it is disappointing and represents a breach of promise. I looked for a way not to disappoint Shimon in what appeared to be one of the major reassuring elements of his analysis and of analysis in general: "I'm here for you; I'm waiting for you." Shimon never missed a single session, despite the danger and financial burden involved. Hence, I felt obligated to consider whether the missing key had to have a determining impact. What would happen to him if I sent him home? He'd be very hurt and feel that I, through the guard, was preventing him from getting what was essential to him. I would not be providing him a safe harbor. The term *safe* is very important here. The gun is usually kept in the safe, like the tiger behind the cage. On this occasion the key was missing, so it was not safe for Shimon to enter the building

I took responsibility for the gun and allowed him to bring it into my car—so I accepted him with all his aggression and protective real needs, and I trusted that it would be okay. The car is like a cage in which we are now together.

Here I am now looking at the tiger with no glass. He is close to me, on my territory, with the gun. I am not frightened, and he feels safe.

He'd be liable to lose the special feeling he'd managed to develop during the analysis that, despite his difficulties in coping with his feelings and experiences, in the therapy sessions he was wanted and taken care of. I wasn't worried he'd stop the therapy. I was concerned he'd be insulted and that all those familiar and arbitrary degradations from his past would be reawakened. I recalled a statement his mother made that came up again and again in the treatment. She would say, as his brother stood smiling beside her, "You're not coming with us because we don't want you to." I didn't want this to be the case here.

The second option was to propose putting the gun in my car, so we could enter the clinic. I rejected this option because it meant I was placing myself in a position of tremendous power and influence by taking his weapon into my custody and putting it in my car. Moreover, the small chance that the weapon or the car with the weapon might be stolen or taken away had the potential for unnecessary legal and ethical complications.

The option of summarizing the situation for Shimon and asking him what he thought was the best thing to do also did not appear to be a good alternative. Shimon, a self-directed person, acted and made decisions for himself. He had not caused the complex situation unraveling around him. His highly agitated state also made me think it was not a good idea to consult him or, alternatively, to place the decision in his hands. Even though I considered him an independent person, I felt responsible for him and for the situation.

The option I chose brought me deliverance fantasies. Was I trying to save him in some miraculous manner? Is this what led me to such an unconventional act? It was hard not to think about this as megalomaniac–heroic behavior. On the other hand, I tried not to give in to the annoying and insurmountable circumstances and to find a solution that, while not perfect, might provide a partial answer to his fundamental expectation that the session would not be cancelled. For Shimon, a therapy session was not a symbol. It was an existential entity. My thoughts and considerations played an important role in selecting the proper professional–ethical alternative. Did my choice stem from my reluctance to frustrate and disappoint Shimon, or was it motivated by the notion that not holding the session would seriously harm him?

Before I proposed the solution, was I aware of its problems and limitations? What is the significance of sitting in a car, of violating the immunity of the analysis by holding it in a car on the street, of the more intimate physical closeness between me and Shimon? In the past, Shimon never hid his desires to get even closer to me, "like children sitting next to each other in kindergarten." He was open with his friends and family about his analysis and never considered it a secret. During the course of the treatment, I never sensed any feelings of an erotic nature from him or towards him. Such feelings, had they existed, could have aroused thoughts of hidden temptation which, had I been conscious of them, would have played a major role in my decision whether or not to choose this alternative. Maybe I sought to impress him with my car? Perhaps I had a need to show my superiority or to brag?

Ultimately, I believe I acted out of my feelings of obligation to Shimon and to his therapy, and out of an inner determination not to give up even one session because he wasn't prepared to do so. He is giving up so much every week, and I am ready to give up something, too. Perhaps I would have conducted myself differently with another patient, one who did not so tangibly express how important the sessions were to him and how much effort he invested in coming to them. Most likely such a choice would not have been appropriate, either professionally or ethically, for a different patient. I am certainly aware now, and even then I understood, that if no practical solution was found and I had sent Shimon away in the same state he came, he might have been terribly let down, reacted emotionally, and had to cope with yet another disappointment.

In the next session, Shimon told me his wife was taking a self-awareness course based on the Adler method. In the course, the students discussed basic human errors. Who makes mistakes? Everyone! They discussed mistakes parents make with their children by yelling at them, frightening them, making them feel they're in the way. These mistakes don't take place only under extreme circumstances, but rather in everyday situations. Parents fail to answer their children's questions, do not pay attention to them, forget promises, and belittle them. They don't care when things happen to their children. They care only about themselves. They must keep running toward their own finish line. This discussion made me think about us. Had I been paying attention to Shimon or to myself, to a mistake that perhaps I didn't make, that I avoided for his sake? I had transformed this seemingly technical problem of "no one is allowed to bring weapons into the building" into a statement of practical action, "I will do my utmost to make sure your analytic session takes place." I was not intimidated by him, whereas the guard was intimidated (understandably, given his role). I took Shimon and his gun into my car—into my private world. It is not just that I didn't miss a session, but I was willing to do something extraordinary for him. I was making an adjustment in the analytic rules—in order to accommodate Shimon—in order to protect and foster the working alliance. And I am sure the analytic work that took place in that hour was different, (but not worse than) any of the other hours we had before and after this event.

This is another example where with deep consideration and thinking, one contributes to the working alliance, while overruling technical and ethical guidelines in their wide context.

The above two examples refer to particular ethical dilemmas involving the analytic setting, in which the ethical problem is clearly a technical therapeutic problem related to the setting. In both examples, the analyst deviated from the setting's fixed boundaries and allowed the setting to change, demonstrating that the borders of the analytic setting are not arbitrarily fixed. Breaching boundaries or making changes is often unavoidable, and like the analytic process itself, construction and definition of the setting are inspired by both participants. In both examples, the analysts decided to adjust the borders to accommodate the new situation—in the first, permanently assimilating the change into the analytic setting, and in the second, adopting the change as an ad hoc solution for a situation with no other fitting solution in view of the patient's potential responses to not doing anything.

There is a conflict here between professional ethics and the patient's needs at the moment, and the alliance. Sometimes they clash, just like ethics and clinical judgment may clash. I had to cope with a dilemma—how to keep the analysis going and attend to patient's needs and to the relationship—and on the other hand, observe the code of fixed setting. My analyst (in the first example) had to cope with the same dilemma. How can the patient feel safe, feel that he is seen by the analyst? In these two examples, preserving the setting would have harmed the sense of safety.

These decisions appear to me to be the correct and ethical choices. Both were professional choices, demonstrating the analyst's profound feelings of responsibility for the patient's welfare. In both cases, the analyst attended not only to the interpretative arena of the analysis but also to the creation or maintenance of the working alliance, a very important element in any treatment. The two examples demonstrate well-taken decisions that actually, by fostering the working alliance, protected the analytic process or enabled it to proceed.

The two examples present a wider dilemma between adherence to the therapeutic model from both an ethical perspective as well as from a dogmatic perspective that analysis works only under strict setting rules. That is the claim that analytic session cannot take place in a car, or that all patients lying on a couch are the same size, or should adapt themselves to the size of their analyst's couch. This is a dilemma between the adherence to the model and the specific needs of the patient and the alliance. Having said so does not eliminate the role of transferencial projections and need of the patient towards the analyst. The tension between these options must activate the analyst's creativity in order to come up with professional yet ethical solutions. In these specific examples, adjusting the setting to the needs of the patient not only did not interrupt the analysis, it also improved the alliance and, thus, the entire analysis. Symington (2012) related to the essence of psychoanalysis and emphasized that the analyst's freedom to believe in and choose among different modes of connecting with the patient. Strict adherence to the setting may cause the loss of the true essence of psychoanalysis.

IMPLICATIONS FOR FUTURE RESEARCH

No studies or research projects are known to me in this field. I think that based on some of the insights gained in this chapter, two research methodologies can be adjusted to study the phenomena I have described.

The first is qualitative interviews-based study, asking analysts and therapist about their experience of extreme or semiextreme situations when they needed to act and decide between the adherence to model approach to adherence to patients understood needs. Such a study can provide us with richer understanding of clinical decision making in psychoanalysis and psychoanalytically oriented psychotherapy. Besides understanding such situations, the proposed qualitative study could enrich our repertoire of clinical vignettes relevant to this subject and the capacity to estimate how frequent such occasions are in psychoanalytic practice.

A second suggestion for optional studies in the field is based on presenting analysts and psychotherapists with clinical vignettes, such as the two described in this chapter, or others that will be gathered in the first qualitative process, and ask them to share their decision-making process.

As for training and supervision, I suggest these dilemmas and similar other ones should come up in supervision and be discussed in a nonjudgmental way. Trainees usually hide such episodes from their supervisors because they feel guilty and ashamed about bending rules. I also think along with Sandler and Godley (2004) and Gabbard (2000) that ethics committees, including those of the International Psychoanalytic Association, the

European Psychoanalytic Federation, and local psychoanalytic societies should initiate study days, case presentations, and seminars, in which cases such as those described in this chapter can be studied and discussed.

CONCLUSION

Psychoanalysis stimulates and creates an illusion that gives rise to wishes, transference projections for the patient, and countertransference for the therapist. Such feelings require the analyst to listen with a sensitive ear to each and every patient, while at the same time applying his unique expertise and insight. Only then can he choose the interventions appropriate for each patient and each situation. These choices affect both patients and analysts who, as we have seen, are not immune to their impact. Perhaps only through understanding the relationship in depth can the analyst allow himself to bend the rules so that the analysis can fit the relationship and still remain an analysis, rather than an analysis that continues according to the rules but loses the patient or the collaborative relationship.

None of the above vignettes touch upon fundamental issues of abuse of human dignity, freedom, and values. Any action the analyst should choose in these dilemmas, after observation and weighing the alternatives, is worthy. Such situations are common and take place every day. By and large, they do not have destructive outcomes and do not touch on matters of morality and integrity. Even so, I believe they are clear examples of professional ethical dilemmas faced by therapists. Without in any way harming the values of the person being treated, the therapist's decision in such dilemmas can facilitate or inhibit development, can enable or block introspection, and can promote or hinder reaching an understanding between therapist and patient.

Contrary to other therapeutic methods that have clearer professional standards, psychoanalysis as a treatment method is based upon tremendous subjectivity, even at its most traditional modalities. Therefore, analysts bear tremendous ethical responsibility, for in many cases it is analysts themselves who set the ethical and professional standard for their actions, backed by their analytic insight and integrity. More than a century ago, Ferenczi (1910) wrote about this in a letter to Freud:

> You once told me that psychoanalysis is a science of facts, a science of what is, that we must not translate what we analyze into some sort of obligatory projection that can only be a set of futile and paranoiac thoughts. From this perspective, there is nothing resembling a psychoanalytic worldview, there are no ethics of psychoanalysis, there is no psychoanalytic code of conduct. I recognize no other ethics than the ethics of pure wisdom.

We must remember that the ensuing 100 years have seen immeasurable changes in the patient–therapist relationship in all areas, including psychoanalysis. The patient has become a partner in the therapy and over the years has become socialized to increased involvement, the right to know, and the right to receive explanations for the analyst's professional actions. These changes did not take place in a vacuum. As I have shown, the analyst's professional obligation and responsibility to understand and often to explain his or her professional behavior clearly, in detail, and meticulously is an expression of the level of his professional ethics. In thinking, understanding, and taking responsibility for his actions, the analyst is acting professionally and ethically, so long as he or she does not cause any harm to the patient.

At the beginning of this chapter, I posed the question of what is the ideal professional standard to which psychoanalysis should strive. Or, in other words, what is an ethical–professional act in psychoanalysis? I propose that the answer lies in the intervention. This intervention must be anchored in theory and based on technical know-how. It must be carried out responsibly by the analyst after having observed, considered, and weighed—both consciously and unconsciously—its potential beneficial and harmful influences on the analytic process, on the patient, and on him- or herself. Finally, it must constitute what the analyst believes to be the most appropriate choice for the situation. Such a definition, which stresses psychoanalysts' ongoing attention and thought as a professional–ethical element in their clinical work, facilitates professional and reasonable dialogue among different factions in psychoanalysis, even if they do not agree on the theoretical approach.

I hope I managed to contribute to this volume not only by demonstrating the issues of analyst–patient relationships in classical psychoanalysis but also by merging ethical principles and thinking, which have crucial importance for patient–therapist relations.

REFERENCES

Akhtar, S. (1999). The distinction between needs and wishes: Implications for psychoanalytic theory and technique. *Journal of the American Psychoanalytic Association*, *47*, 113–151. http://dx.doi.org/10.1177/00030651990470010201

American Psychological Association. (2017). *Ethical principles of psychologists and code of conduct* (2002, Amended June 1, 2010 and January 1, 2017). Retrieved from http://www.apa.org/ethics/code/index.aspx

Bleger, J. (1967). Psycho-analysis of the psycho-analytic frame. *The International Journal of Psychoanalysis*, *48*, 511–519. Retrieved from http://psycnet.apa.org/record/1968-12190-001

Chetrit-Vatine, V. (2003). On responsibility towards the other, and on asymmetry in the psychoanalytical encounter. *Psychoanalysis in Europe: Bulletin of the European Psychoanalytical Foundation, 57*, 153–165.

Chetrit-Vatine, V. (2004). Primal seduction, matricial space and asymmetry in the psychoanalytic encounter. *The International Journal of Psychoanalysis, 85*, 841–856. http://dx.doi.org/10.1516/QYVT-7TCU-C5CW-4YUX

Erikson, E. H. (1964). *Insight and responsibility: Lectures on the ethical implications of psychoanalytic insight*. New York, NY: W. W. Norton.

Etchegoyen, R. H. (1991). *The fundamentals of psychoanalytic technique*. London, England: Karnac Books.

Ferenczi, S. (1910). Letter to Sigmund Freud, 3 October, 1910. In E. Brabant, E. Falzeder, & P. Giampieri-Deutch (Eds.), *The correspondence of Sigmund Freud and Sándor Ferenczi* (Vol. 1: 1908–1919, pp. 217–221). Cambridge, MA: Harvard University Press.

Freud, S. (1913). On beginning the treatment (further recommendations on the technique of psychoanalysis I). In J. Strachey (Ed.), *The standard edition of the complete works of Sigmund Freud* (Vol. 12, pp. 121–144). London, England: Hogarth.

Freud, S. (1915). Observation on transference love (Further recommendations on the technique of psycho-analysis III). In J. Strachey (Ed.), *The standard edition of the complete works of Sigmund Freud* (Vol. 12, pp. 157–171). London, England: Hogarth.

Freud, S. (1919). Lines of advance in psychoanalytic therapy. In J. Strachey (Ed.), *The standard edition of the complete works of Sigmund Freud* (Vol. 17, pp. 157–168). London, England: Hogarth.

Gabbard, G. O. (2000). Consultation from the consultant's perspective. *Psychoanalytic Dialogues: The International Journal of Relational Perspectives, 10*, 209–218. http://dx.doi.org/10.1080/10481881009348532

Gabbard, G. O. (2003). Miscarriages of psychoanalytic treatment with suicidal patients. *The International Journal of Psychoanalysis, 84*, 249–261. http://dx.doi.org/10.1516/WEDV-CUFA-9T91-ELDY

Gabbard, G. O. (2008). Boundaries, technique, and self-deception: A discussion of Arnold Goldberg's "Some limits of the boundary concept." *The Psychoanalytic Quarterly, LXXVII*, 877–881. http://dx.doi.org/10.1002/j.2167-4086.2008.tb00364.x

Gabbard, G. O., & Lester, E. (1995). *Boundaries and boundary violations in psychoanalysis*. Washington, DC: American Psychiatric Association.

Goldberg, A. (1999). Boundaries as pre-conditions. *The Psychoanalytic Quarterly, LXVIII*, 248–263. http://dx.doi.org/10.1002/j.2167-4086.1999.tb00533.x

Goldberg, A. (2008). Some limits of the boundary concept. *The Psychoanalytic Quarterly, LXXVII*, 861–875. http://dx.doi.org/10.1002/j.2167-4086.2008.tb00363.x

International Psychoanalytical Association. (2015). *Ethics code*. Retrieved from https://www.ipa.world/ipa/en/IPA1/Procedural_Code/Ethics_code_new.aspx

Joseph, B. (2003). Ethics and enactment. *Psychoanalysis in Europe: Bulletin of the European Psychoanalytical Foundation*, *57*, 147–153.

Kasher, A. (2005). Professional ethics and collective professional autonomy: A conceptual analysis. *Ethical Perspectives: Journal of the European Ethics Network*, *11*, 67–98.

Kasher, A. (2007). Professional ethics. In Y. Achmon, G. Weil, & G. Shefler, (Eds.), *Ethical issues for professionals in counseling and psychotherapy* (3rd ed., pp. 15–29). Jerusalem, Israel: Magnes Press.

Klimovsky, G., Dupetit, S., & Zysman, S. (1995). Ethical and unethical conduct in psychoanalysis. Correlations between logic, ethics and science. *The International Journal of Psychoanalysis*, *76*, 977–989.

Levinas, E. (1996). *Ethics and infinity: Conversations with Philip Nemo*. Jerusalem, Israel: Magnes.

Michels, R. (1976). Professional ethics and social values. *The International Review of Psycho-Analysis*, *3*, 377–384.

Sandler, A. M., & Godley, W. (2004). Institutional responses to boundary violations: The case of Masud Khan. *The International Journal of Psychoanalysis*, *85*, 27–43. http://dx.doi.org/10.1516/LP8G-5A70-9FFR-U62Q

Segal, H. (1981). *The work of Hanna Segal: A Kleinian approach to clinical practice*. New York, NY: Jason Aronson.

Symington, N. (2012). The essence of psycho-analysis as opposed to what is secondary. *Psychoanalytic Dialogues*, *22*, 395–409. http://dx.doi.org/10.1080/10481885.2012.700872

Winnicott, D. W. (1975). Clinical varieties of transference. In D. W. Winnicott (Ed.), *Collected papers: Paediatrics to psycho-analysis* (pp. 295–299). New York, NY: Basic Books. (original work published 1955)

7

THE THERAPEUTIC RELATIONSHIP: A WARM, IMPORTANT, AND POTENTIALLY MUTATIVE FACTOR IN COGNITIVE–BEHAVIORAL THERAPY

LOUIS G. CASTONGUAY, SOO JEONG YOUN, HENRY XIAO, AND ANDREW A. McALEAVEY

A substantial number of therapists and scholars from non–cognitive–behavioral therapy (CBT) orientations hold the view that CBT essentially involves a cold and mechanistic application of prescribed or manualized sets of techniques. For instance, the fourth author of this chapter (Andrew McAleavey) recently attended a talk by a senior clinician who informed the audience that he has a colleague who "combines CBT with a warm and friendly approach in a really neat way." Similarly, when Andrew informed a fellow psychotherapist-in-training that he was writing a piece on the working alliance in CBT, the student (who happens to be primarily psychodynamically oriented) playfully replied, "Oh, is there one?" Many CB therapists and scholars, it must be recognized, have not always been warm and enthusiastic about the importance of the therapeutic relationship. The first author of this chapter (Louis Castonguay) remembers when a graduate student working with him returned demoralized from his first poster presentation, which had

http://dx.doi.org/10.1037/0000093-008
Developing the Therapeutic Relationship: Integrating Case Studies, Research, and Practice, O. Tishby and H. Wiseman (Editors)

been given at the annual meeting of the Association for the Advancement of Behavior Therapy (ABCT) in the late 1990s. After briefly reading the title and abstract of a study demonstrating a significant relationship between alliance and outcome in CBT for generalized anxiety disorder, a senior therapist said, rather dismissively in both her tone and manner, "You know, young man, we are not really interested in this sort of thing at ABCT." Louis also remembers how disheartened he felt at the way a highly respected and generally very kind scholar reacted to a lecture that he gave as a postdoctoral fellow at Stanford University. The talk included his dissertation findings, where he found, among other things, a positive correlation between the alliance and outcome in cognitive therapy for depression, as well as suggestions about ways that CBT might improve its efficacy by addressing ruptures in the alliance—in line with the integrative perspective described later in this chapter. A polite (friendly, respectful, supportive, encouraging) reflection of the senior scholar's reaction would have been: "Louis, I think that you are wasting your time by focusing on these issues." A more verbatim report was: "Man, this is BS!"

Interestingly, though, things have changed with time. At the same conference mentioned above (now known as the Association of Behavior and Cognitive Therapy) a few years ago, Louis and Jacques Barber were both invited to be discussants on a clinical roundtable about the importance for clinicians to regularly collect outcome data in order to monitor the progress of their clients and the effectiveness of their interventions. One of the panelists started his talk by saying that there are two types of practitioners: those who rely on research data (as most CBT proudly do or should be doing), and those who do not give attention or credit to any empirically based construct or measure. The panelist nonequivocally identified Freud as the most well-known, infamous representative figure of the second breed of clinicians. He then went on to encourage clinicians to go beyond the measurement of symptom change and to also pay particular attention to the empirically based construct of the alliance. To Louis's chagrin, the panelist appeared to be surprised when Louis began his comment by informing him that the concept of alliance actually emerged from the psychoanalytic literature and that, as early as 1913, Freud implored psychoanalysts to never provide an interpretation before a good *rapport* had been established. This talk was a reminder of what Donald Levis (1988), known for his work on implosive therapy, called the behaviorists' phobia of anything that could be viewed as Freudian. Even more recently, Louis spent a few days with the esteemed professor at Stanford mentioned above, who told him about the exciting effectiveness research that he is currently doing, which involves training therapists on what to do when clients do not change. "The first thing I tell them," he said, "is to make sure that you are using the right techniques.

The second is: check the alliance. This is so important." Without missing a beat, he then went on and asked, "By the way, Louis, are you still involved in the very interesting research on the relationship that you were working on ages ago?"

These brief anecdotes suggest that up until very recently, the practice of CBT has been viewed as somehow at odds with being warm and friendly, and that in CBT, the relationship is not a crucial factor. However, the history of research on these issues is much less clear than many people (including CBT therapists) assume, and in fact, the literature suggests that CBT has always required a warm relationship. In this chapter, we address the issues of whether the therapeutic relationship in CBT is best characterized as "cold," whether CBT assumes the relationship to be an unimportant factor in change, and specific ways cognitive–behavioral therapists have used the relationship as part of the therapy process. We then provide suggestions, based on research and constructs outside of mainstream CBT, that might further improve our understanding of the role of alliance in this approach and, possibly, improve its effectiveness. While offering a new conceptualization of the relationship in CBT is beyond the scope of this chapter, we present a case example that illustrates how traditional CBT and non-CBT relationship–based interventions can be integrated in clinical practice.

IS THE RELATIONSHIP IN COGNITIVE–BEHAVIORAL THERAPY COLD?

This question is raised with surprising frequency, particularly given CBT's long history of endorsing warmth, empathy, and collaborative affiliation in theory, practice, and research. Going back to the pioneers of behavioral, cognitive, and then cognitive–behavioral therapies, experts have long encouraged practitioners to adopt a warm and engaging interpersonal style in order to improve the relationship. For example, one of the founding figures of behavior therapy noted that when clients seemed to like him, they showed signs of improvement even before the specific application of his therapeutic interventions (Wolpe, 1958). Beck, Rush, Shaw, and Emery (1979) also wrote that "cognitive and behavior therapies probably require the same subtle therapeutic atmosphere that has been described explicitly in the context of psychodynamic therapy" (p. 50). Further, they went on to discuss warmth, accurate empathy, and genuineness as important characteristics of cognitive and behavioral therapists. The emphasis on basic qualities of the therapeutic relationship has not been lost in the midst of the energy invested in the development of CBT therapy manuals and empirically supported therapies. As one example, Hembree, Rauch, and Foa (2003) noted that trust is an absolutely essential element of the therapeutic relationship in prolonged exposure therapy because of the difficult and sometimes distressing nature of the process of exposure therapy with trauma victims.

Given this theoretical writing on the CBT relationship, one might wonder how CBT has acquired such an infamous reputation. We propose that there are primarily two reasons for this. The first is that the therapeutic relationship *is* different in CBT, at least theoretically, than in some other orientations of psychotherapy. A second reason is that historically, CBTs have emphasized therapeutic interventions (techniques) as the primary causes of therapeutic change, while other therapies have placed more emphasis on the therapeutic value of working with the relationship. This first point will be addressed next, while the second requires more space and will be addressed after.

The particular qualities of the CBT relationship that have emerged over the years can be summarized by a term coined by Beck and colleagues (1979): *collaborative empiricism*. While, as we mentioned above, these authors were not the first in the CBT literature to note the importance of the relationship, this term has become widely used and might just as pithily reflect the entire CBT approach to treatment as it does describe the relationship that takes place within it. *Collaborative empiricism* at once captures a relationship that is highly interactive, democratic, task oriented, and based on the exploration of reality as best defined by the knowledge of the senses. This has also been described as a sense of teamwork that is necessary in CBT, perhaps as a function of its fairly directive stance (Raue & Goldfried, 1994). Collaboration is no doubt important in other therapies as well, and a strong and explicit "dose" of it is likely to be particularly needed for the successful implementation of any kind of directive treatment. When the psychotherapist seeks to engage the client in planned activities or tasks, whether they are cognitive (e.g., Socratic dialogue in the service of cognitive restructuring), behavioral (e.g., exposure), experiential (e.g., a one-chair technique aimed at assisting the client to identify his or her experience), interpersonal (e.g., taking an extensive history of interpersonal relationships), or any other type, the process is made much more difficult in the absence of a collaborative relationship. Nevertheless, cognitive and behavior therapists deserve some credit for pioneering and popularizing this attitude.

There is also substantial empirical evidence to suggest that CBT therapists are not cold with clients, and this literature extends back nearly 4 decades. One of the more well-known examples is the study by Sloane, Staples, Cristol, Yorkston, and Whipple (1975), who found that behavior therapists displayed significantly more empathy, genuineness, and interpersonal contact, as well as comparable warmth, than did psychoanalysts.

More recently, evidence from meta-analyses (e.g., Horvath, Del Re, Flückiger, & Symonds, 2011) suggests that while the alliance in CBT is not stronger than the alliance in other orientations, it is not at all weaker.

Does Cognitive–Behavioral Therapy Assume That the Working Alliance Is an Unimportant Factor in Treatment Outcome?

One of the early behavioral attitudes towards the relationship was Wolpe and Lazarus's (1966) belief in a positive relationship providing "non-specific reciprocal inhibition." By this, the authors indicated that a strong relationship helps to reduce clients' anxiety in general when in the presence of the therapist, and this decreased arousal could be helpful when applied to the clients' specific presenting problems. Thus, this perspective essentially takes the therapeutic relationship as useful insofar as it provides a productive context for working on the identified psychopathological issue for therapy.

However, it may be that this perspective, which has certainly been a main trend in the CBT literature, undervalues the mutative power of a strong therapeutic relationship. This may have less to do with the clinical importance of the relationship as CBT is implemented than its historical roots in experimental psychology and learning theory. Consistent with their empirical approach to therapy, CBT scholars and researchers have frequently separated therapeutic components into two distinct categories: specific and nonspecific variables. Specific variables are those that are identified by a particular theory as the primary cause of change. They can be defined operationally and are assumed to be unique to a specific approach. In contrast, nonspecific factors are assumed to be present in all orientations and perceived as being difficult to measure. For many CBT scholars, nonspecific variables have been viewed, scientifically, as variables to be controlled (in order to establish the causal effect of specific factors) and, clinically, as factors that are auxiliary to the primary means of change (see Castonguay, 1993, for a more extensive discussion on specific and nonspecific factors). And for most of its history, CBT has viewed the techniques based on learning principles (e.g., systemic desensitization) as specific variables par excellence and the therapeutic relationship as an archetypal nonspecific variable.

However, the construct of the alliance has been clearly defined, and several instruments have been able to measure it reliably and validly. In addition, even though there are notable exceptions (e.g., DeRubeis & Feeley, 1990; Feeley, DeRubeis, & Gelfand, 1999), the empirical evidence as a whole suggests that the working alliance is a correlate of outcome in CBT (see Waddington, 2002). The fact that it has been operationalized and found to be predictive of clients' change (although there is still controversy about its causal impact) indicates that therapists, including CBT therapists, should not consider the alliance and other relationship variables (see Castonguay & Beutler, 2006; Norcross, 2011) as nonspecific (unspecified) factors that are merely auxiliary to the prescribed techniques. Consistent with the view that the therapeutic relationship is a potential mechanism of change, clinicians and researchers have integrated interventions designed to enhance this element within a CBT treatment in their practice. The next section focuses exactly on this subject.

How Do Cognitive–Behavioral Therapy Therapists Use the Relationship?

Rather than seeing the therapeutic relationship as being mostly an auxiliary to techniques, a number of influential figures of CBT have adopted ways to purposefully and actively use it as a medium of change. Several of the adopted interventions are similar to strategies that have been used for many years by therapists identified in other orientations, and many of the therapists that have professed the clinical merits of such interventions have either pointed out such similarities or explicitly recognized having borrowed these interventions from psychodynamic–interpersonal and humanistic approaches. From a Piagetian perspective, this can be viewed as an assimilation of constructs and techniques in order to better adapt to the complexity and difficulty of clinical reality.

Several contemporary researchers and theoreticians have proposed different uses of the therapy relationship in CBT, sometimes in ways that may seem very surprising to those unfamiliar with this literature. For instance, Young (1999) suggested that therapists treating clients with personality disorders use the therapy relationship to more effectively activate schemata, and the author explicitly highlighted how similar this is to the use of transference in analytic tradition. Kohlenberg and colleagues also developed a CBT-oriented treatment that relies on the use of the therapeutic relationship and in vivo interpersonal interventions, which often directly address the relationship (Kohlenberg & Tsai, 1991). Hayes and colleagues, who have developed their own approach to CBT (acceptance and commitment therapy; Hayes, Strosahl, & Wilson, 1999) have similarly written that the therapeutic relationship may not be the end purpose of therapy, but that it may be curative if it provides an example of a loving, accepting relationship.

However, it is important to note that CBT writing on how to work with the therapeutic relationship to directly bring change is not new, in and of itself. Arnkoff (1981), for one, made the point that the relationship in cognitive therapy can be as fruitful a source of information and therapeutic focus as in a transference-focused psychodynamic treatment. Goldfried (1985), in an almost radical stance, suggested that not only are relationship-focused interventions (therefore including, most famously, transference interpretations) fully appropriate within CBT, but should be considered in vivo interventions that may possess more power than imaginal interventions. Goldfried argued that the clients' behaviors during session provide unique, here-and-now opportunities to observe and modify how they interact with others. Thus, he essentially suggested that client improvement can be directly fostered by working with the relationship itself.

There have also been other scholars who have studied the way that CBT-oriented therapists can better address or, indeed, utilize any naturally occurring difficulties in the therapy relationship (e.g., Burns, 1989; Leahy, 2001; C. F. Newman, 1994, 1997; Persons, 1989; Safran, Crocker, McMain, & Murray, 1990; Safran & Muran, 1996; Young, 1999). Burns (1989), for example, described what he called "listening skills," which can help cognitive therapists address problems such as clients' resistance to treatment or a disagreement regarding treatment. This set of skills, briefly, includes inviting clients to express their subjective state, responding empathetically to the client's response, and, finally, using the "disarming" technique, which means to explicitly validate the criticism or negative emotion, and find something true about it to agree with. Burns argued that by employing these tools, CBT therapists might find success in deescalating conflicts in the relationship. These skills are consistent with the techniques of "acceptance" that have been emphasized by Marsha Linehan (1993) in her dialectical behavior therapy for borderline personality disorder. These techniques (including the validation of the client's negative experience of the therapist) are used in part to address alliance difficulties—the resolution of which can provide clients' skills for dealing with interpersonal difficulties in real life.

In a program of research regarding alliance ruptures and repairs, Safran and colleagues have described productive ways to treat alliance ruptures in several types of psychotherapy, including cognitive therapy (e.g., Eubanks-Carter, Muran, & Safran, 2010; Muran et al., 2009; Safran et al., 1990; Safran & Muran, 2000; Safran & Segal, 1990). Based on a series of empirical studies, these authors have suggested that therapists, when confronted with any alliance rupture, would do well to recognize it explicitly and to collaboratively explore their client's as well as their own experience of this relationship breach. In using these metacommunication skills, they emphasize the importance of the therapist's adopting an open stance, which includes recognizing their own contribution to the alliance rupture. Safran and colleagues have also suggested that the exploration of alliance ruptures can lead to the client's awareness of needs that are related to the conflict in the therapy relationship and potentially to extratherapy interpersonal problems.

These and other interventions have received some empirical support as useful skills for cognitive and behavioral therapists. For instance, research from Safran, Muran, and colleagues suggests that directly exploring rupture experiences within sessions can help resolve the alliance rupture and may contribute to psychotherapy outcome (Muran et al., 1995; Safran et al., 1990; Safran & Muran, 1996). Relying on the contributions of Burns as well as Safran and Muran, Castonguay et al. (2004) developed a treatment protocol called integrative cognitive therapy (ICT) that assimilates techniques to repair alliance ruptures into cognitive therapy for depression. ICT has demonstrated promise both as compared to a wait-list control group in an initial study (Castonguay et al., 2004) and compared with a standard cognitive therapy for depression (Constantino et al., 2008). In sum, there is evidence, albeit preliminary, supporting the assertion that cognitive- and behavioral-oriented therapists can treat problems in the relationship not only as obstacles to therapeutic gains but also as possible opportunities to promote therapeutic growth.

How Could Cognitive–Behavioral Therapy Therapists Make Further Use of the Relationship?

In the remaining part of this chapter, we provide additional suggestions based on research findings and/or non-CBT concepts and interventions (e.g., psychodynamic, interpersonal, humanistic) that may help us understand more fully how the therapeutic relationship might be mutative in CBT, and thus possibly improve its effectiveness (e.g., helping therapists to anticipate and cope with alliance ruptures). These potentially therapeutic functions are first briefly stated and some of them are then described as part of a case presentation. As with some of the contributions described in the previous section, these conceptual and clinical suggestions illustrate the potential benefits that CBT could gain by assimilating contributions of scholars working within other fields or theoretical orientations.

As diverse sources of research have demonstrated (Cacioppo & Cacioppo, 2012; Holt-Lunstad, Smith, & Layton, 2010; Luo, Hawkley, Waite, & Cacioppo, 2012), loneliness may be one of the worst curses for the physical and emotional health of human beings (Wampold & Imel, 2015). As most clinicians know, many of our clients feel isolated socially, and several of them refuse to or are unable to reach out to others. Whether or not this is in part due to the shame and/or demoralization they experience vis-à-vis their symptoms, such social withdrawal is likely to increase their sense of distress and impairment. Regular contact with a person who is able and willing to discuss difficult aspects of life can go a long way in combatting a sense of demoralization and loneliness. The link between alliance and outcome could in part be due to the possibility that feeling a mutual respect and experiencing an active sense of collaboration are direct evidence that "I am not alone."

The therapeutic relationship might also facilitate a diversity of corrective experiences. For example, research has shown that a subset of individuals with depression are victims of inappropriate parenting (neglect and abuse) in childhood, and thus, a close relationship with a warm, accepting, engaged, and validating therapist might lead some clients (and not only depressed ones) to develop new and more positive thoughts about self and significant others (LeMoult, Castonguay, Joorman, & McAleavey, 2013). Providing evidence to support such a corrective quality of the relationship, a recent study found that the association between alliance and outcome in a primarily CBT treatment for adolescents with substance abuse problems was moderated by the client's attachment history. Specifically, the relationship between the alliance and outcome was significantly higher for clients with poorer attachment than for clients with better attachment histories (Zack et al., 2015). In other words, those who most failed to experience a positive relationship with their parents benefited more from a positive relationship with their therapists. Similarly, another study found that the addition of techniques aimed in part at exploring past and current relationships to CBT (including the use of metacommunication interventions designed to repair alliance ruptures in therapy) led to incremental therapy gains for clients with dismissing attachment styles (M. G. Newman, Castonguay, Jacobson, & Moore, 2015).

We posit that the corrective nature of the therapeutic relationship can take place without the therapist directly "working" on the relationship—by simply allowing clients to experience a relationship that is different from what they experienced before with a significant figure. This is, in fact, one type of corrective experience that Anderson, Ogles, Heckman, and MacFarlane (2013) identified across different forms of therapy. Categorized as the "positive impact of therapist warmth," these events were defined as the clients reporting that the positive relationship in general with their therapist "provided a unique contrast to their prior experiences in which those positive qualities were absent or neglected" (Anderson et al., 2013, p. 294). We also believe that the alliance can be corrective when the relationship is the focus of the therapy, such as when distorted thoughts about or maladaptive ways of behaving toward the therapist are emphasized (Arnkoff, 1981; Goldfried, 1985). As noted by Safran and Segal (1990), the repair of alliance rupture via metacommunication can help clients disconfirm interpersonal schema. Exploring the client's constant control of the session as an attempt to avoid being criticized, for example, can increase the client's awareness of his or her own negative impact on the therapist, especially if this is done in a disarming and noncritical way. Processing how such maladaptive ways of responding are characteristic of clients' interpersonal relationships with significant others can be clinically helpful (see Castonguay et al., 2013). Interestingly, these different mutative natures of the relationship correspond to two general but distinct types of corrective experiences (CEs) identified by Hill et al. (2013). The first type is "new or unexpected thoughts, emotions, sensations, behaviors, or feelings about one's self that result from the client encountering an event that is different from (and thus disconfirming of) his or her frame of reference" (p. 356). By contrast, in the second type of CE, "the client actively does something different in situations that typically have triggered apprehension and negative emotion, leading to a new outcome" (p. 356).

The therapeutic relationship might also provide opportunities for clients to change specific maladaptive patterns of relating to others that are associated with the etiology or maintenance of particular clinical problems. As described by LeMoult et al. (2013), for example, basic research indicates that depressed individuals are frequently angry with others, excessively seek reassurance, and prefer to interact with others who confirm their negative view of self. Needless to say, such patterns are likely to decrease an individual's ability to find and maintain warm, supportive, and validating relationships. By providing client feedback about these ways of relating, by interacting with the client in ways that do not reinforce these styles of interaction, and by genuinely acting with autonomy-granting and validation, the therapist might create an interpersonal world where the client can learn to behave differently without being rejected or dismissed.

More inferentially, we would also posit that a good relationship can at times become a source of internalization for the client. This psychodynamic concept, in our view, goes beyond modeling. It is more than learning vicariously by observing the therapist or someone else. It refers to clients' ability to bring thoughts about the therapist into their awareness, from which they could remind themselves or imagine what the therapist would say and think about how to deal with stressful situations. The therapist, then, becomes a "part" of the client—a new, more soothing, reinforcing, validating, source of evaluation, guidance, and motivation (see examples in Castonguay et al., 2013). The internalization of the therapist is also consistent with the central goal in client-centered therapy, which is to have clients internalize the therapist's genuine praise and acceptance and learn to treat themselves the way the therapist treats them (Rogers, 1951). In this form of therapy, the therapist's stance toward the client and the client's internal discourse are described as optimal ways to foster a new, more positive, relationship with the self. Assuming that the internalization of the therapist is more than a mere epiphenomenon of behavioral changes, this mutative function of the therapeutic relationship is very much in line with the acquisition of positive thoughts and the increase of self-efficacy expectations that are aimed at in CBT. What it may do, above and beyond these traditional CBT concepts, however, is to provide an explanation for why the alliance is predictive of change, even when the therapist does not explicitly focus or work on the therapeutic relationship. It may well be, however, that focusing on the relationship is particularly therapeutic (and may further foster the internalization of a more praising sense of self) when clinicians work with clients who consistently engage in maladaptive patterns (e.g., dismissing) of interpersonal relationships (Castonguay et al., 2013; M.G. Newman et al., 2015).

Most of these suggestions reflect, directly or indirectly, the importance of attachment. This psychodynamically based construct has not only generated substantial research in applied and basic psychology (Cassidy & Shafer, 2008), it has also received support from evolutionary science. MacLean (1985) argued that attachment is one of the three characteristics that distinguish mammals from reptiles—the other two being communication and play. Considering the evolutionary importance of attachment and interpersonal support, we could make the argument that the therapeutic relationship is likely to be mutative in CBT because it addresses one of the fundamental needs of human beings. We find it interesting, however, that positing a role of needs in human functioning requires some CBT therapists to pay closer attention to an element of human functioning—one of which many of them appeared to have been particularly avoidant. While CBT has challenged Skinner by recognizing the instrumental role of cognitions and emotions, in our opinion, it has yet to fully integrate motivations as determinants of behaviors. Again in our opinion, this could be viewed as yet another manifestation of the phobia of Freudian concepts (Levis, 1988) to which we alluded before. However, we believe that some behaviors (of self and others) are more reinforcing (positively and negatively) than others. We would posit that the reason for this is that some events or contingencies are fulfilling crucial needs (biological, psychological, social). Metaphorically, needs can be viewed as "receptors" of reinforcements. As much as cell receptors are required for synapses to fire and for information to be transmitted through the nervous system, needs may be necessary in order for contingencies to be reinforcing. Simply put, monographic and idiographic needs might be helpful for CBT clinicians to figure out what motivates clients and what are ways of behaving (and thinking) that they can adopt to meet these needs while having a less distressing and more fulfilling life. As part of a greater recognition of basic human needs, for example, CBT therapists may want to attend to how maladaptive behaviors and thoughts might relate to clients' attempt to maintain interpersonal attachments and connections, and how these basic needs can be met by developing healthier relationship patterns with significant others, including the therapist (Benjamin, 1993, 2003).

Interestingly, more than 20 years ago, CBT-oriented scholars integrated the concept of attachment within their proposed view of pathology and therapeutic change (Guidano & Liotti, 1983; Safran & Segal, 1990). While the concept has retained the attention of more contemporary CBT scholars (e.g., Chorpita & Barlow, 1998), one could argue that the wealth of basic and applied research on attachment should guide a reformulation of human functioning and change in CBT. Because CBT is at its core an epistemological approach aimed at applying empirically supported interventions and constructs, it should integrate the strong scientific contribution offered by the attachment literature. For the sake of this chapter, we simply provide an illustration of how some of these attachment-related suggestions can play a role in CBT, with the hope that this might generate more extensive conceptual work from other scholars.

CASE EXAMPLE

Presenting Problem and Patient Description

Robert was a 25-year-old, single, White, heterosexual man, from an upper middle-class household, who presented to a community mental health center for therapy to address his skin-picking disorder.[1] He reported a significant history of skin-picking that started when he was in elementary school; since then, he has continuously experienced distress and interference in his daily functioning. He also shared having difficulties in establishing and maintaining relationships in his life due to shame and fear of rejection from others if they were to discover his skin lesions. Thus, the client denied ever having been in a romantic relationship, but he had a desire for one. In terms of past treatment, Robert had experience with previous psychotherapy and psychiatric treatment for his symptoms, but he stated that these had, at best, been only temporarily helpful, and that he had not been able to sustain any of the short-term gains made during the course of the treatments. His treatment goals included working on his skin-picking symptoms and becoming a "better person" in general. After a comprehensive diagnostic initial evaluation as part of routine clinical care, the client was diagnosed with excoriation (skin-picking) disorder (*Diagnostic and Statistical Manual of Mental Disorders*, 5th ed.; American Psychiatric Association, 2013; F42.4 ICD–10, *International Statistical Classification of Diseases and Related Health Problems*; World Health Organization, 1993).

Initial Interview and Case Formulation

The therapist was an Asian, third-year PhD candidate in clinical psychology in her late 20s, with training in both cognitive–behavioral and

[1]Details of this case example have been altered to protect confidentiality.

psychodynamic theories and clinical practice. Treatment initially consisted of a manualized, evidence-based treatment for skin-picking disorder, which started with a functional analysis of the behavior. Robert struggled with this process as he resisted talking about his symptoms with others, including the therapist, but also because he himself did not like monitoring his symptoms, the extent and pervasiveness of the skin-picking, or the damage to his skin that resulted from these behaviors, since it led to increased distress. Despite the initial difficulties, the therapist was able to conceptualize the resistance as avoidance and encouraged the client to engage in this monitoring process, which allowed them to develop a comprehensive assessment and understanding of the picking behavior, including its frequency, severity, extent, and function. For example, it was determined that Robert picked his face mostly, but also his arms and chest area, leading him to spend a significant amount of time choosing clothes and getting ready in the morning in order to hide the skin lesions that resulted from years of repeated skin-picking. Robert's skin-picking only took place when and where he was alone, such as in his bedroom and bathroom; it was both an automatic and conscious behavior; and the skin-picking served an emotion regulation function, mostly used to alleviate distress and anxiety, especially when it was done consciously. For example, Robert described frequent and significantly distressing worries and fears related to his academic performance despite achieving good grades and all academic milestones. Through functional analysis, the therapist and Robert concluded that his skin-picking served a maladaptive emotion regulation function during these times, as he engaged in this behavior as a way to bring about relief from his anxiety symptoms as well as avoid his emotions.

Course of Treatment

The first 6 months of treatment focused on decreasing the frequency and the severity of the skin-picking behavior by introducing competing behaviors. Additionally, treatment helped the client develop alternative emotion regulation skills including relaxation training and cognitive restructuring. Treatment was successful: Robert gradually decreased the frequency and severity of his skin-picking, and towards the end of the 6 months, he had not skin-picked for 2 months and was successfully implementing alternative coping skills and competing behaviors to manage the incidents of picking as well as his distress and anxiety symptoms. After discussion, both therapist and client decided to gradually terminate treatment by meeting once every 2 weeks for an additional month before scheduling the last session in order to ease the transition.

However, a few weeks into this new schedule, Robert's skin-picking incidents started to increase, as well as his suicidal ideation and self-harm behaviors (e.g., burning). The therapist and client jointly decided to resume weekly sessions, and the subsequent months continued with sporadic episodes of improvement followed by deterioration. The therapist and Robert attempted to understand this significant change further by conducting functional analyses of the increased self-harm behaviors and the decreased use of the alternative coping skills that Robert had successfully implemented in his life, and by discussing whether termination may be contributing to the changes seen. The client dismissed the therapist's suggestions and reiterated that he was not concerned by treatment ending, and that he would be able to manage his symptoms by himself.

Treatment continued in this manner for a few months, until an incident led to a significant alliance rupture. As part of homework, Robert was asked to bring in log sheets tracking his skin-picking behavior. The therapist pointed out the discrepancy between the client's high reported frequency of skin-picking on the log sheet and the low frequency shared in session, which the client brushed off as a confusion. However, he then failed to show up for the next two sessions and did not return any of the therapist's phone calls, which was very unusual for him. The therapist continued to leave messages, despite the silence, and eventually was able to get ahold of Robert and schedule a session. The client proceeded to tell the therapist that he felt judged during the last session, and how this had been especially worse for Robert because of the fact that these feelings of judgment had occurred in the context of the therapeutic relationship.

This marked an important moment in the dyad's relationship, as it was the first alliance rupture openly discussed in session by the client. The therapist could have used the client's behavior (i.e., missing sessions), and utterance (i.e., sharing that he felt judged) as additional examples of the client's cognitive biases, but instead, the therapist incorporated techniques from other orientations to augment the CBT treatment at this moment.

Consistent with the conceptualized insecure–avoidant attachment style and Robert's negative self-view that he is not good enough for anyone to care for him or listen to him and his needs, the therapist hypothesized that applying cognitive restructuring skills in the moment could have been felt as invalidating by Robert and even as blaming him. Therefore, instead, the therapist thanked Robert for having shared a difficult experience with her and acknowledged her own contributions that may have led to the rupture in the relationship between the two, such as not allowing enough time in session to discuss the discrepancy noted. She also shared that based on the conversations that they had had regarding feeling judged by his parents, the therapist could have been more explicit in sharing that the few seconds of silence post noting the discrepancy were used to think whether there was, in fact, enough time to discuss the topic during the session or to leave it for the next session, as she understood how this period of silence could have been perceived as judgmental by Robert.

The therapist hypothesized that by accepting Robert's feelings towards the therapist and her behavior, it could potentially allow the client to share his own further. The therapist and client continued to use the session time to further encourage Robert to share his negative reactions towards the therapist, which the therapist validated and accepted, consistent with the disarming technique (Burns, 1989) of finding the subjective truth in the client's criticisms, regardless of whether the criticisms are fair or warranted as a way to address the alliance rupture. Halfway through the appointment, Robert told the therapist that he was surprised by her reaction, and that he was confused about what to do or say next as this interaction between the two of them had been very different from his previous experiences. The therapist and client discussed the similarities and differences in Robert's experience when compared with other relationships in his life, and used this information to increase his awareness of the schema that was activated across these situations. For example, Robert and the therapist talked about how the feeling of being judged by others was a common thread perceived by the client across relationships, such as with his parents, family members, coworkers, and acquaintances. The client was able to verbalize that the fact that this also occurred within the context of the therapeutic relationship was especially hurtful to him, as he had felt that he had opened up to the therapist about his most vulnerable issues, such as his skin-picking. Robert and the therapist also discussed that the therapist accepting his experience and her role in contributing to his reactions were new to him, as his past interactions with others had repeatedly left him believing that he was always at fault, and that he needed to "get over it," as others were always right.

This alliance rupture continued to be referenced throughout the treatment as a way to highlight and change the client's views of what relationships are, and how he expects himself and others to react in them. The therapist and Robert talked about how his core schema—that he is not good enough or is at fault—may be impacting his automatic thoughts when relating to others and to the behaviors that he engages in as a way to deal with these, such as avoiding contact or accepting full blame and picking his skin as a way to cope with the negative emotions.

A second alliance rupture occurred when the therapist introduced the idea of termination 6 months after the first rupture. Robert initially responded by agreeing, stating that he thought he had learned everything he could, and that he wanted to try employing the skills learned on his own. However, he failed to show up for the next three sessions and even left a message in response to the therapist's attempt at contacting him, saying that he would not be returning to treatment. These behaviors were viewed as consistent with Robert's avoidant attachment style, with a tendency to be overly autonomous and deal with perceived rejection by maintaining a distance from others (M.G. Newman et al., 2015). The therapist sent Robert a letter, sharing that she wanted to validate him expressing his thoughts and reinforce his sense of agency in making this decision for himself, but that she was also hoping for a final session if possible. Robert called the clinic and agreed to one more session. During this time, he said that he had felt abandoned by the therapist when she had brought up termination during their last appointment together, and that he felt that the therapist didn't understand that ending treatment also meant that he would be alone in dealing with his difficulties. The therapist and client discussed the role that the therapeutic relationship played, not only in terms of helping the client learn new skills that he could use to manage his symptoms but also in having another person (i.e., the therapist) understand and mitigate the loneliness the client had felt in relation to others due to his symptoms.

The therapist and Robert met for six more sessions after this second alliance rupture. During these, they processed the changes and gains that Robert made during their work together. The client shared having noticed increased monitoring and understanding on his picking behaviors, as well as being able to reduce the incidents of picking as a major goal achievement. However, he also added that the alliance ruptures had been helpful as well, especially since they had provided him with an opportunity to experience a new way of relating to others, such as by discussing his emotions with people when in conflict rather than avoiding or detaching himself from others and in light of potential relational difficulties. He said that, especially since the first incident, he had reminded himself of the interaction with the therapist every time a difficult interpersonal situation arose as an example of evidence that contradicted his core schema about his self-worth as well as his role in interpersonal relationships.

SUMMARY AND MECHANISMS OF CHANGE

In this chapter, we have considered the questions (a) "Is the relationship in CBT cold?" (b) "Does CBT assume that the working alliance is an unimportant factor in treatment outcome?" and (c) "How do CBT therapists use, and can further use, the relationship?" In examination, it seems clear that the relationship in CBT has never been defined by even the slightest coolness, and that while CBT has often emphasized learning and behavior change as the central mechanisms of change, there is evidence to support the hypothesis that the relationship itself may have positive effects within a CBT treatment. Moreover, within the last several years many CBT scholars have begun to conceive the relationship in a new, more encouraging light, and some researchers have been investigating the impact of non-CBT interventions to work directly with the relationship.

For example, studies mentioned above have shown promise that specific interventions of metacommunication about alliance ruptures (e.g., inviting clients to discuss these events, collaboratively exploring their meaning) may be one avenue to improve the impact of cognitive therapy (Castonguay et al., 2004; Constantino et al., 2008). From these and other studies (see Safran, Muran, & Eubanks-Carter, 2011), one might argue that the successful resolution of alliance breaches is a potentially worthwhile strategy to reduce obstacles (e.g., disagreement about some tasks or goals of therapy) preventing the client's full engagement in and benefit from therapy. If such strategies can reduce confusion and frustration about the treatment process, they might indeed help the client to perform the prescribed exercises that are aimed at decreasing negative thoughts and increasing behavioral activation. However, it has also been argued that open and genuine exploration of internal experiences related to in-session difficulties, as well as recognition of therapist and client contributions to therapeutic impasses, might lead to new insights about the client's wishes and ways of relating to others, as well as new skills to foster conflict resolution and the fulfillment of interpersonal needs (Eubanks-Carter et al., 2010).

Using the relationship as a direct therapeutic tool, as we also mentioned before, might be particularly important for clients with pronounced interpersonal and developmental problems. This is suggested by the findings of a research program aimed at improving the impact of CBT for generalized anxiety disorder by the addition of techniques focusing on emotional experiences and interpersonal issues into an integrative treatment. Among the interventions used in this integrative treatment were the exploration of past and current relationships, and the use of metacommunication skills. These metacommunication skills were implemented to repair alliance ruptures, as well as to challenge clients' interpersonal schemas and maladaptive interpersonal functioning. Although a preliminary study showed promising results (M. G. Newman et al., 2008), a subsequent randomized clinical trial failed to find the integrative treatment to be superior to traditional cognitive therapy (M. G. Newman et al., 2011). A third study, however, identified a moderator of these outcome findings: Clients with high levels of dismissive attachment styles (individuals who tend to avoid intimacy and distrust others) benefited significantly more from the integrative treatment than from traditional CBT (M. G. Newman et al., 2015).

Based on these and other findings (e.g., Zack et al., 2015), as well as the conceptual and clinical observations made above, we believe that a full consideration (way beyond the scope of this chapter) of basic and applied research on attachment and related interpersonal concepts, might be a fruitful way to better understand the robust link between alliance and outcome in CBT. The recognition of the attachment as a fundamental need of human beings could provide a theoretical framework to explain why some clients may benefit from a good alliance even when the therapist does not focus on the relationship, why the emergence and repair of alliance ruptures can lead to therapeutic change, and why some clients may need to work more on the relationship than others and/or for whom a good relationship will be more mutative than others. As such, we suggest that an assimilation of concepts and interventions attached to other theoretical orientations can offer ways to improve the impact of CBT.

PRACTICE IMPLICATIONS AND RECOMMENDATIONS FOR CLINICIANS AND SUPERVISORS

A number of clinical and training recommendations can be derived from the findings and observations presented above. First, there is no reason to assume that CBT should be conducted in a cold, mechanical, and inflexible way. There is absolutely no empirical evidence suggesting that therapists should be hostile and rude to their clients (Castonguay, Constantino, & Holtforth, 2006), and there is no indication that the implementation of techniques based on learning principles and cognitive constructs are irreconcilable with empathy, positive regard, and authenticity. Accordingly, we suggest that therapists in training who are exposed to CBT principles and manuals would benefit clinically by being trained in basic helping skills (Hill, 2014), as well as in the Rogerian attitudes that embodied an accepting and validating perspective toward the client. Such skills and attitudes, irrespective of the clinician's level of experience, are likely to facilitate client engagement in treatment tasks, as has been emphasized by some of the earliest and most influential contributors of the CBT movement. We would also suggest that therapist warmth and support might at times counterbalance the sense of isolation and/or negative experiences that many of our clients have had in their lives. This may not only have a positive impact on some symptoms, such as depression, it may also improve the client's general quality of life.

We would also suggest that therapists should learn and constantly improve their ability to monitor and address alliance ruptures. Breaches in the quality of the relationship are to be expected in any form of therapy, and evidence suggests that some ways of dealing with them, such as the rigid and increased adherence to prescribed techniques, may not be optimal to resolve them (Castonguay, Goldfried, Wiser, Raue, & Hayes, 1996; Piper et al., 1999: Schut et al., 2005). In contrast, pointing out the relationship difficulties when they emerge, empathizing with the emotions that are associated with the ruptures and their discussions, recognizing one's own contribution to the therapeutic impasses, and facilitating the client's exploration of the meaning of these events may be more effective. Therapists should also be aware that these metacommunication techniques may not only be helpful to repair alliance ruptures, they can also lead to clients' recognition of their own negative impact on others, greater awareness of their interpersonal wishes and fears, and the acquisition of more appropriate thoughts and behaviors in relation to others.

REFERENCES

American Psychiatric Association. (2013). *Diagnostic and statistical manual of mental disorders* (*DSM–5*). Washington, DC: American Psychiatric Association.

Anderson, T., Ogles, B. M., Heckman, B. D., & MacFarlane, P. (2013). Varieties of corrective experiencing in context: A study of contrasts. In L. G. Castonguay & C. E. Hill (Eds.), *Transformation in psychotherapy: Corrective experiences across cognitive behavioral, humanistic, and psychodynamic approaches* (pp. 281–316). Washington, DC: American Psychological Association.

Arnkoff, D. B. (1981). Flexibility in practicing cognitive therapy. In G. Emery, S. D. Hollon, & R. C. Bedrosian (Eds.), *New directions in cognitive therapy* (pp. 203–223). New York, NY: Guilford Press.

Beck, A. T., Rush, J. J., Shaw, B. F., & Emery, G. (1979). *Cognitive therapy of depression.* New York, NY: Guilford Press.

Benjamin, L. S. (1993). Every psychopathology is a gift of love. *Psychotherapy Research, 3*, 1–24. http://dx.doi.org/10.1080/10503309312331333629

Benjamin, L. S. (2003). *Interpersonal reconstructive therapy: Promoting change in nonresponders.* New York, NY: Guilford Press.

Burns, D. D. (1989). *The feeling good handbook: Using the new mood therapy in everyday life.* New York, NY: William Morrow.

Cacioppo, S., & Cacioppo, J. T. (2012). Decoding the invisible forces of social connections. *Frontiers in Integrative Neuroscience, 6*, 51. http://dx.doi.org/10.3389/fnint.2012.00051

Cassidy, J., & Shafer, P. R. (Eds.). (2008). *Handbook of attachment: Theory, research, and application* (2nd ed.). New York, NY: Guilford Press.

Castonguay, L. G. (1993). "Common factors" and "nonspecific variables": Clarification of the two concepts and recommendations for research. *Journal of Psychotherapy Integration, 3*, 267–286. http://dx.doi.org/10.1037/h0101171

Castonguay, L. G., & Beutler, L. E. (Eds.). (2006). *Principles of therapeutic change that work.* New York, NY: Oxford University Press.

Castonguay, L. G., Constantino, M. J., & Holtforth, M. G. (2006). The working alliance: Where are we and where should we go? *Psychotherapy, 43*, 271–279. http://dx.doi.org/10.1037/0033-3204.43.3.271

Castonguay, L. G., Goldfried, M. R., Wiser, S., Raue, P. J., & Hayes, A. M. (1996). Predicting the effect of cognitive therapy for depression: A study of unique and common factors. *Journal of Consulting and Clinical Psychology, 64*, 497–504. http://dx.doi.org/10.1037/0022-006X.64.3.497

Castonguay, L. G., Nelson, D. L., Boswell, J. F., Nordberg, S. S., McAleavey, A. A., Newman, M. G., & Borkovec, T. D. (2013). Corrective experiences in cognitive behavioral and interpersonal–emotional processing therapies: A qualitative analysis of a single case. In L. G. Castonguay & C. E. Hill (Eds.), *Transformation in psychotherapy: Corrective experiences across cognitive behavioral, humanistic, and psychodynamic approaches* (pp. 245–279). Washington, DC: American Psychological Association.

Castonguay, L. G., Schut, A. J., Aikins, D., Constantino, M. J., Laurenceau, J. P., Bologh, L., & Burns, D. D. (2004). Integrative cognitive therapy for depression: A preliminary investigation. *Journal of Psychotherapy Integration, 14*, 4–20. http://dx.doi.org/10.1037/1053-0479.14.1.4

Chorpita, B. F., & Barlow, D. H. (1998). The development of anxiety: The role of control in the early environment. *Psychological Bulletin, 124*, 3–21. http://dx.doi.org/10.1037/0033-2909.124.1.3

Constantino, M. J., Marnell, M. E., Haile, A. J., Kanther-Sista, S. N., Wolman, K., Zappert, L., & Arnow, B. A. (2008). Integrative cognitive therapy for depression: A randomized pilot comparison. *Psychotherapy, 45*, 122–134. http://dx.doi.org/10.1037/0033-3204.45.2.122

DeRubeis, R. J., & Feeley, M. (1990). Determinants of change in cognitive therapy for depression. *Cognitive Therapy and Research, 14*, 469–482. http://dx.doi.org/10.1007/BF01172968

Eubanks-Carter, C., Muran, J. C., & Safran, J. D. (2010). Alliance ruptures and resolution. In J. C. Muran & J. P. Barber (Eds.), *The therapeutic alliance: An evidence based guide to practice* (pp. 74–94). New York, NY: Guilford Press.

Feeley, M., DeRubeis, R. J., & Gelfand, L. A. (1999). The temporal relation of adherence and alliance to symptom change in cognitive therapy for depression. *Journal of Consulting and Clinical Psychology, 67*, 578–582. http://dx.doi.org/10.1037/0022-006X.67.4.578

Goldfried, M. R. (1985). In vivo intervention or transference? In W. Dryden (Ed.), *Therapist's dilemmas* (pp. 63–75). London, England: Harper & Row.

Guidano, V. F., & Liotti, G. (1983). *Cognitive processes and emotional disorders*. New York, NY: Guilford Press.

Hayes, S. C., Strosahl, K. D., & Wilson, K. G. (1999). *Acceptance and commitment therapy: An experiential approach to behavior change*. New York, NY: Guilford Press.

Hembree, E. A., Rauch, S. A. M., & Foa, E. B. (2003). Beyond the manual: The insider's guide to prolonged exposure therapy for PTSD. *Cognitive and Behavioral Practice, 10*, 22–30. http://dx.doi.org/10.1016/S1077-7229(03)80005-6

Hill, C. E. (2014). *Helping skills: Facilitating exploration, insight, and action* (4th ed.). Washington, DC: American Psychological Association. http://dx.doi.org/10.1037/14345-000

Hill, C. E., Castonguay, L. G., Farber, B. A., Knox, S., Stiles, W. B., Anderson, T., . . . Sharpless, B. A. (2013). Corrective experiences in psychotherapy: Definition, processes, consequences, and research directions. In L. G. Castonguay & C. E., Hill (Eds.), *Transformation in psychotherapy: Corrective experiences across cognitive behavioral, humanistic, and psychodynamic approaches* (pp. 355–370). Washington, DC: American Psychological Association.

Holt-Lunstad, J., Smith, T. B., & Layton, J. B. (2010). Social relationships and mortality risk: A meta-analytic review. *PLoS Medicine, 7*, e1000316. http://dx.doi.org/10.1371/journal.pmed.1000316

Horvath, A. O., Del Re, A. C., Flückiger, C., & Symonds, D. (2011). Alliance in individual psychotherapy. In J. C. Norcross (Ed.), *Psychotherapy relationships that work* (2nd ed., pp. 25–69). New York, NY: Oxford University Press.

Kohlenberg, R. J., & Tsai, M. (1991). *Functional analytic psychotherapy: Creating intense and curative therapeutic relationships*. New York, NY: Springer. http://dx.doi.org/10.1007/978-0-387-70855-3

Leahy, R. L. (2001). *Overcoming resistance in cognitive therapy*. New York, NY: Guilford Press.

LeMoult, J., Castonguay, L. G., Joorman, J., & McAleavey, A. A. (2013). Depression. In L. G. Castonguay & T. G. Oltmanns (Eds.), *Psychopathology: From science to clinical practice* (pp. 17–61). New York, NY: Guilford Press.

Levis, D. J. (1988). Observations and experience from clinical practice: A critical ingredient for advancing behavior theory and practice. *The Behavior Therapist, 11*, 95–99.

Linehan, M. M. (1993). *Cognitive-behavioral treatment of borderline personality disorder*. New York, NY: Guilford Press.

Luo, Y., Hawkley, L. C., Waite, L. J., & Cacioppo, J. T. (2012). Loneliness, health, and mortality in old age: A national longitudinal study. *Social Science & Medicine, 74*, 907–914. http://dx.doi.org/10.1016/j.socscimed.2011.11.028

MacLean, P. D. (1985). Brain evolution relating to family, play, and the separation call. *Archives of General Psychiatry, 42*, 405–417. http://dx.doi.org/10.1001/archpsyc.1985.01790270095011

Muran, J. C., Gorman, B. S., Safran, J. D., Twining, L., Samstag, L. W., & Winston, A. (1995). Linking in-session change to overall outcome in short-term cognitive therapy. *Journal of Consulting and Clinical Psychology, 63*, 651–657. http://dx.doi.org/10.1037/0022-006X.63.4.651

Muran, J. C., Safran, J. D., Gorman, B. S., Samstag, L. W., Eubanks-Carter, C., & Winston, A. (2009). The relationship of early alliance ruptures and their resolution to process and outcome in three time-limited psychotherapies for personality disorders. *Psychotherapy, 46*, 233–248. http://dx.doi.org/10.1037/a0016085

Newman, C. F. (1994). Understanding client resistance: Methods for enhancing motivation to change. *Cognitive and Behavioral Practice, 1*, 47–69. http://dx.doi.org/10.1016/S1077-7229(05)80086-0

Newman, C. F. (1997). Maintaining professionalism in the face of emotional abuse from clients. *Cognitive and Behavioral Practice, 4*, 1–29. http://dx.doi.org/10.1016/S1077-7229(97)80010-7

Newman, M. G., Castonguay, L. G., Borkovec, T. D., Fisher, A. J., Boswell, J. F., Szkodny, L. E., & Nordberg, S. S. (2011). A randomized controlled trial of cognitive–behavioral therapy for generalized anxiety disorder with integrated techniques from emotion-focused and interpersonal therapies. *Journal of Consulting and Clinical Psychology, 79*, 171–181. http://dx.doi.org/10.1037/a0022489

Newman, M. G., Castonguay, L. G., Borkovec, T. D., Fisher, A. J., & Nordberg, S. S. (2008). An open trial of integrative therapy for generalized anxiety disorder. *Psychotherapy, 45*, 135–147. http://dx.doi.org/10.1037/0033-3204.45.2.135

Newman, M. G., Castonguay, L. G., Jacobson, N. C., & Moore, G. A. (2015). Adult attachment as a moderator of treatment outcome for generalized anxiety disorder: Comparison between cognitive–behavioral therapy (CBT) plus supportive listening and CBT plus emotional processing therapy. *Journal of Consulting and Clinical Psychology, 83*, 915–925. http://dx.doi.org/10.1037/a0039359

Norcross, J. C. (Ed.). (2011). *Psychotherapy relationships that work: Evidence-based responsiveness* (2nd ed.). New York, NY: Oxford University Press. http://dx.doi.org/10.1093/acprof:oso/9780199737208.001.0001

Persons, J. B. (1989). *Cognitive therapy in practice: A case formulation approach.* New York, NY: W. W. Norton.

Piper, W. E., Ogrodniczuk, J. S., Joyce, A. S., McCallum, M., Rosie, J. S., O'Kelly, J. G., & Steinberg, P. I. (1999). Prediction of dropping out in time-limited interpretive individual psychotherapy. *Psychotherapy, 36*, 114–122. http://dx.doi.org/10.1037/h0087787

Raue, P. J., & Goldfried, M. R. (1994). The therapeutic alliance in cognitive–behavior therapy. In A. O. Horvath & L. S. Greenberg (Eds.), *The working alliance: Theory, research and practice* (pp. 131–152). New York, NY: Wiley.

Rogers, C. R. (1951). *Client-centered therapy*. Boston, MA: Houghton Mifflin.

Safran, J. D., Crocker, P., McMain, S., & Murray, P. (1990). Therapeutic alliance rupture as a therapy event for empirical investigation. *Psychotherapy, 27*, 154–165. http://dx.doi.org/10.1037/0033-3204.27.2.154

Safran, J. D., & Muran, J. C. (1996). The resolution of ruptures in the therapeutic alliance. *Journal of Consulting and Clinical Psychology, 64*, 447–458. http://dx.doi.org/10.1037/0022-006X.64.3.447

Safran, J. D., & Muran, J. C. (2000). *Negotiating the therapeutic alliance: A relational treatment guide*. New York, NY: Guilford Press.

Safran, J. D., Muran, J. C., & Eubanks-Carter, C. (2011). Repairing alliance ruptures. In J. C. Norcross (Ed.), *Psychotherapy relationships that work: Evidence-based responsiveness* (2nd ed., pp. 224–238). New York, NY: Oxford University Press. http://dx.doi.org/10.1093/acprof:oso/9780199737208.003.0011

Safran, J. D., & Segal, Z. V. (1990). *Interpersonal process in cognitive therapy*. New York, NY: Rowman & Littlefield.

Schut, A. J., Castonguay, L. G., Flanagan, K. M., Yamasaki, A. S., Barber, J. P., Bedics, J. D., & Smith, T. L. (2005). Therapist interpretation, patient–therapist interpersonal process, and outcome in psychodynamic psychotherapy for avoidant personality disorder. *Psychotherapy, 42*, 494–511. http://dx.doi.org/10.1037/0033-3204.42.4.494

Sloane, R. B., Staples, F. R., Cristol, A. H., Yorkston, N. J., & Whipple, K. (1975). *Psychotherapy versus behavior therapy*. Cambridge, MA: Harvard University Press. http://dx.doi.org/10.4159/harvard.9780674365063

Waddington, L. (2002). The therapy relationship in cognitive therapy: A review. *Behavioural and Cognitive Psychotherapy, 30*, 179–191. http://dx.doi.org/10.1017/S1352465802002059

Wampold, B. E., & Imel, Z. E. (2015). *The great psychotherapy debate: The evidence for what makes psychotherapy work* (2nd ed.). New York, NY: Routledge.

Wolpe, J. (1958). *Reciprocal inhibition therapy*. Stanford, CA: Stanford University Press.

Wolpe, J., & Lazarus, A. (1966). *Behavior therapy techniques: A guide to the treatment of neuroses*. New York, NY: Pergamon Press.

World Health Organization. (1993). *ICD–10, international statistical classification of diseases and related health problems*. Geneva, Switzerland: Author.

Young, J. E. (1999). *Cognitive therapy for personality disorders: A schema-focused approach* (3rd ed.). Sarasota, FL: Professional Resource Press.

Zack, S. E., Castonguay, L. G., Boswell, J. F., McAleavey, A. A., Adelman, R., Kraus, D. R., & Pate, G. A. (2015). Attachment history as a moderator of the alliance outcome relationship in adolescents. *Psychotherapy, 52*, 258–267. http://dx.doi.org/10.1037/a0037727

8

NEGOTIATING MULTIPLE ROLES AND STANCES IN COGNITIVE–BEHAVIORAL THERAPY

YONI ELIZUR AND JONATHAN D. HUPPERT

Cognitive–behavioral therapy (CBT) is a therapeutic orientation with many specific types of treatment that fall under its umbrella. Common to most CBT treatments is integrated work on thoughts, emotions, and behaviors of the individual in general, as well as work on the client's response to given contexts or situations. A basic assumption of CBT is the belief that an individual can change and improve her life via adopting patterns of thoughts, beliefs, behaviors, and emotions that are more adaptive. Building the therapeutic relationship is a precondition for helping the therapy reaches its specific, individualized goals, which are naturally related to the "real world" outside of the therapeutic setting. Therapy helps the client learn new skills and tools, internalize the therapeutic messages, and eventually become her own therapist. The overarching goal is to help the client develop a direct, flexible, and open approach to life that will help her reduce symptoms and

http://dx.doi.org/10.1037/0000093-009
Developing the Therapeutic Relationship: Integrating Case Studies, Research, and Practice, O. Tishby and H. Wiseman (Editors)

vulnerabilities or deficits and enhance personal strengths that were not expressed previously, thereby improving quality of life and functioning.

The standard assumption in psychotherapy research is that the therapeutic relationship is a nonspecific factor across all orientations. However, Bordin (1979), Weinberger (1995), and others have suggested that the nature of the therapeutic relationship may differ greatly across different orientations. In fact, Weinberger argued that the relationship has not received much attention in the literature on CBT. In this chapter, we focus on the alliance as the central aspect of the relationship in CBT. That is, the here-and-now bond and the agreement on tasks and goals (cf. Bordin, 1979). Those who have previously examined the relationship in CBT have predominantly focused on alliance, empathy, and other immediate experiences of the relationship and their connection to the proposed operative mechanisms of treatment (e.g., Gilbert & Leahy, 2007; Persons, 2012). Other, wider aspects of the relationship such as how interpersonal relationships and the history and attachment styles of the therapist and client play out in the therapeutic dance will not be addressed.

The lack of research and theory regarding the role of the therapeutic relationship in CBT is notable due to the fact that the alliance is very important in CBT.[1] The therapist puts forth many "demands" on the client, and it is incumbent upon the client to comply and participate in order to achieve the joint goal of creating change or improvement. The client must believe in the therapist and rely on the methods the therapist is proposing. For this to occur, a sufficiently positive relationship must exist. Indeed, research supports that the relationship in CBT is characterized as warm, positive, supportive, and caring (e.g., Keijsers, Schaap, & Hoogduin, 2000), and that the alliance is frequently related to outcome (e.g., Huppert et al., 2014; Webb et al., 2012).

Indeed, Beck (1976) and others (e.g., Persons, 2012) have emphasized the importance of establishing a therapeutic relationship in CBT. However, most theories of mechanisms of action in CBT do not propose that the therapeutic relationship is a major ingredient or factor (e.g., Beck & Haigh, 2014; Craske et al., 2008; Lorenzo-Luaces, Keefe, & DeRubeis, 2016), which has led to little writing or research on the specific nature of the therapeutic relationship in CBT (see Gilbert & Leahy, 2007, for an exception). As Persons (2012) indicated, some of the lack of elaboration on the intricacies of the relationship in CBT is due to the traditional view that the relationship is necessary but not sufficient. The alliance is not seen as the main mechanism of

[1]It is important to note that CBT techniques have had significant success when administered in self-help forms such as bibliotherapy and Internet-based treatments, and therefore outside of the context of a typical alliance. Nevertheless, it does appear that therapist assistance leads to more effective outcomes in self-help. It is likely that the relationship is most important in treating clients who require more motivation, skills, and help to engage in and benefit from treatment.

action but instead as the "glue" or the foundation that facilitates the active ingredients. Whether the alliance is "just" the glue or plays a larger role facilitating or inhibiting progress in treatment, it is important to elaborate on the therapeutic relationship in CBT. We focus here on CBT for anxiety disorders, which is an exemplar of an active process. Most of the specifics here can be generalized to other forms of CBT and for other disorders.

ASPECTS OF THE THERAPEUTIC RELATIONSHIP IN COGNITIVE–BEHAVIORAL THERAPY

CBT is a collaborative process in which each party brings unique capabilities and is responsible for fulfilling her own part of the therapeutic contract. Both sides must fulfill their parts in order to achieve the goal. The therapist's professional role is to bring her expertise on the nature and treatment of the problem and to provide evidence-based methods for addressing the problem within the framework of both a general and tailored conceptualization of the client and her problems or symptoms. The client is expected to provide her own personal data and to apply the strategies and methods suggested by the therapist in and outside the sessions.

The *therapeutic contract* in CBT includes explicit and implicit agreements. Most explicit agreements, such as the therapist working to try to help the client obtain her goals (typically of relief from distress), are supported by the therapist's actions and attitudes towards the client. She commits to transparency, appropriate explanation, and clarification of requirements. She also typically agrees to be available to the client after the end of the current acute and maintenance phases of treatment for "boosters" or follow-up visits. Implicit agreements such as acting only according to the client's best interest, without any interest of her own, and with integrity are also indicated via the therapist's actions.

The client commits to actively work toward the agreed-upon goals, to do homework, and to try to push herself even in difficult situations. She also agrees to provide reliable reports (e.g., about homework being done or not, treatment progress, symptoms), and to speak as openly and honestly as possible. The client is assumed to be motivated to reduce suffering and function better, and since she does not know how to achieve these goals she is seeking the therapist's guidance. Moreover, the client is perceived as lacking both scientific-based knowledge about her problems and empirically supported strategies and methods for effective coping. That is, suffering is not assumed to be necessarily derived from pathological personality problems related to self and identity unless there is explicit information (e.g., behavioral, emotional lability) that demonstrates such psychopathology.

The Contribution of the Therapeutic Alliance to Cognitive–Behavioral Therapy

The therapeutic alliance is considered a nonspecific therapeutic factor; a moderate but robust predictor of outcomes across different treatment approaches, presenting problems, and practice contexts (Flückiger, Del Re, Wampold, Symonds, & Horvath, 2012; Horvath, Del Re, Flückiger, & Symonds, 2011). Furthermore, a poor alliance may hinder the work of therapy. The alliance also has particular effects in CBT, being a directive form of therapy in which the client is expected to commit "to work" and take responsibility and an active role in the process of change. Following are some explanations for the particular role of the alliance on outcomes in CBT:

- The client comes to therapy immersed in powerful cognitive, affective, and behavioral tendencies and habits that constitute her difficulties—often feeling demoralized and criticized due to the responses of individuals around her to her suffering. CBT focuses mainly on providing a supportive, active, and trusting relationship, which is conducive to and facilitates change. From a CBT perspective, it is essential to change the cognitive, affective, and behavioral tendencies and habits that are theorized to maintain suffering, otherwise the problem is not going to change. Often, the client imagines that if she confronts the problem, it will grow worse and may eventually destroy her mentally or physically. Being overwhelmed, the client may be unable to observe the beliefs and actions that aggravate her difficulties from "the outside" with a more "objective," distant, critical view. Under such conditions, it is improbable that therapy will be able to motivate the client to actively engage in the process of change just by the psychoeducational presentation of research findings and explanations of the therapeutic rationale. By building a trusting, empathetic relationship with the client, the therapist is able to help provide guidance to seeing the world more rationally, objectively, and effectively. Such a relationship provides the setting to help the client develop an active coping mindset, a commitment for change, an attitude of risk-taking and the readiness to act contrary to what she perceives as mortal dangers. Indeed, a relationship that can inspire confidence is a clear factor that can assist in developing the motivation for this demanding therapy. Client avoidance, difficulties in regulating or tolerating distress, and hopelessness all require therapist creativity, flexibility, and skill, particularly in adapting herself to the vicissitudes of the particular client (cf. responsiveness; Stiles, Honos-Webb, & Surko, 1998). One particular challenge of the therapist is to flexibly move between joining and leading: balancing and continuously shifting when to demand and push and when to withdraw and soften.

- The alliance promotes emotional security that facilitates the development of attitudes that are vital to the process of change in CBT (cf. Hofmann, 2014, on interpersonal emotion regulation). It helps enhance realistic hope and confidence to counter the initial helplessness and hopelessness of the client. It may also encourage balanced self-consciousness and candor that help to counter the client's habitual tendency for overgeneralizations and denial.

The collaborative alliance promotes the client's readiness and ability to become an observer and active researcher of the paralyzing threats she experiences to counter being overwhelmed. It provides a safe distance from the emotional overload by "looking together at the anxiety." The therapist's readiness to assist the client to courageously risk facing danger "eye to eye" helps to counter the avoidance and automatic thoughts. The therapist supports the client in her willingness and ability to broaden attention so as to notice progress, "baby steps," and personal resources—not only failures. This, too, counters the overfocusing on pathology, self-criticism, and failure. Moreover, this is a way of building an alliance that will facilitate collaboration while also enhancing an attitude of curiosity and, at times, adventurousness in order to counter the client's clinging to comfort zones.

What Describes the Therapist's Stance That Helps Create the Safe Space for the Client?

We view the therapist as assertive but not aggressive, authoritative but not authoritarian. She conveys a respectful attitude towards the client and others. She should also transfer an egalitarian approach to the collaborative inquiry and work with the client, be flexible and capable of changing the specific interventions and tempo when needed, and know how to adapt flexibly to inevitable obstacles and the unexpected turns of life events. And, of course, the therapist must attempt to always be attentive to the client's ideas and feelings.

The therapist should explain the therapeutic principles to the client in her own words and context. While doing so, her goal is to create an atmosphere of collaborative perseverance and goal-directedness without despairing when obstacles occur. She should be attuned to what the client needs in order to collaborate. She should be tolerant and forgiving with the client's mistakes and failures, yet not paternalistic or overly yielding. Finally, the therapist should be truthful and frank, congruent with her words, attitudes, and actions.

The Many Roles of the Therapist in Cognitive–Behavioral Therapy

One way of considering the therapist in CBT is to consider the many roles that a therapist plays in CBT metaphorically. These include being an expert, a salesperson, an ally, and a coach. The next section emphasizes some important dimensions of the therapist's role. The therapist shifts to a different relational position in each role, often flexibly moving among the roles. This requires skill and sensitivity to each client in order to know when to demand and push and when to withdraw and soften, as well as how to fluidly transition back and forth among approaches.

The therapist as an *expert* provides a model based on of the most current state of the field in terms of techniques and mechanisms of treatment, integrated with an idiographic understanding and conceptualization of the client's presenting problems (for more on psychoeducation, see the engagement stage in Table 8.2). The therapist also needs to provide a rationale for the interventions and to execute her interventions with the client in a way that makes the client feel both understood and cared for, with a sense of trust that the therapist knows what she is doing and why. The goals of treatment are set as increasing the functioning and quality of the client's life. The role of an expert here provides both the distant relationship, like that of a surgeon consulting about an operation, while at the same time providing the warmth and empathy of someone who genuinely "sees" the client and wants to help her improve.

As a *salesperson*, the therapist "sells" the treatment, motivates the client, and negotiates with the client flexibly. She manifests confidence and trust in the work model on the bases of the evidence and her clinical experience. Exposure and behavioral experiments require encouraging the client to do things that she does not typically do or even avoids doing. Therefore, they require "selling" the rationale of the treatment and of the exercises themselves. The more the client "buys in" to the rationale and accepts doing exposures, the more they are likely to progress. In times where the client is not immediately sold on the idea, the therapist often should lower the expectations a bit to lower level exposures as an attempt to "put her foot in the door." This role meshes with the expert but focuses more on a relationship that is distant, with the therapist trying to "sell" the therapy to a (typically) somewhat reluctant buyer. However, as any good salesperson knows, part of the sale is relating well to the client, helping her feel that they are on the same side and that the salesperson understands her needs.

As an *ally against avoidance*, the therapist is empathetic, yet persistent. She is understanding of the client's hesitations and anxiety, yet pushes gently towards change. She is skilled in externalizing the problem, flexibly translating the professional understanding and action to the client's unique language, values, and views. One way of externalizing the anxiety is using a metaphor of anxiety as a benign bully. It screams and yells and threatens, but the more she looks it in the face, stands up to it, and then chooses to ignore it while engaging in valued behaviors, the more the client regains control of her life and her anxiety.

The therapist also acts at times as *coach* or cheerleader for exposure. She keeps a positive attitude of encouragement and reinforcement. She believes in the client even when the client feels unsure or discouraged. She keeps teamwork collaborative and makes a big deal of the smallest steps. She is skillful in creating enactment interventions in the here and now that foster cognitive and emotional shifts. At the same time, she is aware that ultimately, it is the client who has to "fight the fight" or "run the race." The therapist is the expert in helping train the client, using experience and research to adapt the most effective techniques and strategizing with the client how to win, but also encouraging independence so that the client can not only win, but also "own the win."

In general, through the therapeutic relationship the therapist engages with the client so as to achieve a joint empathetic understanding of the client's unique issues and a clear and specific direction for change. And last but not least, she is intent on seeing the client as a whole person in her full human complexity.

The Importance of the Therapeutic Alliance in All Stages of Treatment

In this section, we separate and categorize stages of treatment (see Table 8.1), identify challenging issues, and define the main objectives of the therapist. Yet, it is important to remember that creating the therapeutic alliance is not a "first stage in therapy"; it is not a stage at all. Therapists' attitudes are indirectly experienced during and through the therapeutic interaction, through responses and actions. Are therapists accepting or judgmental when homework is not done? How do they respond to client doubts about the therapist or the therapy? How do they respond to criticism: do they counterattack or contain? Do they respectfully listen or are they defensive?

TABLE 8.1
Stage 1—Evaluation

Challenging issues/treatment needs	*Principles of treatment.* The role of the therapist and the changes in the relationship	CBT *techniques*
A. Cognitive–behavioral therapy (CBT) is client oriented.	*The client is an expert regarding her experience.* The therapist allows the client the opportunity to express her feelings, emphasizing that there are no right or wrong answers. The implied assumption is that the client is the authority on her experience. This promotes an open, nondefensive relationship.	Typically, the therapist can rely on her expertise on the nature and treatment of the problem, review the current professional literature, and use pretreatment consultations with an expert on treating "same diagnosis" clients.
B. A highly demanding treatment combined with client anxiety can lead to client dropping out.	The therapist is bound to *transparency and ethical commitment.* The client is entitled to an educated prognosis and timeline. The therapist informs the client about the expectations and requirements from the client, while emphasizing the collaborative nature and that no demands will be forced on the client.	Conducting a *comprehensive intake* and administering reliable and *valid questionnaires* enable the creation of a client-specific treatment plan. After explaining the treatment rationale and discussing its demands, the client gives *informed consent*, which is beneficial in reducing the chance of dropping out.
C. CBT is a time-limited treatment.	To provide evidence-based methods for addressing the problem within a limited period of time.	The *treatment manual* assists therapist's use of evidence-based principles and preparedness and promotes the client's utilization of the treatment.

D. *Evaluation* is a product of a dynamic interaction between the client and the therapist. The challenge is to better understand the difficulties of the client, to assess her motivation for change, and to harness her strengths.	The therapist is attuned to the client, especially to those things that seem to bother her and/or make her more defensive. The therapist and the client have a common goal to evaluate the level of flexibility in response to different kinds of challenges. a. If a client tends to withhold from new relationships and takes a passive stance during therapy, the therapist should encourage her to take a more active stance in later sessions. b. If the client is too active and controls the session, the therapist may need to actively discuss the need for her to be more collaborative.	The therapist uses *microinterventions* during evaluation to observe and analyze how the client responds to them, for example, gradually using more open-ended questions to measure client's self-confidence. *Socratic questioning* is derived from the Socratic method; it helps the client discover the "truth" for herself as opposed to being told what the "truth" is by the therapist (cf. Kazantzis, Fairburn, Padesky, Reinecke, & Teesson, 2014; Padesky, 1993). Another advantage to this method is that the client is more likely to internalize the cognitive changes that occur due to the questioning.
E. *Redefining the problem.* The uniform and rigid conception the client has of the problem plays a role in maintaining the problem.	The therapist can have a different solution from those that derive from the client's narrative. She is active and initiates new cognitive and behavioral options. Doing so, she helps the client redefine the problem and develop a more useful way of thinking about it.	The Socratic method teaches the client the skill of critical thinking. *Socratic inquiry of the problem* guides the client to evaluate her assumptions and modify her thinking so she can reach her goals. It can be used to redefine the essence of the problem, for example, to shift the focus from the upsetting physical sensations to the avoidant reactive "solutions."

And so forth. Therapists' attitudes are thus indirectly perceived through the therapeutic interaction. If therapists are aware of these implicit aspects of the interaction, they can enhance the therapeutic alliance through them. This is both consistent with the literature that the client's perspective of the alliance is often a better predictor of outcomes than the therapist's as well as the work on teaching therapists how to manage resistance and ruptures (Safran, Muran, & Eubanks-Carter, 2011).

The presentation of the stages of treatment includes a demonstration via a clinical case, followed by a summary of the challenging issues and the main objectives of the therapist (Tables 8.1–8.4).

CLINICAL CASE STUDY

The Reason for Referral

Noa (a pseudonym) applied for treatment due to extreme shyness and anxiety in social situations.[2] She described her shyness as interfering with her studies and social situations, and she was worried that it was being interpreted as lack of interest in others. She avoided social events and parties. These difficulties greatly interfered with her social functioning, and adversely affected her mood (Liebowitz Social Anxiety Scale [LSAS] score = 112, Social Phobia Inventory [SPIN] score = 52). Her scores on these measures suggested very severe social anxiety: significant fear and avoidance of a wide variety of social situations. On the other hand, she did not suffer from related problems at work.

The Client's Background

Noa was 26 years old, single, a second-year undergraduate in French literature and education. She was attractive, had pale skin, and a tendency to blush. She spoke softly and rarely made eye contact. She lived in downtown Tel Aviv with two roommates. Noa had worked for the last 2 years at a desk job, and she enjoyed the working environment. During the treatment, she was not in a relationship, but she mentioned having been in a brief romantic relationship in the past.

Noa had five good friends, two of whom were childhood friends and three of whom she met at the university. She said that she did not approach new people, so new relationships had to be initiated by the other person. And since she did not initiate meetings or even phone calls, she lost contact with many people from her past.

[2]Details of this case example have been altered to protect confidentiality.

She felt that whereas social situations are trivial for others, they were very difficult for her. She stated that she almost always avoided people and could not bring herself to talk with them; she often even did not greet friends when she encountered them. She felt that this had given others a negative impression of her as a snob. Most social situations caused her anxiety, and she tried to avoid them. Also, she said she was very sensitive to criticism, and experienced a rapid change in mood mainly due to criticism she received or when things did not go according to her plans, which could make her angry and cause her to "shut down."

Treatment included 17 weekly individual sessions of comprehensive CBT for social phobia (60–90 minutes; Huppert, Roth, & Foa, 2003; Ledley, Foa, & Huppert, 2005).

Assessment and Evaluation

The therapist inquired about the impact of Noa's social anxiety on her life and how she coped with her anxiety. This included discussion of overt and more subtle avoidance and safety behaviors. The therapist worked with Noa to determine her core fear: that others will think that she is stupid. She engaged in many avoidance behaviors to try to prevent this from happening, including refraining from asking questions in class and wearing a scarf to hide possible blushing when she went for a job interview. The therapist's challenge was to build the relationship by expressing empathy for her difficulties and affirmation for her understanding of the problem, combined with a challenging approach and an invitation for a common quest for an alternative way. At the same time, they worked on raising motivation, teamwork, and on creating a joint contract for change.

In the initial stage, the therapist asked predominantly closed-ended questions so that the client did not feel overly pressured or tested (i.e., to come up with "the right answer"). As the session progressed, the therapist felt that the relationship was developing and that Noa had gained confidence; her approach changed accordingly, to asking mainly open-ended questions. In the beginning, due to Noa's tendency to be passive, the therapist had to be more active, leading more than joining. To help the client feel comfortable and not under examination, the therapist noted that there were no right or wrong answers to these questions. The therapist emphasized that Noa was the authority of her experience, and the therapist wanted to understand her subjective experience. Noa said that sharing her avoidance behaviors made her think of herself as irrational and even ridiculous. In response, the therapist told her that her coping methods were rational and legitimate, and there was no reason to feel guilty about them. However, she said that that while these methods have served an immediate need of reducing the anxiety in the short term, in the long run they are harmful. This exchange demonstrated many important principles in the establishment of the therapeutic relationship in CBT. The therapist balanced empathy and introduction of new perspectives for change, came across as authoritative and with expertise (but not authoritarian), yet collaborative. She adjusted to the client and the client's abilities and comforts while being directive.

A key theme at the evaluation stage is *redefining the presenting problem.* Noa held the view that her anxiety is a problem in and of itself. The therapist worked on understanding why anxiety was seen as the problem in order to help reframe the problem as Noa's attempts to manage her anxiety and her interpretations of threat, and not the anxiety itself. This also ended up reframing the goal of therapy from anxiety reduction to learning to cope more in the face of anxiety.

Engagement: Teaching the Client About Therapy Change

Noa spoke quietly and made little eye contact at first. The therapist felt that despite this, there was a feeling of an initial alliance and therapeutic connection. At the beginning of her treatment, Noa received an explanation as to the nature of the treatment and clarification of its principles. The first part is reminiscent of a course and is called *psychoeducation*. Psychoeducation establishes the role of the therapist as an expert, while creating a sense of being collaborative and on an equal footing by emphasizing that both parties have expertise and knowledge: the therapist about treatment and the client about herself.

At this point, the therapist gave Noa facts about the disorder, answered the questions she raised, and tried to make the learning interesting and relevant to her life. The conversation created positive distance between her and the problem, helped her to view the disorder in a broader perspective than usual, and gave a distinct notion of objectivity or at least the pursuit of objectivity. The purpose was to encourage Noa to conceptualize the problem and to normalize it, and strengthen her optimistic feeling that the problem could be solved or at least managed. They focused on her skills and merits and achieved normalization of the disorder, which helped her take comfort and encouragement from the realization that she is not the only one suffering from it. By actively providing the information and allowing Noa to be more passive at first, the therapist was doing a combination of leading (by literally leading the discussion) and joining (by allowing Noa to stay in her comfort zone of more actively listening and not participating significantly). This approach mixed the therapist's empathy and understanding with a bit of frustration at not being able to engage Noa more in treatment and move it along more collaboratively.

Next, they discussed the question "Why does the anxiety persist over time?" The therapist explained to Noa that anxiety may continue for many years, even though the person who has it is aware of its excessive or illogical nature. The therapeutic model suggests that avoidant behavior is a major factor responsible for the ongoing nature of anxiety. Avoidance can be overt or covert: Noa used both types. She avoided meeting new people by refraining from going to places where there was a high likelihood of meeting them, such as cafés (overt avoidance); or, in unavoidable situations where she did meet new people, such as family social gatherings, she would "lighten up" her mood by drinking very large quantities of alcohol (covert avoidance).

After psychoeducation, the therapist and client jointly constructed a model that described Noa's particular social anxiety. This model was a personal adaptation of the general model of social phobia (Clark, 2001). It helped create a case conceptualization and served as a road map for the treatment. Noa understood the model well and pointed out the connection between its different parts. The main emphasis for her was the connection between her negative thoughts and her avoidance behaviors (overt and covert). She saw that avoiding new acquaintances did not allow her to change her mind about the way people initially perceive her. In addition, she mentioned that focusing her attention inwardly increased her physiological symptoms, which in turn invited her to increase her self-focus. Looking at the model, Noa said that she felt overwhelmed by putting it all out there "in her face." The therapist responded by first empathizing, stating that it is hard to look at everything in front of her (i.e., joining). At the same time, she encouraged Noa to take a "researcher mode" of objectivity and distance that facilitated her discovering connections and effects: observing without being overwhelmed, investigating ineffective aspects of her conduct (leading). The therapist also reminded her of what they discussed at the beginning of therapy: that directly dealing with her problem would initially increase anxiety. This normalization allowed her anxiety to subside, and she was ready to continue the session. The therapeutic stance included observing, identifying, and only then acting and supporting. This is a good example of the dance between empathy and encouraging change.

The therapist continued to function as a coach, a team member, a coresearcher, and a salesperson as well. She listened attentively and showed respect, working together to understand how the model of treatment applied to Noa. This enabled Noa to open up gradually; it fostered her self-awareness and ability to observe herself from some distance. The normalization of her behaviors helped her to adopt a more compassionate view of herself rather than "believing and following" self-criticism.

The therapist encouraged Noa to raise doubts whenever she felt them, and indeed she spoke of disappointment, frustration, and even despair throughout. The therapist related to her feedback, not necessarily to oppose it but to emphasize the importance of intentional action, of the values Noa aspired to live by, and her ability to choose according to those values rather than to be guided by her fears (i.e., joining). Noa took responsibility for defining her personal values. She was then asked to examine the gap between her values and the reality determined by her avoidant behavior. The therapist encouraged her to describe her desired future self as specifically as she could, thus activating not only the cognitive aspects but also positive imagination that would foster hope for the future (i.e., leading).

In the *engagement* stage (see Table 8.2), the issues of mobilizing motivation and dealing with ambivalence are pertinent, and the dilemma of the "optimistic coach" versus the "neutral observer" forcefully surfaces. Therapists who take the stance of an optimistic coach will tend to encourage their clients, expressing positivity regarding the chances of progress (i.e., leading). In contrast, therapists who take the stance of a neutral observer will not try to lower uncertainty, nor will they respond to the ambivalence expressed by the client. They will, rather, encourage full expression of the pessimism (i.e., joining) and only then will inquire if other sides exist. They may even play the "devil's advocate" role and present the negative and critical arguments, hoping to drive the client to assume the opposite attitude and respond in a more committed manner, thus helping the client to find assertive strength within. Therapists have to move flexibly between those poles, being always attentive to clients' needs.

Intervention

The *intervention* stage includes predominantly working on gradual exposure and behavioral tests to the factors that trigger anxiety (see Table 8.3). This is a critical stage that necessitates significant motivation on the client's part, because exposure runs contrary to the client's habitual motivation: to avoid any encounter with those factors at all costs. Generally speaking, exposure aims at fulfilling one's values of freedom of choice and action, and of a more authentic life. Goals are selected according to the client's aspirations, interests and self-image (i.e., joining). Noa wanted to focus first on dancing parties, a social activity she had been yearning to do for years (this is an example of social anxiety not mapping well onto introversion). When she discovered that enduring exposure gave her tremendous joy and a sense of freedom due to the courage she experienced, she later agreed to cope later with less enjoyable events that were still meaningful for her self-image, such as academic discourse.

First, the therapist explained that exposure would inevitably bring about discomfort and fear, but would probably be less difficult than what Noa was

TABLE 8.2
Stage 2—Engagement in Treatment

Challenging issues/treatment needs	*Principles of treatment.* The role of the therapist and the changes in the relationship	CBT *techniques*
A. Teaching the client about her specific disorder. Anxious (and/or depressed) clients are constantly suffering from intrusive thoughts that may hinder progress.	The cognitive–behavioral therapy (CBT) therapist is committed to *transparency.* She is required to give an explanation about the nature of the disorder. *Demystify and normalize* the disorder. Externalize the problem and teach the client the importance of looking at her problem objectively.	*Psychoeducation* includes informing the client about her disorder, answering her questions, and making the learning interesting and relevant to her life. Psychoeducation for anxiety includes teaching about the nature of anxiety, the conditions and behaviors that maintain it over time, and the way it is being mediated by automatic thoughts. Clinical experience suggests that objective information (as opposed to the therapist's values and opinions) has a better chance of being utilized by the client.
B. Creating a "client tailored" case conceptualization—constructing a model of the individual's cognitive emotional and behavioral pattern. Methodical investigation of a specific situation allows for identifying the components of the problem.	Investigating a specific event while noticing incongruent or self-handicapping aspects of conduct increases the client's awareness and understanding of her problematic pattern: the consequences of continued avoidance and the ways and benefits of decreasing or stopping it. The client is taught to take a "researcher stance," to observe without being overwhelmed when countering and evaluating feared events.	Creating an *idiographic model* with the client. The model includes situational, behavioral, physical, and cognitive elements, which the client discusses in a specific context. Then she discusses the connection between them (e.g., focusing attention inwardly increases physiological symptoms leading to negative thoughts, promoting avoidance behaviors, and eliminating the chance of new learning: that the anxiety would have decreased naturally).

(*continues*)

TABLE 8.2
Stage 2—Engagement in Treatment (*Continued*)

Challenging issues/treatment needs	*Principles of treatment.* The role of the therapist and the changes in the relationship	CBT *techniques*
C. Enhancing motivation and commitment to change before the intervention stage is advised when dealing with clients who suffer from low motivation and/or high self-criticism. However, if the client exhibits readiness for change, the therapist should advance directly to intervention, even if the client predicts a high level of anxiety.	The therapist should be attentive to the needs of the client, while shifting between being a "neutral observer" and an "optimistic coach." On the one hand, she should not force-feed a low-motivated client, as sustainable motivation and commitment to change come from within. On the other hand, a pessimistic and discouraged client may drop out or avoid dealing with what she fears. A good rule of thumb is to counter the specific client's tendencies. Dependency and relying on others to set goals should be answered by neutrality and Socratic questions. Perfectionism and self-criticism should be replaced or shifted toward a more compassionate view of the self.	The therapist aids the client in exploring feelings of ambivalence and conflict between her avoidant behavior and her personal values and general life goals (e.g., independence, freedom). Asking the client *questions about the consequences of her disorder that are in contrast with her personal values and goals* may enhance her commitment to change. Low motivation might result from high self-criticism and fear of failure. Creating a positive scenario of the future encourages hope that the problem can be solved, or at least better managed.

TABLE 8.3
Stage 3—Intervention

Challenging issues/treatment needs	*Principles of treatment.* The role of the therapist and the changes in the relationship	Cognitive–behavioral therapy *techniques*
A. Encountering a refusal to engage in exposures because of fear of anxiety rising high. A client who is highly avoidant dreads the experience of feeling anxiety, is convinced that she will not stand the tension caused by the exposure, and is asking for methods for relaxation.	The therapist should validate the client's feelings of ambivalence and encourage a stance of exploration, acknowledgment, and acceptance toward them. At the same time, the therapist should encourage the client to challenge her avoidant approach without judgment. Keeping in mind that in most cases, high levels of anxiety will reduce as the client approaches social situations. Supplying the client with methods for relaxation sends the message that she cannot handle social situations by herself, which is the opposite of the treatment rationale.	The appropriate interventions mentioned above (e.g., psychoeducation, building an idiographic model with the client, Socratic questioning, comparing values with current life) should increase the client's awareness of the consequences of continued avoidance and the benefits of decreasing or stopping it. But if all these fail, the therapist can equip the client with methods for managing the anxiety such as mindfulness. Some therapists include tools like *muscle relaxation, breathing techniques*, and other methods that promote relaxation, which are not a part of current evidence-based treatment for many anxiety disorders.
B. Exposure is the gold standard for treating anxiety. The challenge is acceptance versus pushing for change. How to be attuned to the client, demanding more, without bringing the client to her breaking point.	The therapist should be attentive to the client's progress—including areas of difficulty. For example, dealing with noncompliance in session or homework, the therapists might "go back" to previous exposures in order to verify their satisfactory completion. When therapists don't value homework assignments, their clients usually ignore them.	Suitable interventions should be applied throughout this stage to achieve optimal exposures (e.g., *building a hierarchy* and doing *in vivo exposures*). Other interventions include: a. Interventions designed to expose the client to situations otherwise impossible (e.g., *imaginal exposures*). b. Getting external feedback about the exposures (e.g., watching the tape and producing a *video feedback*, getting *feedback from conversation partners*). c. Interventions that tackle client's nonadaptive schemes or misperceptions (e.g., *cognitive restructuring*, which is challenging dysfunctional beliefs and *surveys*, which are useful to counter unrelenting standards).

imagining it to be (i.e., leading). The therapist emphasized that exposure would be done in a gradual, controlled manner, and that Noa would not be required to do things she was not ready to do. Through this intervention, the therapist anticipated Noa's anxiety about doing the exposures, was empathetic, but did not relent (both leading and joining). She was sensitive to Noa's capabilities and limitations, in tune with her individual rhythm and timing, and tried to create experiences in the here and now, instead of just discussing verbally the "then and there" (joining).

Following this, they created a *hierarchy of Noa's fears*: Noa had to write a list of social situations that frightened her and rate them from 0 to 100 according to the level of fear she expected. The hierarchy promoted externalization and created an "us versus anxiety" framework. Indeed, sitting and looking at the list of the situations on a computer screen where the therapist and patient are positioned next to each other, opposite the list of the anxiety-provoking situations is an instantiation of the cooperation against the externalized anxiety. Building the hierarchy also promoted collaborative inquiry by practicing curiosity and exploration.

At a later stage of the treatment, the therapist asked Noa to identify the situations which especially scared her, those which she couldn't deal with earlier (leading). They thought together how to divide these into stages, create external and internal aids for coping and building exposure events that she could handle. This stage of the treatment was therapeutic in a number of aspects: first, in the behavioral approach, actions and experiences speak louder than words (though words help prepare and process the experience). Second, through the exposure, the empirical element of the collaborative inquiry comes through. When Noa began checking her assumptions like a research scientist, she found she could handle situations that she had thought were too hard. This led her to realize her anxiety was inaccurate. Here the therapist acted as a coach: accompanying her along the way, encouraging action, and reinforcing competence. Through the therapist's collaboration and warm engagement, Noa could gradually manage and accept her anxiety and cope actively with challenges that at first seemed impossible.

The main objective of these meetings was learning through social encounters with people inside and outside the clinic, with or without a defined purpose, designed to resemble the stressful situations which Noa met or avoided in her life. The tasks assigned to Noa increased in difficulty, from having "small talk," participating in a lively discussion and being assertive about controversial subjects, and finally having to make a speech with or without preparation in front of a group of people (i.e., leading). The rationale was that the more Noa experienced the feared social situations, online or within the therapy session, she would learn new things about these situations, reduce her anxiety, readjust cognitive distortions about herself, and strengthen her confidence. The exposures were designed accordingly. For example, Noa assumed that making deliberate eye contact on her side would be inappropriate during small talk with a stranger, and she viewed her blushing as a sign of weakness. Noa was surprised to find that her perception was very different from what others found to be acceptable behavior (when it was inquired about after the conversations): More eye contact on her part led to an improvement in the quality of conversation in both her experience and (according to feedback) from others. Her blushing, however, was "missed" by all of her partners except one, a young man who mentioned it and wrote that it made him feel more comfortable and made Noa more likeable in his eyes.

In addition to the feedback, the therapist and patient would observe the video taken of the exposure during the therapy session, which included close-ups of Noa's facial expressions. During this stage, the therapist's reactions moved from empathy with the weakness Noa felt to directing her attention to the positive sides of her behavior. On one occasion, the therapist had to stop the video every few seconds to promote an exact and not general or negative processing of the information. The first time they used video feedback was effective for Noa, but later on she didn't feel helped by it. It seemed that Noa's negative perception of herself influenced the way she observed the video, which made it less useful for her. It was therefore decided to stop using it. More importantly, it started a dialogue about her tendency to focus on the negative aspects of social situations, and the role of memory, attention, and interpretation biases in maintaining social anxiety disorder. Note the flexible with which the therapist was persistent, on message, but also adapting to Noa's needs and abilities via collaboration and empathy.

At one midtreatment session, Noa behaved more ambivalently than she had previously. She was anxious about in vivo exposures. During an exposure that was a conversation with a stranger, her hands trembled, and it made her upset and disappointed with herself. In addition, she had difficulty with the exposures she was asked to perform for homework, sometimes neglecting them completely. The therapist initially felt a bit of frustration and fear that the therapy was not progressing. She sought supervision, which helped her see the refusal as avoidant behavior, so the therapist invested considerable time in understanding Noa's exact fears. The therapist then offered alternative ways of looking at the exposure exercises to make them less threatening, by breaking them down to manageable parts (foot in the door), while supporting and encouraging her to undergo the task. In most cases it was effective, and Noa agreed to participate in the exposures during the meeting that she had avoided during the previous week.

However, when Noa described her struggle to talk during university classes and the catastrophic fears she had about the students ridiculing her, the therapist realized Noa needed more time to gradually cope with exposures in the academic realm (i.e., joining). The mere thought of such exposure made her feel anxious: her face went pale and her respiratory rate increased rapidly. After they discussed it at length, and the therapist expressed empathy to her difficulty and agreed to postpone the exposures in class, Noa relaxed a bit (more joining; only three sessions later she agreed to such exposure and, as a first step, only in a small classroom). The therapist shifted from the role of a *coach* or cheerleader to a role of an emphatic ally. In regard to the relational process, she focused on joining rather than leading at this point. Considering Noa's reluctance at this stage, although she had some concern that the therapy was slowing, the therapist felt it more accurate to focus on imaginal exposures in the following sessions. For this, Noa and the therapist built together an extreme and dramatic imaginary scenario based on her catastrophic fears, aimed to help her process the ultimate fears, and reduce them (i.e., going back to leading). In the following weeks, Noa listened to a recorded description of the scenario, four times a day for 5 minutes each. They then discovered the intensity of feeling reduced, and it became a kind of "vaccination" against avoidance during similar situations relevant to her real life. The cooperative building of the scenario and the therapist's not completely giving up on exposure, but rather shifting to another type of exposure that Noa was willing to engage in, impacted the relationship on a number of levels. The therapist demonstrated empathy, but also that she had additional techniques in her armamentarium that could help Noa acquire the same principles that the in vivo exposures and other behavioral exercises were aiming at. The therapist exhibited persistence, suggesting that she still believed in the overall conceptualization, and that she was optimistic that the patient would improve. This was a good example of balancing empathy and change.

The general stress levels Noa felt at a specific point in her life influenced her willingness to use exposures. When she felt more stress, related to her work or studies, it was harder for her to agree to exposures. For example, at the beginning of the treatment, Noa saw herself as a recluse with no social circles at university. The therapist told Noa that there are many social situations she would need to deal with when she was under pressure and it would be an opportunity to learn, but Noa wasn't convinced. While the therapist felt a bit frustrated, she was able to contain this and persist. When asked what would happen if she agreed to exposures, and they lead to a positive outcome, Noa replied that it would not really help and the effect would pass quickly. However, if the outcome was negative, she claimed it would have a negative impact. It appeared that Noa was avoiding exposures because of her fear of a negative outcome, making it difficult for her to imagine a positive outcome that increased her confidence at university. Nevertheless, during this period of time, she dealt with social situations such as parties and social gatherings, demonstrating her desire to progress, although the social demands in her academic environment seemed more difficult and increased her anxiety. Her fear touched the deepest, core levels of her self-image, particularly the fear that she was not smart or successful enough. When they spoke about these feelings she became tearful. This made the therapist feel closer to Noa. The therapist was empathetic, reflecting how significant it was for Noa to be successful and how afraid she was to fail. She paused momentarily from active encouragement of these exposures and allowed the patient to consider what she wanted from treatment (joining). The shift from being active to passive was a conscious choice, given the apparent resistance the therapist felt from Noa. By shifting gears, the therapist was able to maintain the working alliance and keep Noa feeling that the therapist was on her side.

Once, Noa came to a meeting during a panic attack following an unpleasant conversation with a lecturer; an attack that intensified as she walked toward the clinic. This was a turning point for Noa, as it was the first time she reacted actively, not avoiding an unpredicted event as she usually did. Even though Noa's anxiety was palpable, the therapist knew that this was a critical opening of which advantage should be taken. The therapist guided her to imagine her anxiety as a rampaging horse in the field. Instead of trying to control it, she asked Noa to let go of the reins and let it run freely, while she's on the saddle, curiously observing it. This image "stuck" to Noa. She later shared that even weeks afterwards, during stressful moments and even during a panic attack, she could let go, watch, and feel the intense physiological and emotional reactions, and allow herself to feel a different sort of presence in the moment. She trusted the horse would steer clear of the cliff, meaning she would avoid destructive behavior during these moments.

The therapist remembered from that same meeting how Noa found it hard to relax, elevating the therapist's anxiety as well. Noa had constantly crunched her fingers and tightened her jaw, saying, "This isn't working. I'm too nervous."

The therapist persisted, saying, "That's right, you feel it's not working and you're nervous. Notice the tension in your hands, this recurring thought of 'it's not working,' the nervous feeling . . . but now (when the hand crunching stopped), notice the brief calmness in your hands . . . and how it passes when they're stretched again . . . and again, the hands are relaxed." These expressions merely followed the physical changes in Noa's voice and body language, and reflected the reduced anxiety in the room. There was no argument, coercion, or objection. There were only two people who were working together to reach a better situation. In Noa's case, the therapist's aim was joining by seeing Noa's fear from the beginning, staying with it and empathizing with it, and then leading her to a more independent and safe position. When the therapy concluded, Noa internalized these two abilities: (a) identifying and staying with the difficulty (not "giving in to it") and (b) dealing with it appropriately.

As the therapeutic relationship gradually grew stronger, Noa felt more comfortable to share experiences and hardships. Noa wasn't a typical socially anxious client: she was an extrovert. Her world of reference was one of parties and nightlife, and many of the objectives referred to this world. However, it was important to expand the reference to the academic realm, not from a judging point of view of it being objectively "more important" but because it was important to Noa. The therapist felt that Noa sensed her efforts, and demonstrated great courage talking about her feelings on these subjects, which were painful to her (joining). The therapist tried to insist and not let her off the hook, despite some concerns that she was pushing too hard (leading). Ultimately, such pushing appeared to have helped in situations in which Noa's motivation was low.

In conclusion, a central challenge of the therapist at this stage is to achieve the *relational process* of joining and leading. *Joining* means communicating with Noa on her level, looking at the values important to her and the objectives derived from them. That is why the first focus was the nightlife realm and not the academic one—Noa loved parties, and an essential value for her is the ability to participate in them authentically. The contrast between this value and the avoidance strengthened her motivation for change. It allowed the therapist to *lead* towards Noa's social avoidance in the academic realm, as opposed to her initial tendency to completely avoid it.

The balance between leading and joining is one of the most important and practical aspects of empathy. Noa needed the therapist's deepest acceptance of who she was, for better or worse. Joining is a cognitive, emotional, and behavioral tool: (a) cognitive, as it allows the therapist to look at the client's hardship and try and understand it, confirming the client's subjective logic; (b) emotional, as it allows the client to accept the reflection of her feelings of disappointment and despair with no judgment, criticism, or preaching; and (c) behavioral, as the therapist walks the client through the exposures, feels the client's anxiety, sees its verbal and nonverbal expressions, and is with the client, strengthening her during breakdowns and despair. But joining isn't enough: Noa had to be led beyond what already existed (otherwise she would not turn to get professional help). The challenge for a therapist is to flexibly move between joining and leading. It requires skill but mainly sensitivity to each client in order to know when to demand and push and when to withdraw and soften. In fact, it is a continuous movement rather than a transition between opposing approaches.

Termination and Maintenance: The Client Establishes New Behaviors on a Long-Term Basis

A positive way of leading toward a treatment's conclusion is to facilitate the client's independence in treatment decisions (e.g., how to conduct an exposure and what to do to make it most effective), which can make the therapist seem redundant. The main objective is to empower clients and give them a sense of independence and competence when dealing with their lives. For example, the therapist may encourage the client to make more use of other sources of support, such as family, friends, and community. Their support is critical for the client to continue practicing exposures. It is also important the client is fully committed to continue following her progress. The therapist should prepare the client for unwanted but unavoidable "slips" in the road, and prepare the client to deal with them without fear, anxiety, or despair. These preparations support maintaining the achievements of the therapy, leading to the follow-up meeting 3 months after the therapy's conclusion, and beyond. At this stage, it is recommended that the client be encouraged to set goals for the posttherapy period. These goals should be realistic and compatible with the client's life circumstances (see Table 8.4).

As the treatment proceeded to a close, Noa became more willing to perform the exposures in "real life," outside of treatment. She went to parties she had previously avoided, formed new relationships, and even enrolled in a psychodrama class to help her improvise and stand in front of an audience. In one session late in treatment, the therapist recalled Noa's radiant face and her big smile when she entered the room and announced, "I did it!" (referring to her ultimate exposure). To celebrate her success, they both made a toast with metaphorical wine glasses. A positive new development occurred in Noa's life using the "approach" attitude. For example, Noa dared to take the initiative to contact a distant cousin with whom she had lost touch. In her studies, she asked for help from a lecturer she used to avoid. She shared her insights on the treatment with a close friend, who showed interest and willingness to support her. It was important, as this particular friend was a role model for Noa because of her social courage.

In their last meetings, the therapist and Noa went through the main insights they had recorded from the sessions (it is recommended to write the main themes from each meeting in the client's log). They checked in which areas Noa had accomplished her objective and how to preserve these successes, and in which ones she still felt she wanted to make progress.

They discussed the values that drove Noa to action currently, and whether they had changed from the beginning of treatment. The values were (a) the courage to be who she is when faced with weakness and (b) doing her best to deal with social challenges. Noa chose objectives that fit with these

TABLE 8.4
Stage 4—Termination and Maintenance

Challenging issues/ treatment needs	*Principles of treatment.* The role of the therapist and the changes in the relationship	CBT *techniques*
A. The challenge here is to finish in the right time: Some clients may benefit from several sessions beyond what was planned; but for most, extending treatment beyond what is necessary may reinforce avoidant behavior and prevent the client from experiencing alternative options.	The therapist should beware of situations in which the current treatment episode has run its course but treatment continues due to dependency or perfectionism. Keep in mind that no therapy is perfect, that it is merely one of many experiences in the client's life, and beware of the erroneous scheme "it's all or nothing." Acknowledging the progress that the client has made is extra important when the termination is due to time constraints, so that the client is not robbed of hope and is more likely to seek treatment in the future. It can still be regarded as a successful treatment, as long as the client is empowered and motivated to keep the change going.	When clients are anxious about the upcoming termination, the clinician should acknowledge the client's feelings and experiences as a normal part of recovery and refrain from alarming the client by demanding to continue the treatment beyond what was agreed upon. Therapists who pressure their dependent and anxious clients, who are probably susceptible to assertiveness, are ensuring the breakdown of the therapeutic alliance. Suitable interventions should be applied throughout this stage to empower the client (e.g., the *client takes charge* of the "therapist's role," planning exposures in and outside of therapy room; creating a *personal journal* of treatment goals, achievements, and life lessons).
B. Even though cognitive–behavioral therapy (CBT) is usually short-term, the client–therapist relationship is perceived as a continuation, over time, while a specific treatment episode is the time-limited experience. An important principle of the therapy is to inform clients that they can always come back for more help.	The therapist encourages the client to take the stance of an *active agent*, who copes with anxiety as it arises. She aids the client by creating and executing an action plan, and encourages her to keep working on skills needed to maintain her progress. A good way to end treatment is to make the therapist unnecessary. The therapist encourages the client to use resources more fully during daily life (e.g., family, friends, community).	The therapist explains about maintenance and *relapse prevention.* She praises the client for her progress but reminds her of her lingering patterns and of what is yet to come. It is important to identify situations that are still being avoided or mishandled. As the problematic patterns are recognized as possible causes for withdrawal, development of an improved course of action is possible. *Follow-up sessions* can be used to reinforce, evaluate present actions, and redefine long-term maintenance plans.

values, and they thought together about how she could achieve them in a realistic time frame. Merely independently writing down these objectives helped Noa realize clearly what was important and realistic, and strengthened her "internal compass" and her belief in herself. Noa wrote these objectives for a follow-up period of 3 months. This included interim tasks to achieve the objectives until the follow-up meeting. This was an important declarative act, announcing she was committed to these values and committed to internalize what she had learned in therapy. She promised herself not to give in to her lack of confidence, her anxieties, and negative thoughts that led to a withdrawn life. She chose to take responsibility: an internal obligation to deal with her fears rather than let them control her.

Noa felt that during the treatment her anxiety levels reduced, and she learned she could deal better with crises, and in fact become her own "cognitive therapist." She emphasized the use of positive imagery as a helpful tool during and after therapy. Her improvements manifested in a decrease of 56 on the LSAS and 27 on the SPIN (LSAS = 66, SPIN = 25 at end point). These are indications of moderate to low anxiety and avoidance, a substantial reduction from pretreatment.

This short-term, time-limited treatment was effective for Noa, as it has been for many others who experience social anxiety and therefore difficulties in creating and preserving relationships. The short time in which an alliance is formed is based on shared emotional experiences and overcoming obstacles. Above all, clients feel actual progress in their lives outside the treatment. Their connection to the therapist is largely based on the concrete help they receive and the constant demand to not give up on themselves. This insistence works well with the demanding and often critical part of the clients' complex characters.

In conclusion, the therapist's role includes many subfunctions, each of which may be critical at some stage of the therapeutic process. Therapists need to have a basic ability to correctly identify obstacles to change and ruptures in the therapeutic relationship. They should possess professional skills for coping with the obstacles, knowing when and how to push, when and how to let go, when to encourage, and when to critique or suggest changes. These aspects of therapy are not usually specified in CBT manuals, because they are specific to the client and the therapist at different points in the process. These are the constantly changing aspects of the treatment process. Gradually, therapists come to know their clients in a more accurate way, and can identify the process a client is going through, sometimes even before the client can. Moreover, therapists can express (verbally or nonverbally) their understanding. All of these aspects of the therapist's role are crucial factors that influence the quality of the therapeutic relationship and the therapeutic outcome.

FROM RESEARCH TO PRACTICE AND BACK

The described case study used an evidence-based practice for the treatment of social anxiety disorder: individual CBT (Mayo-Wilson et al., 2014). Processes that have been demonstrated to be related to the specific psychopathology, such as interpretation biases, attentional focus, and taking an observer perspective (Clark, 2001), were all addressed and techniques such as exposure, video feedback, and confederate feedback were administered. All of these methods have good research evidence. Indeed, even the use of individual instead of group treatment for social anxiety is evidence-based (Aderka, 2009). Nonetheless, treatment was tailored to the patient, and the subtle interpersonal dance that we have described here often remains unwritten. It is either passed from supervisor to therapist during supervision discussions that don't make it into written works or conveyed nonverbally.

Striking the balance between being active and passive, or leading and joining, has not been studied in CBT to the best of our knowledge. Microprocess research, perhaps via identification of either ruptures and repairs (Safran et al., 2011) or resistance (Westra, 2011; Westra et al., 2012), may help reveal more about the importance of these processes, how they unfold, and how to improve them to make the treatment more effective. Alternatively, a new coding system that identifies therapist activity versus passivity or leading versus joining could be developed. Such a system would need to try to identify appropriate triggers for either leading versus joining (either matched or mismatched to patient needs), which would be an indicator of appropriate therapist responsiveness (Stiles et al., 1998).

Additionally, a coding system could be developed to try to categorize the various roles of the therapist as described here to determine whether use of each of the roles is related to outcomes and how the therapist switches across the different roles. This too, would ideally be integrated with how these roles shift according to patient reactions, responses, or needs. Such research would help better describe the processes that occur in therapy, provide more detailed information about the therapist–patient relationship than typical alliance studies provide, and help to advance research and potentially improve treatment outcomes.

IMPLICATIONS FOR SUPERVISION AND TRAINING

As noted above, much of what we have written here is a form of "oral tradition" that is often passed down from supervisor to therapist, though it is less frequently written down. We have found that emphasizing these issues, in the context of adhering to evidence-based principles, can assist both novice and more experienced therapists who are less used to conducting more active treatments to incorporate these practices into their therapeutic repertoire. The current chapter avoids engaging in the academic debate about techniques versus relationship as the main factor leading to treatment outcomes (cf. Wampold & Imel, 2015) by taking a third stance: in most cases of psychotherapy, including CBT, the challenge is using the relationship to facilitate the principles of treatment via various techniques. The dance of leading and joining is one that many therapists attempt to manage without directly addressing the issue in supervision. Some novice CBT therapists overfocus on the technique to the detriment of the treatment (e.g., Castonguay, Goldfried, Wiser, Raue, & Hayes, 1996), while others may overemphasize the need to build the relationship at the expense of the treatment interventions. Raising the issue with supervisees and trainees and working with them to find the ideal "window" for a given patient is part of the transmission of the art of CBT.

REFERENCES

Aderka, I. M. (2009). Factors affecting treatment efficacy in social phobia: The use of video feedback and individual vs. group formats. *Journal of Anxiety Disorders, 23*, 12–17. http://dx.doi.org/10.1016/j.janxdis.2008.05.003

Beck, A. T. (1976). *Cognitive therapy and the emotional disorders*. New York, NY: Penguin.

Beck, A. T., & Haigh, E. A. (2014). Advances in cognitive theory and therapy: The generic cognitive model. *Annual Review of Clinical Psychology, 10*, 1–24. http://dx.doi.org/10.1146/annurev-clinpsy-032813-153734

Bordin, E. S. (1979). The generalizability of the psychoanalytic concept of the working alliance. *Psychotherapy, 16*, 252–260. http://dx.doi.org/10.1037/h0085885

Castonguay, L. G., Goldfried, M. R., Wiser, S., Raue, P. J., & Hayes, A. M. (1996). Predicting the effect of cognitive therapy for depression: A study of unique and common factors. *Journal of Consulting and Clinical Psychology, 64*, 497–504. http://dx.doi.org/10.1037/0022-006X.64.3.497

Clark, D. M. (2001). A cognitive perspective on social phobia. In W. R. Crozier & L. E. Alden (Eds.), *International handbook of social anxiety: Concepts, research and interventions relating to the self and shyness* (pp. 405–430). Chichester, England: Wiley.

Craske, M. G., Kircanski, K., Zelikowsky, M., Mystkowski, J., Chowdhury, N., & Baker, A. (2008). Optimizing inhibitory learning during exposure therapy. *Behaviour Research and Therapy, 46*, 5–27. http://dx.doi.org/10.1016/j.brat.2007.10.003

Flückiger, C., Del Re, A. C., Wampold, B. E., Symonds, D., & Horvath, A. O. (2012). How central is the alliance in psychotherapy? A multilevel longitudinal meta-analysis. *Journal of Counseling Psychology, 59*, 10–17. http://dx.doi.org/10.1037/a0025749

Gilbert, P., & Leahy, R. L. (Eds.). (2007). *The therapeutic relationship in the cognitive behavioral psychotherapies*. New York, NY: Routledge.

Hofmann, S. G. (2014). Interpersonal emotion regulation model of mood and anxiety disorders. *Cognitive Therapy and Research, 38*, 483–492. http://dx.doi.org/10.1007/s10608-014-9620-1

Horvath, A. O., Del Re, A. C., Flückiger, C., & Symonds, D. (2011). Alliance in individual psychotherapy. *Psychotherapy, 48*, 9–16. http://dx.doi.org/10.1037/a0022186

Huppert, J. D., Kivity, Y., Barlow, D. H., Gorman, J. M., Shear, M. K., & Woods, S. W. (2014). Therapist effects and the outcome–alliance correlation in cognitive behavioral therapy for panic disorder with agoraphobia. *Behaviour Research and Therapy, 52*, 26–34. http://dx.doi.org/10.1016/j.brat.2013.11.001

Huppert, J. D., Roth, D. A., & Foa, E. B. (2003). Cognitive–behavioral treatment of social phobia: New advances. *Current Psychiatry Reports, 5*, 289–296. http://dx.doi.org/10.1007/s11920-003-0058-5

Kazantzis, N., Fairburn, C. G., Padesky, C. A., Reinecke, M., & Teesson, M. (2014). Unresolved issues regarding the research and practice of cognitive behavior therapy: The case of guided discovery using Socratic questioning. *Behaviour Change, 31*, 1–17. http://dx.doi.org/10.1017/bec.2013.29

Keijsers, G. P. J., Schaap, C. P. D. R., & Hoogduin, C. A. L. (2000). The impact of interpersonal patient and therapist behavior on outcome in cognitive–behavior therapy. A review of empirical studies. *Behavior Modification, 24*, 264–297. http://dx.doi.org/10.1177/0145445500242006

Ledley, D. R., Foa, E. B., & Huppert, J. D. (2005). *Comprehensive cognitive behavior therapy for social phobia*. Unpublished manual.

Lorenzo-Luaces, L., Keefe, J. R., & DeRubeis, R. J. (2016). Cognitive behavioral therapy: Nature and relation to non-cognitive behavioral therapy. *Behavior Therapy, 47*, 785–803. http://dx.doi.org/10.1016/j.beth.2016.02.012

Mayo-Wilson, E., Dias, S., Mavranezouli, I., Kew, K., Clark, D. M., Ades, A. E., & Pilling, S. (2014). Psychological and pharmacological interventions for social anxiety disorder in adults: A systematic review and network meta-analysis. *The Lancet: Psychiatry, 1*, 368–376. http://dx.doi.org/10.1016/S2215-0366(14)70329-3

Padesky, C. A. (1993, September). *Socratic questioning: Changing minds or guiding discovery*. Keynote address delivered at the European Congress of Behavioural and Cognitive Therapies, London, England. Retrieved from https://padesky.com/newpad/wp-content/uploads/2012/11/socquest.pdf

Persons, J. B. (2012). *The case formulation approach to cognitive–behavior therapy*. New York, NY: Guilford Press.

Safran, J. D., Muran, J. C., & Eubanks-Carter, C. (2011). Repairing alliance ruptures. *Psychotherapy*, *48*, 80–87. http://dx.doi.org/10.1037/a0022140

Stiles, W. B., Honos-Webb, L., & Surko, M. (1998). Responsiveness in psychotherapy. *Clinical Psychology: Science and Practice*, *5*, 439–458. http://dx.doi.org/10.1111/j.1468-2850.1998.tb00166.x

Wampold, B. E., & Imel, Z. E. (2015). *The great psychotherapy debate: The evidence for what makes psychotherapy work*. New York, NY: Routledge.

Webb, C. A., DeRubeis, R. J., Dimidjian, S., Hollon, S. D., Amsterdam, J. D., & Shelton, R. C. (2012). Predictors of patient cognitive therapy skills and symptom change in two randomized clinical trials: The role of therapist adherence and the therapeutic alliance. *Journal of Consulting and Clinical Psychology*, *80*, 373–381. http://dx.doi.org/10.1037/a0027663

Weinberger, J. (1995). Common factors aren't so common: The common factors dilemma. *Clinical Psychology: Science and Practice*, *2*, 45–69. http://dx.doi.org/10.1111/j.1468-2850.1995.tb00024.x

Westra, H. A. (2011). Comparing the predictive capacity of observed in-session resistance to self-reported motivation in cognitive behavioral therapy. *Behaviour Research and Therapy*, *49*, 106–113. http://dx.doi.org/10.1016/j.brat.2010.11.007

Westra, H. A., Aviram, A., Connors, L., Kertes, A., & Ahmed, M. (2012). Therapist emotional reactions and client resistance in cognitive behavioral therapy. *Psychotherapy*, *49*, 163–172. http://dx.doi.org/10.1037/a0023200

9

AFFIRMING THE CASE FOR POSITIVE REGARD

BARRY A. FARBER AND JESSICA Y. SUZUKI

There are moments, we imagine, in every therapist's work with virtually all their clients, in which they are moved to express their deep-seated care or support for that client. It may be a verbal or nonverbal expression, solicited or not, expanded upon or not, explicitly acknowledged by their client or not. "That was brave of you." "I do care about you." "You're handling those situations so much better now." "I'm proud of you." "You're a good person." Or perhaps a smile, a laugh, or several (affirming) nods of the head. All are means of expressing positive regard for one's client. Carl Rogers's remark to Gloria in that famous filmed therapy session (Shostrom, 1965)—"You look to me like a pretty good daughter"—may be criticized as excessively personal and even seductive (Daniels, 2014), but there can be little doubt that Rogers meant it as an affirmation of Gloria's basic worth.

It is possible to conceptualize the therapist's provision of positive regard in a rather straightforward manner, one consistent with Rogers's original

http://dx.doi.org/10.1037/0000093-010
Developing the Therapeutic Relationship: Integrating Case Studies, Research, and Practice, O. Tishby and H. Wiseman (Editors)

writings on this subject—the therapist's conveyance of unconditional support and/or caring for his or her client. But like many concepts in our field, pinning down more specifically the constituent components of positive regard or the many ways in which it manifests in therapeutic situations is a far trickier proposition. Thus, a somewhat more nuanced understanding includes an awareness that the clinical manifestation of this attitude may vary significantly as a function of therapist or client preferences or therapist–client interactions, that different kinds of clients may have quite discrepant responses to different expressions of positive regard, and that the same client may shift his or her perceptions of the meaningfulness or salience of different types of positive regard over the course of psychotherapy.

In this chapter, we draw our inspiration from Carl Rogers's client-centered (later person-centered) framework and align ourselves with his contention that positive regard is an essential facilitative condition of the therapeutic process. We further propose that positive regard—alternately referred to in the literature as nonpossessive warmth, affirmation, support, prizing, and caring—is a wide-ranging construct that has a great deal of overlap with Rogers's other facilitative conditions of empathy and authenticity.

My (BAF) treatment with Carole, described below, demonstrates the diversity of ways in which positive regard may be communicated from therapist to client. We argue on behalf of the hypothesis that positive regard in therapy is most effectively conveyed through multiple and ever-changing expressions of both verbal and nonverbal communication. Stated somewhat differently, we believe that consistent expression of but one type of positive regard—for example, verbal statements supportive of a client's basic worth—is insufficient, or at least a less potent means, to effect significant and enduring change in clients who have suffered from early and persistent trauma. To provide a better context for these clinical observations, we first review the theoretical and empirical literature on positive regard in psychotherapy.

THEORETICAL/CONCEPTUAL BASIS

Over the last several decades, psychotherapy researchers and clinicians alike have increasingly emphasized the clinical necessity of an effective therapeutic relationship, one which includes the therapist's expression of warmth, support, empathy, and overall responsiveness to the client's changing needs. Though Freud's writings on psychoanalysis emphasized the scientific nature of the treatment and encouraged analysts to remain as neutral in the room as possible, accounts of successful therapy by many of his patients suggest that he offered many of these fundamental "relational" aspects of the healing relationship in the treatment room (Breger, 2009). Today, an intervention that classical Freudians might once have pejoratively labeled as "gratification of the patient" would likely today be embraced across a variety of therapeutic approaches as quite helpful or even critical for the client's progress in therapy.

This transformation is due in large part to the work of Rogers, one of the earlier theoreticians to make a bold case for the therapeutic relationship as a profoundly human and healing one. In Rogers's form of humanistic therapy, the therapist's provision of positive regard, congruence (i.e., genuineness and openness) and empathy were considered not just necessary but also sufficient for facilitating client growth and change. Even as studies continued to investigate the role of an extraordinary variety of client, therapist, and process variables as potential contributors to therapy outcome (e.g., Bergin & Garfield, 1994), psychotherapy research and practice in the second half of the 20th century increasingly recognized and emphasized the value of the relationship per se. Among other consequences of this increasing focus on the therapeutic relationship and specifically, Rogers's facilitative conditions, studies began to investigate the effectiveness of therapists' conveyance of positive regard. This research has consistently found a significant positive association between positive regard and therapeutic outcome (Farber & Doolin, 2011; Farber, Suzuki, & Lynch, in press).

Where does positive regard fit within Rogers's overall theory? Rogers (1961), crediting Standal with originating the term, argued that psychotherapy should strive to enable clients to access their inherent tendency toward self-actualization by increasing their openness to the full range of internal experience. This process, he contended, facilitated a liberation from *conditions of worth* that threaten clients' ability to experience and accept their true and authentic self. Conditions of worth are those internalized rules or strictures primarily laid down early in life that a child must adhere to in order to feel valued or good enough. To the extent, then, that the child comes to believe that he or she is valuable only when meeting these conditions, much of his or her life is constrained (i.e., unable to take in or feel the full range of life's experiences) and infused with anxiety and distress. Thus, the goal of therapy, per Rogers, was to help the client become more *congruent*, such that perceptions of the self and one's internal experience more nearly reflect all of one's actual experiences: "All the available experiential data will be available to awareness and used" (Rogers, 1959, p. 235). The therapist abets this process by acting congruently and authentically, by being empathetic toward the client's self-experience on a moment-by-moment basis, and by adopting an attitude of *unconditional positive regard* in order to demonstrate to the client that all aspects of his or her internal experience are equally valid and acceptable. According to Rogers, this overall approach will inevitably result in change: "Gradually the client can feel more acceptance of all of his own experiences, and this makes him again more of a whole or congruent person, able to function effectively" (Rogers, 1959, p. 208).

Although, as noted above, there have been some studies of the relationship of positive regard to therapeutic outcome (for a review, see Farber et al., in press), far more research has been conducted on an overlapping construct, that of empathy (for a review, see Horvath, Del Re, Flückiger, & Symonds, 2011)—a more easily defined and assessed variable. Moreover, empirical study of positive regard has generally lagged behind its actual implementation in practice. Practitioners across multiple orientations, especially psychodynamic, have implicitly acknowledged its value by adopting theoretically consistent justifications for its use. They have blended Rogers's ideas about positive regard (and the other facilitative conditions) into their own theoretical perspectives—if typically without attribution (Farber, 2007).

The self-psychology of Heinz Kohut (1984), for example, provides a bridge between psychoanalysis and humanistic psychotherapy (Kahn, 1985). Kohut posited a universal human need for empathy, recognition, attunement, and soothing that, if not met in early life, could lead to profound difficulties in functioning and relationships. In self psychology, the therapy relationship, particularly the ability of the therapist to impart these needs, offers one path to reparation of these early deficits. Kohut's notions of "mirroring," "idealizing," and "twinship" are distinctly self-object terms that nonetheless echo Rogers's sentiments on nonpossessive warmth and prizing in client-centered therapy (Kahn, 1985). Relational psychoanalysis (e.g., Mitchell & Aron, 1999; Wachtel, 2008), with its focus on the cocreated nature of the psychotherapy relationship and the authentic exchange between two subjective individuals, also provides theoretical space for the therapist's provision of positive regard. Existential psychoanalysis, too, emphasizes the therapist's honest provision of interpersonal feedback in the here and now—much of which can be affirming and supportive—as a significant factor in client progress (Yalom, 1980, 2002). Even cognitive–behavioral and other manualized treatments, which tend to implicate specific techniques as the mechanisms of symptomatic improvement, have increasingly recognized the importance of relationship factors like positive regard; in these therapies, the therapist inhabits a reliably affirming and supportive stance as a means to set the stage for a strong working alliance and the implementation of specific, targeted interventions (Beck, Rush, Shaw, & Emery, 1987; Leahy, 2001; Linehan, 2014; Weissman, Markowitz, & Klerman, 2000).

This incorporation of positive regard as a fundamental condition of successful therapy across diverse theoretical orientations belies the fact that few studies have investigated either the specific mechanisms by which positive regard contributes to psychotherapy outcomes or the precise nature of the concept itself. In regard to this latter point, until very recently (e.g., Suzuki & Farber, 2016), virtually no research had addressed the question of the domain of positive regard, that is, investigating what kinds of therapist statements or behaviors fall within its scope, or what forms of therapist-provided positive regard clients find most meaningful or most affirming. The disconnect between research and practice can be explained in part by the difficulty of clearly defining positive regard. Even Rogers's (1957) best attempts to operationalize the construct allow for ample slippage:

> To the extent that the therapist finds himself experiencing a warm acceptance of each aspect of the client's experience as being a part of that client, he is experiencing unconditional positive regard . . . It means that there are no conditions of acceptance, no feeling of "I like you only if you are thus and so." It means a "prizing" of the person, as Dewey has used that term. It is at the opposite pole from a selective evaluating attitude—"You are bad in these ways, good in those." It involves as much feeling of acceptance for the client's expression of negative, "bad," painful, fearful, defensive, abnormal feelings as for his expression of "good," positive, mature, confident, social feelings, as much acceptance of ways in which he is inconsistent as of ways in which he is consistent. It means a caring for the client, but not in a possessive way or in such a way as simply to satisfy the therapist's own needs. It means a caring for the client as a separate person, with permission to have his own feelings, his own experiences. (p. 829)

Rogers's (1957) definition here implies a kind of attitude toward the client. But of course attitudes may have specific behavioral manifestations—and this is where part of the ambiguity lies. In addition, Rogers's initial conceptualization of unconditional positive regard consists of two components: *unconditionality* and *regard*. While conceptually distinct, these components are here inextricably linked, in that the therapist is to convey a warm, positive, and caring response to the client *regardless of* the experiences or attitudes he or she may bring to bear in therapy. Furthermore, Rogers appears to emphasize more heavily the unconditionality component than the regard component, as indicated by sample items he goes on to propose in the same paper: "I feel no revulsion at anything the client says"; "I feel neither approval nor disapproval of the client and his statements—simply acceptance"; "I feel warmly toward the client—toward his weaknesses and problems as well as his potentialities"; "I am not inclined to pass judgment on what the client tells me"; and "I like the client" (Rogers, 1957, p. 829). Of these five proposed items, only one ("I feel warmly towards the client . . .") integrates unconditionality with regard, while three items focus exclusively on unconditionality, and only one item ("I like the client") is keyed to regard alone.

Reflecting the intrinsic duality in Rogers's conception of unconditional positive regard, the research literature has tended to separate these two components. The best validated and most commonly used measure of the facilitative conditions, the Barrett-Lennard Relationship Inventory (BLRI;

Barrett-Lennard, 1962, 2015), utilizes two subscales to assess this overall construct—Level of Regard, "the overall level or tendency of one person's affective response to another," and Unconditionality of Regard, the extent to which "regard . . . is stable, in the sense that it is not experienced as varying with or otherwise dependently linked to particular attributes of the person being regarded" (Barrett-Lennard, 1986, p. 441). Subsequent research found, however, that the Unconditionality of Regard subscale was less reliable and valid than the other three subscales (Barrett-Lennard, 1962; Cramer, 1987); furthermore, its association with expected therapy relationship and outcome variables has been weaker, or not consistent with the associations obtained with the other three subscales (e.g., Cramer, 1987; Handley, 1982; Lanning & Lemons, 1974; Mann & Murphy, 1975; Mills & Zytowski, 1967). As a result, the Unconditionality of Regard subscale has sometimes been excluded in studies using the other three BLRI scales (Level of Regard, Empathic Understanding, and Congruence). Meanwhile, the "Unconditional" specifier has often been dropped from the label of "positive regard," and clinical and research conceptualizations in recent decades have tended to focus more on the "regard" strand of Rogers's operationalization than the "unconditionality" strand.

To summarize, Rogers's ideas about the importance of positive regard have been widely adopted and empirically validated. Despite the fact that many questions remain to be answered regarding the exact nature of positive regard, it seems certain that clients who experience consistent support and caring from their therapist benefit considerably, regardless of the exact form this attitude takes. The case study below is one in which the therapist conveyed his support and caring for his client in multiple ways over the course of a long-term therapy, a seemingly significant factor in the positive outcomes in this case.

CLINICAL CASE STUDY

Carole (a pseudonym), a Caucasian woman from a working-class, Irish American family with divorced parents, was 25 years old when she first presented for psychotherapy.[1] She came to see me (BAF) complaining of persistent anxiety, sleep difficulties, sadness, and bitterness over the recent breakup of her marriage, suicidal thoughts (without a plan), low self-esteem, financial difficulties, and uncertainty regarding career goals. She allowed that she was usually a "moderate" drinker (several glasses of wine and/or bottles of beer

[1]Details of this case example have been altered to protect confidentiality.

each week) and weekend user of marijuana but no other substances; however, she also noted that she occasionally drank to the point of inebriation, and that she had experienced several "blackout bouts" within the past year, including at least two occasions when she woke up the next morning in a strange man's apartment. Carole was a high-school graduate, working full time as a cashier in a local supermarket (a job well below her abilities), and living in a small apartment with two other women with whom she had no prior relationship. She appeared thin, even gaunt, was dressed plainly, and spoke somewhat haltingly and with a somewhat depressed affect, though she answered all my questions and gave a thorough history. That history included a gruesome period during her childhood and early adolescence of being physically and sexually abused by her father, abetted by her mother's inability or unwillingness to intervene. The abuse only ended when her mother, likely also physically abused, left her father, took Carole (her only child) to a new apartment in a new part of the city, and subsequently filed for divorce.

Despite these difficulties, Carole presented then and still does now—8 years, two marriages, several other long-term relationships, and two children later—as intelligent, thoughtful, and psychologically minded, but also as wounded, needy, and fragile. My sense was that she was someone who, paradoxically, was both quite resilient ("I know I will get through this") and constantly in the throes of chaos.

No formal assessment instruments were administered, but my first diagnostic impressions were of a young woman suffering from agitated depression, precipitated by the recent breakup of her marriage and distally influenced by her experiences as an abused child and adolescent. Given this history, as well as current indications of her inability to emotionally self-regulate, I also noted the need to rule out a diagnosis of borderline personality disorder.

Course of Treatment

Whereas early in our work together, in fact for 5 years, Carole came to therapy once or sometimes twice a week (and, according to my notes, missed but two sessions over these years), over the past 3 years, we have met on an as-needed basis—on average meeting once every 2 to 3 weeks. In part, this reflects the fact that Carole is doing better (i.e., has far more control over her life and is less dependent on weekly sessions); in part, it reflects the realities of her having moved a fairly substantial distance from my office.

Our work was and still is primarily integrative, mostly a blend of relational psychodynamic therapy (a contemporary variation of the psychoanalytic approach that I learned in my doctoral program 40 years ago) and client-centered therapy (an approach that I began using clinically and studying empirically about 30 years ago). I've argued elsewhere (Farber, 2007) that these two approaches have a great deal in common, in particular their shared emphasis on the here-and-now connection between therapist and client, the elements of which can be traced back to Rogers's (1957) seminal work on the necessary and sufficient ingredients of effective psychotherapy.

As noted above, Carole was physically and sexually abused by her father during her childhood and adolescence and wore the scars of these acts as so many do—barely ever feeling good enough or that someone could value her. Particularly in the first few months of our work, she shared many of the awful details of her abuse, often with a mixture of tears and intense, even homicidal, anger. Trying somehow to "make sense" of these horrors—including continuous attempts to find a new narrative that emphasized that the abuse was not her fault—occupied a great deal of space in these early sessions. Two other prominent themes were explored in the early stages of our work: the "failure" of her marriage, including the extent to which Carole saw that as her fault; and somewhat relatedly, her inherent "likability." What was entirely clear, almost from the first session on, was that regardless of what we were focused on, Carole was intensely committed to the work of therapy and intensely sensitive to my perceptions of her.

Several other themes emerged over time in our sessions, including our work together, especially the nature of our relationship; her role as mother to her two children; her hobbies (including painting and computer-generated photography); her interpersonal relationships, including her romantic partnerships and friendships; and her work as an administrator in a banking company. Each of these themes (along with those noted earlier, which featured more prominently in the first stages of our work) provided ample opportunities for me to question, clarify, provide advice, self-disclose, empathize, and—most germane to this paper—provide positive regard to Carole.

What follows is an annotated list of the most affirming statements and actions therapists take to demonstrate their positive regard for those with whom they work, as rated by the hundreds of clients, engaging in a variety of forms of therapy, who participated in our research study (Suzuki & Farber, 2016). Each of these items was rated at 3.5 or higher on a 5-point Likert-type scale that assessed client perceptions of how "affirming" each of these therapist-generated behaviors have felt or might feel to them. We then illustrate how each of these was enacted in Carole's therapy.

"My Therapist Offers Me a New Way of Understanding a Part of Myself That I Usually View as a Weakness."

On the one hand, this highest rated item is not a true reflection of Rogers's writings about the essence of positive regard. It is not, strictly speaking, an affirmation of a client's basic worth nor even an acceptance of a client's self-perceived weakness, but rather an attempt to construct a new narrative, a new perspective on an old way of viewing oneself. It is an amalgam of a client-centered attitude with the principles of narrative psychotherapy. On the other hand, there is something about this item that is reminiscent of Rogers's remark to Gloria (Shostrom, 1965) that suggested an alternative, far more positive way of viewing herself.

How did this type of positive regard manifest in my work with Carole? Primarily through reminding her that her efforts to take care of her mother in her old age—at least to a minimal extent—was not a weakness, not a "pathetic response to giving her what she doesn't deserve" (in her words) but rather an indication of her own humanity, of her own hard-earned ability to transcend the experiences and values passed on to her. "In fact," I said to her on more than one occasion words to this effect:

> I respect greatly your finding a compromise between the part of you that doesn't want to care for her at all and your sense that you don't want to act in ways that reflect either her values or those of your father. You've tried hard to be decent, to live up to your own moral values, and though it may irk you to give to her, I suspect there's a piece of you that gives yourself some credit.

Tearfully, Carole nodded in assent.

"My Therapist Shows S/He Is Listening Through Her/His Body Language."

Again, while this is not an action that is noted explicitly in any of Rogers's writings, it is nonetheless consistent with his sense that positive regard is more of an attitude than an action per se. With Carole—as with any client who has been abused—I had to be enormously considerate of the balance between excessive closeness, which can be experienced by the client as threatening, and excessive distance, which can be experienced as rejecting and thus evidence of perceived unworthiness, the antithesis of positive regard.

In general, I tend to err on the side of closeness and certainly did so with Carole. She needed to know that I was fully present and my posture—feet flat on the floor, leaning toward her, and often nodding my head to signal my understanding—indicated as much. She also remarked to me that I grimaced and sometimes shook my head from side to side when she recounted some of the details of her abuse, actions that she noted made her feel that I understood her pain.

"My Therapist Makes a Connection Between My Current Experience and Something I Have Discussed in the Past."

Whereas this action in any therapy is reflective of great attentiveness on the therapist's part, essentially affirming the client's importance, it is far more consistent with the tenets of a psychodynamic approach than a person-centered approach. And while the psychodynamic literature has not emphasized the ways in which making connections between the past and present may lead to perceptions on the client's part of being affirmed, the value of doing so is now empirically indicated.

There was at least one significant aspect of my work with Carole that exemplified how making this kind of connection could lead to her feeling positively regarded. I had the opportunity to point out how her fear of my disappointing her—of not caring enough about her—seemed to be related to similar (and realistic) expectations of her parents' disappointing and hurting her. From a psychodynamic perspective, this is no more or less than a classic transference interpretation; imbued though with a humanistic touch, this kind of remark can have greater emotional resonance.

> I understand why you'd feel like I could disappoint you—other important people in your life have certainly done so—but I'm glad we're talking about this now, I'm glad you can hear this, and I hope we can keep working on this.

In other words: I accept fully that this is happening—it's entirely understandable—and I also believe in your ability to learn from this, to work together, and eventually to see me and others as more trustworthy. To my words, "I hope we can keep working on this," Carole responded, "Yes, somehow, and thanks for believing in me. I know I can be difficult."

"My Therapist Summarizes What I Have Said Accurately."

On the face of it, this item seems far more consistent with Rogers's ideas about empathy, specifically in terms of attempting to understand fully the client's world. But like many actions both inside and outside of therapy, accurate summaries are both empathetic and affirming. The affirming quality contained in this action resides in the therapist's attentiveness to the client's disclosures and may consist of two components: the therapist's ability to accurately reflect discrete comments of his or her client (as per Rogers's tendency); and his or her ability to point out salient, overall themes in a client's life. Future research may help determine which of these components feels most affirming to clients—that is, makes them feel especially important, cared for, and fully accepted. In either case, though, the client comes to believe that the therapist has been listening intently, trying hard to make sense of what most needs to be heard and addressed.

I believe that I was able to do this consistently with Carole. Moreover, she needed me to do this. Having not been heard, or worse, having her words and actions maligned and distorted by her parents, she needed someone whom she respected to accurately summarize—without critical commentary—her thoughts, feelings, and beliefs. This is not to say that during our time working together I always summarized her words or synthesized multiple strands of her narrative with sufficient accuracy. It is to say, though, that when I got it right—"Sounds like no one in your household really listened to you at all or believed in your worth as a human being"; "Winning that high school achievement award was a real turning point in your life"—my interventions made Carole feel valued, respected, and cared for.

"My Therapist Is Understanding if I Need to Cancel/Reschedule."

With so many other items on our survey, it is perhaps somewhat surprising that this action would have been ranked highly in terms of its affirming capacity. Perhaps its value as a form of affirmation can be understood if we view this action as the antithesis of the stereotypical image of therapists as too formal and rule-bound. This action then allows clients to believe they are valuable and worthy enough for their therapist to be flexible in terms of scheduling—to find ways to continue the work, even as obstacles to the work arise.

In fact, on a fairly regular basis—perhaps on average once a month—situations arose in Carole's life (e.g., childcare issues) that occasioned a need on my part to find a new appointment time for us to meet. I chose not to pursue this from a psychodynamic stance. That is, rather than viewing her requests as a form of resistance that needed to be discussed and worked through, I simply accepted them, and we found new times to meet. This did not lead to Carole "taking advantage" of my flexibility by requesting more frequent reschedules. It led instead to her increasing belief that I cared for her and that I could help—though of course this was not a linear pathway.

"My Therapist Remembers the Name or the Details of Someone or Something I Spoke of Long Ago."

When therapists are attentive in this way, they demonstrate their caring and their belief in the importance of their client. They show that their attention is not just focused on what is going on in the immediate moment, as important as that might be, but directed as well to the client's life as a whole.

I remembered some, though certainly not all, of the important figures in Carole's life. I am able, as I imagine most therapists are, to access many of the most important details about clients' immediate family members, children, and many if not all the significant others in their lives. When I didn't remember some details about Carole's life (including figures from her childhood), I would either refer to my notes (especially the family tree I constructed for her, as I do for all my clients, in the first or second session), or I would ask her to remind me of who so-and-so was, and why and how this person was or is important in her life. While not ideal—that is, I wished I was able to remember more details, more people in her life without having to ask—I believe I was able to demonstrate a great deal of positive regard for Carole by remembering a good deal and by pursuing those details I did not remember.

"My Therapist Maintains Eye Contact With Me."

This item is clearly a variation on the earlier noted item regarding the importance of the therapist's body language. Here, the focus is not on body language as a general indication of positive regard but more specifically on the therapist's ability to maintain eye contact per se. While people can "fake it"—that is, look squarely into a person's eyes and still lie or remain essentially disengaged—research indicates that, in general, people who are good at maintaining eye contact are perceived as warmer and more honest. "A looker's frank gaze is widely interpreted as positive regard" (Riggio, 2014).

I attempted with Carole to meet her gaze whenever possible. The problem for me in consistently doing this was that I tend to gaze upward and to my right whenever I'm thinking intently about something. I mention this tendency of mine to my clients and did so with Carole: "I'm listening to what you're saying but sometimes when I'm thinking I look up or stare away. I'm still with you, though." I'd say that this part of my overall interaction with Carole—my ability to maintain eye contact—was affirming to her; nevertheless, this felt like a less critical aspect of her feeling positively regarded by me than some of the more specifically affirming comments or reframing I was able to offer. Still, it may well have added to the overall gestalt of feeling unconditionally regarded and accepted.

"My Therapist Compliments Me on Something I Feel Is a Strength of Mine."

Most of us—whether therapists, clients, or otherwise—greatly enjoy being complimented on a part of ourselves that we feel we good about. Such statements fit or strengthen our self-image. Perhaps in some ways, too, the affirming quality of complimentary statements is related to the theory (e.g., Berglas, 2012) that feeling unappreciated or underappreciated is a nearly ubiquitous phenomenon, one that may lead to significant distress. Whether or not this is true, rarely does a therapist encounter a client, especially someone who has been traumatized early in life, who does not feel affirmed and positively regarded by comments that indicate the therapist is aware of and impressed by some behavior or characteristic that this client has spoken about or displayed in the therapeutic interaction.

Over the years of our work together, I've made the following remarks to Carole, some repeatedly: "You've been the strength of your extended family, you've essentially held it together"; "You have great artistic talent" (after she had brought some of her artwork into session); "You're very gracious"; "You're a very sensitive, loving mother"; "You're remarkably resilient"; "You're quite sensitive"; "That's a very smart way of looking at things"; "That's very kind of you" (following her sending me a condolence card after a death in my family). Her reaction to these and similar complimentary remarks—sometimes smiles, sometimes tears, sometimes simple gratitude—strongly indicated how much this type of positive regard meant to her.

"My Therapist Encourages Me to Take Pride in the Things I Do Well."

This item clearly overlaps with the previous one, again suggestive of the strong affirming quality of the therapist's explicit recognition of the client's strengths. The distinction, of course, is that rather than directly complimenting the client on his or her talents, the therapist in this case entreats the client to do this for him or herself—that is, to be self-affirming.

In this regard, I would often follow up complimenting Carole on something she did well (e.g., a painting of hers she'd show me on her phone; an astute conversation with one of her children) with a plea for her to give herself credit for her ability. "It's easy for me to see that you're a loving parent with really good instincts, but the task is for you to realize this." Over time, I think she began to internalize this to a greater extent. That is, she began to accept the reality that she had many quite admirable attributes and talents and also began to believe more in her own innate goodness.

"My Therapist Speaks to Me in a Gentle Tone of Voice."

This item speaks to the kind of affirmation that comes from paralinguistic cues. What we as therapists say to our clients is what is most often written about in books and journals and talked about in classes and supervision. Yet researchers suggest that up to 70% of what we communicate is through paralanguage. Contrast the paralinguistic cues among the therapy participants in those "Gloria" videos: Rogers's gentle tone of voice distinguishes him greatly from Perls and Ellis. And while immediately after the filming, Gloria appeared to endorse Perls as her therapist of choice, it was Rogers with whom she maintained a decades-long correspondence.

Both by nature and by identifying with Rogers as a therapeutic model, I tend to speak calmly (at least outside the realms of faculty meetings and sporting events). In the terminology of Bion (1962), I believe I function well as a "container" of intense client affect. Many, if not most, of the clients in my part-time practice have been abused as children, and I tend not to get upset or flustered by the occasional therapy-interfering behaviors such clients typically engage in. I suspect that Carole appreciated and perhaps even sometimes was soothed by my tone of voice, though I also suspect that this aspect of any therapist's presentation is inextricably connected to other paralinguistic aspects of a therapist's overall demeanor.

Over time, though certainly not in any linear fashion, my expressions of positive regard began to "take." This may have been a function of my repeated efforts; it may have been a function, too, of the fact that the ways in which I demonstrated my liking and caring for Carole varied greatly over the course of therapy. That is, the particular nature of my positively regarding actions and statements changed both within sessions and over time—a reflection of her needs (and perhaps my moods and needs) at different points of our work together. But Carole increasingly believed my words and actions. In the language of psychodynamic theory, they became ego syntonic, consistent with the changes in the way she viewed herself. That said, it may be important to reiterate that no one technique or attitude can fully explain changes in a client's life, including self-image. My attitude and expressions of positive regard were likely significant contributors to improvements in Carole's life, but they need to be considered in the context of my provision of the other facilitative conditions Rogers (1957) enumerated (i.e., empathy and genuineness/openness) and in the context of my approach to therapy that was not purely Rogerian or otherwise humanistic. That is, there were other "ingredients" thrown in the mix, including the kinds of interpretive comments, challenging questions, and direct suggestions that Rogers typically eschewed.

It's important to note that despite my commitment to maintaining an attitude of positive regard toward Carole, I could not do so unfailingly, nor do I believe that any therapist can do so with any client. Therapists are fallible; many clients, including Carole, are at least occasionally provocative, resistant, or frustrating; and alliance ruptures in long-term therapies are nearly inevitable. At times I erred in not providing strong enough words, quick enough responses, or sufficiently explicit nonverbal cues of attentiveness. One example: my intended compliment for one of Carole's artistic efforts—"that's a nice piece of work"—felt flat and tepid to her and resulted in several sessions' worth of apologies and discussion. A related example: My praise for her artistic efforts led to Carole's sharing such efforts via e-mail attachments, leading in turn to expectations of further attention and then to therapeutic ruptures when I failed to respond with sufficient positive regard in a timely enough manner. A final example: my consistent praise for her increasing degrees of self-acceptance and emotional resilience turned, on several occasions, into a fear on Carole's part that I was preparing her for termination. More generally, and not surprisingly, when I was either "off" (e.g., tired, preoccupied, sick) or when Carole was especially needy and therefore almost entirely refractory to my efforts to be caring and affirming, our clinical work floundered. Trainees in particular should be aware that despite a resolve to consistently demonstrate an attitude of positive regard, clients will not be consistently responsive. Thus, alongside the provision of positive regard, empathy, and other facilitative conditions, clinicians must consistently monitor the extent to which and circumstances under which different clients respond to different forms of their best-intentioned efforts.

Outcome and Prognosis

I consider my work with Carole to be largely successful, a judgment that she herself has often rendered unasked. Indeed, she credits our work with the fact that she is still married and still alive today, though she also has occasionally expressed the thought that this last outcome is very much a mixed blessing. Her life is still sometimes wrought with anxiety, including interpersonal insecurities and fears of abandonment. "Disturbances in the field"—including arguments with friends, family members or coworkers; feeling judged, misunderstood, unappreciated or rejected; and ruptures in our therapeutic relationship—continue to make life occasionally difficult for her, though not nearly as much now as when she first began therapy. These struggles are, of course, inevitable for virtually all of us, but for Carole, they still have the potential to escalate rapidly to despondency, with feelings of hopelessness ("What's the point?") and even occasional suicidal ideation.

Still, Carole's life is far more emotionally regulated, pleasurable, and free of drama now than it was decades ago. She has good, consistent friendships and reciprocally loving relationships with her children. She has a steady job and is well-respected and liked by most of her coworkers at the bank where she's employed in a managerial capacity. She is far less self-deprecating and far more nuanced in her judgments of others; moreover, her suicidal ideation is less frequent and less enduring.

Summary of Mechanisms of Change

It is impossible to determine with any certainty which aspects of therapy are most responsible for therapeutic improvement in any individual case. There are far too many uncontrolled variables and far too much bias on the parts of both client and therapist. Among clinicians themselves, there's still a strong divide between those who believe in the mutative power of specific interventions ("empirically supported treatments") and those who believe it's the therapeutic relationship per se that primarily accounts for therapeutic effectiveness. Moreover, many therapists, especially as they grow more experienced, become more eclectic in their work, thus rendering judgments about what exactly worked for whom extremely tenuous. And even though individual elements of the therapeutic relationship (e.g., empathy, repair of alliance ruptures, therapist disclosure) have been shown to be significantly associated with therapeutic improvement (Norcross, 2011), these associations tend to be modest, with much of the variance in outcome unexplained. Many researchers and clinicians have come to believe that it is some idiographic mix of elements common across therapeutic approaches—including an effective therapeutic alliance; therapist support, care, and empathy; encouragement to clients to try out new behaviors, thoughts, and feelings; emotional release ("catharsis"); and the formulation of new, more adaptive personal "narratives"—that account for therapeutic success in any individual case.

Nevertheless, my sense, one corroborated by Carole, is that the improvements in her life, including her ability to better tolerate ambiguity and uncertainty and to consider herself and others as rich and complex mixtures of both weaknesses and strengths (or, in her words, "problems and talents"), is attributable in great measure to my providing for her over the years a steady stream of positive regard. Importantly, too, these expressions of my positive regard felt quite genuine to me—that is, they reflected an attitude of authentic caring. Expressions of positive regard, like empathetic attunements toward children (Stern, 1985), can exist on a continuum of authenticity, and clients, perhaps especially clients who have been traumatized, can invariably discern such distinctions. The point here, consistent with Rogers's (1957) theorizing, is that ultimately the therapist's provision of positive regard—or for that matter, any of the facilitative conditions—is of little consequence unless and until the client experiences it as such. And I'm convinced that Carole did, at least most of the time, and that it made a difference.

We are thus suggesting that in this case my (BAF's) clinical expressions of positive regard exceeded the "baseline" level of outcome variance that can be attributed to this relational condition. This is hardly a remarkable assertion inasmuch as we imagine that there is considerable variability in the extent to which specific therapeutic attitudes or interventions are manifest in individual therapy cases, even among those who profess to adhere to a single therapeutic tradition. Indeed, one element of "evidence-based treatment" is the clinician's judgment of what works best for a specific client, including those elements of treatment not "officially" validated. In this regard too, we are reminded of Yalom's (1980) comment:

> Formal texts, journal articles, and lectures portray therapy as precise and systematic, with carefully delineated stages, strategic technical interventions, the methodical development and resolution of transference, analysis of object relations, and a careful, rational program of insight-offering interpretations. Yet I believe that when no one is looking, the therapist throws in the "real thing" . . . such qualities as compassion, "presence," caring, extending oneself, touching the patient at a profound level, or—that most elusive one of all—wisdom. (pp. 3–4)

Our specification of positive regard as a primary determinant of treatment effectiveness in this work with Carole, while justifiable in our judgment, is also somewhat simplistic. There were so many other elements of Carole's treatment—psychodynamic interpretations, cognitive–behavioral therapy–like attempts to change self-deprecating self-statements, dialectical behavior therapy–like banter (irreverence), and existentially focused discussions of values and meanings in life, just to name a few. The question of how these interventions (as well as more than a few clinical mistakes and therapeutic ruptures) affected the treatment, and how these interacted with the therapist's consistent adoption of an attitude of positive regard with Carole, remains unknown and essentially unknowable. In a similar vein, we believe that the effect of providing clients with consistent positive regard is actually intensified by the therapist's occasional introduction of other (somewhat non-Rogerian) conditions, including challenges and questioning. In this way, instances of positive regard may be felt as less automatic and perhaps especially genuine. This contention, though, is speculative and would certainly be challenged by those more firmly entrenched in the classic tenets of client-centered therapy. Most fundamentally, what does remain for us is the conviction that for Carole, and likely for others whose early lives leave them desperate for a sense that important others respect and care deeply for them, the therapist's consistent provision of multiple forms of affirmation is a critical and too often underappreciated aspect of psychotherapeutic treatment.

RESEARCH TO PRACTICE AND BACK

The meta-analysis conducted by Farber et al. (in press) indicated that positive regard has a modest positive association (effect size, g = 28) with psychotherapy outcome. The authors noted that, like many other relational variables, positive regard is a significant but not exhaustive part of the process–outcome equation. A meta-analysis, of course, offers an aggregate snapshot of many pairs of associations between variables; individual cases included in the analysis may deviate considerably in terms of the correlation obtained between the variables of interest.

The positive outcome obtained in this case is consistent with the results of this meta-analysis supporting the clinical effectiveness of positive regard. Moreover, the specific and varied ways in which the therapist (BAF) conveyed this attitude toward the client were consistent with the recent research findings of the authors (Suzuki & Farber, 2016). In that study, therapy clients ($N = 540$) were asked to respond to an extensive inventory of possible therapist statements (e.g., "That was brave of you," "I look forward to us talking about this some more") and actions (e.g., "My therapist laughs at a funny comment I make," "My therapist summarizes what I have said accurately"), rating first how *affirming* it might feel for each to take place in their therapy, and next rating how *likely* each given statement or action would be, coming from their therapist.

These data were subjected to a principal components analysis, the results of which suggested that positive regard (or "affirmation," the more easily comprehensible stand-in term used in this study), can be seen as consisting of a few distinct dimensions. The first factor extracted, Supportive/Caring Statements, consisted of *statements* such as "I'm glad you shared that with me," "This is a space for your own healing and growth," and "That must have been very difficult." The second factor, Unique Responsiveness, consisted of therapist *actions* that reflect attentiveness and sensitivity to the client's history and needs; representative items here included "My therapist summarizes what I have said accurately," and "My therapist remembers the name/details of someone or something I have discussed in the past." Finally, the third factor that emerged, Intimacy/Disclosure, included therapist *actions* that represent extensions of the typical boundaries that exist in the therapeutic relationship, for example, "My therapist puts his/her hand on my shoulder," "My therapist has tears in his/her eyes as I relate a sad story," and "My therapist hugs me."

Additional analyses indicated that among these three factors, therapist behaviors falling under the category of Unique Responsiveness are both the most potentially affirming to clients and also the most likely to occur in therapy. A therapist's unique responsiveness can be manifest through reflective listening, empathetic comments, accurate recall of previously shared information, interpretations, support, and positive feedback—all of which reflect a sense of truly knowing the client. The items comprising the Supportive and Caring Statements factor seemingly reflect less personal understanding than items within the Unique Responsiveness factor but nonetheless are also able to effectively convey a sense of reassurance and prizing; taken together, the items on this factor were endorsed by clients as high in affirming quality and high on likelihood of occurrence in therapy—though in both cases, somewhat less so than for Unique Responsiveness. Important too, is that both these factors correlated significantly with the BLRI Level of Regard subscale, as well as with a measure reflective of the strength of the therapeutic relationship, the Working Alliance Inventory Short-Form (Tracey & Kokotovic, 1989).

Unlike the other two factors, items from the third factor (Intimacy/Disclosure), reflecting instances of therapist boundary extensions, were rated low in their affirming potential as well as in their likelihood of occurring in therapy. Furthermore, greater likelihood of therapist Intimacy/Disclosure behaviors in this study was associated with lower BLRI ratings of positive regard. Boundaries are an important component of any therapeutic relationship (Gutheil & Gabbard, 1998), and clients may be as keen as therapists themselves to preserve them (Johnston & Farber, 1996). In one sense, then, these results are unsurprising. However, the literature suggests that certain boundary extensions, especially therapist self-disclosures, can be important tools for client progress, as long as they are applied sparingly and with careful consideration of the client's needs and issues (Henretty & Levitt, 2010; Knox & Hill, 2003). Our ongoing research, including a qualitative study, will aim to clarify the contexts in which therapist expressions of intimacy and disclosure are experienced by clients as reflective of positive regard or as antithetical to this feeling.

Our research also investigated which specific therapist expressions of positive regard were considered by clients to be most potent (i.e., most affirming), as well as which were perceived as most likely to occur in their therapy. The most affirming items—all noted earlier in the section on course of treatment—were thematically diverse, including promotion of self-acceptance ("My therapist offers me a new way of understanding a part of myself that I usually view as a weakness"), nonverbal indications of active listening ("My therapist shows s/he is listening through her/his body language"), provision of insight ("My therapist makes a connection between my current experience and something I have discussed in the past"), reflective listening ("My therapist summarizes what I have said accurately"), and flexibility in scheduling ("My therapist is understanding if I need to cancel/reschedule"). Notably too, the top five most highly rated items in regard to likelihood of occurrence were all therapist *actions* and again spanned different domains, including eye contact ("My therapist maintains eye contact with me"), tone of voice ("My therapist speaks to me in a gentle tone of voice"), flexibility in scheduling ("My therapist is understanding if I need to cancel/reschedule"), nonverbal indications of active listening ("My therapist shows s/he is listening through her/his body language"), and promotion of self-esteem ("My therapist encourages me to take pride in the things I do well").

These findings suggest that from the client's perspective, positive regard is a wide-ranging construct, and that therapists have at their disposal multiple means of demonstrating this attitude. Undoubtedly, the frequency and perceived intensity (potency) of these actions and statements differ considerably across therapeutic dyads and even within the same therapeutic dyad over the course of a single session or treatment.

PRACTICE IMPLICATIONS AND RECOMMENDATIONS FOR CLINICIANS AND SUPERVISORS

Not only do studies indicate that therapists' provision of positive regard is mutative—that is, significantly associated with therapeutic effectiveness—but the emerging data reveal that this general attitude can be conveyed effectively in a great variety of ways. Clinicians, we believe, can and should offer positive regard to their clients in both instinctual and carefully considered ways, emanating in either case from a basic attitude of acceptance and affirmation. Our sense, in part based on the data, is that most clinicians already do so; that is, as part of their focus on developing an effective working relationship early in the treatment, clinicians are engaging in the kinds of behaviors that fall within the broad range of a positively regarding attitude, and their clients perceive and are affected positively by this attitude.

That said, we also believe there is room in most therapists' practices for more of a good thing. While, as noted above, virtually every school of therapy has endorsed the importance of an effective working alliance, and while most therapists have implicitly adopted a positively regarding stance toward their clients in the service of developing that good relationship, we suspect that many therapists are still somewhat reluctant to explicitly and/or consistently affirm and support their clients. That reluctance may be a vestige of clinical training that still privileges therapeutic boundaries and the adoption of a strict "professional" stance; it may reflect a hesitancy to adopt a stance that is so closely associated with a client-centered approach; or it may be that some clinicians hold to the notion that explicit affirmation colludes with clients' defenses, essentially accepting rather than challenging maladaptive or ineffective thoughts, feelings, or patterns of behavior. While excessive praise or affirmation may, in fact, be unproductive or even undermine change with certain clients, we contend that there is far greater danger in withholding this primarily helpful attitude. So many of our clients, regardless of diagnosis, struggle with issues of self-esteem or with feelings of "demoralization" (Frank & Frank, 1991). They need to feel our support and caring for them in order to ultimately internalize a sense of being good enough. Thus, we recommend that therapists across all theoretical orientations and all levels of experience adopt multiple ways of demonstrating their positive regard for their clients, adjusting their choices in accord with their clients' responses. Consistent with this perspective, we recommend that supervisors support and promote beginning therapists' efforts to find the most comfortable and effective ways of demonstrating their positive regard for their clients.

REFERENCES

Barrett-Lennard, G. T. (1962). Dimensions of therapist response as causal factors in therapeutic change. *Psychological Monographs: General and Applied*, *76*, 1–36. http://dx.doi.org/10.1037/h0093918

Barrett-Lennard, G. T. (1986). The Relationship Inventory now: Issues and advances in theory, method, and use. In L. S. Greenberg & W. M. Pinsof (Eds.), *The psychotherapeutic process: A research handbook* (pp. 439–476). New York, NY: Guilford Press.

Barrett-Lennard, G. T. (2015). *The Relationship Inventory: A complete resource and guide.* Chichester, England: Wiley.

Beck, A. T., Rush, A. J., Shaw, B. F., & Emery, G. (1987). *Cognitive therapy of depression.* New York, NY: Guilford Press.

Bergin, A. E., & Garfield, S. L. (1994). *Handbook of psychotherapy and behavior change* (4th ed.). New York, NY: Wiley.

Berglas, S. (2012, May 29). Do you feel underappreciated? You're only 5 (small) steps away from ending the pain. *Forbes.com*. Retrieved from http://www.forbes.com/sites/stevenberglas/2012/05/29/do-you-feel-underappreciated-youre-only-5-small-steps-away-from-ending-the-pain/#5d387d4f2877

Bion, W. R. (1962). *Learning from experience.* London, England: William Heinemann.

Breger, L. (2009). *A Dream of undying fame: How Freud betrayed his mentor and invented psychoanalysis.* New York, NY: Basic Books.

Cramer, D. (1987). Self-esteem, advice-giving and facilitative nature of close personal relationships. *Person-Centered Review, 2*, 99–110. Retrieved from http://psycnet.apa.org/record/1989-25840-001

Daniels, D. (2014). Permanently cheated—Part I. *Contemporary Psychotherapy, 6.* Retrieved from http://www.contemporarypsychotherapy.org/volume-6-no-1-summer-2014/permanently-cheated/

Farber, B. A. (2007). On the enduring and substantial influence of Carl Rogers' not-quite necessary nor sufficient conditions. *Psychotherapy, 44*, 289–294. http://dx.doi.org/10.1037/0033-3204.44.3.289

Farber, B. A., & Doolin, E. M. (2011). Positive regard and affirmation. In J. C. Norcross (Ed.), *Psychotherapy relationships that work: Evidence-based responsiveness* (2nd ed., pp. 168–186). New York, NY: Oxford University Press. http://dx.doi.org/10.1093/acprof:oso/9780199737208.003.0008

Farber, B. A., Suzuki, J. Y., & Lynch, D. (in press). Positive regard and affirmation. In J. Norcross and M. Lambert (Eds.), *Psychotherapy relationships that work* (3rd ed.). New York, NY: Oxford University Press.

Frank, J. D., & Frank, J. B. (1991). *Persuasion & healing: A comparative study of psychotherapy* (3rd ed.). Baltimore, MD: Johns Hopkins University Press.

Gutheil, T. G., & Gabbard, G. O. (1998). Misuses and misunderstandings of boundary theory in clinical and regulatory settings. *The American Journal of Psychiatry, 155*, 409–414. http://dx.doi.org/10.1176/ajp.155.3.409

Handley, P. (1982). Relationship between supervisors' and trainees' cognitive styles and the supervision process. *Journal of Counseling Psychology, 29*, 508–515. http://dx.doi.org/10.1037/0022-0167.29.5.508

Henretty, J. R., & Levitt, H. M. (2010). The role of therapist self-disclosure in psychotherapy: A qualitative review. *Clinical Psychology Review, 30*, 63–77. http://dx.doi.org/10.1016/j.cpr.2009.09.004

Horvath, A. O., Del Re, A. C., Flückiger, C., & Symonds, D. (2011). Alliance in individual psychotherapy. *Psychotherapy, 48*, 9–16. http://dx.doi.org/10.1037/a0022186

Johnston, S. H., & Farber, B. A. (1996). The maintenance of boundaries in psychotherapeutic practice. *Psychotherapy, 33*, 391–402. http://dx.doi.org/10.1037/0033-3204.33.3.391

Kahn, E. (1985). Heinz Kohut and Carl Rogers: A timely comparison. *American Psychologist, 40*, 893–904. http://dx.doi.org/10.1037/0003-066X.40.8.893

Knox, S., & Hill, C. E. (2003). Therapist self-disclosure: Research-based suggestions for practitioners. *Journal of Clinical Psychology, 59*, 529–539. http://dx.doi.org/10.1002/jclp.10157

Kohut, H. (1984). *How does analysis cure?* Chicago, IL: University of Chicago Press. http://dx.doi.org/10.7208/chicago/9780226006147.001.0001

Lanning, W. L., & Lemons, S. L. (1974). Another look at the factor structure of the Barrett-Lennard Relationship Inventory. *Measurement & Evaluation in Guidance, 6*, 228–231. Retrieved from http://psycnet.apa.org/record/1974-20059-001

Leahy, R. (2001). *Overcoming resistance in cognitive therapy*. New York, NY: Guilford Press.

Linehan, M. (2014). *DBT skills training manual* (2nd ed.). New York, NY: Guilford Press.

Mann, B., & Murphy, K. C. (1975). Timing of self-disclosure, reciprocity of self-disclosure, and reactions to an initial interview. *Journal of Counseling Psychology, 22*, 304–308. http://dx.doi.org/10.1037/h0076694

Mills, D. H., & Zytowski, D. G. (1967). Helping relationship: A structural analysis. *Journal of Counseling Psychology, 14*, 193–197. http://dx.doi.org/10.1037/h0024480

Mitchell, S. A., & Aron, L. (1999). *Relational psychoanalysis: Vol. 1. The emergence of a tradition*. New York, NY: Routledge/Taylor & Francis Group.

Norcross, J. C. (Ed.) (2011). *Psychotherapy relationships that work: Evidence-based responsiveness* (2nd ed.). New York, NY: Oxford University Press.

Riggio, R. E. (2014, April 3). 5 secret powers of eye contact: Surprising reasons why the eyes always have it [Web log post]. *Psychology Today*. Retrieved from https://www.psychologytoday.com/us/blog/cutting-edge-leadership/201404/5-secret-powers-eye-contact

Rogers, C. R. (1957). The necessary and sufficient conditions of therapeutic personality change. *Journal of Consulting and Clinical Psychology, 21*, 95–103. Retrieved from http://citeseerx.ist.psu.edu/viewdoc/download?doi=10.1.1.587.7605&rep=rep1&type=pdf

Rogers, C. R. (1959). A theory of therapy, personality, and interpersonal relationships as developed in the client-centered framework. In S. Koch, (Ed.), *Psychology: A study of a science: Vol. 3. Formulations of the person and the social context* (pp. 184–256). New York, NY: McGraw-Hill.

Rogers, C. R. (1961). *On becoming a person: A therapist's view of psychotherapy.* Boston, MA: Houghton Mifflin.

Shostrom, E. L. (Producer) (1965). *Three approaches to psychotherapy (Part I)* [Film]. Orange, CA: Psychological Films.

Stern, D. (1985). *The interpersonal world of the infant: A view from psychoanalysis and developmental psychology*. New York, NY: Basic Books.

Suzuki, J. Y., & Farber, B. A. (2016). Toward greater specificity of the concept of positive regard. *Person-Centered and Experiential Psychotherapies, 15,* 263–284. http://dx.doi.org/10.1080/14779757.2016.1204941

Tracey, T. J., & Kokotovic, A. M. (1989). Factor structure of the Working Alliance Inventory. *Psychological Assessment: A Journal of Consulting and Clinical Psychology, 1,* 207–210. http://dx.doi.org/10.1037/1040-3590.1.3.207

Wachtel, P. L. (2008). *Relational theory and the practice of psychotherapy*. New York, NY: Guilford Press.

Weissman, M. M., Markowitz, J. C., & Klerman, G. L. (2000). *Comprehensive guide to interpersonal psychotherapy*. New York, NY: Basic Books.

Yalom, I. (2002). *The gift of psychotherapy: An open letter to a new generation of therapists and their patients*. New York, NY: HarperCollins.

Yalom, I. D. (1980). *Existential psychotherapy*. New York, NY: Basic Books.

10

EMPATHY AND RESPONSIVENESS IN EMOTION-FOCUSED THERAPY

JEANNE C. WATSON

Emotion-focused therapy (EFT) emphasizes the delicate balance between leading and following. Rooted in client-centered psychotherapy with its emphasis on the therapeutic relationship, EFT stresses the importance of empathic attunement and understanding as well as acceptance of the client's inner world to facilitate changes in clients' emotion schemes and emotional processing, as well as their relationships with self and others. Embedded within the relationship conditions of empathy, acceptance, congruence, and prizing, EFT therapists offer process guiding techniques to focus clients on problematic aspects of emotional experience. These techniques include increasing clients' awareness of their emotions; facilitating the labeling and differentiation of emotional experience; identifying negative ways of relating to self and regulating experience including dismissing, avoiding, and silencing it; and learning new ways to express their emotions and meet their

http://dx.doi.org/10.1037/0000093-011
Developing the Therapeutic Relationship: Integrating Case Studies, Research, and Practice, O. Tishby and H. Wiseman (Editors)

needs. These processes must be harmonized and integrated into treatments tailored to fit each client's problem set and way of working in therapy.

EFT therapists try to be fully present in their interactions with clients, providing warmth, empathic attunement, and acceptance along with being congruent and transparent. These characteristics are seen as providing a restorative relationship, fostering clients' growth and healing to enable them to overcome distress, develop their capacities for more optimal affect regulation, and transform their relationships with self and others (Greenberg & Watson, 2005; Watson & Greenberg, 2017). Therapists in EFT communicate acceptance and understanding of their clients' experiences by reflecting and providing a mirror to their clients of their inner subjective experiences as well as their ways of being in the world. Empathic reflections are offered tentatively to communicate that clients are the experts on their experience—including the goals and tasks that are seen as optimal at any one time. EFT therapists try to be optimally responsive to their clients as they provide structure and support to facilitate clients' emotional processing and regulation and the development of new ways of relating to self and other. In this chapter, the focus will be on therapists' empathic attunement and responsiveness in the context of a healing therapeutic relationship characterized by presence, empathy, warmth, acceptance and congruence to address a client's problems with affect regulation and hypertension.

THEORETICAL BASE

Research on therapists' empathy reveals that it is an essential component of successful therapy across all modalities (Elliott, Bohart, Watson, & Greenberg, 2011; Norcross & Wampold, 2011). However, in many approaches empathy is viewed as an essential background condition that facilitates the implementation of more active interventions and techniques to facilitate change. In contrast, in EFT empathy and the other relationship conditions are viewed as *active ingredients of change*. Empathic reflections serve four important functions, including (a) establishing a positive working alliance to facilitate the work of psychotherapy, (b) deconstructing clients' internal perspectives and subjective worldviews, (c) facilitating affect regulation, and (d) developing more positive introjects to develop a stronger and more resilient sense of self (Watson, 2001, 2015).

The Interpersonal Function of Empathy

Empathic attunement and responsiveness develops and maintains a positive therapeutic alliance in therapy enabling therapists to understand their clients' goals and negotiate the tasks of therapy. Being attuned, therapists are better able to tailor their interventions and be more responsive to their clients' concerns as they monitor their interactions with clients and modify their responses to tailor their treatments. Being sensitive to the impact of their interventions and to the overall quality of the alliance, empathetic therapists are alert for ruptures as well as moment-to-moment shifts in the relationship during a session and over the course of therapy. Therapists' presence, empathy, and acceptance create conditions of safety that facilitate clients' exploration of their problems and their emotional experiences. The conditions help clients to turn their attention inward, confident that their therapists are following along attentively with respect and prizing as clients begin to examine aspects of their experience that has been denied or remained unsymbolized. In the process, clients apprehend their implicit experience, putting it into words to inform their understanding of themselves and the world.

The Deconstructive Function of Empathy

EFT therapists offer reflections of their clients' experience in a tentative and probing manner, communicating that clients are the experts on their own experience and encouraging them to check and evaluate what they are saying against an inner felt sense to determine its fit and accuracy. Thus empathic reflections help to deconstruct clients' worldviews and assumptions about self and others, sometimes referred to as the hermeneutic aspect of empathy (Keil, 1996; Watson & Greenberg, 1998). As clients' feelings, perceptions, ways of being, and worldviews are reflected, their implicit knowledge and experience is accessed and their meanings and intentions become visible. The subjectivity of their perceptions is revealed. This opens up alternative worldviews and ways of behaving as clients become more hypothetical in their formulations of events thereby increasing their degrees of freedom.

The Affect-Regulating Function of Empathy

Empathic reflections serve to process and regulate emotions. They modulate the intensity of feelings and soothe clients in moments of distress. Clients who come to therapy are often experiencing acute and chronic conditions related to dysregulation in their affective systems. Empathic responding in the context of an accepting, congruent and prizing relationship begins to help clients regulate their emotions both within the session and in the longer term. Effective emotional processing begins with awareness and labeling of feelings, so that clients can reflect on them to understand the impact of events and identify what they need to protect and nourish themselves. The expression and symbolization of emotions acts to contain and moderate them in much the same way that rating them on a scale of 1 to 10 has been observed to do.

The important role of interpersonal experiences in the development of affect regulation is recognized by social, developmental, and neuropsychologists (DeSteno, Gross, & Kubzansky, 2013; Feshbach, 1997; Schore, 2003; van der Kolk, 1994, 1996, 2005). Early attachment experiences with primary caretakers play a pivotal role in the development and acquisition of affect regulation capacities (Schore, 2003; Siegel, 2012). In interaction with caregivers, human beings learn to process and regulate their emotional experience—attend to and label it and develop ways to modulate and express it optimally for their own well-being. In addition, there is a sense of relief and comfort when we feel understood, especially when experiencing intense and painful emotions.

Strengthening Self and Developing Positive Introjects

Listening to their clients, and attending to and accepting their experience, EFT therapists model positive ways of being with their clients' experience. Barrett-Lennard (1997) referred to this as the development of self-empathy. As clients learn to attend to their emotions, label them, and accept them, they acquire self-compassion. Clients internalize their therapists' attitudes and develop positive, nurturing introjects and ways of responding to themselves that are affirming, accepting, protective, and soothing and that contribute to changes in their own self-concepts. In the process, they become less judgmental of themselves and their experiences and more self-confident. (Barrett-Lennard, 1997; Bozarth, 2001; Rogers, 1975; Watson, 2001, 2015).

Therapists' empathetic understanding of clients develops over the course of therapy. Empathy requires therapists to understand their clients both intellectually and emotionally, as they try to grasp the range of meanings and feelings expressed by their clients as well as the implications and impact of events (Watson, 2015). Intellectual understanding is insufficient—it allows only comprehension of the surface meaning of what clients are sharing and not the full significance of events that guide their perceptions and reactions moment to moment. In sum, empathetic therapists distill the essence of clients' experiences (Bohart & Greenberg, 1997).

In EFT, clients are encouraged and supported to focus on the pain that is at the root of their distress. To effectively support clients' processing of painful experiences, empathetic therapists recognize clients' proximal zones of development (Vygotsky, 1978) in terms of their capacity to regulate affect, their capacity to represent their experience, and their self-structure. For example, clients may be unable to attend to their emotional experience, if they do not have a coherent narrative or adequate construction of what is currently contributing or has contributed to their distress. Clients who have not adequately processed and assimilated their experiences may need to develop a coherent life narrative before they will be more ready to focus on the impact of specific events and see how they learned to process and regulate their emotional experience. Therapists can facilitate the process by attuning to the primary task, which is the focus of clients' attention at different points in therapy. At times, clients may be more focused on making sense of their experience, at others on learning to process their emotional experience, and at yet others developing the capacity for empathy toward self and others in order to transform their relationships and self-structures. Each of these tasks supports clients to become more agentic and differentiated. Some clients may have to address all three tasks while others may need to focus on only one or two. The more negative and traumatic clients' early experiences, the less likely they are to develop adequate representations of their life history, adequate emotional processing capacities, or positive self-structures. A healing therapeutic relationship provides the context for clients to work on these tasks. However, some clients may not have the capacity to receive therapists' empathy and acceptance initially and may have to build this capacity over the course of therapy, as they experience their therapists' responsiveness and resulting physiological transformations and internalize therapists' empathy, acceptance, and care.

CLINICAL CASE

Presenting Problems and Patient Description

Edwin, who was 58 years of age, presented with depression and dangerously high blood pressure.[1] He was unable to take medication to remediate his blood pressure because of other medications he was taking and thus was actively seeking alternatives to lower his blood pressure as well as his stress levels. Before he began therapy, he was diagnosed with major depressive disorder on Axis I; no diagnosis on Axis II; hypertension and diabetes on Axis III; problems with his primary support group manifesting in marital discord on Axis IV; and some social and occupational problems on Axis V, characterized by few social supports and problems transitioning to retirement. From the beginning, the client formed a good alliance with his therapist. He would comment often in the session that he appreciated her concern and that speaking with her was helpful. The experience reminded him of time spent with his mother, in whom he had been able to confide after suffering

[1]Details of this case example have been altered to protect confidentiality.

debilitating injuries in a car accident when he was young. His ratings on the Working Alliance Inventory (WAI; Horvath & Greenberg, 1989) ranged from 5.33 to 7, with an average of 6.4 to 7 over the course of therapy. It is notable that after Session 8, the client's score on the WAI dropped from 6.83 to 6.08, suggesting a rupture in the session. A review of the session showed that the client had begun to question a previously accepted way of coping and was feeling less confident about the tasks and goals of therapy. This uncertainty was resolved the following session, after which his scores rose to previous levels with a peak of 7 at Sessions 14 and 16.

On a measure of Client Task Specific Change (Watson, Greenberg, Rice, & Gordon, 1998), a self-report questionnaire that asks clients to rate the types of changes they are experiencing in therapy (e.g., whether they see a significant other in a new way, or feel less self-critical), the client reported moderate to high change after each session. The scores on change increased from an average of 5.38 on a 7-point scale in the first quartile to 6.36 in the last quartile. This indicates that the client was experiencing changes in how he viewed himself, that he was resolving difficulties with significant others, and viewing himself with more compassion.

Initial Interviews and Case Formulation

Edwin felt trapped and burdened in his marriage and was filled with regret that many of his dreams would not be realized. After giving birth to their third child, his wife suffered a psychotic breakdown. Subsequently, she suffered from extreme mood swings and was unable to care for her family or work outside the home. Strong cultural values prevented Edwin from hospitalizing her for fear of bringing shame on the family, particularly his children, of whom he was very protective. He had shielded them from their mother's illness and mood swings when they were growing up.

As Edwin and his wife had emigrated from Vietnam over 30 years previously, they were without extended family to help them cope with his wife's illness. Life was lonely as he struggled to care for his wife and three children. In spite of the pressures at home, he was successful at work, which provided him with relief from the stresses at home. He enjoyed interacting with his colleagues and missed this social interaction after he retired. He observed that he had very little time as he juggled work and family. But now that the children were grown and pursuing their own lives and he had retired, he had time to assess his current life situation and think about the future. He had dreamed that he would pursue his hobbies, reconnect with friends, and travel in retirement. However, his life had become narrowly focused on caring for his wife, as he was fearful that she would injure herself or someone else. He had become a loner—his social circle was constricted and he felt unable to socialize with his wife. She refused to travel and he did not want to leave her alone. He saw his life as meaningless, without joy or fulfillment. Although he contemplated leaving the marriage, he was reluctant to do so; instead, he continued to hope that his wife's condition would improve and that she would recover.

The primary emotion schemes that operated for Edwin were intense sadness, loneliness, and shame. An important theme in Edwin's life was stepping up and assuming the care of others, often at the expense of his own needs and desires. As an oldest son, he had had to assume responsibility for his siblings after his father died, becoming the head of the family as a teenager to support his mother. He gave up going to university and instead went to work in his father's business. He recalled that his mother was warm and supportive. She was appreciative of his efforts, and they had a good relationship. She provided emotional support and guidance, as he would consult with her about the business and they would make decisions together.

The pattern of assuming responsibility for others' well-being at his own expense continued into his marriage. He recalled that when he first met his wife, she had turned to him for support and comfort to deal with difficult members of her own family. In retrospect, he felt duped by his in-laws and was angry that they did not reveal that some family members suffered from intense mood swings. He silenced and suppressed his feelings, keeping them out of awareness. He did not express them to others and was not able to use them as a guide to his needs and goals. However, he was resentful and angry at his wife's condition and easily became frustrated and angry when he perceived her as being out of control and imprudent.

Course of Treatment

Over the course of therapy, Edwin became aware of how his feelings of anger impacted his blood pressure and hypertension. In the first three sessions, the therapist worked to establish a safe working alliance and negotiate a focus for the treatment. As this was a short-term treatment of 16 sessions, it was important to establish agreement on the tasks and goals early in therapy to try to ensure a positive outcome. The client responded well and engaged in therapy, recalling how he had been able to speak with his mother before his marriage. He had found their interaction to be very soothing and comforting, and this positive experience likely colored his experience of the therapeutic relationship. Initially, the client focused on his feelings of being trapped by his wife's condition. He was torn between staying in the marriage and leaving. Part of him wished he could leave, so that he could pursue his interests and enjoy his retirement years. At first, the therapist felt daunted by the client's goal to reduce his blood pressure and hypertension. Focusing on the client's depression, she framed the treatment around the client's conflict about his marriage and the extent to which he silenced his emotions and needs. Thus, an early focus in the treatment was how he could take better care of himself. In Session 2, the therapist observed that Edwin's needs tended to get lost as he focused on caring for others. The client agreed that it was important to try to find a way to balance his needs with those of others. To the therapist's surprise and relief, in Session 3 the client reported a significant decrease in blood pressure over the previous week. However, although he was relieved, he still felt sad and hopeless about his wife's condition. He felt intense social pressure to care for her and was committed to supporting his daughters. He spent a lot of time helping with his grandchildren, who were a source of joy and pride.

In the following sessions, the client began to access and explore his feelings of sadness and despair about his wife's condition. He still hoped that her condition would improve, so things could be different. As it was, her behavior made him angry, particularly when he perceived her as stubborn and she refused to be guided by him. As he began to examine his marriage, Edwin explored how he had arrived at this point in his life. He became aware of his feelings and expressed them as he processed his emotions of sadness, anger, hopelessness, and grief. He longed for a close loving relationship with a supportive other in whom he could confide and was worried about growing old and being unable to care for his wife or having to be cared for by her.

To address his conflicted feelings about his marriage, the therapist suggested a two-chair dialogue in Session 6. The client explored the two sides of his conflict, the side that wanted to flee and the other side that said he must stay. The part that wanted to flee, expressed how fatigued he was and how burdened and exhausted he felt from monitoring his wife's behavior. He also shared how disappointed he was that his life had not turned out as he had dreamed. He had hoped things would be easier in Canada, and that he and his wife would be part of the Vietnamese community. He wanted to return home to visit relatives in his country of origin. In contrast, speaking from the side that said he must stay in the marriage, he expressed his deep commitment to caring for his children. He was concerned that if he left his marriage, the burden of caring for his wife would fall to his daughters. He did not want them to be overburdened. In Session 7 he continued to explore his conflicting feelings as he recognized that he needed to regroup and do things differently. He realized that walking away from his marriage at this stage would negate all that he had worked for over the last 20 years. His life's project would be destroyed. He recognized that he had devoted his life to caring for his children and felt good about how well they were doing. He took great joy and pride in their accomplishments and enjoyed helping his daughters with his grandchildren. After this session, to his therapist's surprise, he reaffirmed the choices that he had made and began to feel more positive.

At this juncture, his therapist was confronted with the importance of his values to protect his children and shield them from the disgrace of their mother's illness and the dissolution of the family unit. She realized that she needed to attune and shift her focus so that the client could find a different balance within his current context that would not take such a significant toll on him physically. Stepping back and heeding the client's direction, the therapist began to focus on Edwin's anger at his wife's behavior. His therapist suggested that it was damaging to his health and well-being for him to be angry all the time. Edwin observed that he became angry when his wife argued with him or contradicted him. He was very worried about how she spent their money. He recalled that his daughter had advised him to let go of his worries and concerns, but he said that was impossible. Other things that angered him were when she left the water running so that it overflowed or put a pot on the stove and let it boil over. Exploring these situations, the client realized how much he bottled his feelings in an attempt to avoid conflict with his wife. He began to see how this was affecting his health. It became clear that his anger was partly fueled by his wish that his wife's condition would improve. Her erratic behavior scared him and made him feel that she was out of control. Thus, he was disappointed and frustrated by any sign of his wife's condition.

The therapist suggested that together they needed to work to find a way that Edwin could accept and come to terms with his wife's condition so that he did not feel angry all the time. His therapist highlighted how at risk he was by continuing to be angry with his wife and not expressing his feelings. Edwin agreed that something had to shift if he was to regulate his blood pressure. After this session the client's score on the WAI dropped a little. This was in contrast to the previous session when his scores had been very high with each item receiving a score of 7 on a 7-point scale. An examination of the transcript revealed that the client felt uncertain about how to tackle his problem and change his perspective. Notwithstanding the drop in the alliance score, the client returned to the next session saying that his blood pressure had dropped dramatically and that he felt lighter and freer.

To help him process his disappointment and frustration with his wife's condition, the therapist suggested an empty chair dialogue with his wife in the following week in, Session 9. During the dialogue, Edwin expressed his anger, sorrow, and disappointment with their life since she became ill. After he assumed his wife's perspective, he realized that she was not responsible for her actions and that her condition was not going to improve. With this shift in perspective, Edwin was able to empathize with his wife and accept that she would not recover. Letting go of his dream of her recovery, he began to focus instead on devising solutions to some of the problems her behaviors caused. For example, he decided to make some changes to the house so that she would not injure herself if she forgot to turn off the stove or left a tap running. After this session, he felt more upbeat and energetic.

This was a major turning point in the therapy that resulted in dramatic physiological changes with respect to his blood pressure readings. Edwin acknowledged how he suppressed his emotions and recognized that he needed to express them more. He noted that while he had tried to suppress his anger only, what happened was that all his feelings were silenced. He resolved to express his feelings and felt more entitled to share when he was angry or sad. Subsequently, he focused on his grief at losing his mother. He recalled how much he valued speaking with her and how comforting she had been. Over the next few sessions, Edwin continued to explore his feelings of sadness and frustration. He resolved to stop worrying and to relax more, as he began to explore ways of pursuing his hobbies and seek short-term relief from caring for his wife with the help of his daughters. He also reconnected with the Vietnamese community and together with his wife planned to entertain a number of friends at home. He recognized that he needed to seek connection and support from a variety of different sources, observing that instead of looking to one person to meet all his needs, it would be better to get a little support from a number of different people, "like little streams feeding a big river," to sustain him over the next phase of his life.

Outcome and Prognosis

The client's physical and psychological functioning improved substantially over the course of treatment. His depression remitted significantly, with his scores on the Beck Depression Inventory (BDI; Beck, Steer, & Brown, 1996) dropping from 23 to 7 at the termination of therapy. Further support that the client had benefited from treatment and made significant changes was provided by his score on the Symptom Checklist-90–Revised (Derogatis, Lipman, & Covi, 1973; Derogatis, Rickels, & Rock, 1976), a 90-item, self-report questionnaire that is used to measure general psychological distress including psychological and physical symptoms. Edwin's score dropped from .41 at the beginning of treatment to .04 at the end.

Additional changes were noted on the Depressive Experiences Questionnaire (Blatt, D'Afflitti, & Quinlan, 1976), a measure of self-criticism, neediness, and dependency. These constructs have been found to be highly related to depression, with the client showing a significant decline on the self-criticism scale and a significant increase in self-efficacy. This suggests that the client became more accepting of himself over the course of therapy, becoming less perfectionistic and bound by excessively high standards. Instead he became more forgiving and tolerant of himself and his wife. He also felt more effective in dealing with his wife and her behavior and validated his life choices, seeing them as important to the stability and well-being of his family.

However, the client did not change on all the outcome measures. There was no significant change on the Rosenberg Self-Esteem Inventory (Rosenberg, 1965), a 10-item self-report measure that evaluates clients' self-esteem. Nor were there changes on the Dysfunctional Attitudes Scale (Weissman & Beck, 1978), a 40-item self-report measure that identifies pervasive negative attitudes toward the self, the outside world, and the future that are seen as being related to or causing depression. Similarly, the client's scores on the Inventory of Interpersonal Problems (Horowitz, Rosenberg, Baer, Ureño, & Villaseñor, 1988), a 127-item self-report inventory that measures behaviors associated with interpersonal problems including difficulties being assertive, being overly needy and dependent in relationships, as well as hostile and rejecting of others, increased at the end of treatment. Lower scores represent more adaptive beliefs and fewer cognitive distortions about interpersonal interactions. His higher score was not surprising, as prior to entering therapy, the client had exercised excessive control of his feelings and silenced their expression to others, which contributed to his high blood pressure and exacerbated his stress levels. One of the major changes at the end of therapy was his decision to share his feelings both positive and negative more with others, including his wife, but he was still learning how to modulate their expression effectively.

To his therapists' initial consternation, an important goal of the client was to reduce his blood pressure. From Session 3 on, he reported a significant drop in blood pressure, which he attributed directly to therapy. He greatly valued the opportunity to share his distress and explore his problems, as he had not confided in anyone since he emigrated. He missed his chats with his mother and had hoped his wife would act as a confidante and provide support and listen to his concerns, but the onset of her psychological problems trumped this. For 18 years he had carried his burdens alone. Speaking with his therapist was the first time in all those years that he had been able to share and explore his concerns with another person. His therapist began to realize that talking about his feelings and exploring the impact of events, putting them in perspective, and allowing himself to freely process his emotions in an empathetic, accepting, prizing and congruent therapeutic relationship could serve an important role in reducing his stress levels and hypertension. He felt less stressed as he acknowledged his resentment, confronted his sadness, and overcame his shame at his wife's condition, trusting that his school friends would support and welcome them into their social group.

Other significant changes were observed in how the client processed and regulated his affect as measured by an Observer Measure of Affect Regulation, called O–MAR (Watson, McMullen, Prosser, & Bedard, 2011; Watson & Prosser, 2004). The O–MAR assesses clients' affect regulation capacity on five dimensions of emotional processing, including (a) level of awareness, (b) modulation of arousal, (c) modulation of expression, (d) acceptance of affective experience, and (e) reflection on affective experience. The client's total score increased from 1.8 to 5.6, a significant difference. A review of the ratings showed that the client improved on all five dimensions of emotional processing and affect regulation, including becoming more aware of and able to label his emotions. He moved from general distress and hopelessness to a more differentiated understanding of his feelings including anger and frustration at being trapped and feeling out of control, sadness at what he had not been able to achieve, grief at his mother's passing, loneliness as a result of disconnection from others and his stoical attitude, and fear of being shamed. He was better able to modulate his levels of arousal as well as his expression of emotion. Over the course of therapy, as he became more accepting and aware of his feelings, he used them to guide his search for solutions and to identify new ways of being that contributed to him feeling more effective, confident, and happy. Further evidence that the client was more accepting and allowing of his emotions was gleaned from a self-report measure of coping, which indicated that the client was not suppressing his feelings as much at the end of therapy as he had at the beginning.

As noted previously, the client reported a positive working alliance over the course of therapy. He felt he and his therapist were focused on finding a solution to his problems—although a number of times he felt he had a solution at the beginning, this would evaporate over the course of the week. Initially, he hoped that his wife would change, however, as therapy progressed he began to realize that it was he who would have to modify his expectations. He accepted that his wife's condition would not improve, and that he needed to find ways to meet his own needs and care for himself while remaining committed to caring for his wife, his children, and grandchildren. He realized how his hope that she would recover made him vulnerable to anger and frustration whenever she exhibited behavior that was evidence of her mental condition. He mourned the absence of support in his life and let go of his sense of being duped and misled by his in-laws. While he wished that things had been different, he was able to see what was positive in his relationships and began to build on this to establish more connection with others and develop his interests.

The focus on how Edwin treated his experience was important to him changing how he processed and regulated his emotions. When he started therapy, he had been self-sacrificing, putting others needs ahead of his own. As a result, by the time he came to therapy he was exhausted, resentful, depressed, and despairing that he would ever have time to enjoy life. Early on his therapist suggested they focus on how he could take better care of himself. At first Edwin thought that it meant leaving his marriage. However, after recommitting to the marriage, he realized that he could balance his needs with those of others. He realized he needed to make space for himself and respect his feelings. He saw that his siblings and friends were eager to support him and reconnect with him now that he was no longer working full time. He felt more entitled to pursue some of his interests and to ask for support with his wife.

Internalizing his therapist's attitudes, Edwin became more caring, accepting, and empathic towards his own experience. He acknowledged and expressed his feelings and accepted that his wife's condition would not improve and, more important, that she did not intentionally mean to harm him. As a result, his blood pressure decreased significantly. He became involved with a nonprofit organization that provided support for individuals and families with a member suffering from psychological distress and started a support group for members of his community. Observing that members of his community had difficulty disclosing feelings and talking about family matters, he hoped to destigmatize the act of sharing feelings and asking for support, so that they could benefit from sharing their experience with others, just as he had done in therapy.

Edwin maintained his gains at 18-month follow-up. In fact he continued to improve on a number of measures including not suppressing his feelings to cope but rather reflecting on them to solve problems. His depression continued to remit showing a score of 2 on the BDI; his score on the Inventory of Interpersonal Problems (Horowitz et al., 1988) dropped from a high of 1.63 posttreatment to 1.13 at 18-month follow-up. This was lower than it had been at the beginning of treatment. At a follow-up interview, Edwin was beaming and said he was enjoying his life. His health had remained stable and he was planning to travel with friends to California. He had remained active in the community and was seeing friends regularly.

MECHANISMS OF CHANGE

Identifying the mechanisms of change as a result of psychotherapy is an ongoing quest that is being fueled by new and exciting developments in the fields of developmental neurobiology, psychology, and psychiatry. Daniel Siegel (2012) observed that "our social experiences can directly shape our neural architecture" (p. 15). Social interactions provide the scaffolding to support, modulate, and change our biology from birth on. The provision of an empathic, prizing, accepting, and congruent therapeutic relationship is one of the best ways to facilitate changes in individuals' emotional experience, its processing and regulation. Porges (2007) suggested that affect is a biobehavioral process that is regulated interpersonally. According to this view effective psychotherapy characterized by positive social interactions and interpersonal behaviors serves to regulate body states and behaviors.

The creation of a safe relationship provides the optimal conditions for clients to begin to regulate their emotions and experience physiological changes. Porges proposes that the vagus nerve, which transmits information between the heart and brain, serves as a vagal brake that can be applied or released to either calm or activate the individual to protective action. In the presence of attentive, calm, soothing others, the brain "neuroceives" a state of safety. Neuroception is a novel construct used to describe how neural circuits discern safety, danger, or life threat based on visceral information outside the realm of awareness. It is the communication of this state of safety and calm by means of posture, gaze, attention, vocal quality, care, warmth, and attunement to the client's experience that may have contributed to the activation of the vagal brake resulting in a lowering of the client's blood pressure and his sense of stress and threat. Lowering clients' apprehension of threat may be even more important if clients are insecurely attached. Edwin responded positively to his therapist's empathic, warm, accepting attitude. He noted that her attentive listening and suggestions reminded him of his talks with his mother. It is highly likely that this type of interaction activated his implicit procedural knowledge of being with his mother as well as the accompanying neurobiological and emotion regulating brain circuits thereby contributing to a sense of calm and a feeling of being soothed (Porges, 2007; Schore, 2003). Activation of this physical state requires therapists to be fully present, empathic, accepting, prizing and congruent in the session with their clients (Geller, Greenberg, & Watson, 2010; Geller & Porges, 2014). No doubt changing his perceptions of his wife's behavior also lowered his sense of being threatened and contributed to his lowered blood pressure.

In addition to promoting these neurobiological processes, EFT therapists actively reflect what their clients are saying and exploring. In this process, therapists' mirror their clients' affective experience; working with them to differentiate and label it so that they can know it better and understand the impact of events. This process enables clients to modulate their levels of arousal and begin to learn new ways of expressing their feelings as well as how to reflect on their experience as a guide for future action. Therapists' empathy has been found to lead to improvement in clients' affect regulation capacities, depression, self-esteem, self-criticism, and neediness (Watson, Steckley, & McMullen, 2014). However, therapist behavior does not exist independently of clients' characteristics but rather interacts with them. An important client characteristic that has been found to mediate the impact of the therapeutic relationship is the level of clients' attachment security. Watson et al. (2014) found that insecurely attached individuals responded better to treatment when they experienced their therapists as empathic. Edwin scored above the median in terms of insecure attachment, thus it is likely that he may have benefited more from his therapist's empathy and acceptance.

To facilitate changes in the client's emotional processing, his therapist suggested they focus on how he could take care of himself. The negative ways that he related to himself and his experience were identified; two-chair dialogues highlighted his negative treatment of self, including self-silencing and self-criticism; and empty chair dialogues with his wife helped him to find alternative ways of relating to his situation and his wife by drawing on his mother's wisdom and love of him.

RESEARCH TO PRACTICE AND BACK

Facilitating clients' emotional processing is clearly an important goal and outcome in psychotherapy across different approaches. Future research will have to consider how emotional processing can be facilitated in psychotherapy and differentiate those clients who are most responsive to the relational conditions. A number of studies have pointed to variations in clients' responding indicating that not all clients require the same level of empathy. While it is likely that a baseline level of the relationship conditions is optimal in all therapies regardless of approach and client characteristics, there are likely some clients who require different levels and types of empathic responding than others. Attachment research has proven fruitful and circumplex models of personality have illuminated the interactions between clients and therapists (Alden, Wiggins, & Pincus, 1990; Benjamin, 1974). Some clients may be particularly responsive to therapists' nonverbal behaviors, while others may require a sense that their therapists "get them" intellectually as well as emotionally. For other clients, their therapists' empathic responses, whether conveyed by tone of voice or content, may be experienced as too cloying or intrusive. This is particularly important as we learn about the neural, physiological, and behavioral changes that ensue as a result of abusive and neglectful environments. Some clients may not respond as expected to their therapist's empathy and acceptance. To provide optimal treatments, it would be helpful to be able to identify these clients early on in therapy, even as therapists continue to be responsive and try to moderate their responses to fit with their clients' needs and styles.

There are a number of measures to assess clients' affect regulation capacity including the O–MAR (Watson & Prosser, 2004) an observer-rated measure. The O–MAR can be used to assess clients' emotional processing during the session in terms of (a) their level of awareness, (b) their ability to label and differentiate their affective experience, (c) how accepting they are of their experience, (d) how well they modulate their levels of arousal and expression, and (e) how reflective they are of their emotional experience. As an observer-rated measure, O–MAR is anchored to behavioral indices that are visible within the session, so it can be employed by clinicians to hone their awareness of clients' emotional-processing capacities. The measure is transtheoretical and applicable to clients' in-session process and narratives across a range of theoretical approaches.

Other measures of clients' emotional processing include the emotional productivity measure developed by Greenberg, Auszra, and Herrmann (2007) and the Client Expressed Arousal Scale–III (Warwar & Greenberg, 1999). The measure of productive emotion rates clients' expressions of emotion in the session to determine whether it is productive or not in terms of criteria relevant for EFT. The measure of emotional arousal assesses the extent to which clients are emotionally aroused in the session after they have acknowledged a feeling or expressed an emotion. Raters assess clients' vocal tone and quality, facial expressions, and body movements. In addition, there are self-report measures including the Difficulties in Emotion Regulation Scale (Gratz & Roemer, 2004), which measures emotional processing. Both self-report and observer rated measures can help to sensitize researchers and clinicians to relevant information in the session.

Measuring therapists' attitudes and behaviors continues to be important. Studies have shown that therapists convey empathy, acceptance, warmth, and prizing congruently in different ways (Bachelor, 1988; Watson, 2001, 2015). However, with the burgeoning work in neurobiology, it may be possible to define the characteristics of therapists' interpersonal behavior at a more granular level. Clearly, there is strong support for Rogers' assertion that the relationship conditions are necessary for successful psychotherapy. With the proliferation of different therapeutic approaches emphasizing different techniques, the jury is still out on whether the relationship conditions are sufficient. Notwithstanding, a more differentiated understanding of therapists' behaviors that promote optimal affect regulation in clients and lead to long-term change is necessary so that therapists can hone their skills and make psychotherapy more effective. An observer measure to assess therapists' empathy, such as the Measure of Expressed Empathy (Watson, 1999), can be helpful in this regard. This measure rates therapists' nonverbal behaviors as well as the verbal content of their reflections and responses to clients to assess their level of empathy in the session. Like other observer measures, it is a useful training tool for both clinicians and researchers. Another enduring measure is the Barrett-Lennard Relationship Inventory (Barrett-Lennard, 1962). This is a self-report measure to assess clients' perceptions of the therapeutic relationship conditions as defined by Rogers. It has strong validity and reliability and is a useful measure over and above the therapeutic alliance to provide an indication of how clients are experiencing their therapists.

PRACTICE IMPLICATIONS AND RECOMMENDATIONS FOR CLINICIANS AND SUPERVISORS

The kinds of relational qualities that we are discussing require therapists to be fully present with their clients. This requires a high level of attention to the moment-by-moment emotional reactions, perceptions, thoughts, and sensations occurring within each participant as well as between participant and therapist. To be present in this manner requires therapists to decenter and to put their concerns, worries, judgments, and worldviews aside so that they can enter fully the client's phenomenological world and experience it as they do. To do this, therapists need to clear a space, put their personal concerns aside, and bracket their assumptions. The Clearing a Space task in EFT can facilitate this. Then as they give their clients their full attention, therapists will be able to resonate more fully with their clients' feelings and experience of events in order to provide the necessary level of empathic responding (Watson & Greenberg, 2009). Empathic therapists attend to their clients' faces, hear their voices and are aware of their physical beings and behavior. Receiving their therapists undivided and focused attention, clients come to feel valued, prized, and accepted (Watson & Greenberg, 2017).

While theoretically most therapists would agree with the premise that therapists' presence encompassing empathy, warmth, and acceptance is the backbone of therapy, there are times when maintaining this stance with clients can be challenging: when therapists feel overwhelmed by their clients' problems, or when clients are hostile or unreceptive to their interventions or ways of working. At these times, it can be helpful for therapists to sit back and try to decenter from their own experience. This requires providing clients the space to disagree and to work at their own pace and in their own way. While this may seem counterintuitive when we believe we have ways of working that are optimal, some clients may need to feel in control of the process, its pace, and its focus, while others may not be able to respond as would be expected given certain neurobiological and physical patterning that has been laid down.

Supervisors and therapists may have to modify their expectations so that they are not too self-critical or focused on outcome. Both these stances can result in us losing sight of the client, leading to ruptures in the relationship. The capacity to decenter and prioritize the client's concerns and goals is central to empathy. This requires therapists to be flexible and fluid in their conceptualizations, case formulations and hypotheses. Supervisors and therapists might deliberately work at developing a number of alternative hypotheses and case formulations to conceptualize clients' problems. To be optimally empathic and accepting, therapists may have to be able to break set quickly so that perspectives and ways of seeing things can dissolve and reform to better take account of their clients' feelings and perceptions in the moment. In this case, Edwin's therapist needed to respect and value his commitment to his children and support him to work out a solution that would enable him to care for himself and honor his commitment to his family, rather than seeing the dissolution of his marriage or the institutionalization of his wife as the solution.

EFT therapists continually monitor and mirror their clients' reactions. They ask clients to attend to their bodies to become aware of their subjective organismic experience and to symbolize it to become more aware of it. EFT therapists use the feedback from clients' organismic experience to guide them. It is clients' organismic experience that provides information about how therapy is progressing as well as what needs to be focused on at any given moment in therapy. One technique that helps clients to bring their organismic experience into awareness is focusing. The process of symbolizing inner experience is fundamental in EFT and goes hand in hand with the other techniques to assist clients to develop more optimal emotional processing and regulation capacities. However, primary and foundational to all of these techniques is the therapeutic relationship, with the therapist remaining empathetically attuned and guided by clients' organismic experience in the session at all times.

REFERENCES

Alden, L. E., Wiggins, J. S., & Pincus, A. L. (1990). Construction of circumplex scales for the Inventory of Interpersonal Problems. *Journal of Personality Assessment, 55,* 521–536. http://dx.doi.org/10.1080/00223891.1990.9674088

Bachelor, A. (1988). How clients perceive therapist empathy: A content analysis of "received" empathy. *Psychotherapy, 25,* 227–240. http://dx.doi.org/10.1037/h0085337

Barrett-Lennard, G. T. (1962). Dimensions of therapist response as causal factors in therapeutic change. *Psychological Monographs: General and Applied, 76,* 1–36. http://dx.doi.org/10.1037/h0093918

Barrett-Lennard, G. T. (1997). The recovery of empathy—Toward others and self. In A. C. Bohart & L. S. Greenberg (Eds.), *Empathy reconsidered: New directions in psychotherapy* (pp. 103–121). Washington, DC: American Psychological Association. http://dx.doi.org/10.1037/10226-004

Beck, A. T., Steer, R. A., & Brown, G. K. (1996). *Manual for the Beck Depression Inventory—II.* San Antonio, TX: Harcourt.

Benjamin, L. S. (1974). Structural analysis of social behavior. *Psychological Review, 81,* 392–425. http://dx.doi.org/10.1037/h0037024

Blatt, S. J., D'Afflitti, J. P., & Quinlan, D. M. (1976). Experiences of depression in normal young adults. *Journal of Abnormal Psychology, 85,* 383–389. http://dx.doi.org/10.1037/0021-843X.85.4.383

Bohart, A., & Greenberg, L. S. (1997). Empathy: Where are we and where do we go from here? In A. C. Bohart & L. S. Greenberg (Eds.), *Empathy reconsidered: New directions in theory research and practice* (pp. 419–449). Washington, DC: American Psychological Association. http://dx.doi.org/10.1037/10226-031

Bozarth, J. (2001). Client-centered unconditional positive regard: A historical perspective. In J. Bozarth & P. Wilkens (Eds.), *Unconditional positive regard* (pp. 5–18). Ross-on-Wye, England: PCCS Books.

Derogatis, L. R., Lipman, R. S., & Covi, L. (1973). SCL–90: An outpatient psychiatric rating scale—Preliminary report. *Psychopharmacology Bulletin, 9*, 13–28.

Derogatis, L. R., Rickels, K., & Rock, A. F. (1976). The SCL–90 and the MMPI: A step in the validation of a new self-report scale. *The British Journal of Psychiatry, 128*, 280–289. http://dx.doi.org/10.1192/bjp.128.3.280

DeSteno, D., Gross, J. J., & Kubzansky, L. (2013). Affective science and health: The importance of emotion and emotion regulation. *Health Psychology, 32*, 474–486. http://dx.doi.org/10.1037/a0030259

Elliott, R., Bohart, A. C., Watson, J. C., & Greenberg, L. S. (2011). Empathy. *Psychotherapy, 48*, 43–49. http://dx.doi.org/10.1037/a0022187

Feshbach, N. D. (1997). Empathy: The formative years—Implications for clinical practice. In A. C. Bohart & L. S. Greenberg (Eds.), *Empathy reconsidered: New directions in psychotherapy* (pp. 33–59). Washington, DC: American Psychological Association. http://dx.doi.org/10.1037/10226-001

Geller, S. M., Greenberg, L. S., & Watson, J. C. (2010). Therapist and client perceptions of therapeutic presence: The development of a measure. *Psychotherapy Research, 20*, 599–610. http://dx.doi.org/10.1080/10503307.2010.495957

Geller, S. M., & Porges, S. W. (2014). Therapeutic presence: Neurophysiological mechanisms mediating feeling safe in therapeutic relationships. *Journal of Psychotherapy Integration, 24*, 178–192. http://dx.doi.org/10.1037/a0037511

Gratz, K. L., & Roemer, L. (2004). Multidimensional assessment of emotion regulation and dysregulation: Development, factor structure, and initial validation of the difficulties in emotion regulation scale. *Journal of Psychopathology and Behavioral Assessment, 26*, 41–54. http://dx.doi.org/10.1023/B:JOBA.0000007455.08539.94

Greenberg, L. S., Auszra, L., & Herrmann, I. R. (2007). The relationship among emotional productivity, emotional arousal and outcome in experiential therapy of depression. *Psychotherapy Research, 17*, 482–493. http://dx.doi.org/10.1080/10503300600977800

Greenberg, L. S., & Watson, J. C. (2005). *Emotion-focused psychotherapy for generalized anxiety disorder.* Washington, DC: American Psychological Association.

Horowitz, L. M., Rosenberg, S. E., Baer, B. A., Ureño, G., & Villaseñor, V. S. (1988). Inventory of Interpersonal Problems: Psychometric properties and clinical applications. *Journal of Consulting and Clinical Psychology, 56*, 885–892. http://dx.doi.org/10.1037/0022-006X.56.6.885

Horvath, A. O., & Greenberg, L. S. (1989). Development and validation of the Working Alliance Inventory. *Journal of Counseling Psychology*, *36*, 223–233. http://dx.doi.org/10.1037/0022-0167.36.2.223

Keil, W. (1996). Hermeneutic empathy in client-centered therapy. In U. Esser, H. Pabst, & G. Speirer (Eds.), *The power of the person-centered approach: New challenges, perspectives and answers* (pp. 65–80). Köln, Germany: GwG.

Norcross, J. C., & Wampold, B. E. (2011). Evidence-based therapy relationships: Research conclusions and clinical practices. *Psychotherapy*, *48*, 98–102. http://dx.doi.org/10.1037/a0022161

Porges, S. W. (2007). The polyvagal perspective. *Biological Psychology*, *74*, 116–143. http://dx.doi.org/10.1016/j.biopsycho.2006.06.009

Rogers, C. R. (1975). Empathic: An unappreciated way of being. *The Counseling Psychologist*, *5*, 2–10. http://dx.doi.org/10.1177/001100007500500202

Rosenberg, M. (1965). *Society and the adolescent self-image*. Princeton, NJ: Princeton University Press. http://dx.doi.org/10.1515/9781400876136

Schore, A. N. (2003). *Affect dysregulation and disorders of the self*. New York, NY: W. W. Norton.

Siegel, D. J. (2012). *The developing mind: How relationships and the brain interact to shape who we are* (2nd ed.). New York, NY: Guilford Press.

van der Kolk, B. A. (1994). The body keeps the score: Memory and the evolving psychobiology of posttraumatic stress. *Harvard Review of Psychiatry*, *1*, 253–265. http://dx.doi.org/10.3109/10673229409017088

van der Kolk, B. A. (1996). The body keeps the score: Approaches to the psychobiology of posttraumatic stress disorder. In B. A. van der Kolk, A. C. McFarlane, & L. Weisaeth (Eds.), *Traumatic stress: The effects of overwhelming experience on mind, body and society* (pp. 214–241). New York, NY: Guilford Press.

van der Kolk, B. A. (2005). Developmental trauma disorder: Toward a rational diagnosis for children with complex trauma histories. *Psychiatric Annals*, *35*, 401–408. http://dx.doi.org/10.3928/00485713-20050501-06

Vygotsky, L. S. (1978). *Mind in society: The development of higher psychological processes*. Cambridge, MA: Harvard University Press.

Warwar, S., & Greenberg, L. S. (1999, June). *Emotional processing and therapeutic change*. Paper presented at the annual meeting of the International Society for Psychotherapy Research, Braga, Portugal.

Watson, J. C. (1999). *Measure of expressed empathy (MEE)*. Unpublished instrument, Ontario Institute for Studies in Education, University of Toronto, Ontario, Canada.

Watson, J. C. (2001). Revisioning empathy: Theory, research and practice. In D. Cain & J. Seeman (Eds.), *Humanistic psychotherapies: Handbook of research and practice* (pp. 445–471). Washington, DC: American Psychological Association.

Watson, J. C. (2015, June). *Mapping patterns of change: Implications for theory, research, practice and training*. Presidential address, 46th Annual Meeting of the Society for Psychotherapy Research, University of Pennsylvania, Philadelphia.

Watson, J. C., & Greenberg, L. (1998). The alliance in short term experiential therapy. In J. Safran & C. Muran (Eds.), *The therapeutic alliance in brief psychotherapy* (pp. 123–146). Washington, DC: American Psychological Association.

Watson, J. C. & Greenberg, L. S. (2009). Empathic resonance: A neuroscience perspective. In J. Decety & W. Ickes (Eds.), *The social neuroscience of empathy* (pp. 125–137). Cambridge, MA: Massachusetts Institute of Technology.

Watson, J. C. & Greenberg, L. S. (2017). *Emotion focused psychotherapy for generalized anxiety disorder.* Washington, DC: American Psychological Association.

Watson, J. C., Greenberg, L. S., Rice, L. N. & Gordon, L. (1998). *Client Task Specific Change Measure—Revised.* Unpublished manual, Ontario Institute for Studies in Education of the University of Toronto, Ontario, Canada.

Watson, J. C., McMullen, E. J., Prosser, M. C., & Bedard, D. L. (2011). An examination of the relationships among clients' affect regulation, in-session emotional processing, the working alliance, and outcome. *Psychotherapy Research, 21*, 86–96. http://dx.doi.org/10.1080/10503307.2010.518637

Watson, J. C., & Prosser, M. (2004). *Observer measure of affect regulation (O–MAR).* Unpublished observer-rated measure of affect regulation, Department of Adult Education and Counselling Psychology, OISE/University of Toronto, Ontario, Canada.

Watson, J. C., Steckley, P. L., & McMullen, E. J. (2014). The role of empathy in promoting change. *Psychotherapy Research, 24*, 286–298. http://dx.doi.org/10.1080/10503307.2013.802823

Weissman, A. N., & Beck, A. T. (1978, March). *Development and validation of the Dysfunctional Attitudes Scale: A preliminary investigation.* Paper presented at the 62nd Annual Meeting of the American Educational Research Association, Toronto, Ontario, Canada. Retrieved from https://files.eric.ed.gov/fulltext/ED167619.pdf

11

WHERE THE ALLIANCE AND SYSTEMS THEORY MEET IN BRIEF FAMILY THERAPY

LAURIE HEATHERINGTON, VALENTÍN ESCUDERO, AND MYRNA L. FRIEDLANDER

Imagine the following scenario: A family in significant distress appears for an initial session, with myriad presenting problems, including the adolescent son's substance abuse and hostility toward his younger sister, and parents who have decided that they are "emotionally divorced" but are keeping this critical information from their children. Moreover, no one in the family believes that he or she needs therapy, but everyone thinks that all the *others* are in urgent need of professional help. Although all four family members are clearly in pain, no one really wants to be there.

How can you engage this family in treatment before they collectively decide to head for the door? Where should the therapy start, and how, ideally, should it unfold? How do you make decisions, in the moment-to-moment process of the therapeutic hour, about how and where to intervene? Not surprisingly, these are among the most important questions for

We gratefully acknowledge the assistance of Natalia Ruiz de Cortrate Gracia in transcribing and translating the clinical material.

http://dx.doi.org/10.1037/0000093-012
Developing the Therapeutic Relationship: Integrating Case Studies, Research, and Practice, O. Tishby and H. Wiseman (Editors)

family therapists—those who are highly experienced as well as those just starting their careers. And happily, these are also important questions for family therapy researchers.

RELATIONSHIP ASPECT: BALANCING ALLIANCES WITH DIFFERENT FAMILY MEMBERS AND THE FAMILY UNIT

In our analysis of this case and in keeping with the theme of this book, we propose that two elements undergird the answers to these questions: (a) the therapist's theoretical or conceptual road map to treatment, and (b) the development and maintenance of therapeutic relationships with each family member and with the family unit as a whole. As in any good therapy, elements related to theory and relationship are equally essential and closely intertwined, especially at significant moments in the treatment, as demonstrated in the following analysis.

We selected this particular case because it demonstrates how an experienced therapist used his relationship, in particular the working alliance, with each family member and with the sibling and parental subsystems, as the major strategy to effect systemic change. With each client and subsystem, it was necessary to tailor the alliance differently and yet be mindful of the needs of the entire family unit, all the while being flexible with each individual in the relationship-building process. Moreover, the therapist used alliance-focused strategies and interventions that reflect each of the four dimensions in our conceptual model of the alliance in conjoint family treatment, the System for Observing Family Therapy Alliances (SOFTA; Escudero & Friedlander, 2017; Friedlander, Escudero, & Heatherington, 2006): (a) engagement in the therapeutic process, (b) emotional connection with the therapist, (c) safety within the therapeutic system, and (d) shared sense of purpose within the family. Finally, the outcome of this brief treatment, 11 sessions, was mostly (but not entirely) successful, as we explain below.

The family was treated from a *systemic therapy orientation* in a research-based outpatient training clinic in northwestern Spain.

THEORETICAL/CONCEPTUAL BACKGROUND

Systemic Family Therapy

The focus of systemic therapy is not primarily on individuals, but rather on the entire psychological system in which people interact with one another on a daily basis. The lens of the systemic therapist is wide, moving back and forth to define, assess, and treat problems contextually. Typically, the context or frame of interest is the couple or the family unit. Even when speaking with individual family members, the therapist is mindful of how the various parts (people and subsystems) in the system mutually influence one another with regard to the problems, and how therapeutic change in one part of the system affects all the other parts.

Despite the many and varied approaches to systemic family therapy (Lebow, 2005), contemporary family therapists tend to use an integrative approach that combines structural, strategic, and constructivist techniques as needed. All systemic approaches share certain defining features, however. Most important is the focus on the *inter*personal and *inter*actional dynamics that shape and maintain problems. Consider, for example, a couple in whom the emotional or physical avoidance of one partner "causes" the other partner to make demands, which in turn begets more avoidance behavior, and then even more demanding behavior. This is the classic "demand–withdraw" or "pursue–distance" dynamic. Although the partners often punctuate their interactions in a linear way by blaming one another and exonerating the self ("She started it;" "I wouldn't bug him if he didn't avoid me"), the systemic therapist takes a "metaperspective" on the couple's dance, reframing the ways in which the partners' pattern of interacting sustains their unhappiness in a circular fashion. Likewise, a child's problem behavior is considered as both an action and a reaction to dynamics within the family system. As an example, a teenager's misbehavior in school may function to draw a distant parent into greater contact with her, or to provide a detour for the parents to avoid discussing their underlying marital conflict.

Generally speaking, family therapists tend to create a multiactor setting for the therapy by inviting different members of the family to join the sessions and thus conjointly share in the therapy. Systemic therapies also share a focus on communication as the means by which relationships (both functional and dysfunctional) are defined and observed. Therapists pay close attention not only to *what* family members say to each other, but also to *how* they say it, nonverbally and paralinguistically. Moreover, systemic therapists assess the patterns of interaction that accompany distress and unhappiness, as well as the positive and negative feedback cycles that accompany these feelings and the meanings that family members attach to their interactions. Indeed, contemporary systemic theories, such as functional family therapy (Sexton & Alexander, 2002), attachment-based family therapy (Diamond, Diamond, & Levy, 2014) and emotion-focused couples therapy (Greenberg & Johnson, 1988; Johnson & Greenberg, 1994) extend the traditional focus in couple and family therapy on interactions to include attention to the roles of cognition, attachment, and emotion.

Although the mechanisms of change in systemic family therapy are not fully understood (Friedlander, Heatherington, & Escudero, 2016; Heatherington,

Friedlander & Greenberg, 2005), it is likely that they include helping families identify and modify negative patterns of interaction, helping individuals find more adaptive constructions of their problems, and encouraging family members to reconnect emotionally with one another. In any case, it is clear that important change processes occur not only between therapist and clients but also *among the clients* themselves, as well as *within* individual members of the system, as illustrated in the present case.

The Therapeutic Alliance in Conjoint Family Therapy

The therapeutic alliance is one of the most robust, if not *the* most robust relationship factor in successful psychotherapy, regardless of modality (Friedlander, Escudero, Heatherington, & Diamond, 2011; Horvath, Del Re, Flückiger, & Symonds, 2011). In family therapy, the alliance has some of the same elements that comprise the working alliance in individual psychotherapy (i.e., emotional connection with the therapist and active involvement in the therapeutic process; see Bordin's [1979] agreement on goals and tasks). In conjoint family therapies, however, the alliance is more challenging, interesting, and dynamic. Family members often have different motives and motivational levels for treatment, and some come to therapy reluctantly or under duress. Once in the consulting room, they may not acknowledge the same problems, they may construe the problems or the solutions differently, or even disagree on the need for professional help (Lambert, Skinner, & Friedlander, 2012).

Thus, the therapist's creation of a psychological space in which family members can agree about the goals and tasks of therapy and experience a strong emotional bond with the therapist is of necessity highly complex (Friedlander, Escudero, & Heatherington, 2006). In systemic therapy, alliances develop not only between individuals and the therapist, but also between and among family members as a group and between the therapist and various subsystems (e.g., parents). At any given point in treatment, these multiple alliances interact systemically (Friedlander, Escudero, & Heatherington, 2006; Pinsof, 1994). For example, the degree to which a father likes the therapist and engages in the treatment may have a facilitating (or hindering) effect on his son's willingness to form a bond with the therapist. If the father and son are in conflict, observing a strong bond between the father and therapist may initially be threatening for the son. Alternatively, in a family in which the father had been initially reluctant to seek the professional help that the mother and son had initiated, observing that a strong bond is developing between son and therapist may boost the father's expectations and thus his engagement in the treatment.

As mentioned earlier, the SOFTA (Friedlander, Escudero, & Heatherington, 2006, Friedlander, Escudero, Horvath, et al., 2006), or the Spanish version, SOATIF (Sistema de la Observacie de la Alianza en Terapia

Familiar; Escudero & Friedlander, 2003), is a multidimensional conceptual model, with accompanying observational rating (SOFTA–o) and self-report (SOFTA–s) measures, of conjoint therapy alliances. We created the SOFTA model and measures to account for the relational complexity of systemic therapy. *Safety within the therapeutic system* is a particularly important dimension, as family members who go home together risk continuing the interpersonal consequences of their revelations and conflicts during the therapy hour. For this reason, a lack of safety can seriously compromise a client's trust in the therapist and involvement in the therapeutic process.

Another important aspect of the alliance in systemic therapy is the *within alliance* (Pinsof, 1994) or, in the SOFTA, the family's *Shared sense of purpose* (Friedlander, Escudero, & Heatherington, 2006). This dimension of the alliance, which is unique to conjoint therapy, refers to family members' willingness to collaborate in treatment with one another as well as a strong emotional bond between and among them. Indeed, family members often see their personal relationships with the therapist differently from their allegiances with each other (e.g., Friedlander, Lambert, & Muñiz de la Peña, 2008). In the SOFTA model, the shared sense of purpose—which develops simultaneously and interacts with all of the client's individual alliances with the therapist—constitutes family members' thoughts, feelings, and behavior toward one another in relation to the problems that brought them to treatment, the proposed goals, and the value of participating with one another in a conjoint format for achieving these goals.

When alliances are "split" (e.g., Heatherington & Friedlander, 1990; Muñiz de la Peña, Friedlander, & Escudero, 2009; Pinsof & Catherall, 1986) or "unbalanced" (Robbins, Turner, Alexander, & Perez, 2003), at least one family member has a stronger bond with the therapist than the others (Friedlander, Escudero, & Heatherington, 2006). Such splits are common (Heatherington & Friedlander, 1990), they vary in severity (Muñiz de la Peña et al., 2009), and their skillful management is needed to sustain treatment progress.

Using the SOFTA–o, trained raters identify behaviors indicative of each alliance dimension from session videotapes or transcripts. As mentioned earlier, these four dimensions include (a) engagement in the therapeutic process (ENGAGEMENT), (b) emotional connection with the therapist (CONNECTION), (c) safety within the therapeutic system (SAFETY), and (d) shared sense of purpose within the family (PURPOSE). In the SOFTA–o, whereas clients' behaviors reflect their thoughts and feelings about each aspect of the alliance, the therapist's behaviors reflect contributions to (or detractions from) each aspect. Operational definitions of each behavior and dimension, as well as the rating guidelines, can be found at http://www.softa-soatif.com.

CLINICAL CASE STUDY

Presenting Problems and Client Descriptions

The present case involves the family introduced above: mother ("Rosa"), father ("José"), son ("Alberto," the identified patient), and daughter ("Ana").[1] The mother was a homemaker and the father a skilled carpenter. The presenting problem was Alberto's antisocial behavior. According to his parents, Alberto started having externalizing problems (using marijuana and being disruptive and disobedient at home) and difficulties in school, such as declining academic performance and lack of motivation, in the past few months. In the initial session, Alberto admitted to his marijuana use, recognized that it was a problem, and agreed to work with the therapist to stop smoking on the condition that his parents not be involved—only he and the therapist would work toward this goal. He was consistently talkative and cooperative in therapy, and his in-session behavior was quite good except in front of his parents, when he was highly defensive and oppositional.

The family excluded Alberto's sister, Ana, from the therapy until the therapist insisted on her attending the sixth session. In this session, Ana presented as quite introverted. Her mother, Rosa, had previously revealed (in Session 4) that Ana had an obsession with germs and cleaning; she felt compelled to wash her hands many times throughout the day and avoided sitting in chairs that someone else had used if she believed that person to be unclean. Ana performed well in school, but she had many worries and was highly sensitive to her parents' concerns about her brother.

Rosa was laid off from her job as a secretary in hospital administration after having been moved to another department due to problems with coworkers. She had been taking antidepressant medication over the previous couple of years. In session, Rosa presented as highly emotional and struggled to control her feelings. She was keenly focused on her son's difficulties and brought a long list (two typed pages) of all his problems to the initial session. Whereas Rosa minimized her daughter's obsessive-compulsive symptoms, she was the first to raise the topic of the couple's difficulties; in fact, when the therapist decided to talk with Rosa alone in Session 4, she felt safe enough to disclose that the couple relationship was irretrievably broken. This disclosure was accompanied by highly intense emotion, as she stated her belief that the couple's and the children's difficulties, as well as the general negative environment at home, were interrelated.

Like Rosa, José, the father, was quite worried about his son and minimized his daughter's problems. José was not expressive, but was nonetheless

[1]Details of this case example have been altered to protect confidentiality.

sincere in responding whenever the therapist asked for his opinions. However, when the couple's history and problems were disclosed, he was quite closed and visibly anxious.

Setting and Therapist

The family was seen at a university-based family therapy outpatient clinic located in a public hospital in Spain. The clinic provides psychotherapy services free of charge to families referred from several agencies (mental health, social services, child protective services, and specific programs for family violence), and training and research are integrated as part of the clinic's practice. All sessions are videotaped for training and research, and family members complete self-report measures as part of routine data collection. Families are seen by a primary therapist and a team composed of another senior therapist and a few graduate students in training, who observe sessions live and serve as consultants for the therapist. The therapist always takes a break of 5 to 10 minutes to consult with the team before ending the session with recommendations to the family from the observing team.

The therapist (Valentín Escudero), director and clinical supervisor at the clinic, is a PhD-level clinical psychologist with more than 20 years of experience, licensed in Spain as a psychotherapist and family therapist. His experience as a systemic therapist has been recognized throughout Europe through invited participations in various prestigious doctoral and training programs. Escudero's family therapy orientation is integrative and based on systems theory (Guttman, 1991) with elements from traditional family therapy models (e.g., structural and strategic) as well as more recent models, such as solution-focused and narrative/constructivist approaches (Lebow, 2005; Nichols & Schwartz, 2006), as described above.

The therapy proceeded for a total of 11 weekly or biweekly sessions, conducted over the course of approximately 3 months. As is common in systemic therapy, different family members were seen in different sessions and, occasionally were seen individually during portions of family sessions. Table 11.1 summarizes the participants, major topics, and length of each session.

Assessment

In systemic therapy, measuring change over time is more complex than in individual therapy and involves multiple goals and several potential loci of change (e.g., the son's behavior, the mother's affect). Thus, we used multiple methods and respondents to assess the treatment: process notes written by the therapist following each session and session ratings by the clients. The client

TABLE 11.1
Brief Session Summaries

Session	Clients	Topics	Duration
1*	Alberto, Rosa, José	Initial interview. Established treatment plan. Decided that Alberto and his parents would be seen separately and conjointly so each of them could discuss their personal issues. [Transcribed segment illustrates managing Alberto's resistance to being considered "the problem," while the therapist tried to expand the therapeutic system to include the parents.]	1 hr 17 min
2	José, Rosa	The work in this session revealed that the parents had a positive outlook regarding change, although it would likely be a long process. Discussed their previously attempted strategies that did not work with Alberto. The parents indicated that if all went as well as it had been recently, in three months they could terminate the therapy.	50 min
3	Alberto, Rosa, José	The focus of this session was how Rosa's issues and depression might be affecting the whole family, especially Alberto.	1 hr 25 min
4	Alberto, Rosa	After a portion of the session with the mother and son together (the father was not able to come and excused himself), the session continued with Rosa alone. She revealed that in addition to Alberto's behavior, José behaves very protectively with the children, and Ana has an obsessive-compulsive disorder focused on cleaning and hygiene. She indicated that the couple relationship is broken; while she had considered couple therapy, her husband was not in favor of it.	47 min
5	Alberto, Rosa, José	Alberto was more collaborative and active in therapy in this session, speaking about his future plans and feelings related to his parents and sister. The therapist invited Ana to join the therapy. The parents (without Alberto) described their relationship in depth; they do not see themselves as a couple anymore, just two parents caring for their children. The homework task for the parents was to come to the next session with two photos, one with the family and another individual picture.	1 hr 19 min

TABLE 11.1
Brief Session Summaries (*Continued*)

Session	Clients	Topics	Duration
6	Ana (and the family)	After seeing the whole family briefly, the therapist continued the session with Ana alone. Ana's perspective on the family was further revealed. She believed that she had no obsessions, that all the problems in the family are due to Alberto. She expressed the belief that her parents were doing fine and did not need to change anything. In general, Ana appeared defensive about the family's problems. The homework task for Ana was to do something "small" to make her parents worry less about her obsessions and to do something "good" to get along better with Alberto.	50 min
7	Rosa, José	Review of the couple's history, and asked them to describe all the stages in their relationship. It became clear that Alberto's behavioral problems keep them united as parents.	1 hr 12 min
8	Alberto, Ana	Talked in-depth about their relationship as siblings, how they get along, how they can support each other, etc.	1 hr 16 min
9	Alberto, Ana, José, Rosa	This session revealed that the emotional emptiness in the couple's relationship is affecting their effectiveness as parents as well as affecting their children. The parents indicated not knowing if they wanted to focus on their own issues as a couple, seemingly fearful of doing so. In their view, Ana was worse than the last time in therapy; Alberto was more unstable, with some moments of disruptive behavior, but with others in which he demonstrated "good behavior."	1 hr 25 min
10*	Alberto, Ana, José, Rosa	Family members reaffirmed their commitment to therapy and that it has been beneficial for everyone so far. After the parents left the room, the therapist used active techniques (using body movement and physical closeness) to make Ana feel comfortable when Alberto touched her. Their strengths as siblings were discussed and reinforced. Ana began to engage in the therapy. The homework task for Ana was to find photos from the happy years in her childhood and create a slideshow, with Alberto helping her. [Transcribed segment illustrates how the therapist worked to create an alliance with each sibling and within the sibling subsystem.]	1 hr

(*continues*)

TABLE 11.1
Brief Session Summaries (*Continued*)

Session	Clients	Topics	Duration
11*	Rosa, José, Alberto, Ana	Although both children seemed to be better, the parents still complained about their behavior. There was a change of focus in the couple therapy, with part of the session being alone with the two of them. They realized how their "emotional divorce" was affecting their children and finally became aware of the consequences. [Transcribed segment illustrates the work of connecting the parents' secret emotional divorce with the children's difficulties and the entire family's lack of well-being.]	1 hr 40 min

Note. *Denotes sessions in which the transcribed material is included in the analysis.

data included (a) a rating of the global impact of the session just completed ("After this session I feel . . .") on a scale from –2 (*much worse*) through 0 (*the same*) to +2 (*much better*), (b) a rating of the usefulness of the previous session on a scale from 1 (*not at all*) to 5 (*very much*) (see Table 11.2), and (c) two brief assessments of clients' views of the therapy's progress: a rating of the current status of his or her target complaints (Battle, Imber, Hoehn-Saric, Nash, & Frank, 1966), on a scale from 1 (*worse than ever*) to 10 (*absolutely perfect*) and a rating of "improvement so far" on a scale from 1 (*not at all*) to 5 (*very much*)—

TABLE 11.2
Family Members' Ratings Over Time

	Session impact (current session)				Usefulness of the previous session			
Session	Son	Daughter	Mother	Father	Son	Daughter	Mother	Father
1	+1		0	0				
2			+1	0	2		3	3
3	–1		0	0			4	3
4	+1		+1		2		4	4
5	+1		+1		3		3	
6	+1	+1	+1	0	1		4	3
7			0	+1	2	3	3	3
8	+2	+1			3	4		
9	+1	+1	–1	+1	2	3	2	3
10	+2	+1			2	3	4	3
11	+1	+1	+2	+1				

Note. Current session impact, rated immediately following each session, was given as follows: –2 = *much worse*, –1 = *worse*, 0 = *the same*, +1 = *better*, +2 = *much better*. Usefulness of the previous session, which the clients rated at the beginning of each session, ranged from 1 = *not at all* to 5 = *very much*.

see Table 11.3. In addition, clients' perceptions of the alliance were collected after Sessions 3, 6, and 9 using the full 16-item SOFTA–s (see Figure 11.1); for clinical feedback, clients completed a brief, 4-item version of the SOFTA–s (one item per alliance dimension) after every session. Each client completed the measure independently.

We used the observational SOFTA–o to identify specific alliance-related behaviors, both positive and negative for each dimension, e.g., "Family members offer to compromise" (Family SHARED PURPOSE); "Therapist shares a lighthearted moment with client" (Therapist ENGAGEMENT) on the part of both client(s) and therapist during the important moments of the case. The self-report SOFTA–s was administered to the clients and therapist independently following Sessions 3, 6, and 9. Together, the self-report SOFTA–s and observational SOFTA–o data provided an empirical assessment of evolving family therapy alliances.

Initial Interviews and Case Formulation: Session 1

The initial assessment included each family member's written target complaints (no maximum number), obtained immediately before the first session. Rosa listed her target complaints as (a) Alberto's aggressive behavior at home (which she described as "violent"), (b) his continuous challenges to the parents' authority, (c) his lack of studying, poor performance, and bad behavior at school, and (d) his marijuana use. José's target complaints were (a) Alberto's lack of respect for his parents and sister, (b) his aggressive behavior, and (c) his marijuana use. Alberto chose not to complete the target

TABLE 11.3
Family Members' Views of the Therapy's Progress

	Problem scale ratings				"Improvement so far"			
Session	Son	Daughter	Mother	Father	Son	Daughter	Mother	Father
1	2		3	4				
2			4	3			1	2
3	10		3	3	3		4	2
4	5		4	4	3		3	
5	9		5	5	4		3	3
6	6	3	5	5	3	2	3	2
7	6		4	4			3	3
8	3	3			4	2		
9	5	4	2	2	3	3	2	1
10	6	8			4	3		
11	3	7	6	6			3	2

Note. The Problem scale reflected the perceived current status of the target problem on a 1 (*worse than ever*) to 10 (*absolutely perfect*) scale. "Improvement so far" was rated on a scale from 1 (*not at all*) to 5 (*very much*).

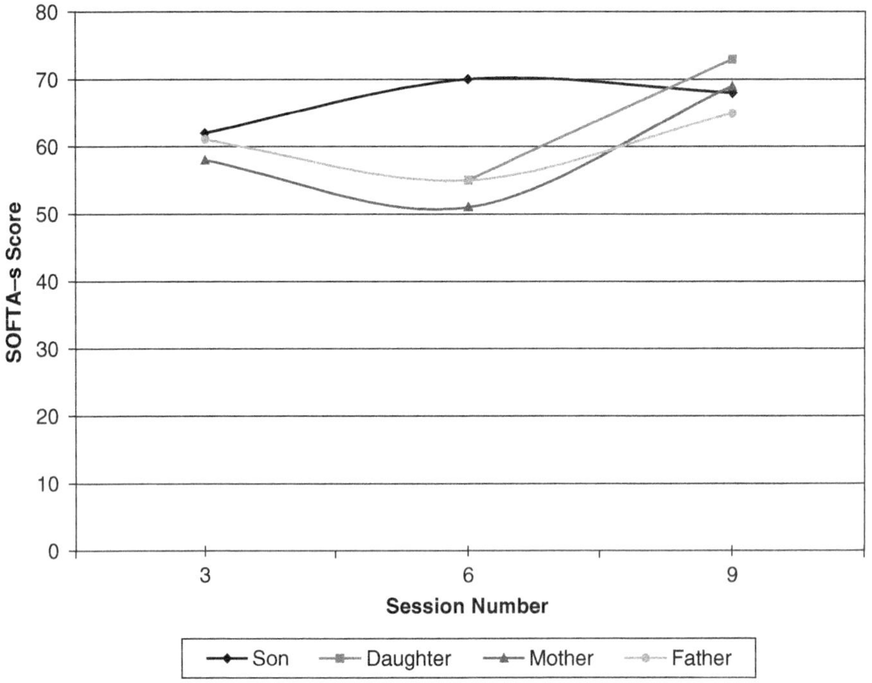

Figure 11.1. Self-report version of the System for Observing Family Therapy Alliances (SOFTA–s) ratings. SOFTA–s scores over time (possible range = 16–80). The daughter began the therapy in session 6.

complaints questionnaire, and Ana did not do so because she did not take part in the therapy until Session 6.

In the first session the therapist began by engaging family members in a brief, social conversation in order to learn about them aside from the problems they were bringing to therapy. Next, he asked each person to describe the problems and explain the severity ratings that he or she had provided on the target complaint questionnaire. In doing so, the therapist the therapist's objective was to explore the interrelations of the presenting problems and to discover why Alberto, the identified patient, chose not to provide any written complaints.

The therapist approached the first session by listening closely to each family member and carefully observing each person's behavior as well as the four family members' interactions with each other in order to develop an initial systemic formulation, including ideas about how the treatment should proceed. However, formulating an assessment–treatment plan and engaging the family's collaboration in the plan are quite different. The "best laid plans" will not work if clients do not feel engaged, safe, and connected with the therapist, as well as motivated to work together toward common goals. The segment below illustrates how the therapist worked to build these four dimensions of the family therapy alliance. (SOFTA–o dimensions and related behaviors are shown in parentheses where they occur in the transcribed segments.)

Prior to this segment, the therapist realized that his intention to work conjointly with this family needed revision because the conflict that family members brought from home to the session produced excessive tension, especially as Alberto was refusing to communicate with his parents. After trying, with little success, to dissolve the tension caused by the son's rejection of his parents by moving the conversation to lighter topics, the therapist decided to see Alberto alone. The purpose of this move was to engage him in treatment by making it safe for him to open up without his parents in the room. (Separating family members is a therapist SOFTA–o SAFETY contribution to the alliance.)

In this case, it was quite evident that Alberto's engagement in the therapy would be interpreted as a positive outcome by the parents. The therapist anticipated that by raising the positive value of the therapy in the parents' eyes, they too would become more engaged in the process. In fact, the parents did not hesitate to accept the therapist's suggestion to continue the session with Alberto alone. Not surprisingly, Alberto's nonverbal behavior clearly showed signs of relaxation and openness the moment his parents left the room—behaviors indicative of positive SAFETY in the SOFTA model.

After confirming that Alberto indeed felt more at ease without his parents in the room, the therapist suggested how they could work together: Alberto would have a confidential space to discuss some of his personal problems, and in doing so, he would not feel pressured by his parents' negative, blaming view that he was the sole cause of all of the difficulties in the family. As shown in the following excerpt, the therapist introduced one condition to this plan: that Alberto tell his parents that they, too, needed to come to therapy (by themselves) in order to be part of the therapeutic system:

Therapist: I would like to propose something to you . . . only if you want to. It's your call. I was thinking that, if you want, I could talk to your parents. You said you don't want to go back to the drug rehab center and be assessed for substance use. If you want, I can talk to your parents and tell them that. I could make a deal with them and tell them that I'll work with you. You'll come here and we'll talk about all the problems related with drugs and other issues that you might want to talk about. At the same time, I'll have some sessions with your parents. I'll focus on their anxiety because probably they're very distressed about this whole situation. This way, whatever we talk about together will be confidential and private. I'll tell them not to talk with you any more about joints. I'll take care of that from now on. If I need to inform them about something really important, I'll do it, but I'll always ask you first for your permission. I think this could make you feel better . . . what do you think? *(Positive SAFETY indicator; therapist provides structure and guidelines for safety and confidentiality.)*

Alberto: Well . . . I don't know . . . if they don't bother me anymore about the smoking thing. . . .

Therapist: Yeah, but well . . . This is something that it will help you get over it . . . Would you like to come back here again so we can talk about how these issues are going? And also I can talk to your parents and help them with their worries . . . *(Positive ENGAGEMENT indicator; therapist encourages the client to articulate goals.)*

Alberto: Are they gonna be coming here by themselves?

Therapist: They might come alone . . . what do you prefer? I think that if you come here, they'd be willing to come as well, and it could be beneficial for them. Also, if you don't continue coming to therapy, they'll be more anxious about you, don't you think? *(Positive SAFETY indicator; therapist creates conditions for the client to feel safe.)*

Alberto: Yes . . . but in the end everything is the same . . . I'm gonna be coming here for a while until something bad happens and then they'll take me to another therapist and so on . . . I already went through this process . . . *(Negative ENGAGEMENT indicator; client questions the value of therapy.)*

Therapist: No, no . . . that's not going to happen.

Alberto: You'll see . . .

Therapist: Look, I'll bet you 20 Euros. *(Positive CONNECTION indicator; therapist shares a lighthearted moment with the client.)*

Alberto: 20?! *(Positive CONNECTION indicator; client shares the lighthearted joke.)*

This suggestion apparently surprised Alberto, because the therapist was neither insisting nor directly trying to convince him that participating in therapy was necessary; rather, the 20 Euro bet seemed to create a positive connection with Alberto. In this way, while the therapist demonstrated his optimism about the therapeutic process, he did not amplify the adolescent's resistance by engaging in an argument with him. Rather, the therapist first created a safe space for Alberto to talk without his parents present and then proposed a scenario in which Alberto would not be the only identified patient, since his parents would need to come to their own session. Yet it was the 20 Euro bet that created the first emotional connection with Alberto, within a safe conversational context. As we show in the following segment, Alberto's emotional tone improved (another positive indicator of SAFETY):

Therapist: I bet you that if you start coming here to therapy, you'll keep coming here and your parents will too. (*Positive ENGAGEMENT indicator; therapist expresses optimism.*)

Alberto: Yes, until I do something bad or wrong and then they'll want to take me somewhere else . . .

Therapist: No, no, that's the good thing about coming here. If something goes wrong, I assure you that we'll get through it. (*Positive ENGAGEMENT indicator; therapist expresses optimism.*) Since I'm going to be working with your parents, I'll help them out and guide them through the process, and I'll help them understand . . . What do they usually do when you're in trouble? Do they overreact?

Alberto: Yeah . . . every little thing that happen is a tragedy for them . . . it's like they never get used to anything . . . I know people who are much worse than me and their parents don't do what mine do . . . Besides, they compare me with my sister all the time, so I'm the bad one . . . (*Positive ENGAGEMENT indicator; client introduces a new problem for discussion. Positive SAFETY indicator; client shows vulnerability by opening up.*)

Therapist: I understand . . . I see a lot of kids here who are troublemakers . . . with criminal records and other problems . . . and I'm used to it. That's why I can help your parents deal with your issues. That's why it could be good for both of you, your parents and yourself, to come here. You can even tell me how your parents are doing, whether things are quieter lately . . .

Alberto: How long do I have to come here?

Therapist: How long do you think you'll be able to?

Alberto: I thought I just had to come once . . .

Therapist: What do you think is a reasonable number of times to come?

Alberto: Including this time?

Therapist: No, in addition to this one.

Alberto: Five.

At this point in the interaction, when Alberto offered to come for five sessions, (perhaps to test whether the therapy could actually help him and his parents), the therapist's nonverbal behavior confirmed their agreement and showed appreciation for his generosity. Alberto's answer represented a commitment to engage in the therapy, or at least the possibility that he had some confidence in the therapist as a person. From here on, the conversation focused on negotiating the goals and conditions for the therapy:

Therapist: You have to think that during that time, I'd see you, but I'd see your parents as well . . . If you could choose the length of time that your parents would come . . . how long would you choose for them?

Alberto: I don't know . . . months . . .

Therapist: So you think your parents need some help.

Alberto: My mom loves therapy. . . . The more therapists she sees the better . . .

Therapist: Well, I could help her with this issue . . . to see why she seeks all this help . . . I suspect they'd come to therapy if you came too. What do you think?

Alberto: Yes, we should try. (*Positive ENGAGEMENT indicator; client indicates the possibility of change.*)

In these exchanges, we see the client and therapist having a dialogue about the process of therapy, with the therapist encouraging the adolescent to articulate his goals, which in this case simply involved deciding whether or not to give therapy a try. This example illustrates the interplay of a technical approach to create an alternative construction of the problem by reframing the parents' exclusive, blaming focus on their son as the only problem and cause of difficulties in the family. That is, the parents' initial presentation of the problem was extremely contaminated with blame, intrusiveness, defensiveness, and avoidance or denial of some highly relevant factors, in particular the couple's "emotional divorce" and extreme anxiety, the daughter's serious symptoms, and so on. The therapist carefully constructed a therapeutic system by cautiously moving around some pieces of the puzzle. The first objective was to see if it was possible to engage the angry adolescent. To do so, the therapist used Alberto's anger at his parents and his real concern for them to motivate him to work on his problems. Indeed, the SOFTA–s data (Table 11.2) show that Alberto rated the impact of this session quite positively (+1).

Course of Treatment: Working With Subsystems to Facilitate Change, or Getting From "There" to "Here"

Throughout treatment the therapist's alliance-focused techniques not only strengthened his relationship with each family member, but also furthered his strategic/systemic strategies of working to strengthen each subsystem (parents and siblings) to reduce conflict between and within the two subsystems, and to reduce the parents' detouring of their marital problems onto their children (Alberto in particular). In this section, we focus on three specific sessions (Sessions 1, 10, and 11), during which significant moments illustrate the interrelation of alliance and technique.

As experienced family therapists know, the heart of therapy comes *after* the initial session, as the therapist gets to know the family, and as they all (hopefully) settle into the hard work of change. The conceptual "map" of the therapist may require some detours between the first and final sessions, as she or he observes what is working and what is not. Doing so certainly requires close attention to the territory on the ground, that is, the relationships between therapist and clients and among the clients themselves that begin to shift and change as the work unfolds.

Following a systemic "map," successful treatment should progress through effecting changes in the interactions of the family, so that the functioning of the whole system changes. This change should be perceived by the family, as they become aware (with the therapist's help) of behaving in a different way, with each person sharing responsibility for acting and reacting differently. The therapist facilitates this change, but the family members are the protagonists in the new system. Along the way, the therapist implicitly asks family members a few key "diagnostic questions" in different ways: What is blocking you from solving your difficulties? What (bio/psycho/social) factors or past experiences are preventing you from changing?

In the case of Alberto and his family, the process of therapy helped them see that their various difficulties were more connected that they had initially thought. That is, the couple's "emotional divorce" was clearly impeding their ability as parents to work together to help their children, and the parents' helplessness with respect to influencing and regulating their children's behavior was making their own relationship even more painful and irreparable. The therapist had to work carefully to engage the family in discussing what they were strongly avoiding: their more painful difficulties. To do so, he created strong alliances with each member and subsystem of the family and reviewed the self-report data after each session to assess the clients' levels of safety and engagement in the developing therapeutic system. The link between the therapeutic techniques and the alliance-facilitating interventions was central to this systemic approach. In other words, creating and sustaining strong therapeutic relationships with individual clients and subsystems was not merely an underlying element of process, but rather a central and critical technical method for advancing the process effectively.

The next two significant moments illustrate the interplay of relationship and technique with, first, the sibling subsystem and, second, with the parental subsystem. In the sibling subsystem, Ana contributed to the maintenance of the problem by behaving in a negative and rejecting manner toward Alberto, which may have been her way of protecting the weak parental system. That is, Ana contributed to the counterproductive blaming of Alberto for every problem in the family by feeding his rebellious and risky behavior. But Ana's position was also terrible for herself, as it made her increasingly lonely and anxious, which she displayed in obsessive–compulsive behaviors and social isolation.

Session 10

In the 10th session, the therapist took the siblings on "field trip to their childhood" in order to repair the emotional attachment between them, in hopes that this repair would benefit both of them and facilitate systemic change in the family as a whole. Since Ana's reticent yet defensive attitude continued when she was alone with her brother in this session, the therapist needed to carefully create an environment where Ana would feel safe and protected. Moreover, he needed to connect emotionally with Ana in order to reattach the siblings with one another. Doing so was challenging, however, because the intervention needed to avoid making Ana feel that she was betraying her parents by interacting positively with her brother.

Therapist [to Ana]: I have the feeling that you're the kind of person who is sort of cautious . . . like shy . . . I think it looks like you keep things to yourself . . . Am I wrong? It seems to me that you're quiet, but also . . . rather sensitive? I was wondering . . . Alberto, do you think that she'd like to take a little field trip to your childhood? For example, pick some pictures from a period of time in her childhood. *[To Ana]* Do you like pictures? Don't you have some photos in your room? Family pictures, friends . . .? (*Positive CONNECTION indicator; therapist expresses interest in the client apart from the problems being treated in therapy.*)

Ana: *[nods]*

Alberto: Yes she does, she even has pictures of me!

Therapist: Okay, then, for example, what period of your life could we use as an example of the happiest moment in your life? You know, that she could take a look at those pictures and remember a very happy time with your family, in your life . . . How old were you then? The happiest years . . .

[Silence . . .]

Ana: *[shrugs her shoulders]* I don't know . . . (*Negative ENGAGEMENT indicator; minimal response.*)

Therapist [to Alberto]: and you . . . What do you think?

Alberto: Between 0 and 6 years old . . . more or less . . .

Therapist: Is that right? *[looking at Ana]*

Ana: Yes, as babies. *[smiling]*

Therapist: I want you to be sure. I want you to be the main actress in this story . . . would you like that? (*Positive CONNECTION indicator; expresses confidence, trust, or belief in the client.*) Would you like us to take a kind of trip exploring your past? What time period would you like to focus on? (*Positive ENGAGEMENT indicator; asks client to agree to a therapy task.*)

Ana: This one . . .

Therapist: Which one? Say it yourself.

Ana [looking at her brother]: Which one did you say? From 0 to . . .

Alberto: *[laughs]*

Therapist: He said from 0 to 6. Do you remember when you were 4?

Ana: I don't know . . . I don't remember . . . (*Negative ENGAGEMENT indicator; minimal response.*)

Therapist: But you do have pictures from that time, don't you? What kind of kid you were? (*Positive CONNECTION indicator; shows interest in the client apart from the problem at hand.*)

Ana: Quiet . . . I don't know . . . the same as now . . .

Therapist: Quiet?

Alberto: Well . . . quiet, quiet. . . . I don't think so! *[smiles]*

Therapist: And how were you as a one-year-old? Do you know if you . . . for example, had hair when you were a baby? (*Positive* CONNECTION *indicator; shows interest in the client apart from the problem at hand.*)

Ana: *[shakes her head]*

Alberto: You were born with a lot of hair! *[laughs]* (*Positive SHARED PURPOSE indicator; family members share lighthearted moment with each other.)*

Therapist: Well . . . now . . . choose a time period.

Ana: From 0 to 6 *[very assertive this time]* (*Positive* ENGAGEMENT *indicator; client agrees to do homework.*)

Therapist: Okay, then. By the way, I hope your parents don't say anything like, "What're you guys doing, playing with those pictures?" or something like that. You guys only need some of them . . . How many do you think it'd be okay to choose?

Ana: I don't know . . .

Therapist: Well, what you have to do is to pick the pictures and then explain to us a little bit about that period of time and what these pictures remind you of . . . Are you okay with this? (*Positive* ENGAGEMENT *indicator; asks clients to agree to a therapy task.*) *[Looking at Alberto]* Do you know how to create a slide show? Scan the pictures and create a Power Point or something?

Ana: Yes . . . he knows how to do it, he's an expert with computers.

Therapist: Okay, so you can give him . . . for example, around 12 to 20 photos . . . from 0 to 6 years old . . . Do you know those programs where they show you someone changing over time? It starts from when the person is a baby until they're old? *[To Alberto)]* Would you be able to do something like that? (*Positive* ENGAGEMENT *indicator; asks clients to agree to a therapy task.*)

Alberto: Yes. *[Ana agrees nonverbally]*

This segment illustrates how the therapist worked carefully to pay special attention to Ana's reticence and engagement difficulties, mainly by encouraging her to play the leading role in the suggested task. The therapist emphasized the playful and positive aspects of the task, giving Ana the choice to decide or at least confirm every aspect of the proposed activity. A very important aspect of this strategy was obtaining the siblings' agreement to work together without raising Ana's level of anxiety.

Therapist: That'd be great. I'll bring my laptop and we can play it here. . . . Okay, however, you, Ana, you're the director and the scriptwriter, all right? This is about your life, so you are the one who selects and chooses. Alberto is going to do the technical part, the "postproduction" bit. How does that sound to you guys? Do you think your parents will be okay with this? Would you be able to work together on this? (*Positive SHARED PURPOSE indicator; therapist encourages clients to compromise with one another, to collaborate as a team, i.e., "work together."*)

Ana: Good, yes, it's fine. Sounds good *[shows enthusiasm for the first time]*. (*Positive SAFETY indicator; client varies her emotional tone during the session and opens her body posture in response to the therapist's comment.*)

This task furthered the therapist's strategy, and indeed Ana's and Alberto's self-reported perceptions (see Table 11.2) of the session's impact (+1 and +2, respectively) and usefulness (+1 and +1, respectively) suggested that this moment likely was significant for both of them. The "field trip to your childhood" served as a metaphor for recalling the positive experiences and emotions that they had shared at a younger time in their lives. At the same time, the "field trip" gave Ana and Alberto a way to do something together that could repair the distance between them and normalize their relationship as siblings. In systemic therapy, strengthening a sibling subsystem serves to reduce anxiety and facilitate symptom change. Further, the therapist was careful, while joining with the sibling subsystem, not to cross boundaries by aligning himself too strongly with them and against the parents.

Session 11

The final significant moment, which in our view came in Session 11 with the parents, likely was the most central vehicle for change in this case. The couple finally approached the hot issue of considering how their "emotional divorce" might be a part of the problem in the family. From a systemic perspective, it is not essential to know if the parental difficulties in regulating their children's behavior *caused* the marital problem, or if the causality goes in the opposite direction, that is, whether the marital problem caused the parental problems (or at least reduced the parents' capacity to be effective with their children). Additionally, from a systemic perspective, it is assumed that causal circularity is an important way to understand negative functioning in a family and to change the vicious cycle of behaviors that maintain the problem.

In practice, a strong therapeutic relationship is essential to help parents understand the link between the marital and parental difficulties so that they can decide on a new way of behaving. Behaving differently is only possible when this new conceptualization of the family's problems is accepted by the parents, but they must also feel safe enough to work together to face the problems head on. The therapist and the therapeutic context have to be the mediators in this change. So once again, we see the relational and technical aspects of the case coming together in the present therapist's strong intervention in the couple session with Rosa and José. Session 11 began with the therapist checking in with the parents about how they were feeling, given the events of the previous session and the week in between. Simultaneously, the therapist redirected the conversation to the couple's stalemate:

Therapist: So . . . how are you both doing? I already told you in the last session, how brave you were . . . in the sense that, besides this entire problem, we can't forget the fact that you both are not okay. Neither of you might be getting the support that you really need from the other person, in the deepest meaning, I mean . . . I'm not talking about making decisions about your kids, which is something that you've been doing well as parents . . . (*Positive SHARED PURPOSE indicator; therapist draws attention to clients' shared values, experiences, needs or feelings.*)

Rosa: But there's other kind of comfort that you can get without being in a couple . . . You can just . . . empathize with someone . . . I think that the comfort and support shouldn't be coming from your partner only.

Later on the clients gave some examples, trying to justify their belief that their problems as a couple were not affecting them as parents. Also, they discussed the emotional bonds within the family as a justification for not disclosing the "emotional divorce" to their children.

Therapist: From what I understand you're having some . . . disagreements that are creating some . . . tension between you two . . . like a general tension in the air . . . (*Positive SHARED PURPOSE indicator; indicating a shared feeling between family members.*)

José: Yes, it's overall . . . and just between us.

Rosa: Sometimes some of the things that we talked about in session come out . . . and that's a sign . . . but I kind of want to postpone it . . . like . . . if we start taking care of our own issues right now . . . this is not the best moment for our family . . . this is not a good time . . .

Therapist: I understand . . .

Rosa: And this is something that I've been thinking for a long time . . .

Therapist: What kinds of things are making you feel this way?

Rosa: Some allusions to . . .

Therapist: Like what? sarcastic comments?

Rosa: No, just . . . like . . . I don't know . . . for example, if our relationship is so bad . . . why are we together?

Therapist: José, I'd like to know how you feel about this . . . Maybe you think that the fact of talking about your relationship could make things worse, maybe distract you from your kids and bring more instability into the family . . . although to be honest, in my opinion . . . (*Positive SAFETY indicator; therapist helps clients to talk truthfully and not defensively.*)

Rosa: It wasn't working that well . . . it's hard to continue this way.

Therapist: Yes, but I'm trying to understand you both . . . it may be reasonable to say, "Okay, let's put this behind us and focus now on what we have to do with our children." (*Positive SHARED PURPOSE indicator; therapist indicates a shared feeling between family members.*)

José: The thing is, we don't have any arguments . . . it's more like . . . we have a problem, but it's frozen, since we can't take care of it right now, it's not the priority.

Therapist: That's the point. There's only one doubt. I also think that it could be reasonable to shut off this topic and, as you said, Rosa, focus on the kids. However, I wonder if . . . I've been thinking about this a lot . . . it's been in my mind from the beginning of the therapy . . . what if things are all related and we're doing just the opposite? *[Long pause, looking at the parents]* I mean . . . all the behavior problems that Alberto is going through . . . also Ana is struggling with many issues . . . all together this makes me feel that everything is interrelated with everything . . .

Rosa: But for them this can't be postponed . . .

Therapist: Well, my point is . . . this is even hard for me to say . . . even though I'm the professional here *[laughs]*. What I think is that we've been focusing on these kids . . . and I feel responsible for this as well. It's obviously necessary to work on their problems. But I want and would like to do that and also try to do so something here in therapy. This is a place where they can relieve some pain and anger; it takes time with adolescents, but it can be done. (*Positive* ENGAGEMENT *indicator; therapist expresses optimism for change.*) Now I realize that this sort of emotional disconnection that you have . . . this "emotional divorce" that you're going through without even talking about it, from a long time ago . . . I can see that there're things that are hurting you both here . . . (*Positive* CONNECTION *indicator; therapist expresses empathy with the clients' struggle.*)

Rosa: Yes . . .

Therapist: So on the one hand, we have what we've been doing, trying to work with the kids and focus on them and see if things get better . . . On the other hand . . . my other scenario is . . . what if . . . what if this is all the other way round? What if you need to be prepared to disclose this secret? Maybe you could tell them, "Well, we're going to therapy because we have some issues . . . nothing is going to happen and we're not letting you down, and besides, we want to talk about these problems that we're having." This is my other hypothesis . . . do you think that they'd be very surprised by this?

José: No. *[confidently and assertively]*

Therapist: I have the sense that we all think our parents are perfect and do everything right . . . however, that's not true, and it could be a big relief for them, especially for Ana, to see this . . . *[Silence]* I'm just trying to be honest with you . . . I feel your pain and I really appreciate you all . . . you've become a very special family to me . . . you are wonderful people and you're suffering a lot . . . and you can even feel in Alberto this . . . (*Positive* CONNECTION *indicator; therapist expresses empathy with the clients' struggle.*)

Rosa: . . . anger.

Therapist: Yes, exactly, his suffering and fury . . . So I'd like that whatever path you decide to take, it would be the right one, so long as you take a firm step . . . to be sure of what you're doing. Besides everything, in the end you're able to become a strong team. (*Positive ENGAGEMENT indicator; therapist expresses optimism.*)

José: There's no hostility in our relationship.

Therapist: Okay, then . . . I wonder . . . whenever you're ready and really sure about it, wouldn't you be able to talk to your kids about the real situation between the two of you? (*Positive ENGAGEMENT indicator; therapist asks clients for their willingness to follow a specific suggestion.*)

[Silence]

José: Maybe.

Rosa: But . . . I think it's a risk.

Therapist: Yes, it could be . . . however, isn't it hard to keep this secret from them? I know perfectly . . . I am a father, too, (*Positive CONNECTION indicator; therapist self-discloses something about his personal life.*) that it is extremely hard to know that something that we did hurt my children . . . I know.

[Silence—but Rosa is clearly agreeing nonverbally with emotion that suggests she feels what the therapist is saying.]

Therapist: Let me tell you something, with affection *[sits up]*. Let me hold your hand *[holds Rosa's hand]* because I'm also very afraid to hurt you . . . (*Positive CONNECTION indicator; therapist expresses caring and touches client affectionately.*) You said before something like, "Well . . . the kids are doing fine, they come here and do fine as siblings," and it's interesting to me because you both come here and you're doing well as a couple . . . but that's not really the truth . . .

Rosa: I see . . . you're right.

Therapist: Then, what I'm wondering is . . . all this anger that they have within them . . . kids tend to figure everything out . . . You guys aren't enemies, you don't let each other down, you have been together in this . . . however, this *[referring to their emotional divorce]* could be affecting your kids, it's like they are following a pattern. (*Positive SHARED PURPOSE indicator; therapist draws attention to clients' shared values.*)

At this point, the discussion turns to how the lack of intimacy between José and Rosa could be affecting the whole family, an indicator that the couple has already accepted the therapist's construction of the interrelated family's problems. The parents also confirm that the children actually *know* what the situation is between them, in some sense.

The therapist's systemic reframing (on a technical level) was effective because it was supported in parallel fashion with a focus on the therapeutic alliance (on a relational level). Specifically, the therapist's interventions were intended to sustain a solid emotional connection, create safety, and offer the couple a way to engage in the therapy for themselves. Indeed, the SOFTA–s self-reported alliance data following Session 9 (see Figure 11.1) indicated that both parents felt a strong alliance with the therapist. From the perspective of SOFTA, the parents' consideration of this new perspective on how to cope with the family's difficulties was likely due to their feeling emotionally understood by the therapist rather than blamed. That is, since previously the parents hid the fact of their "emotional divorce" in order to avoid hurting their children, the therapist needed to reframe their strategy as a positive one, while simultaneously recognizing its evident negative result and raising the possibility of an alternative—being truthful and sincere with their children.

Outcome and Prognosis

This case had a mixed result. Session 11 turned out to be the last one. A couple of weeks later, Rosa telephoned the therapist to say that she and José had indeed spoken with their children about the marital difficulties. Rosa indicated being grateful to the therapist and the clinic because their relationship with the children had become much easier, and in fact the children's behavior had improved. Yet they were unwilling to tackle the emotional divorce, indicating clearly that they wanted some time to think about how to proceed as a couple. After that phone call, the therapist sent the parents a letter that commented positively on their decision and indicated that, in his view, the changes they had made were both honest and brave. The therapist congratulated them on the positive changes in the family and encouraged them to continue working together.

As shown in Table 11.1 and Figure 11.1, the process of therapy was complex, and the impact and value of the sessions were being seen as more positive toward the end of the treatment, as were the self-reported therapeutic alliances. With regard to specific improvements, Alberto's smoking and trouble in school diminished, and his relationship with Ana was more peaceful and unstrained.

The quantitative self-report data (family members' problem ratings, see Figure 11.1) showed a mixed picture. Rosa's and Ana's Session 11 ratings, the highest they had been to that point, indicated improvements. Alberto's ratings, however, despite showing clear improvement in the early sessions, were low in the final session, and José's ratings stayed fairly low over the course of treatment. It is, however, difficult to compare these ratings across family members, as each client had listed different sets of problems on which these session ratings were based. On the other hand, family members' ratings of "improvement so far" over the course of therapy were more positive, especially Alberto's and, only to a slightly lesser extent, Ana's and Rosa's. Relative to the others' ratings, José's ratings of improvement were relatively low and unchanging.

SUMMARY AND MECHANISMS OF CHANGE

Since the family did not continue in therapy after Session 11 and we have no objective ratings of the children's symptomatic behaviors, it is not possible to determine the final outcome of this case. Nonetheless, our aim in selecting this case was to illustrate the interplay of technical and relational aspects in systemic therapy, by relating the verbatim case material to the therapist's intentions and to the clients' perceptions of the process of therapy, especially in three significant moments.

The case illustrates the complexities and opportunities involved in working conjointly with family members who are in conflict with one another, as well as the editors' assertion that "in the reality of clinical practice, technique and relationship are intertwined, and cannot be neatly separated—the therapy process consists of a synergy between technique and relationship." There are moments when a specific technique makes a strong impact, and other moments when something happens in the relationship that moves the process along on other dimensions as well. For example, in the work to engage Alberto in Session 1 (specifically, the "I'll bet you 20 Euros" exchange) the therapist's emergent emotional connection gave him a platform to reframe the presenting problem systemically, as one that required therapeutic attention to the parents' worries.

Through various creative alliance-focused interventions, the therapist first managed to obtain the family members' commitment to engage in therapy and then led them to shift their relations with one another to work together toward problem-solving. This work was facilitated by having a clear model of the alliance with concrete indicators that allowed the therapist to create and evaluate the consequences of specific "alliance interventions" and to use the evaluation as a feedback to the therapy process.

FROM RESEARCH TO PRACTICE: IMPLICATIONS AND RECOMMENDATIONS FOR CLINICIANS AND SUPERVISORS

While the alliance is a common factor across therapies, that does not mean that it is an "everywhere and nowhere" (or elusive) phenomenon. Nor is it something that arises only spontaneously in the therapeutic interactions.

Rather, as demonstrated in this case, alliance-building is comprised of concrete interventions, and therapists can be trained in alliance-fostering skills and techniques (Carpenter, Escudero, & Rivett, 2008; Escudero, Friedlander, & Heatherington, 2011). Below are some suggestions based on our study for clinicians, supervisors, and trainees.

First, didactic instruction in psychotherapy training should include the analysis of entire cases, not only individual sessions or specific interventions taken out of context. The therapeutic alliance in the context of systemic family therapy is actually a dynamic *set* of alliances (between subsystems and within the family system) that unfold over time and across sessions. Providing trainees with entire cases, either from clinic files or supervisors' cases, as well as published case material such as Friedlander, Angus, et al. (2016) and cases in the journal *Pragmatic Case Studies in Psychotherapy*, can help trainees learn how different levels of the alliance develop and interconnect over the entire course of a family treatment. Whether the alliances are strong or weak in any given case, case material will allow trainees to see how they develop and how ruptures are repaired (well or less well). Full (ideally) or partial transcripts or videos should be used whenever possible in order to most closely approximate the clinical situation.

Second, if students are instructed in the conceptual and technical aspects of the SOFTA, they can use these tools to study and discuss what worked and did not work for them and why. By stopping a video at strategic moments, trainees could role-play skills learned from observation of others' work.

Once familiar with the SOFTA system, trainees and their supervisors can use specific observations about the alliance as material during the supervision process (see Escudero & Friedlander, 2015). Feedback from clients' self-reports about the alliance can enrich the process of therapy; further, observations from the SOFTA–o can be used in the therapy process as well. For example, introducing "data" (using SOFTA–o observations) to a couple about the emergent risk of a split alliance might affect the treatment process and outcome.

Moreover, the present case suggests that we (clinicians, supervisors, trainees) remember to attend to metacommunication, which contributes to alliance building and repair throughout the treatment. Systemic theory has always emphasized that interpersonal communication (in therapy as well as in other contexts) has relational as well as content levels; that is, the *ways* in which people deliver verbal and nonverbal messages serve to communicate implicitly how they define the relationship and how they feel about each other. The relational level of the therapeutic communication (vs. the purely content level) is an often overlooked medium by which the therapeutic alliance is built. And relational communication occurs constantly in therapeutic communication, including during the delivery of specific interventions. In the present case, for example, the therapist's "bet" with Alberto signaled a kind of playful willingness to meet the boy on his own terms, as well as a kind of genuineness that seemed to engage him. We hope we have conveyed a different perspective from the traditional assumption that the alliance is merely a platform to be built early in therapy to allow the technical interventions to be more accepted or successful. Simply put, technical interventions and relationship/alliance-building interventions are recursively connected.

FROM PRACTICE TO RESEARCH

Studies of this kind (those closely grounded in clinical material) have implications for research as well as practice. The recommendation to study entire cases for clinical training also holds for research, as well; it is only in the unfolding interactions over time that we will truly be able to capture the process of change. Thus, research questions about patterns of change over time and research methods such as sequential analysis and other time series strategies are preferable to cross-sectional questions or methods in which behaviors of therapists and clients are counted and summed over time.

Paying attention to metacommunication or relational communication along with the content of communication helps strengthen alliances throughout treatment. This also has implications for research. We suggest that systematically studying the relational effects of certain techniques, such as the reframing illustrated in this chapter on alliance-building, is a potentially fruitful area of future investigation. Having a concrete model of the alliance, as illustrated in this chapter, allows the study of how certain techniques affect specific dimensions of the alliance, such as creating safety or fostering a shared sense of purpose for the treatment in the family.

Echoing the practice implications suggestions, another major focus of interest for future research is the *impact* of integrating feedback of information about the alliance into the therapy process over the course of therapy. It would be interesting to systematically study the effects of using alliance-related feedback in treatment. A first step would be simply to compare the course and outcomes of treatment when feedback about the alliance is shared with the participants and used versus not shared and not used in the therapy. In this kind of study it would also be relatively easy and potentially fruitful to assess therapists' and clients' opinions (posttherapy) about the feedback intervention.

In any case, recognizing that research (both large scale and small scale) is indispensable for the progress of psychotherapy, we humbly acknowledge that the best therapy is still partially an "art"; sensing how and when to harness the twin engines that drive the therapy with families—alliance interventions and systemic interventions—requires a respectful attitude toward the family, careful listening, good timing, and emotional responsivity. We hope that this case study will inform readers' own journeys toward working responsively with families in conflict.

REFERENCES

Battle, C. C., Imber, S. D., Hoehn-Saric, R., Nash, E. R., & Frank, J. D. (1966). Target complaints as criteria of improvement. *American Journal of Psychotherapy, 20*, 184–192.

Bordin, E. S. (1979). The generalizability of the psychoanalytic concept of the working alliance. *Psychotherapy, 16*, 252–260. http://dx.doi.org/10.1037/h0085885

Carpenter, J., Escudero, V., & Rivett, M. (2008). Training family therapy students in conceptual and observation skills relating to the therapeutic alliance: An evaluation. *Journal of Family Therapy, 30*, 411–424. http://dx.doi.org/10.1111/j.1467-6427.2008.00442.x

Diamond, G. S., Diamond, G., & Levy, S. A. (2014). *Attachment-based family therapy for depressed adolescents*. Washington, DC: American Psychological Association. http://dx.doi.org/10.1037/14296-000

Escudero, V., & Friedlander, M. L. (2003). El sistema de observación de la alianza terapéutica en intervención familiar (SOATIF): Desarrollo trans-cultural, fiabilidad, y aplicaciones del instrumento. *Mosaico (Journal of the Spanish Federation of Family Therapy Associations), 25*, 32–36.

Escudero, V., & Friedlander, M. L. (2015). e–SOFTA: A video-based software for observing the working alliance in clinical training and supervision. In T. Rousmaniere & E. Renfro-Michel (Eds.), *Using technology to enhance clinical supervision* (pp. 223–238). Alexandria, VA: American Counseling Association.

Escudero, V., & Friedlander, M. L. (2017). *Therapeutic alliances in families: Empowering clients in challenging cases*. New York, NY: Springer. http://dx.doi.org/10.1007/978-3-319-59369-2

Escudero, V., Friedlander, M. L., & Heatherington, L. (2011). Using the e–SOFTA for video training and research on alliance-related behavior. *Psychotherapy, 48*, 138–147. http://dx.doi.org/10.1037/a0022188

Friedlander, M. L., Angus, L., Wright, S. T., Günther, C., Austin, C. L., Kangos, K., . . . Khattra, J. (2016). "If those tears could talk, what would they say?" Multi-method analysis of a corrective experience in brief dynamic therapy. *Psychotherapy Research*, 1–18. Advance online publication. http://dx.doi.org/10.1080/10503307.2016.1184350

Friedlander, M. L., Escudero, V., & Heatherington, L. (2006). *Therapeutic alliances in couple and family therapy: An empirically informed guide to practice*. Washington,

DC: American Psychological Association. [(Also published in Spanish as *La Alianza terapeutica: En las terapia familiar y de Pareja* (2009). Barcelona, Spain: Paidós Iberica; and in Italian as *La Alianza Terapéutica* (2009) Rome, Italy: Edizioni CarloAmore] http://dx.doi.org/10.1037/11410-000

Friedlander, M. L., Escudero, V., Heatherington, L., & Diamond, G. M. (2011). Alliance in couple and family therapy. *Psychotherapy*, *48*, 25–33. http://dx.doi.org/10.1037/a0022060

Friedlander, M. L., Escudero, V., Horvath, A. S., Heatherington, L., Cabero, A., & Martens, M. P. (2006). System for observing family therapy alliances: A tool for research and practice. *Journal of Counseling Psychology*, *53*, 214–225. http://dx.doi.org/10.1037/0022-0167.53.2.214

Friedlander, M. L., Heatherington, L., & Escudero, V. (2016). Research-based change mechanisms: Advances in process research. In T. L. Sexton & J. Lebow (Eds.), *Handbook of family therapy* (pp. 454–467). New York, NY: Routledge.

Friedlander, M. L., Lambert, J. E., & Muñiz de la Peña, C. (2008). A step toward disentangling the alliance/improvement cycle in family therapy. *Journal of Counseling Psychology*, *55*, 118–124. http://dx.doi.org/10.1037/0022-0167.55.1.118

Greenberg, L. S., & Johnson, S. M. (1988). *Emotionally focused therapy for couples*. New York, NY: Guilford Press.

Guttman, H. A. (1991). Systems theory, cybernetics, and epistemology. In A. S. Gurman & D. P. Kniskern (Eds.), *Handbook of family therapy*, Vol. 2 (pp. 41–62). New York, NY: Brunner/Mazel.

Heatherington, L., & Friedlander, M. L. (1990). Couple and family therapy alliance scales: Empirical considerations. *Journal of Marital and Family Therapy*, *16*, 299–306. http://dx.doi.org/10.1111/j.1752-0606.1990.tb00851.x

Heatherington, L., Friedlander, M. L., & Greenberg, L. (2005). Change process research in couple and family therapy: Methodological challenges and opportunities. *Journal of Family Psychology*, *19*, 18–27. http://dx.doi.org/10.1037/0893-3200.19.1.18

Horvath, A. O., Del Re, A. C., Flückiger, C., & Symonds, D. (2011). Alliance in individual psychotherapy. *Psychotherapy*, *48*, 9–16. http://dx.doi.org/10.1037/a0022186

Johnson, S. M., & Greenberg, L. S. (Eds.). (1994). *The heart of the matter: Perspectives on emotion in marital therapy*. New York, NY: Brunner/Mazel.

Lambert, J. E., Skinner, A. H., & Friedlander, M. L. (2012). Problematic within-family alliances in conjoint family therapy: A close look at five cases. *Journal of Marital and Family Therapy*, *38*, 417–428. http://dx.doi.org/10.1111/j.1752-0606.2010.00212.x

Lebow, J. (2005). *Handbook of clinical family therapy*. Hoboken, NJ: Wiley.

Muñiz de la Peña, C., Friedlander, M., & Escudero, V. (2009). Frequency, severity, and evolution of split family alliances: How observable are they? *Psychotherapy Research*, *19*, 133–142. http://dx.doi.org/10.1080/10503300802460050

Nichols, M. P., & Schwartz, R. C. (2006). *Family therapy: Concepts and methods* (3rd ed.). Boston, MA: Pearson/Allyn & Bacon.

Pinsof, W. M. (1994). An integrative systems perspective on the therapeutic alliance: Theoretical, clinical, and research implications. In A. O. Horvath & L. S. Greenberg (Eds.), *The working alliance: Theory, research, and practice* (pp. 173–195). Oxford, England: Wiley.

Pinsof, W. M., & Catherall, D. R. (1986). The integrative psychotherapy alliance: Family, couple and individual therapy scales. *Journal of Marital and Family Therapy, 12*, 137–151. http://dx.doi.org/10.1111/j.1752-0606.1986.tb01631.x

Robbins, M. S., Turner, C. W., Alexander, J. F., & Perez, G. A. (2003). Alliance and dropout in family therapy for adolescents with behavior problems: Individual and systemic effects. *Journal of Family Psychology, 17*, 534–544. http://dx.doi.org/10.1037/0893-3200.17.4.534

Sexton, T. L., & Alexander, J. F. (2002). Functional family therapy for at-risk adolescents and their families. In F. W. Kaslow & T. Patterson (Eds.), *Comprehensive handbook of psychotherapy: Cognitive–behavioral approaches* (Vol. 2, pp. 117–140). Hoboken, NJ: Wiley.

12

THE USE OF IMMEDIACY IN SUPERVISORY RELATIONSHIPS

CLARA E. HILL AND SHUDARSHANA GUPTA

Imagine that Joan (a supervisee) is very angry at Dr. S. (her supervisor) because Dr. S. constantly interrupts the supervision session and takes phone calls, but Joan says nothing to Dr. S. about the disruptions and acts as if everything is fine. Or, consider that Dr. S. has overheard people talking in the lunchroom about Joan's dissatisfaction with supervision, but Joan has said nothing to Dr. S. How should Joan and Dr. S. deal with these situations?

We propose that immediacy, or the supervisor and supervisee talking together directly about the relationship, could help to resolve some of the problems in the above situations. Unfortunately, although there is talk in the supervision literature about the importance of openly processing the supervisory relationship (e.g., Mueller & Kell, 1972; Stoltenberg & McNeill, 2012), there is minimal empirical research. Hence, we first briefly review the literature about immediacy in psychotherapy, and then we make propositions about how immediacy could be used in supervision. We next review a study on working with

http://dx.doi.org/10.1037/0000093-013
Developing the Therapeutic Relationship: Integrating Case Studies, Research, and Practice, O. Tishby and H. Wiseman (Editors)

conflict in supervision (Nelson, Barnes, Evans, & Triggiano, 2008) because the results of this study have implications for this chapter. Finally, we present some data about how immediacy was used in 18 supervision dyads in one clinic.

THEORETICAL AND CONCEPTUAL BASES FOR THE USE OF IMMEDIACY

Immediacy in the therapeutic relationship (between client and therapist) has been defined as talking about the therapeutic relationship in the here and now (Hill & Knox, 2009). This skill has also been called metacommunication (Kiesler, 1988) or processing the relationship (Hill & Knox, 2009). Immediacy can be considered a subtype of self-disclosure, but the focus is on the immediate relationship, whereas self-disclosure involves personal information not related to the client (e.g., "I feel anxious, too, when I have to give a public speech," "I learned about supervision in graduate school").

The first reference to the term *immediacy* that I (CEH) recall is Carkhuff (1969) writing about immediacy as an advanced skill that communicated high levels of empathy. For Carkhuff, the therapist is able to see that the client is covertly communicating something and makes the implicit statement explicit (e.g., "You say that you are angry at everyone lately. I wonder if you're angry at me?")

Theoretical support for therapist use of immediacy in psychotherapy comes from relational and interpersonal theorists (e.g., Cashdan, 1988; Kiesler, 1988, 1996; Safran & Muran, 2000), who have conceptualized immediacy (or metacommunication) as a key mechanism of therapeutic change. These theorists suggested that both therapist and client contribute to the therapy relationship, and therapy involves a process of negotiating the relationship. They note that every communication is at some level about the relationship (e.g., with each interaction, the client wants something from the therapist, and the therapist wants something from the client). In terms of steps for metacommunication, these theorists suggest that all interventions must be grounded in the immediate experience; hence, such interventions cannot be fabricated or used as an experiment. The therapist must first become aware of strong emotion about the relationship (e.g., become bored, distracted, angry, attracted, or what can be called becoming "hooked"). The therapist then needs to disembed (i.e., step back or disengage) from the strong emotion and reflect about what is happening. By becoming curious and gaining insight into the situation, the therapist is typically able to reapproach the client with insight and compassion. The therapist then articulates what is going on between the two of them, owning his or her feelings and asking about the client's feelings (making the implicit explicit). By then exploring openly and dialoguing about what is going on between them, the therapist and client can emerge with a new understanding of their relationship and new ideas for how to approach the relationship differently. By no means is this experience easy, and in fact, it is often difficult and anxiety-producing for both people to talk openly about negative feelings. Metaphorically, the temperature in the room rises, with both people feeling vulnerable and anxious, but with (we hope) at least the therapist having confidence that relationship issues can be resolved through open communication.

Empirical Support for the Use of Immediacy in Psychotherapy

Some empirical support exists for the use of immediacy in psychotherapy (see Hill & Knox, 2009). A number of empirically based case studies have shown that, although used infrequently, immediacy has been found to help to build the therapeutic relationship, negotiate and resolve problems within the therapeutic relationship, and model for the client how to deal with relationships outside of therapy (Berman et al., 2012; Friedlander et al., 2018; Hill et al., 2008; Kasper, Hill, & Kivlighan, 2008; Kuutmann & Hilsenroth, 2012; Mayotte-Blum et al., 2012).

Building on these case studies, Hill et al. (2014) conducted an intensive study of 16 cases of open-ended (10–59 sessions) individual psychodynamic/interpersonal psychotherapy conducted by doctoral student therapists with adult community clients. After each session, therapists responded yes or no to the question "Did you use immediacy in today's session (i.e., did you disclose about your feelings about the client, yourself in relation to the client, or the relationship)?" Research teams, each responsible for one to three entire cases, watched the intake and all sessions with identified immediacy events. The research team members coded types of immediacy, quality of each immediacy event, and the direct consequences of each immediacy event. At the end of each case, the judges combined all the evidence and wrote a narrative about the observed consequences in the case. Another team of judges then went through all the evidence for each case and coded the consequences into categories (e.g., gained insight) established from the data.

In the 16 cases, there were 234 events, ranging from 3 to 40 events per case. There was an average of less than one event per session ($M = .61$, $SD = .31$), and therapists spent an average of about 5% of their time in immediacy. The average length of an immediacy event was about 5 minutes, and therapists initiated 85% of the events.

The first and most frequent type of immediacy was of unexpressed feelings or making the covert overt, with these occurring on average once every other session. An example here is of an intake session with a young female therapist paired with an older male client.

The therapist asked, "How do you feel about working with a younger female therapist?"

The client responded, "It's a little startling but I understand that younger people have expertise. I expect you to guide the process not have all the answers."

The therapist said, "I appreciate you sharing that with me because it's important to keep the communication open."

The client then turned it back to the therapist and said, "How do you feel working with someone much older than you?"

The therapist replied, "It's a little different—we have different life experiences, but we can work on it together." This event set the tone for the remainder of the case, with the therapist and client able to deal with many difficulties openly.

The second type of immediacy involved negotiating the tasks and goals of therapy; this type occurred about once every four sessions. For example, in a middle session of therapy the therapist asked, "How do you feel about how it's going right now . . . is this a good direction for you, talking about your family?"

The client responded, "I am fine talking about my family, but I want to focus on myself and my own change. I don't think insight will be enough to help me change. Does that make sense?"

The therapist replied, "Yes, sometimes making that realization isn't good enough." Thus, they negotiated the terms of their relationship, with the client directly stating what she needed and the therapist being responsive to the client's needs. They were able to collaboratively determine the scope and focus of their work.

The third type involved drawing parallels between what was going on in the client's life with what was going on in therapy; this type occurred about once every four sessions. For example, in a session where the therapist came in with a cold and was visibly not feeling well, the client talked at length about being at a mentoring event. She complained that she felt less important to others than they were to her. To the therapist's query "Between us, you feel that too?" the client responded, "Yes, I feel like a burden to you. I get the feeling that, on the day that I'm sick, I don't want to hear people's problems." The therapist reassured the client that she did not view her as a burden. By drawing the parallel, the therapist was able to make explicit what the client was hinting at, thus enabling them to openly process and correct the client's projection that the therapist did not want to be at the session.

The final and least frequently occurring (once every eight sessions) type was repairing ruptures. At the end of a session where the therapist was concerned that the client may have had some negative reactions, the therapist asked, "How did this session feel for you?"

The client responded, "I felt a little uncomfortable talking about my husband and all the clutter in my life."

The therapist said, "I know I pushed you more than usual."

To which the client responded, "You didn't make me feel uncomfortable, but it's just that I don't want to see myself like that. I'd rather come across in a more positive light." This exchange prevented a rupture from worsening by getting the client's feelings out in the open. The therapist was also able to show that he valued the client and the therapeutic relationship by being sensitive to potential problems.

The consequences of the immediacy as judged at the end of the cases based on a review of all the data (these were not mutually exclusive) were (a) clients expressed feelings about therapist/therapy (50% of cases); (b) clients opened up and gained insight (50% of cases); (c) boundaries were clarified (44% of cases); (d) clients felt validated, cared for, or reassured (12% of cases); (e) the relationship was established (12% of cases); (f) ruptures in the relationship were repaired (12% of cases); or (g) clients had a corrective relational experience (12% of cases). In 19% of the cases, no effects were observed. Negative effects (e.g., ruptures, dropouts) were not judged as having occurred in any of the cases.

In a reanalysis of the Hill et al. (2014) data, Shafran, Kivlighan, Gelso, Bhatia, and Hill (2017) found that sessions with more immediacy were rated higher in session quality by clients across all of therapy, and higher in working alliance later in treatment. Similarly, in 60 cases of psychotherapy, Lingiardi, Colli, Gentile, and Tanzilli (2011) found that sessions that were rated as having more of a focus on the therapy relationship were also rated as having more depth and working alliance.

Thus, from the evidence, it appears that immediacy occurs infrequently within psychodynamic/interpersonal psychotherapy and can be helpful. In their summary, Hill and Knox (2009) suggested that if immediacy is used appropriately in psychotherapy, "feelings will be expressed and accepted, problems will be resolved, the relationship will be enhanced, and clients will transfer their learning to other relationships outside of therapy" (p. 13).

Empirical Support for the Use of Immediacy in Supervision

Given that therapist immediacy can benefit the process and outcome of psychotherapy, it makes sense that it could also be useful in supervision, since both endeavors involve relationships. We recognize, however, that psychotherapy and supervision differ in some fundamental ways, particularly in relation to the evaluative component of supervision (see Burke, Goodyear, & Guzzard, 1998). Indeed, in their recent review of the supervision literature, Stoltenberg and McNeill (2012) suggested that, "For the supervision process to be effective and impactful, there needs to be a clear, relevant, and open communication between the supervisor and supervisee within professionally appropriate interpersonal boundaries" (p. 304).

We would thus expand Hill and Knox's propositions about immediacy in psychotherapy to suggest that if immediacy is used appropriately in supervision, feelings will be expressed and accepted, problems in the supervisory relationship will be resolved, the supervisory relationship will be enhanced, and supervisees will transfer their learning to their conduct of therapy with their clients. If supervisees/therapists then use immediacy with their clients, the consequences for clients noted above will be realized. In other words, we propose that the use of immediacy in supervision is not only beneficial for the supervision relationship but is also one avenue for trainees/supervisees to learn about how to use immediacy in their provision of psychotherapy.

We found only one empirical study that focused, albeit indirectly, on immediacy in supervision. Nelson, Barnes, Evans, and Triggiano (2008) noted a lack of a clearly defined skill set for handling conflicts within supervision. They noted that conflict is typical in supervision for many reasons: (a) supervisees need to learn skills and take risks, and hence they are in a vulnerable position relative to their supervisors, (b) the supervision relationship is an evaluative one, and supervisees often fear that they can jeopardize their future careers if they misstep the boundaries or get a bad evaluation, (c) supervision relationships are often brief, not allowing for much time to work through conflicts, (d) supervisees are expected to embrace their supervisor's philosophy even though they may have very different world assumptions, and thus may have very different ideas for how to intervene with clients, and (e) parallel process from the supervisee's/therapist's work in therapy may infect supervision (e.g., if the client feels helpless and hopeless in the therapy, the supervisee may feel helpless and hopeless with the supervisor).

Because of this lack of information, Nelson et al. (2008) felt a need for a study that would provide some preliminary information about managing conflict. Hence, in their qualitative study, they interviewed 12 supervisors who had been nominated for being highly qualified and "wise" about supervision. They asked these supervisors about their perceptions of working with conflict in supervision. They discovered a core theme: These supervisors were open to working through conflict, even though it was painful and anxiety producing, because they believed that conflict is necessary and beneficial, and that supervision is a good place to learn about how to deal with conflict. In general, these supervisors said that supervision needs to be a safe place to deal with conflict especially given the power imbalance, and that supervisors need to set clear expectations, have good boundaries, and give feedback to help supervisees grow.

The wise supervisors described three skill sets for supervisors in working with conflict:

- They highlighted reflective strategies: stepping back and gaining insight into themselves, the supervisees, the supervision relationship, and parallel process; using self-coaching, such as working to recognize their own limitations; not taking conflicts personally, given that they could be due to transference or distortions; and seeking consultation and support.
- They suggested several interpersonal strategies: not shaming or embarrassing supervisees when giving feedback; disengaging from power struggles; listening carefully and empathetically; disclosing feelings and owning responsibility; and interpreting transference, countertransference, and parallel process. These interpersonal strategies sound very similar to immediacy and have been recommended by the relational and interpersonal theorists for psychotherapy (e.g., Cashdan, 1988; Kiesler, 1988, 1996; Safran & Muran, 2000).
- Supervisors recommended some technical interventions that could be used to strengthen supervision: becoming more active with teaching skills, observing therapy sessions to assess skills/style, providing early and timely feedback, and focusing on supervisee's strengths.

The Nelson et al. (2008) study is incredibly rich and important, but clearly, more research is needed to identify the specific skills that can be used not only to work with conflict, but to help supervisors process the supervision relationship. In addition, the Nelson et al. study only focused on dealing with conflicts in supervision, whereas there may be other reasons for talking openly about the supervision relationship (e.g., negotiating goals, dealing with transferences). Given the research cited above about immediacy in psychotherapy, our experiences in training therapists in the skill of immediacy (Spangler et al., 2014), and our experiences in individual and group supervision, the skill we focus on in this chapter is immediacy.

RESEARCH TO PRACTICE AND BACK: THE USE OF IMMEDIACY IN ONE CLINIC

We investigated the use of immediacy in supervision in one small psychology department clinic that served community clients using a psychodynamic/interpersonal approach, with advanced doctoral students serving as therapists. Doctoral student trainees started working at the clinic after they had participated in a prepracticum that focused on helping skills and had been in at least two practica. Supervisors were highly experienced, psychodynamically oriented psychologists chosen by the clinic directors for their expertise in providing supervision.

For this investigation, we had two sets of data. First, we drew data from a qualitative study with nine counseling psychology doctoral student trainees who were at the end of their training (1–2 years) or who had already been in the clinic for 3 years (Hill et al., 2015). Using semistructured interviews, we asked therapists about changes they had made during their time in the clinic, to what they attributed any changes, and about their experiences in individual supervision. All talked extensively about helpful aspects of the individual supervision, with three spontaneously describing immediacy events as helpful.

Second, we did a survey of the 12 supervisor–supervisee dyads who were currently active or who had terminated within the past 6 months (individual supervision with the same supervisor had lasted from 3 months to 4 years). We asked both the supervisors and supervisees separately if immediacy had occurred within their supervision. If not, we asked them why not and what prevented them from using immediacy. If yes, we asked them which of three types of immediacy (negotiating the tasks and goals of supervision, parallels between therapy and supervision, and repairing distortions/ruptures in supervision) had occurred, and to give us examples. All but one supervisor and one supervisee indicated that at least one type of immediacy had occurred.

Three of the supervisees were participants in both samples, so we report here on a total of 18 unique dyads. Interestingly, of the three supervisees who were in both samples, only one spontaneously mentioned immediacy in the qualitative study, whereas all three indicated in the survey that it had occurred, which undoubtedly speaks to differences in results based on different methods of asking about immediacy. In this chapter, we combined the results from the two studies because our intent was to provide descriptions of how immediacy was used in supervision, rather than to catalog the frequency or quality of the immediacy (which would have required observing the occurrence of immediacy within recordings of supervision sessions, as was done in the Hill et al., 2014, study on immediacy in psychotherapy). In addition, because of the intensity of the rupture experience in one case, I (CEH) also interviewed the supervisor and supervisee for this chapter (thus, we had more information about this case than about the other cases).

We (the coauthors) examined all the information we had about the cases and consensually coded the data into five types. In terms of nonuse, there were two types: (a) no immediacy used or needed, and (b) no immediacy used, but it could have been helpful. We identified three types of immediacy: (a) immediacy used to negotiate or monitor the relationship, (b) immediacy used to draw parallels between what happened in the supervisee's therapy cases and what was happening in the supervision, and (c) immediacy used to challenge distortions/transferences or to repair ruptures. In the next section, we provide examples of these five types of immediacy. When we provide quotations, minimal verbal responses such as "mhmm" and "you know" were removed to make reading easier.

No Discussion of Immediacy: Smooth Sailing

In one supervision dyad, which had been together for 3 years, the supervisor and supervisee indicated that immediacy was not used. The supervisor said it was not needed because the focus of the supervision was on clients, and things were going well. She said that no problems had emerged, and there were no interpersonal issues between them. This supervisor was very gentle and accepting, which may have limited the potential for distortions and ruptures.

No Discussion of Immediacy: Problems Kept Underground

In two cases, supervisees indicated that immediacy had not been used but could have been helpful. In both cases, the supervisors were traditionally psychoanalytic, believing in more of a blank slate and a distant supervisory relationship focused primarily on client dynamics and possible interventions that the supervisee-therapist could use in sessions. For example, the supervisee in one dyad (3 months in duration at time of survey) said that immediacy was rarely if ever used, because the focus was on clients and things were going well. But she said that immediacy could have been helpful. According to this supervisee, what prevented the use of immediacy was that it did not seem to be important to the supervisor's model of supervision. On the survey, the supervisee said that the supervisor

> comes across as more blank slate versus warm and personal, and this makes me feel as though it would be tough to bring up personal things. At the same time, if something was important to address, I believe I would bring it up. Since things are going pretty well, I don't feel a strong pull towards initiating immediacy. At the same time, I feel like I would like it sometimes anyway, even if there are no problems.

Because of participating in the survey, the supervisee initiated immediacy with the supervisor in the next supervision session. The supervisor was receptive, and they discussed their relationship for the full session. Although the supervisee felt awkward bringing up the topic, the relationship improved because the supervisee was able to explore previously unexplored feelings, and then they were able to better negotiate their relationship. The supervisor realized that the supervisee needed a warmer, more personal relationship and was able to change her behavior to meet the needs of the supervisee.

Immediacy Used to Negotiate the Terms of the Relationship or Monitor the Relationship: Prophylactic Immediacy

Prophylactic immediacy was used in most of the dyads. For example, one supervisor generally was interested in talking about their relationship, and was open to talking about the supervisor's own mistakes, which the supervisee said made her feel comfortable admitting mistakes. In addition, the supervisee had intense feelings of sadness about the supervision relationship coming to an end. She did not want the supervisor to feel bad, and so tried to hide her feelings. Because the supervisor noticed and responded, they were able to have a very memorable event talking about the feelings. According to the supervisee:

Supervisee: I think my relationship with [supervisor] is generally I would say is really great. I think at the beginning I do have doubts about "Is she going to understand me?" or "Is she going to be okay if I'm not very skilled?" or "How would she respond if she saw my mistake?" or "How is she going to give feedback to me?" But then I think, over time, we kind of make this an open dialogue and she would be— I would say, she would be open to my feedback; she always asked me "How is that working, how is our supervision working?" Yeah, and I think she is not afraid of admitting that what she feels about her mistake, or things that she did, which gives me space and room to be like it's actually okay to make mistakes sometimes as a therapist.

Interviewer: So she was very open, you talked about your relationship?

Supervisee: Yeah she did, yeah—not a lot, but from time to time we did go back to see what's working, what's not working with us. Yeah, she was like my role model—

Interviewer: So it's going to be kind of hard to leave her I'm sure at this point?

Supervisee: Oh yeah, we also kind of processed that during supervision, and I did not know how much I was feeling sad. Well of course, I kind of make it seem like that's just normal, we just move on, and we do other extra—you know, she has other professional responsibilities, so she decided also not to be with the clinic, supervise students. So I just didn't notice. Maybe I noticed, but I kind of don't want to deal with it when I first learned that we're not going to work together. Then it also happened that one of my clients dropped out, so I felt a very intense feeling of loss and just confused and frus— . . . a lot feelings, a lot of intense emotions. I think the supervisor was not afraid to bring this up, "Hey, I noticed that's also happening between us too that, you know, the fact is that we're going to end at the end of August." So through that, I also noticed more about myself, to be more self-aware of how protective I am of her, I just don't want her to feel bad saying that she is not supervising me anymore. So I told her that I just want to hide off all my feelings with her. So we kind of talked about that actually. So I think that was one very memorable experience I think I had with [the supervisor].

Another perspective about prophylactic immediacy comes from a supervisor from a different dyad that had been together over a year. She said,

> As for the supervision, I check in with the supervisee frequently during the supervision regarding how it is going for her, am I being helpful, how does she feel about my suggestion, does she believe it would either fit her style or be something she would like to try to expand her style, etc. We speak before the session on how her life is going, school, family, etc. to make sure she is in a good place to hear what I have to say (not that I am particularly critical, but just to make sure she is *here*). I think, in some ways (duh) I treat our sessions like psychotherapy sessions, investigating how I am heard, am I understanding what the person is saying, etc.

Likewise, the supervisee in this dyad said, "We used immediacy occasionally, mostly to check in on the relationship. On another occasion, she and I saw the client differently, and she mentioned being glad that I was able to disagree with her." Hence, there was good agreement between the supervisor and supervisee about how immediacy was used.

Two other supervisees provided a slightly different perspective on how this type of immediacy was used in their supervision. The first supervisee (in supervision over a year) said,

> A few weeks after we started out work, my supervisor asked me how we were doing and asked about my goals. She said she had been filling out the working alliance measure and wondered about the goals aspect, as we don't always discuss my goals in supervision. I'm glad she brought this up as it allowed me to talk about my hopes for supervision.

Another supervisee (in supervision for 3 months) said,

> We have occasional conversations to check in on how our work together is going, and whether it is meeting my needs. For example, once we had a discussion about whether or not I felt our supervisory sessions were

goal-oriented enough. He expressed that he felt the way we were working felt appropriate but wondered if I felt things were too aimless. I shared my opinion about how our work was going.

Not all occurrences of this type of immediacy, however, revealed problems. Supervisees also mentioned times when immediacy was used to express appreciation or gratitude. For example, one supervisee (in supervision over a year) said,

> We used immediacy occasionally, mostly to check in on the relationship. On another occasion, she and I saw the client differently, and she mentioned being glad that I was able to disagree with her. I then spoke to her about how it felt comfortable to be honest with her.

Another (who had been in supervision over 4 years) said,

> Mainly after semester or annual evaluations, I would share with my supervisor my feelings in relation to working with him. Specifically, tell him how grateful I was, and how I enjoyed working with him. I would also say something like I thought we had a strong real relationship and working alliance.

These examples illustrate that immediacy can be used prophylactically to negotiate the terms of the relationship (e.g., "What do you want or need?") and monitor the relationship (e.g., "How are we doing?"). Supervisors who checked in with their supervisees had fewer surprises and were better able to manage the relationship because issues were out in the open.

Immediacy Used to Draw Parallels Between Therapy and Supervision

Using immediacy to draw parallels (from what was going on in the supervisee's relationships with clients to the supervision relationship) was also used frequently in this sample. In the following example, both the supervisor and supervisee (who had been together over a year) described exactly the same event. We provide here the supervisee's description because she nicely shows how the use of immediacy in supervision provided a model for how she could use immediacy with her client:

> I was talking about how I felt the need to introduce immediacy into my work with a specific client . . . [the supervisor] asked if there was ever a time that I concealed something from her regarding my needs. A timely example came to mind immediately: just prior to beginning our supervision that day, she asked me if I wouldn't mind reuploading all my older session notes onto our shared Dropbox because she likes to be able to check back on past notes while she is watching current sessions [the supervisor had accidentally deleted the file]. I said I didn't mind,

> but internally I felt burdened because I didn't have an electronic copy of my past notes . . . After I disclosed my true feelings, we processed my motivations a bit more, and the whole experience modeled how I could use immediacy with my client. In fact, I did so shortly after this supervision session, and even ended up using the same intervention: "Have you ever censored yourself in here or concealed something from me?" The intervention had a positive outcome with this client.

Another example of using immediacy to draw a parallel between therapy and supervision comes from another supervisee (supervision was more than a year):

> It's actually hard to give an example of this because we do it all the time! I recently had a session with a client in which he acted very helpless. Not only did he act helpless, he also seemed to be very harsh on himself. It was hard for me to sit with this client's emotions in the session. During supervision I discussed this with my supervisor, who then pointed out that she was sensing from me a similar helplessness and harshness. We processed our interaction and the parallel process that was happening.

These examples show how immediacy can be used to draw parallels. Whether the supervisee was actually covertly referring to the supervision process when talking about the client, or whether the therapy process was "infecting" the supervision is not clear, and in fact it is probably a two-way process. It is clear, however, that it can be helpful to think about these parallels between therapy and supervision.

Immediacy Used to Process Distortions and Resolve Ruptures

All of the above examples are relatively benign. Immediacy can also, however, be used to work with conflicts that arise in the supervision relationship, similar to what Nelson et al. (2008) described in their study of wise supervisors. Although there were far fewer examples of this type of immediacy, the events seemed to be more intense emotionally.

We identified three kinds of such events. One type involved supervisee distortions within the context of a strong alliance. The second type involved both distortions and dissatisfactions that the supervisee did not reveal until a breaking point. The third type involved a boundary problem between the supervisor and supervisee. The ruptures were eventually successfully resolved in all cases.

Distortions

Occasionally, when George (a pseudonym) would wonder whether his supervisor (Dr. L.) was getting frustrated with him, Dr. L. would say that she was not frustrated (this was a 3-year supervision).[1] They would then talk a lot about the relationship and clarify misperceptions. They talked about their relationship, and worked through the misperceptions, providing a model that the supervisee was to use with his clients. In his interview, George said,

Supervisee: I was able to see the supervisor more for who she was. I think she, because she's not going to give the advice or, often she's just able to sit with things and ask more about them. It left a lot of space for me to project that she's not happy with the work I'm doing or she's, she's worried about, she's, this is what I would think, I would think that she's frustrated that I'm not changing faster, that came up in our supervision work. She would say, "Why are you so, what's going on with this fast thing? Why do you gotta do things so fast?" So later I think I came to see that when she's there with me, she cares about me, whereas before I was sort of rejecting that . . . We actually would talk about times when I might say something like—just every now and then she might ask, "Is there something else you're thinking?" I might say I just realize that working on a certain issue for several sessions, you must be getting kind of frustrated with that, which she'd say, "well that really isn't my experience, actually. But let's [talk more]." She wanted to talk more about what was happening so and then—

Interviewer: So you used a lot of immediacy?

Supervisee: Oh yeah, yeah. She and I spoke in the here and now a lot about our relationship.

Interviewer: And that helped clarify misconceptions?

Supervisee: Yup. She would clarify, but she was also real good about not letting it drop there. It wasn't just sort of like "No, that's not what I'm thinking." It was, "No, that's not what I'm thinking. Now let's explore this." And that was so helpful because with my last client, it was like he had all these misperceptions and it was important, "Well that wasn't my intention" or "I'm not so sure I said that." . . . But it was like what's important here, what does it mean that these are the thoughts you're having, what does it mean that this is how you see me? And she did that with me, so I guess staying with him I think in part because I watched her, experienced her stay there with me. She also—and I told her in our last session—I thought she became more, a little more real.

[1]Details of case examples have been altered to protect confidentiality.

Hidden Reactions That Were Ultimately Worked Through

Chin Ho (a pseudonym), a female Asian doctoral student in her mid-20s, was initially paired for supervision with Dr. F., an older male Caucasian professor, for her first year in the clinic. Although the relationship was initially rocky, Chin Ho and Dr. F. eventually formed a close relationship. According to Chin Ho:

> In the beginning it was kind of rough to develop a relationship. The first 3 weeks we were like, "what's going on?" [because of confusion over scheduling, they missed three sessions] . . . I think it was a very corrective experience for me in the end. I was able to develop a relationship with him and almost, like, grow. I had the experience of, like, a good father transference to him, a good father figure who I trusted a lot . . . He was interested in what I was doing and what I was having reactions of, and how to help me in supervision. So I think in the beginning it was hard but I grew fond of him and he helped me. He was mean at times, and pointed things out that were not easy, but I noticed myself I had a difficult time letting him go in the end.

What Chin Ho was referring to as "mean" as that Dr. F. confronted her directly about a number of things. He gave Chin Ho a lot of feedback about her accent being problematic, because it was hard for clients to understand her. He also gave her feedback about her being too giving and supportive as a therapist. He encouraged her to be more curious about deeper dynamics and allow clients to go deeply into emotions. At the end of the year of supervision, Dr. F. suggested that Chin Ho switch to another supervisor so that she could have a different learning experience.

In sum, Chin Ho and Dr. F. were able to resolve the initial difficulties and establish a good working relationship. Because they had a strong alliance and Chin Ho had positive transference toward Dr. F., she was able to forgive difficult moments in the relationship. Clearly, however (as will become apparent in the next supervision experience), Chin Ho was left with unresolved feelings about ending the supervisory relationship. These feelings were apparently not adequately discussed and therefore lingered and influenced the next supervision.

Chin Ho was then paired with Dr. B., a Jewish female psychologist in her mid-30s, for 2 years. During the first 6 months of her supervisory relationship with Dr. B., Chin Ho became increasingly angry at Dr. B. but successfully masked her discontent to such an extent that Dr. B. was completely unaware of any problems. About this time, Chin Ho presented a case in group supervision (CEH was the group supervisor), and became very upset. Chin Ho talked about her dissatisfaction with the supervision. She was particularly upset about having supervision in the dining room of Dr. B.'s home, because the family walked through and there was a lack of privacy. In group supervision, we suggested that Chin Ho talk directly with Dr. B. about her concerns.

Chin Ho did talk to Dr. B. but did not tell her the extent of her dissatisfaction with the supervision as a whole and in particular about the supervision being in Dr. B's home. Instead, Chin Ho softened her anger and, in effect, blamed herself for feeling that she was infringing on Dr. B.'s family. Dr. B. asked Chin Ho what she needed to feel comfortable. Chin Ho said that she would like to meet the family, and so Dr. B. introduced them and thought things were resolved. Chin Ho, however, expressed in group supervision a few weeks later that she was still angry and was dissatisfied with the quality of the supervision with Dr. B. With Chin Ho's permission, I called Dr. B. because I was very concerned about the rupture. Dr. B. was shocked, because she thought they had resolved their problems. After the phone call, Dr. B. processed the relationship with Chin Ho and moved the supervision to an office outside the home.

After this, Dr. B. and Chin Ho spoke frequently about their relationship. When there was an option to shift to another supervisor, Chin Ho indicated that she wanted to continue to work with Dr. B. because they were getting along. Things were not easy, however, and they continued to use immediacy to process their relationship. Dr. B. frequently asked how Chin Ho was feeling about the relationship and about their work together. Chin Ho tried to reveal her feelings, but clearly it was hard for her to be completely honest with Dr. B. To our knowledge, Chin Ho and Dr. B. did not process how Chin Ho felt about transferring from Dr. F. to Dr. B., even though her idealization of Dr. F. may have made it more difficult for Chin Ho to work with Dr. B.

Because of differences related to beliefs and expectations about directiveness, power dynamics, and values and perspectives related to culture and gender, conflict arose in the supervisory relationship. From Dr. B.'s perspective:

> There was a time that I could just sense or feel that there was something going on, and I thought it was around the work, like literally some of the things I was suggesting that she do, and those moments that I would have called reaching out for immediacy, of "I wonder how you're feeling, what I'm suggesting, what's going on for you when I suggest," because I really suggested some circumscribed work with her people, which was different from what she was trained to do specifically. And I acknowledged that, and sort of tried to get feedback from her about that, and she in the moment said she understood. Did she ever say I'm happy to do that—probably not, but she didn't push back. . . . That's when she said, that's when the whole conversation about that she didn't feel connected to me and she was losing, and she was sad that she wished she had more of a connection to me and so we talked about it, and then that was a really immediate conversation . . . in that conversation, we talked about her parents and how she was having, there was a rupture with them, and

how there was so much repair that she felt like she wanted there, and so much she needed from them that she wasn't getting, and somehow that was being played out in our relationship that she couldn't satisfy, and that was the disconnection. It felt really fruitful to have that [discussion] . . . The cultural dynamics, maybe, come into play in that, there's a part of her that I think was what I thought culturally nontraditional in that she was really telling me, in a lot of ways, that I'm not happy. But then I would say, "Well, maybe you're not happy because of this," and then she would say, "Yeah, that must be it," so then I think she was very accepting of like, was influenced by what she thought, my position of authority or her supervisor, and it got complicated, so there was this, "I'm able to tell you I'm really unhappy, but I'm not really able to articulate what it is exactly." I started to sense that that was a pattern of what was happening, maybe I was offering or she was suggesting the safest thing to be unhappy about. So I just said, "I'm sensing there's more, I'm sensing you're really unhappy; it's okay to be unhappy with me, I just need to know what it is so I can change, so I can be different," and that conversation was probably our best. She said, all sorts of things came out . . . that I wasn't interested enough in her and her countertransference, and what was going on for her, and how she was reacting internally to the work, so I got that was one piece of it, that she felt like I was doing something different than that. I think she didn't think I was paying attention to the cultural piece either, her own sort of multicultural identity of herself as an Asian woman therapist, or that I didn't care or understand what it felt like to be her in the room, that I wasn't sensitive to cultural issues . . . And then there was the gender thing and the power thing and sort of, I use that language in my work and that I had sort of been encouraging her to, what I call, own some power in the room and take some risks and that I think triggered stuff with her in terms of her own relation with her gender identity in [country of origin], her gender identity and her family, her gender identity and her relationship with her now fiancé, so I think it started, all of that was triggered and really, somehow, stirring up . . . I could have done more with the cultural piece . . . there were so many cultural pieces that were complicated in terms of both her being able to articulate her needs but for me being able to understand her needs, so like where she was coming from or if there was anything going on even, I mean even just sort of the typical body language, you know, reading someone, being felt, that was cultural but it was difficult, you know, so all of those pieces—so like not even having any idea that she was unhappy and all of the sudden feeling like not only am I unhappy, I'm actually quite miserable, and actually the intensity of that I only sort of heard through you.

From Chin Ho's perspective:

Supervisee: It has been a big learning experience for me, too, how to deal with conflict, because my own history dealing with conflict has been avoidance. It's never been somebody who holds power is interested in me to know your opinions and to discuss and negotiate your needs. Doing that, it was very foreign to me. So, being able to, when there is a conflict, meet my needs and hearing where they come from and negotiate was very challenging. For me, it was a great insight from my supervision, but if there is some conflict or difference of opinion, that meant to me like I cannot relate to that person on a different level, I am not having a good relationship.

Interviewer: Kind of all or nothing. If there's conflict you can't get anything out of it.

Supervisee: Almost like I cannot have a relationship with that person. If there is conflict I cannot.

Interviewer: You just want to run away.

Supervisee: Avoid, avoid, yeah.

Interviewer: So having stuck through the conflict with your supervisor—two major conflicts—has been a big thing for you.

Supervisee: It was really hard, really, really, really hard, knowing how to deal with it, knowing how to bring it up. I mean it was my viewpoint, but she is really want to be equal. But, and she's the type that really kind of assure me, too. She'll say I hope there is no power difference between you and me, you can say whatever you need to say, so she showed me, in a way, right away and, in my viewpoint, that made me want to shut down. Like what do you mean that there is no power difference, what do you mean that I can say whatever I can say? In my mind if I say something, because it was so closely related to her, I mean if it was a conflict about something else, I probably would be able to talk. But, I felt like it was so closely tied in to her style, maybe her lifestyle, maybe her way of supervision. I felt like it was too difficult to say.

Interviewer: It was criticizing her too much.

Supervisee: Criticizing her for the things that she—

Interviewer: For who she is almost.

Supervisee: Yeah, like about her house, and about her office setting, or about her husband. I mean, it just felt kind of weird. So it was very conflicting experience for me. She is very inviting, and she said she want to hear my opinion and she assured me in saying that I don't want to have power over you. But she would say those things a lot to me and to assure me, but to me for some reason that wasn't—

Interviewer: It was not believable.

Supervisee: Yes, and it wasn't enough for me . . . When I struggle with my supervisor I think there was also an aspect of me feeling a little misunderstood as an Asian person. In that aspect, I don't know. But, I had a difficult time telling her . . . It was quite challenging . . . I'm dealing with my anxiety, yes, about conflict. It has been a big learning experience for me too, how to deal with conflict, because my own history dealing with conflict has been avoidance. It's never been somebody who holds power is interested in me to know your opinions and to discuss and negotiate your needs. Doing that it was very foreign to me. So, being able to, when there is a conflict, meet my needs and hearing where they come from and negotiate was very challenging. For me, it was a great insight from my supervision, but if there is some conflict or difference of opinion that meant to me like I cannot relate to that person on a different level. I am not having a good relationship . . .

Many issues relevant to immediacy came up in this case, all of which may have been influenced by their cultural backgrounds. The second supervisor and the supervisee had different styles in the way they processed things, in that the supervisor liked to talk through things, but the supervisee liked to avoid conflict. They also held different beliefs about power dynamics, such that the supervisor did not believe that there were power differences, whereas the supervisee did. Another key issue was that Chin Ho did not completely reveal how she felt about the supervision relationship. Indeed, she was so good at hiding her reactions that Dr. B. was completely unaware of Chin Ho's distress.

There were also transference issues going on here. Chin Ho had difficulty transitioning from a previous, idealized supervisor; she was envious of her second supervisor's status and family; and she felt competitive with the second supervisor about physical size and age. In addition, Chin Ho was having problems with her own family and may have transferred these onto supervision. This case demonstrates the complexity of immediacy, even when the supervisee and both supervisors were committed to working on the relationship and repairing ruptures. The Dr. B., in fact, was tenacious at addressing the relationship problems once she recognized that there were problems. Both she and Chin Ho wanted to make the supervision relationship work.

Interestingly, parallel process from work with clients influencing the supervision did not seem to operate in the second supervision. Rather, the parallel process was in the direction of problems in the supervision negatively affecting the supervisor's/therapist's ability to do therapy. Chin Ho actually seemed to deteriorate in her therapy skills during the worst time of the rupture in the supervision relationship (which, of course, may have been exacerbated by her family problems). Chin Ho was hesitant to go deep with her clients or to confront problems in the therapy relationships. Fortunately, after considerable time and effort, Chin Ho and Dr. B. were able to resolve things between them so that both felt good about their supervisory relationship. As a result of their resolving their problems, the supervisee improved in her work with clients.

Boundary Problems

In another dyad entering their second year of working together, a problem arose related to boundaries. The supervisee asked the supervisor to do her a favor and minimally supervise her on nonclinic cases (the supervisee was being supervised at another site by a nonpsychologist and needed a psychologist to provide oversight). The supervisor initially agreed, but in a supervision of supervision meeting (all the supervisors met occasionally to talk about their cases), the supervisor disclosed that she was annoyed about having agreed to do the extra work, since it seemed beyond the boundary of what she had signed up for, and she was not able to adequately supervise these other cases given the time limitations. The group encouraged the supervisor to talk with the supervisee about the problem, and the resulting interaction occurred. From the supervisee perspective:

> Recently my supervisor told me she would be unable to supervise me for my second externship at a place other than the clinic. She said this probably brings up feelings in me for her. I agreed, and said I felt shocked and upset. In our next session we revisited this interaction, and I felt comfortable disclosing some of my reactions to her. My supervisor disclosed agreeing to the second supervision without thinking it through and in an effort to help me in some way. On the whole I believe I share feelings about our relationship more so than my supervisor (including this episode). There was some immediacy used here that addressed the discomfort from the previous session. However, we soon moved away from immediacy, and the issue was not completely resolved. Apart from this incident, my supervisor has communicated care for me previously and I believe that helped in resolving the rupture in some way . . . I was talking about being gentle and not assertive in session. My supervisor wondered if she should have been more assertive in our relationship and said no to supervision for the second externship. I felt her response came out of the blue and was confused by the parallel.

Fortunately, the supervisor and supervisee were able to work on their relationship and this conflict in particular. They returned to it several times over the course of 3 months and used immediacy to resolve problems between them. At last report, both were very pleased with the supervisory relationship. Of particular interest here is that the supervisees were often the ones to bring up problems in the supervisory relationships, perhaps because there was so much emphasis in the doctoral program training about immediacy.

These three different cases clearly illustrate how distortions and ruptures occur with supervision. If not dealt with openly and sensitively, problems continue to get worse and can damage the therapeutic relationships in addition to the supervisory relationship. But fortunately, if dealt with openly, problems can be resolved, although much effort and pain is often involved. It is important to note that culture, gender, power dynamics, transferring supervisors, and ending supervision can make supervisory relationships difficult, especially when there are unexpressed expectations and feelings.

PRACTICE IMPLICATIONS

Based on our data (from a qualitative study and an informal survey) and our knowledge of these cases, it appeared that immediacy was used at least occasionally in 10 of 12 supervision dyads. Immediacy was used infrequently for the most part; the most typical types of immediacy were the negotiation or monitoring of the relationship, parallels, and resolution of distortions and ruptures.

Immediacy Is Not Always Needed

It appears that it is possible to have good supervision without immediacy. It is possible to focus on client dynamics, supervisee countertransference, and possible skills that the supervisee could use with clients without ever addressing immediacy. *But* we know that supervisees leave many things unsaid, often for fear of political suicide (e.g., Ladany et al., 1996). We also know from the psychotherapy literature that clients often hide things from therapists (Hess et al., 2008) and that therapists are unable to read clients' minds, especially related to negative reactions. So, we stress that supervisors cannot trust intuition. *If supervisors don't ask, supervisees probably won't tell.* Thus, monitoring the supervisory relationship is important, even when things seem to be going well. Supervisors can ask how the supervisee is feeling about the supervision, what is working, and what is not working.

Suggestions for When to Use Immediacy

Our results showed that immediacy can particularly be useful when there are distortions or ruptures in the relationship. We would also highlight that perceived dissimilarities (e.g., culture, theoretical orientation) might be useful to address. As with the repair of ruptures in psychotherapy (Hill & Knox, 2009), tear and repair can often make the relationship stronger.

But immediacy is clearly appropriate not just for working with conflict. It can be helpful for establishing expectations, negotiating the terms of the relationship, and monitoring the relationship. By getting things out in the open, making the implicit explicit or turning the covert into overt, we suspect that ruptures are prevented from occurring. In addition, immediacy can be used to express gratitude.

Immediacy Can Be Used to Establish Open Communication in Supervision

We suspect that it is important to establish a culture within supervision in which it is permissible to talk about the supervisory relationship. Thus, supervisors can be genuinely curious about supervisees' feelings rather than just asking for validation that everything is okay. Furthermore, supervisors may need to educate supervisees about why they are using immediacy, so that supervisees can understand the rationale and benefits of immediately working on the supervisory relationship. Thus, supervisors can let supervisees know that immediacy is useful to resolve problems in the supervisory relationship as well as for modelling how immediacy can be used in therapy relationships.

Immediacy Is Helpful With Parallel Process

Immediacy also seems to be useful when parallel process is occurring, to make the implicit processes more explicit. Parallels can go both ways, such that events in therapy can influence supervision, but also that events in supervision can influence therapy. We especially recommend that immediacy be used if the supervisee seems to be indirectly talking about the supervisory relationship.

Modeling Is Helpful in Teaching Supervisees to Use Immediacy in Their Therapy

One supervisor said it well: "They [supervisees] have to experience the same thing we are trying to get them to do with their clients." In several of the examples provided earlier in the chapter, supervisees talked about how they were able to implement with their clients what their supervisors had done with them. Clearly, there was a ripple effect.

Importance of Culture in Use of Immediacy

It is important and humbling to remember that supervisors and supervisees come from different cultures, with some being more discrepant than others. In some cultures (e.g., Asian, as in the above example), it is almost forbidden for people to talk openly and directly about reactions to another person. For such people, directly talking about the supervision relationship and revealing problems may be particularly threatening.

Importance of Not Using Immediacy as a Gimmick

If immediacy is used inappropriately, it can come across as fake and self-centered, and it can actually damage the relationship. One of our supervisors was quite concerned that supervisors and therapists would be overly eager to use immediacy without being appropriately cautious about the possible effects. He said,

> I think that caution is warranted in how we teach students to use immediacy, as well as how we use it. I worry about its overuse, and there can be an overdetermined element to its incorporation in the therapeutic and supervisory process, such that it becomes more of a gimmick than an organic aspect of the rich and developing therapeutic (or supervisory) relationship. The effective use of immediacy, I believe, comes out of the ongoing process of becoming a psychotherapist, which involves years of development, supervision, and self-examination, as well as our ongoing study of our emotional reactions to our clients and our supervisees. I think of it is an advanced tool, which should be used judiciously, especially by students of psychotherapy, but also by experienced clinicians. In this way, it is another effective tool to further client growth, and not a mechanism for the discharge of countertransference feelings that the supervisee or therapist cannot adequately contain.

IMPLICATIONS FOR RESEARCH

Several ideas for research emerge from this preliminary work (see Hill & Knox, 2013, for a more extensive review of the complete supervision literature and recommendations for research). First, we need to replicate the Hill et al. (2014) study of immediacy in psychotherapy with a study of immediacy in supervision. Thus, it would be important to observe and code recorded supervision sessions, see what happens, and judge the consequences. Second, we need to investigate characteristics of supervisors, therapists, clients, and situations that call for immediacy. Given that in the Hill et al. study (2014), therapists focused more on feelings and less on ruptures, and initiated immediacy more often with fearfully attached than with securely attached clients, it would be interesting to see how supervisor and supervisee attachment style influences supervision. Third, we need to study the impact of culture on supervision given the intriguing findings in this study. Finally, given the paucity of findings on the transmission of effects from supervision to psychotherapy (see also Hill & Knox, 2013), we need to examine the transmission of immediacy from supervision to therapy. If the transmission indirect through modeling, how it can be used? Or is it more direct, through the supervisor recommending that the supervisee use it? Finally, perhaps a qualitative study could be conducted of supervisees recalling how immediacy used in supervision sessions enabled them to use immediacy with their clients.

CONCLUSION

Immediacy can take many forms and can be used for different reasons/intentions (e.g., negotiating and monitoring the relationship, drawing parallels, and resolving distortions and ruptures) in supervision. Furthermore, immediacy can be very helpful if used appropriately given that it can help to resolve problems in the supervision, can provide the supervisee with an experience about how powerful immediacy can be, and can provide a model for how supervisees can use immediacy in their work with clients. We recommend, however, that it be used carefully and with extensive processing between the supervisor and supervisee to enhance the benefits and reduce the possibility of misunderstanding and harm. Thus, we conclude this chapter suggesting that immediacy is a mechanism of change in supervision that can directly impact the supervision and indirectly impact the supervisees'/therapists' clinical work.

REFERENCES

Berman, M. I., Hill, C. E., Liu, J., Jackson, J., Sim, W., & Spangler, P. (2012). Relational events in acceptance and commitment therapy for three clients with anorexia nervosa: What is corrective? In L. G. Castonguay & C. E. Hill (Eds.), *Transformation in psychotherapy: Corrective experiences across cognitive behavioral, humanistic, and psychodynamic approaches*. Washington, DC: American Psychological Association. http://dx.doi.org/10.1037/13747-012

Burke, W. R., Goodyear, R. K., & Guzzard, C. R. (1998). Weakenings and repairs in supervisory alliances: A multiple-case study. *American Journal of Psychotherapy*, *52*, 450–462.

Carkhuff, R. R. (1969). *Human and helping relations: A primer for lay and professional helpers* (Vols. 1 & 2). New York, NY: Holt, Rinehart, & Winston.

Cashdan, S. (1988). *Object relations therapy: Using the relationship*. New York, NY: Norton.

Friedlander, M. L., Angus, L., Wright, S. T., Günther, C., Austin, C. L., Kangos, K., . . . Khattra, J. (2018). "If those tears could talk, what would they say?" Multi-method analysis of a corrective experience in brief dynamic therapy. *Psychotherapy Research*, *28*, 217–234. http://dx.doi.org/10.1080/10503307.2016.1184350

Hess, S. A., Knox, S., Schultz, J. M., Hill, C. E., Sloan, L., Brandt, S., . . . Hoffman, M. A. (2008). Predoctoral interns' nondisclosure in supervision. *Psychotherapy Research*, *18*, 400–411. http://dx.doi.org/10.1080/10503300701697505

Hill, C. E., Baumann, E., Shafran, N., Gupta, S., Morrison, A., Rojas, A. E., . . . Gelso, C. J. (2015). Is training effective? A study of counseling psychology doctoral trainees in a psychodynamic/interpersonal training clinic. *Journal of Counseling Psychology*, *62*, 184–201. http://dx.doi.org/10.1037/cou0000053

Hill, C. E., Gelso, C. J., Chui, H., Spangler, P. T., Hummel, A., Huang, T., . . . Miles, J. R. (2014). To be or not to be immediate with clients: The use and perceived effects of immediacy in psychodynamic/interpersonal psychotherapy. *Psychotherapy Research*, *24*, 299–315. http://dx.doi.org/10.1080/10503307.2013.812262

Hill, C. E., & Knox, S. (2009). Processing the therapeutic relationship. *Psychotherapy Research*, *19*, 13–29. http://dx.doi.org/10.1080/10503300802621206

Hill, C. E., & Knox, S. (2013). Training and supervision in psychotherapy. In M. J. Lambert (Ed.), *Bergin and Garfield's handbook of psychotherapy and behavior change* (6th ed., pp. 775–811). New York, NY: Wiley.

Hill, C. E., Sim, W., Spangler, P., Stahl, J., Sullivan, C., & Teyber, E. (2008). Therapist immediacy in brief psychotherapy: Case study II. *Psychotherapy*, *45*, 298–315. http://dx.doi.org/10.1037/a0013306

Kasper, L. B., Hill, C. E., & Kivlighan, D. M., Jr. (2008). Therapist immediacy in brief psychotherapy: Case study I. *Psychotherapy*, *45*, 281–297. http://dx.doi.org/10.1037/a0013305

Kiesler, D. J. (1988). *Therapeutic metacommunication: Therapist impact disclosure as feedback in psychotherapy*. Palo Alto, CA: Consulting Psychologists Press.

Kiesler, D. J. (1996). *Contemporary interpersonal theory and research: Personality, psychopathology, and psychotherapy*. New York, NY: Wiley.

Kuutmann, K., & Hilsenroth, M. J. (2012). Exploring in-session focus on the patient–therapist relationship: Patient characteristics, process and outcome. *Clinical Psychology & Psychotherapy*, *19*, 187–202. http://dx.doi.org/10.1002/cpp.743

Ladany, N., Hill, C. E., Corbett, M. M., & Nutt, E. A. (1996). Nature, extent, and importance of what psychotherapy trainees do not disclose to their supervisors. *Journal of Counseling Psychology*, *43*, 10–23. http://dx.doi.org/10.1037/0022-0167.43.1.10

Lingiardi, V., Colli, A., Gentile, D., & Tanzilli, A. (2011). Exploration of session process: Relationship to depth and alliance. *Psychotherapy*, *48*, 391–400. http://dx.doi.org/10.1037/a0025248

Mayotte-Blum, J., Slavin-Mulford, J., Lehmann, M., Pesale, F., Becker-Matero, N., & Hilsenroth, M. (2012). Therapeutic immediacy across long-term psychodynamic psychotherapy: An evidence-based case study. *Journal of Counseling Psychology*, *59*, 27–40. http://dx.doi.org/10.1037/a0026087

Mueller, W. J., & Kell, B. L. (1972). *Coping with conflict: Supervising counselors and psychotherapists*. New York, NY: Appleton–Century–Crofts.

Nelson, M. L., Barnes, K. L., Evans, A. L., & Triggiano, P. J. (2008). Working with conflicts in clinical supervision: Wise supervisors' perspectives. *Journal of Counseling Psychology*, *55*, 172–184. http://dx.doi.org/10.1037/0022-0167.55.2.172

Safran, J. D., & Muran, J. C. (2000). *Negotiating the therapeutic alliance: A relational treatment guide*. New York, NY: Guilford Press.

Shafran, N., Kivlighan, D. M., Jr., Gelso, C. J., Bhatia, A., & Hill, C. E. (2017). Therapist immediacy: The association with working alliance, real relationship, session quality, and time in psychotherapy. *Psychotherapy Research*, *27*, 737–748. http://dx.doi.org/10.1080/10503307.2016.1158884

Spangler, P. T., Hill, C. E., Dunn, M. G., Hummel, A., Walden, T., Liu, J., Jackson, J., . . . Salahuddin, N. (2014). Training undergraduate students to use immediacy. *The Counseling Psychologist*, *42*, 729–757. http://dx.doi.org/10.1177/0011000014542835

Stoltenberg, C. D., & McNeill, B. W. (2012). Supervision: research, models, and competence. In N. A. Fouad (Ed.), *APA handbook of counseling psychology* (Vol. 1, pp. 295–327). Washington, DC: American Psychological Association.

II

MAPPING MODELS AND CONCLUSIONS

13

MAPPING MODELS OF THE THERAPEUTIC RELATIONSHIP: IMPLICATIONS FOR INTEGRATIVE PRACTICE

STANLEY B. MESSER AND DANIEL B. FISHMAN

The most general observation emanating from our review of the chapters in this volume is that therapists holding alternate theoretical orientations use different kinds of interventions to develop and maintain the therapeutic relationship. To capture these differences, we introduce a set of terms for two types of therapeutic interventions: *relationship-focused interventions* (RFIs) and *non–relationship-focused interventions* (N-RFIs). RFIs are directed towards establishing, maintaining, and enhancing the therapeutic relationship. N-RFIs, on the other hand, are directed towards other aspects of therapy, such as correcting clients' distorted thinking, helping clients to better regulate their emotions, or fostering insight into dynamics that are largely independent of the therapeutic relationship. We further characterize therapist interventions as those designed to address the relationship directly versus those that do not, but the way they are implemented has an impact on the

This chapter represents the equal contribution of both authors.

http://dx.doi.org/10.1037/0000093-014
Developing the Therapeutic Relationship: Integrating Case Studies, Research, and Practice, O. Tishby and H. Wiseman (Editors)

relationship. The two dimensions form a 2 × 2 Therapeutic Relationship Matrix, described later, in which the psychotherapies can be classified and compared.

A second general observation relates to the frequent reference in the therapy literature to relationship-building between therapist and client as a "common factor" in therapy. The fact that different therapies use different RFIs in the process of developing and maintaining an effective therapeutic relationship means that relationship-building is a common factor only at a certain level of abstraction (cf. Messer and Winokur's [1981] critique of Goldfried's [1980] proposal of two common factors in psychotherapy.) In other words, it is our view that relationship-building is more of a "common theme" across therapies than it is a true common factor. As we will discuss, the view of relationship-building as a common theme versus a common factor means that it may look quite different in various therapy models as it flows from its underlying theory of therapy.

THE PURPOSE AND ORGANIZATION OF THE CHAPTER

In light of the above, this chapter recognizes the differences in relationship-building among the various models described in the preceding chapters and seeks to map them on a matrix in order to clarify the underlying similarities and contrasts among them and to explore the ensuing practical implications, especially for the possibilities of psychotherapy integration. For each chapter, we (a) discerned its main theoretical understanding and use of the therapy relationship; (b) provided one or two clinical vignettes that illustrate that understanding as reflected in the presentation of representative RFIs; and (c) placed the approach in a particular cell of the matrix, with an explanation of why it belongs there. We checked each other's placement of the model in the Therapeutic Relationship Matrix for reliability purposes, with resulting high agreement. We then reflected on the implications of the matrix groupings of interventions for their integrative potential, especially regarding the process of assimilative integration (Messer, 2015a).

A focus of this volume is to embody the role of the therapeutic relationship within clinically important moments in therapy. As is evident in our other work (e.g., Fishman, Messer, Edwards, & Dattilio, 2017), we are strong advocates of studying clinical phenomena in context through case studies and mixed methods. As case studies and case examples are accumulated, a complementary perspective is to step back and look for general principles and themes that emerge through cross-case comparison, which the 2 × 2 matrix illustrates. We conclude the chapter with a discussion of how the matrix can be helpful in practice, returning in more detail to the concept of assimilative integration.

THE MODELS AND CASE EXAMPLES IN THE INDIVIDUAL CHAPTERS

The Columns in the Matrix

Table 13.1 presents the Therapeutic Relationship Matrix, with the placement of the various chapters indicated, as explained in the text below. The columns vary along a dimension of the therapist's goal in establishing a relationship vis-à-vis therapeutic change. The first column—the Relationship as Necessary but Insufficient (RNBI)—is the traditional model in cognitive–behavioral therapy (CBT), in which the relationship provides leverage for the therapist to motivate the client to try out the N-RFIs—like cognitive restructuring or exposure to feared stimuli—that lead to improvement in disorders such as anxiety and depression (Fishman, 2016). Brady (1980) presented an early version of this approach in CBT: "Equally important is the quality and tone of the relationship [the patient] . . . has with the therapist. That is, if he feels trusting and warm toward the therapist, this generally will facilitate following the treatment regimen" (p. 285).

In contrast, the second column—the Relationship as Treatment (RasT)—represents the traditional psychoanalytic therapy view that therapeutic change is directly tied to the evolving therapeutic relationship. Specifically, in this view the client projects onto the therapist the client's own relationship difficulties, and those difficulties are worked out in their relationship (Messer, 2015b). Persons (2008) described how his view has been adopted by some cognitive–behavioral therapists, including Persons herself, although it is not a mainstream view:

> The relationship-as-treatment view of CBT is based on the notion that the patient's behaviors in the session are samples of behaviors that also occur outside the session. As a result, the presence of these behaviors in the session provides opportunities for assessment, conceptualization and intervention. Moreover, in some therapies guided by this model . . . the therapist works actively to elicit patient problem behaviors that might not otherwise appear in the session. (pp. 168–169)

Relationship Between RFIs and N-RFIs Within the Matrix

The relationship between RFIs and N-RFIs differs between the columns in the matrix. In the Relationship as Necessary but Insufficient column, the purpose of RFIs is to create a therapeutic relationship to facilitate the effectiveness of N-RFIs. Thus, in this column, the interaction between RFIs and N-RFIs is very prominent. In the Relationship as Treatment column, the focus is primarily on RFIs, since these are a major constituent of the therapy (with the exception of the cognitive–behavioral-based integrative therapy).

TABLE 13.1
The Therapeutic Relationship Matrix With Chapters Coded by Primary Cell Emphasized

II. How Directly Do the Therapist's Actions Address the Therapeutic Relationship?	I. The Goal of Establishing a Relationship to Bring About Therapeutic Change: 1. Relationship Necessary but Insufficient	2. Relationship as Treatment
	Cell A	Cell B
A. Therapist's actions are designed to address the therapeutic relationship directly	Chapter 11: family systems therapy (Heatherington, Escudero, & Friedlander)	Chapter 2: psychodynamic therapy (Kohberger, Safran, & Muran) Chapter 3: psychodynamic therapy (Schattner & Tishby) Chapter 4: psychodynamic therapy (Wiseman & Atzil-Slonim) Chapter 5: psychodynamic therapy (Zilcha-Mano & Barber) Chapter 7: cognitive–behavioral therapy/ assimilative integration (Castonguay, Youn, Xiao, & McAleavey) Chapter 12: psychodynamic therapy (Hill & Gupta)
	Cell C	Cell D
B. Therapist's actions are *not* designed to address the therapeutic relationship directly—but the way they are implemented impacts the therapeutic relationship	Chapter 7: cognitive–behavioral therapy/ assimilative integration (Castonguay, Youn, Xiao, & McAleavey) Chapter 8: cognitive–behavioral therapy (Elizur & Huppert)	Chapter 6: psychoanalytic therapy (Shefler) Chapter 7: cognitive–behavioral therapy/ assimilative integration (Castonguay, Youn, Xiao, & McAleavey) Chapter 9: Rogerian/ client-centered therapy (Farber & Suzuki) Chapter 10: emotion-focused therapy (Watson)

The Rows in the Matrix

Cross-cutting the columns in Table 13.1 are two rows, which vary in terms of how directly the therapists' actions address the therapeutic relationship. These columns flow less from models embedded in the therapy literature and more from the logic of RFIs and N-RFIs. The first row represents true RFIs—that is, therapist actions that are designed to address the therapeutic relationship directly.

The second row represents therapist's actions that are not designed to address the therapeutic relationship directly—that is, actions that are designed as N-RFIs—but the way they are implemented impacts the therapeutic relationship. In other words, while the therapist's actions are designed as N-RFIs, they also function indirectly as RFIs.

THEORY, CASE VIGNETTES, AND MATRIX PLACEMENT FOR EACH CHAPTER

Chapter 2: Kohberger, Safran, and Muran (Psychodynamic/Relational)

Main Theoretical Concept

In this version of psychodynamic therapy, known as brief relational therapy (BRT), the negotiation of ruptures in the therapeutic relationship is considered the main pathway to change. These are said to be inevitable. "A key ingredient in resolving ruptures is helping clients to recognize that they can assert their needs without destroying the relationship [with the therapist]. Resolving ruptures can empower clients confront conflicts in their lives, acknowledge parts of themselves that they have disowned, and negotiate their needs for relatedness and agency in a more effective way . . ." (p. 32). This leads to the development of new relational schemas as a central mechanism of change.

Clinical Vignette

The client was a 31-year-old, Caucasian woman who had been married for 4 years and had no children.[1] She described her parents as having been overly strict and controlling; she also complained of lack of self-esteem, feelings of sadness and anger, and trouble expressing her feelings directly.

[1]Details of case examples have been altered to protect confidentiality.

In a written statement following Session 6 (of 30) of a second round of BRT, she wrote in her therapy diary that a two-chair exercise the therapist wanted her to do seemed pointless to her, and later she and the therapist talked openly and nondefensively about the client's view on the exercise. In response to a written question about what was helpful, she wrote, "Being honest and able to trust that it was okay to doubt the process. The therapist didn't take it personally" (p. 47). The therapist was also open to exploring the client's discomfort in discussing her anger toward her husband. The client stated, "How he [the therapist] handled the conflict in the process showed me it was okay to disagree in the session and it was not the end of the world" (p. 47).

Position on the Relationship Grid

Cell B. This approach emphasizes the therapist–client relationship itself as the locus of change. More specifically, therapist interventions are designed to bring out the disagreements, conflicts, or tensions that arise in the relationship (i.e., addressing the therapeutic relationship directly) in order for the client to have a chance to express them in a safe environment and to have a corrective experience. This then enables the client to apply that experience in her life outside therapy, such as being better able to express her feelings more openly and honestly to significant others.

Chapter 3: Schattner and Tishby (Psychodynamic/Relational)

Main Theoretical Concept

According to the authors, therapy is a process of cocreation of meaning, often focusing on patient–therapist enactments, where the patient's dynamics come to life, as they touch on or trigger emotions and cognitions within the therapist, which, in turn, evoke their own characteristic interpersonal patterns. Patient and therapist can each get stuck in old familiar patterns. However, in working through these enactments, unlike interpretations in the one-person model, the fantasy worlds of both parties are called upon.

Clinical Example

Amanda, a 23-year-old, female, single, undergraduate student, sought treatment for her difficulties in interpersonal relationships. Her background included a past eating disorder, experiences of sexual harassment, and coping with a learning disability.

Amanda's mother was experienced as a "friend," confusing, childish, and lacking in authority, which is why Amanda wished for a therapist that would be "mature"—strong, guiding, consistent. The therapist's aversion to filling that role may have stemmed not only from the psychodynamic principle of neutrality, but also from her experience of her own mother as too strict, "educational," and not warm or loving enough (p. 76).

After two sessions, the therapist learned from a colleague that Amanda was dissatisfied with the treatment and had requested to change therapists. Responding nondefensively, in the next session the therapist raised the issue.

Amanda said that she felt that talking to the therapist was "like talking to a friend," and she "needed someone more directive to 'manage' her," like her previous psychotherapist. The therapist responded that she was glad Amanda had been able to speak her mind, but considered her wish to be an indication of the problem: "I'm not willing to take that role. You're looking for someone to tell you what to do, but that's just what we're going to tackle in therapy. The solution isn't for me to tell you what to do in your life" (p. 69).

This dynamic, of Amanda pressing for more direction from the therapist in Amanda's decision making—as Amanda's previous therapist had done—and the therapist resisting this by validating Amanda and encouraging her autonomy by supporting her in making her own decisions became a main theme in subsequent therapy, leading to Amanda eventually accepting this role and leading her to feel much better about herself and to make psychologically healthy decisions.

Position on the Relationship Grid

Cell B. The thrust of the therapy is the relationship and commenting directly on the evolving nature of the relationship. In this case, the client wanted direction, advice, and guidance, and the therapist parried this request by saying she wanted to help the client become more autonomous and empowered, which the client eventually accepted. At the same time, the therapist, at a later point in therapy, became more willing to give direct advice to the client, indicating that she was willing to change as well.

The therapy was not only about addressing the relationship directly but had a variety of other interventions, such as supportive and empathic ones, that indirectly affected the therapeutic relationship. Hence, Cell C can be seen as a secondary classification.

Chapter 4: Wiseman and Atzil-Slonim (Psychodynamic/Attachment-Oriented)

Main Theoretical Concept

The authors view the development of the therapeutic relationship from the perspective of attachment theory and contemporary psychodynamic relational theory regarding the mutual impact of client and therapist. They point out that "the similarity or dissimilarity in attachment style of client and therapist will affect these dynamics . . . it has been suggested from both the perspective of interpersonal theory and attachment theory that 'contrasting' (dissimilar) interpersonal orientations of the client and therapist are optimal for the process and outcome of psychotherapy" (p. 83).

Clinical Vignette

The case vignette involves Hannah, a single, 25-year-old, female graduate student with feelings of depression and anxiety. Hannah began therapy with especially high attachment avoidance (and relatively high anxiety). When the therapist, with her own high anxiety (and high avoidance relative to the therapist sample), insisted upon engaging, Hannah experienced it as a repetition of her object relations and resisted the therapist's attempts to get close. However, gradually, when the therapist became more attuned to Hannah's needs and accepted her request to get close at her own pace, a more secure attachment was developed (p. 96).

As an indication of client and therapist attuning their attachment needs to each other, in one session the client came in and "didn't want to sit in the chair, . . . and sat on the carpet" (p. 95). After internal deliberation, the therapist decided to join Hannah on the carpet, and "it opened up a new kind of relationship with us" (p. 95).

Position on the Relationship Grid

Cell B. This is a good example of "relationship as therapy." The intervention by the therapist of choosing to sit on the carpet with the client is carried out in the service of responding to the client's need for the right amount of closeness in the relationship and having to deal with her own conflicts over closeness and attachment. It is in the direction of providing a corrective emotional experience for the client and may, in fact, do the same for the therapist.

Secondarily, the intervention can be seen as fitting in Cell A, because the improvement in the degree of closeness able to be tolerated by both client and therapist allows for a deeper exploration of the client's issues. In this sense the relationship can be seen as necessary but insufficient (RNBI).

Chapter 5: Zilcha-Mano and Barber (Psychodynamic/Relational)

Main Theoretical Concept

According to the authors, a particular concrete focus in the therapeutic relationship should be on creating the interpersonal conditions between clinician and client so that the client feels understood. This process is measured by a "Feeling Understood in Treatment" (FUT) coding system. This measure encompasses three aspects: "(a) the extent to which the therapist communicates, actively or passively, that he or she is trying to understand the patient, (b) the extent to which the patient seems to show feelings of being understood by the therapist, and (c) the extent to which patients seem to show during the session that they feel understood by significant others in their lives" (p. 110).

Clinical Vignette

The authors describe the case of Dan, a single, depressed, African American man in his 40s. During the second stage of therapy (Sessions 8–15), Dan began to discuss his need for close intimate relationships in which he would feel understood and respected, along with his fears of being in a vulnerable position in which he could be mistreated and hurt by other people. For example, Dan described feeling upset when his son did not call him on Father's Day and was angry at his son's mother for not reminding him to call. Simultaneously, Dan began to mention concerns of not being understood by his therapist (p. 110).

The therapist reacted empathetically, as she did in the course of other ruptures that occurred during this phase of treatment. This process of rupture–resolution seemed to strengthen the relationship between Dan and the therapist. Dan started to communicate feeling understood by the therapist and began to bring up examples of his experiences in vulnerable situations to work on in treatment (e.g., feeling offended after someone he was romantically interested in spurned his overture) (p. 116).

This change in feeling understood was reflected by rising scores on the FUT scale.

Position on the Relationship Grid

Cell B. The intention of the empathetic intervention was to make the patient feel understood and to provide a corrective experience, which constitutes use of the relationship as a change agent. The interventions were also designed to address the therapy relationship directly.

Chapter 6: Shefler (Classical Psychoanalysis)

Main Theoretical Concept

Chapter 6 focuses on one aspect of the therapeutic relationship within classical psychoanalysis (vs. psychodynamic therapy) and that is the issue of psychoanalyst–patient boundaries in the context of the therapy setting. Shefler affirms the importance of well-defined boundaries in order for the analyst to be able to concentrate primarily on interpretations, especially of the transference–countertransference interaction, but speaks to the occasional need to cross boundaries through, for example, altering features of the setting, in order to maintain the therapeutic alliance or to meet a specific patient's needs.

Clinical Example

In one of his two examples, Shefler describes a client named "Shimon," who began treatment "to cope with outbursts of rage, particularly toward his young son" (p. 145). It was enormously challenging, both logistically and financially, for Shimon to come to the clinic for his therapy sessions. One day in the third year of therapy, Shimon appeared at the clinic carrying a weapon, for which he had a license, but the policy of the clinic was no weapons in the building. The only option was for Shimon to leave his weapon with the guard, which Shimon refused to do. What to do? Again, the author, in deviating from the setting's fixed boundaries, enhanced the working alliance with his patient. In the therapist's words:

> When I remembered how much effort Shimon invested in coming to each session, the financial hardship and the physical endangerment, it was difficult for me to accept there was no solution. . . . There was no public place to sit anywhere near the clinic. I also felt Shimon would not even consider canceling the session. I made a suggestion to Shimon. "What do you think about sitting in my car?" "Great idea," he answered. (p. 147)

The therapist–patient interaction in the car was quite positive in terms of the therapy. For example, Shimon said to the therapist:

"And you didn't get into an argument with the guard." . . . [And the therapist said] "Just like what happens with you with your son, when he doesn't capitulate to your authority." [Shimon replied:] "Yes, that's me. I need to learn from you how to control my emotions" (p. 148).

Position on the Relationship Grid

Cell D. Although typically psychoanalysis might be placed in Cell B due to its emphasis on the relationship as therapy, the focus in Chapter 6 is on breaching the usual psychoanalytic boundary in the service of the working alliance, in this case, the therapist's willingness to meet with his patient in his own car.

Chapter 7: Castonguay, Youn, Xiao, and McAleavey (Cognitive–Behavioral Therapy/Assimilative Integration)

Main Theoretical Concept

The home theory in Chapter 7 is CBT but it is widened to include concepts from other theories in an assimilative integrative manner. Regarding CBT proper, a core concept is "collaborative empiricism," in which the CBT therapist presents herself as ally and expert as described in the other CBT-oriented chapter in this volume by Elizur and Huppert (Chapter 8).

In terms of extending the traditional CBT approach to include making use of the therapeutic relationship, Castonguay, Youn, Xiao, and McAleavey point to a variety of examples, such as Linehan's (1993) validation of the client's negative experience of the therapist in order to address alliance difficulties. The authors add their own ways of integrating concepts from other therapies into the home base of CBT. These include the therapist being with the client in such a way as to combat demoralization and loneliness; providing various corrective experiences, such as disconfirming interpersonal schemas; and being a good model (honest, trustworthy, caring, etc.) for the client to internalize.

Clinical Vignette

The authors introduce the client as follows:

> Robert is a 25-year-old, single, heterosexual man, who presented to a community mental health center for therapy to address his skin picking disorder. (p. 168)

In response to a manualized, evidence-based CBT treatment for skin picking disorder, the client was at first successful, but then the effect tapered off, at which point the skin picking incidents and suicidal ideation and other self-harm behaviors increased. In addition, Robert then started expressing upset that he felt judged for his lack of progress and "failed to show up for the next two sessions, and did not return any of the therapist's phone calls, which was very unusual for him" (p. 170).

Then a critical choice point occurred:

> The therapist could have used the client's behavior (i.e., missing sessions), and utterance (i.e., sharing that he felt judged) as additional examples of the client's cognitive biases, but instead, the therapist incorporated techniques from other orientations to augment the CBT treatment at this moment. . . . The therapist thanked Robert for having shared a difficult experience with her and acknowledged her own contributions that

> may have led to the rupture in the relationship between the two. . . . The therapist and client continued to use the session time to further encourage Robert to share his negative reactions towards the therapist, which the therapist validated and accepted, consistent with the disarming technique (Burns, 1989) of finding the subjective truth in the client's criticisms, regardless of whether the criticisms are fair or warranted as a way to address the alliance rupture. (p. 171)

The therapist then compared her relationship with Robert to other experiences in Robert's life, to good effect.

Position on the Relationship Grid

Cells C, D, and B. As Chapter 7 integrates the traditional approach to the relationship in CBT with other models, it belongs in more than one cell. Insofar as it emphasizes the directive function of the therapist it belongs in Cell C, like Chapter 8. But as it assimilates outlooks from humanistic approaches that view the relationship as therapy (even if not addressed directly) and from psychodynamic therapy (relationship as therapy and interventions that address it directly), it also belongs in Cells D and B.

Chapter 8: Elizur and Huppert (Cognitive–Behavioral Therapy)

Main Theoretical Concept

According to Elizur and Huppert, within a CBT framework, "Building the relationship is a precondition for helping the therapy reach its specific, individualized goals, which are naturally related to the 'real world,' outside of the therapeutic setting" (p. 181). In order to bring about change, a positive relationship must exist that is warm, positive, supportive and caring. However, the alliance is "not seen as the main mechanism of action, but instead as the 'glue' or the foundation that facilitates the active ingredients" (p. 183). Elizur and Huppert describe the roles that the CBT therapist plays in the relationship as including that of expert, salesperson, ally against avoidance, and coach. Throughout Chapter 8, there is no mention of the relationship being interpreted or analyzed.

Clinical Vignettes

Noa was a 26-year-old, single, second-year undergraduate who "applied for treatment due to extreme shyness and anxiety in social situations. She described her shyness as interfering with her studies and social situations, and was worried that it was being interpreted as lack of interest in others. She avoided social events and parties" (p. 190).

Some examples of how the therapist exhibited the different roles included the following:

- Understanding why anxiety was seen as the problem in order to help reframe the problem as the client's attempts to manage her anxiety and her interpretations of threat, and not the anxiety itself (role of expert);
- Helping the client identify the situations that especially frightened her, those which she couldn't deal with earlier. They thought together how to divide these into stages and created external and internal aids for coping and building exposure events that she could handle (role of coach); and
- Helping the client determine her core fear: that others would think that she was stupid and expressing empathy for the client's difficulties and affirmation for her understanding of the problem, combined with a challenging approach and an invitation for a common quest for an alternative way (p. 191) (role of ally against avoidance).

Position on the Relationship Grid

Cell C. In CBT, as it is described in Chapter 8, the therapeutic relationship is not considered to be the focus of therapy or a major mechanism of change. The exploration of the relationship or the nature of the relationship are not relied upon to directly lead the client to make changes. However, it is an important feature of the therapy in the ways described above because without a supportive and facilitative relationship, the client may not be amenable to working with the therapist to implement the techniques to deal with her social anxiety. As described in Cell C of the grid, the techniques are not designed to address the therapeutic relationship directly, but the way they are implemented impacts that relationship. These can be intended as such or unintended but are impactful, nevertheless.

Chapter 9: Farber and Suzuki (Rogerian/Client-Centered)

Main Theoretical Concept

Based on Rogerian client-centered theory, the major approach to the relationship in Chapter 9 is the therapist conveying positive regard for the client, which is useful to the extent that the client experiences it as such. There are a variety of ways in which positive regard may be communicated from therapist to client, which are "most effectively conveyed through multiple and ever-changing expressions of both verbal and nonverbal communication" (p. 212) (e.g., affirmation, nonpossessive warmth, praising, and acceptance).

Clinical Vignette

Farber first saw Carole when she was 25. She presented with a history that "included a gruesome period during her childhood and early adolescence of being physically and sexually abused by her father, abetted by her mother's inability or unwillingness to intervene" (p. 217).

Farber and Suzuki describe the therapy with Carole in terms of "affirming statements and actions therapists take to demonstrate their positive regard for those with whom they work" (p. 218). Farber illustrates such affirming remarks that he made to Carole over the years of working together:

> "You've been the strength of your family, you've essentially held it together"; "You have great artistic talent" (after bringing into session some of her artwork); "You're very gracious"; "You're a very sensitive, loving mother"; "You're remarkably resilient"; "You're quite sensitive"; "That's a very smart way of looking at things"; "That's very kind of you" (following her sending me a condolence card after a death in my family). Her reaction to these and similar complimentary remarks—sometimes smiles, sometimes tears, sometimes simple gratitude—strongly indicated how much this type of positive regard meant to her. (p. 223)

Position on the Relationship Grid

Cell D. This is a good example of the relationship as therapy—namely, conveying positive regard in the relationship is meant to help the client become congruent with all of their experience and to undo the lack of unconditional positive regard experienced in the past. It falls under Cell D rather than Cell B because the therapist's interventions are not necessarily addressing the relationship per se but rather are designed to impact the relationship. To compliment the client ("You've tried hard to be decent"; "You're a very sensitive, loving mother," etc.) is not addressing the relationship directly as required in Cell B, but the content of these interventions and the way in which they are conveyed has an impact on the therapeutic relationship.

Chapter 10: Watson (Emotion-Focused/Client-Centered)

Main Theoretical Concept

A quote from Watson in Chapter 10 nicely conveys her theoretical approach:

> [Emotion focused] EFT [emotion-focused therapy] therapists try to be fully present in their interactions with clients, providing warmth,

> empathic attunement, and acceptance along with being congruent and transparent. These characteristics are seen as providing a restorative relationship, fostering clients' growth and healing to enable them to overcome distress, and develop their capacities for more optimal affect regulation, and transform their relationships with self and others. (p. 236)

Clinical Vignette

When Edwin, a 58-year-old Vietnamese man, entered treatment, he suffered from major depressive disorder, felt trapped and burdened in his marriage to a wife with very serious mental illness, and manifested a serious heart condition together with diabetes and high blood pressure. The therapy is reflected in the following quotes from Chapter 10:

> [Edwin's therapist worked with him] to process his emotions of sadness, anger, hopelessness and grief. He longed for a close loving relationship with a supportive other in whom he could confide and was worried about growing old and being unable to care for his wife or having to be cared for by her. (p. 242)
>
> His therapist began to realize that talking about his feelings and exploring the impact of events, putting them in perspective, and allowing himself to freely process his emotions in an empathetic, accepting, prizing and congruent therapeutic relationship could serve an important role in reducing his stress levels and hypertension. (p. 245)
>
> It is the communication of this state of safety and calm by means of posture, gaze, attention, vocal quality, care, warmth and attunement to the client's experience that may have contributed to the activation of the vagal brake resulting in a lowering of the client's blood pressure and sense of stress and threat. (p. 248)

By therapy's end, Edwin's depression had been very significantly reduced and his blood pressure had dropped substantially.

Position on the Relationship Grid

Cell D. The nature of the relationship is all-important in this model, although there is no indication that the therapist–client relationship is addressed directly. For example, when the patient talked about how he had been able to converse with his mother in an open way but not with his wife, the therapist did not consider it necessary to connect herself to the mother and explore this comparison further or contrast it with what he missed in his marital relationship. That is, the transference is not explored as it might have been in a psychodynamic therapy. What carry the therapy are conditions like safety, empathy, and congruence, which allow the client to introject the benign features of the therapist and to become more self-accepting.

Chapter 11: Heatherington, Escudero, and Friedlander (Family Systems)

Main Theoretical Concept

Chapter 11 uses a systemic model, where the work is with a whole family but also with some of its subsystems, such as a couple, siblings, and even individuals. It stresses the therapist's role in engaging in the therapeutic process and establishing emotional connection with the clients. Safety is established within the therapeutic system and a shared sense of purpose is fostered.

Clinical Vignette

To illustrate their systems approach, Heatherington, Escudero, and Friedlander present the following scenario:

> A family in significant distress appears for an initial session, with myriad presenting problems, including the adolescent son's substance abuse and hostility toward his younger sister, and parents who have decided that they are "emotionally divorced" but are keeping this important fact from their children. (p. 257)

As one example of working with different relationships in the family:

> in the 10th session, the therapist took the siblings on a "field trip through their childhood" in order to repair the emotional attachment between them, in hopes that this repair would benefit both of them and facilitate systemic change in the family as a whole. (p. 274)

As one way of bonding with the siblings, the therapist thus expressed an interest in them apart from the problems being treated in therapy.

Position on the Relationship Grid

Cell A. Establishing a relationship between the therapist and each of the subsystems in the family was a central goal and allowed the therapist to introduce the N-RFI techniques that he felt would help the members of the family to do better and to lower the tension in their interactions. The therapeutic relationship is not explored or addressed directly and so the approach doesn't belong in Cell B. The relationship does not constitute the therapy itself but allows the techniques to be instituted much as in CBT. It does not belong in Cell C because the interventions are deliberately designed to address the therapeutic relationship directly.

Chapter 12: Hill and Gupta (Psychodynamic/Interpersonal)

Main Theoretical Concept

Hill and Gupta propose that *immediacy*, or the supervisor and supervisee talking together directly about the relationship in the here and now, can help to resolve problems that might arise between them, such as dissatisfaction by the supervisee with some aspect of the supervision. Modeling immediacy in the supervisory relationship is a way of training supervisees to apply it with their clients.

Clinical Vignette

In this vignette, in which the researcher interviewed the supervisee, immediacy was used to process misperceptions in the supervisor–supervisee relationship, which helped the therapist to conduct the therapy with her client more in the here and now.

> *Interviewer:* So you used a lot of immediacy [in your supervisory relationship]?
>
> *Supervisee:* Oh yeah, yeah. She [the supervisor] and I spoke in the here and now a lot about our relationship.
>
> *Interviewer:* And that helped clarify misconceptions?
>
> *Supervisee:* Yup. She would clarify, but she was also real good about not letting it drop there, you know. It wasn't just sort of like "No, that's not what I'm thinking." It was, "No, that's not what I'm thinking. Now let's explore this." And that was so helpful because with my last client, it was like he had all these misperceptions and it was important, "Well that wasn't my intention" or "I'm not so sure I said that." . . . But it was like what's important here, what does it mean that these are the thoughts you're having, what does it mean that this is how you see me? (p. 302)

Position on the Relationship Grid

Cell B. Immediacy is designed to use the supervisory relationship as a way for supervisees to learn about their interpersonal dynamics from the working through of misperceptions, ruptures, clarifications, validations, etc., in the supervisory relationship itself.

It should be noted that within the therapy for which Hill and Gupta's supervision takes place, rupture dynamics and dealing with attachment issues are less central than in the other therapy models shown in Cell B. For this reason, we would secondarily place the Hill and Gupta therapy model in Cell A, in which the role of the relationship is necessary but insufficient.

COMPARISON OF MODELS AND IMPLICATIONS FOR PRACTICE

The models from Chapters 2 through 12 are mapped in Table 13.1 in terms of their primary approach to the therapeutic relationship. Not unsurprisingly, Table 13.1 cell placement reflects how similar theoretical orientations cluster in the same cells, that is, the Table 13.1 cells differentiate the models by theoretical orientation, as follows. Cell A is associated with the family systems in Chapter 11. Cell B is associated with the psychodynamic Chapters 2, 3, 4, 5, and 12. Cell C is associated with the "pure" CBT model in Chapter 8. Cell D is associated with the two Rogerian/client-centered-derived models, Chapters 9 and 10, and with the particular emphasis on relationship bonding in the psychoanalytic Chapter 6. As a model of assimilative integration, which we will discuss below, Chapter 7 is coded in Cell C for its connection to its CBT roots; in Cell B, for its assimilation of the relationship–rupture dynamics associated with the psychodynamic therapies; and in Cell D, for its assimilation of client-centered interventions.

Within the psychodynamic models, and despite their carrying the same theoretical label, there are some noteworthy contrasts in what they emphasize. Kohberger, Safran, and Muran's model in Chapter 2 emphasizes a focus on finding and resolving ruptures, while Zilcah-Mano and Barber's model in Chapter 5 emphasizes the need to maximize a patient's feeling understood. Hill and Gupta's model of immediacy in Chapter 12 emphasizes both ruptures and validations between supervisor and supervisee with the result that the therapist becomes more willing to use immediacy to deal with problems in therapy. Wiseman and Atzil-Slonim in Chapter 4 and Schattner and Tishby in Chapter 3 emphasize the connection between the therapist's and patient's enactments, based in their individual attachment histories, with Wiseman and Atzil-Slonim emphasizing the advantages of contrasting dynamics, and Tishby and Schattner stressing the advantages of similar dynamics.

Although traditionally the field has distinguished between "technique" and "relationship" in therapy, we propose that the different strategies and interventions described and clinically illustrated in Chapters 2 through 12 present different types of RFIs. It is in this sense that the therapy relationship is not so much a clearly specified "common" factor as it is a common theme across therapies. Specifically, each model emphasizes one or more particular types of intervention for enhancing the therapeutic relationship in the service of strengthening the effectiveness of that therapy. A main intervention associated with each model is presented in Table 13.2. As can be seen across the 11 items listed in Table 13.2, these are all interventions in so far as they involve intentional, reasoned-out decisions for therapist action that are made at ongoing choice points in therapy. For example, Farber and Suzuki's Chapter 9 stresses interventions that positively frame their client's thoughts and behaviors.

As can also be seen by viewing across the 12 interventions in Table 13.2, they provide contrasting options at clinical choice points (cf. Messer's, 1986, comparison of behavioral and psychoanalytic interventions at therapeutic choice points). This is exemplified in Castonguay et al.'s Chapter 7, in which the authors turned to non-CBT relational interventions (RFIs) when the usual CBT interventions for extratherapy problems (N-RFIs) ran into barriers. As another example of differences, Chapter 2 (Kohberger et al.) and Chapter 12 (Hill and Gupta), which both emphasize ruptures and conflict in the relationship, contrast with the approaches of Zilcha-Mano and Barber in Chapter 5, Farber and Suzuki in Chapter 9, and Watson in Chapter 10, which all emphasize validating the client and focusing on the positive in the relationship. This emphasis on the positive is similar to Elizur and Huppert's role of the therapist as coach and ally against client avoidance (Chapter 8).

It is important to note that the dialectic between a rupture focus and a validation focus appears in the CBT tradition, being resonant with Linehan's (1993) dialectical behavior therapy (DBT), in which the therapist is always aware at clinical choice points of the dialectical tension between acceptance and validation of clients versus challenging them to look at their problems and to change. This dialectic is also represented in the psychodynamic tradition in terms of the contrast between insight-oriented therapy, which challenges patients to confront difficult parts of themselves, and supportive therapy, which emphasizes acceptance and reassurance of patients. Frequently, psychodynamic therapists orchestrate both types of therapy in the same treatment, especially with more emotionally disturbed patients (Messer, 2015b).

Linehan's DBT is instructive because the dialectical nature of the opposing approaches to the client—acceptance and validation versus change and challenge—is built into the therapy's name. In line with this, DBT is actually a combination of very different elements: those from hermeneutically inspired Buddhist ideas have been incorporated into a home theory of positivistic behaviorism. (Another example of this combination of opposing elements is Hayes's acceptance and commitment therapy [ACT], in which Buddhist elements are incorporated into a home theory of radical behaviorism.)

TABLE 13.2
Major Relationship-Focused Interventions Proposed by the Chapter Authors

Chapter 2 (Kohberger, Safran, & Muran)	Take notice of and work through ruptures in the therapeutic relationship.
Chapter 3 (Schattner & Tishby)	Focus on patient and therapist enactments played out in the therapeutic relationship to promote positive change for both therapist and patient—arriving thereby at a healthy middle ground (similar to Wiseman & Atzil-Slonim).
Chapter 4 (Wiseman & Atzil-Slonim)	Focus on attachment style conflict between the therapist and the patient as it plays out in the therapeutic relationship to promote positive change for both—by facilitating movement in both therapist and client toward a healthy middle ground of relating.
Chapter 5 (Zilcha-Mano & Barber)	Strive to have the client feel accepted by the therapist.
Chapter 6 (Shefler)	Consider breaking traditional therapy boundaries if they impede the therapist–patient bond in order to enhance this bond for the sake of progress in therapy.
Chapter 7 (Castonguay, Youn, Xiao, & McAleavey)	Incorporate relationship perspectives from non–cognitive–behavioral therapies, such as providing corrective experiences and being a good role model to internalize.
Chapter 8 (Elizur & Huppert)	Employ four roles (expert, salesperson, ally, and coach) to create a positive relationship as a motivator to help the client overcome obstacles and complete extratherapy tasks.
Chapter 9 (Farber & Suzuki)	Provide clients with varieties of acceptance, positive framing of their strengths, and encouragement of their best.
Chapter 10 (Watson)	Use warmth and empathy to encourage clients' emotional expression in order to combat the damaging effects of negative emotions that have not been properly identified and worked through.
Chapter 11 (Heatherington, Escudero, & Friedlander)	In a family setting, orchestrate and enhance multiple positive relationships, both between the therapist and family members, and among family members.
Chapter 12 (Hill & Gupta)	Employ immediacy—that is, focus on the present relationship between supervisor and supervisee, whether the relationship is ruptured or validating—to enhance supervisees' learning, positive psychological development, and their application of immediacy in the therapies they conduct.

Messer (2017) has developed the model of assimilative integration to explain how a therapist can incorporate interventions or clinical perspectives from other therapies:

> [Assimilative integration] can be seen as a middle ground between a full theoretical integration as proposed, for example, by Paul Wachtel for psychoanalytic and cognitive behavioral therapy (CBT), and technical eclecticism, in which any empirically supported techniques can be combined without a theoretical anchor point. As mental health practitioners become more clinically experienced, they typically include some features from outside their favored theoretical approach in order to make therapy more effective or allow it to be briefer. Thus, assimilative integration can be defined as a way of conducting psychotherapy by incorporating into one's home or preferred therapeutic approach, concepts, techniques or perspectives from another form of therapy. In this fashion, therapists modify and extend their usual mode of practice by integrating other methods. For example, one might incorporate homework or relaxation training—that is, CBT techniques—into a psychodynamic or humanistic–experiential therapy, or pay attention in CBT to the way in which clients play out their problems in the interpersonal interaction with their therapist—a major feature of psychodynamic therapy. (p. 314)

Pluralism is one of the underlying epistemological principles within assimilative integration that explains how, for example, a behavioral home theory can integrate contrasting Buddhist concepts, or how—in the instance of Castonguay et al.—psychodynamic and client-centered concepts can be integrated within CBT. According to Messer (2015a),

> Pluralism holds that one theory or model can never preclude an alternate, competing theory. This is because, according to pluralism, we do not discover what is in nature but, rather, invent our theories and conceptual categories and view reality through them. What follows is that there are, and always will be, multiple ways of conceptualizing and interpreting human experience. So, rather than viewing contradictions among theories as negative or a challenge to be overcome, pluralism sees them as a way of spurring on the creation of yet other ideas and theories. Such differences are not to be viewed as mere deviations from one accurate way of understanding or treating people, but as expressions of the many ways in which human experience can be conceptualized and ameliorated. We will always have several theories of therapy because the way to the truth is via the confrontation and dialogue among them. Assimilative integration can be thought of as comprising a bridge between these two outlooks. Even while a theory of therapy, in accordance with a modernist view, should be grounded in observation and empirical evidence, there are a multitude of ways to construct

valid theories, including by assimilating techniques or concepts into one's home theory and therapy. (p. 65)

For an example of the use of a pluralistic approach to case conceptualization and clinical decision making, see the Case of Mrs. B in Fishman and Messer (2013).

In line with a pluralistic approach to assimilative integration, we propose that this volume provides interventions pertaining to the therapy relationship that psychotherapists from a different home base can assimilate into their practice. The variety of these interventions, as illustrated in Table 13.2, can be useful as alternative relationship-based tools at various choice points in the clinical process (Messer, 1986). For example, at a particular choice point the therapist can consider:

- Is this a time to enhance the relationship through Farber and Suzuki's and Watson's validation and positive regard interventions, or a time to use Hill and Gupta's immediacy stance or Kohberger et al.'s focus on bringing to the surface the tension and rupture in the therapy relationship?
- Is this a time to enhance problem-solving in the client's extra-therapy life by considering adopting one or more of the four CBT roles of expert, salesperson, ally against avoidance, and coach that Elizur and Huppert discuss?
- Is this a time to bring in other members of a client's family? If so, the therapist should consider orchestrating a variety of relationships—between the therapist and each of the family members, and among the family members, as in Heatherington et al.
- In psychoanalytic therapy, is this a time to focus on whether the role of the therapist's attachment style (as described by Wiseman and Atzil-Slonim and by Schattner and Tishby) is properly aligned with the client's attachment style?

In considering such an assimilative psychotherapy integration, a therapist should be aware that integrating a new perspective or intervention is not always straightforward or without its perils. Therapists have to introduce it in such a way that it fits as seamlessly as possible within their home or preferred therapy.

In closing, we want to underscore that what is particularly helpful in terms of understanding the nature and use of the relational interventions in Table 13.2 are their theoretical and empirical backgrounds and their embodiment in clinical vignettes, as presented in each chapter. We believe that the scope of this book and the therapeutic relationship matrix provide a general framework for expanding upon our knowledge of useful relational interventions. We encourage the further development of this framework, including its use with comprehensive and systematic case studies, as represented in such journals as *Clinical Case Studies* (Hersen, 2002) and *Pragmatic Case Studies in Psychotherapy* (Fishman, 2005). We believe that the study of such cases is needed to do justice to the complexity and multilayered nature of the therapeutic relationship and its potential to facilitate psychotherapeutic change.

REFERENCES

Brady, J. P. (1980). Some views on effective principles of psychotherapy. *Cognitive Therapy and Research*, *4*, 271–306. http://dx.doi.org/10.1007/BF01371318

Fishman, D. B. (2005). Editor's introduction to PCSP—From single case to database: A new method for enhancing psychotherapy practice. *Pragmatic Case Studies in Psychotherapy*, *1*, 1–50. http://dx.doi.org/10.14713/pcsp.v1i1.855

Fishman, D. B. (2016). Behavioral theories. In J. C. Norcross, G. R. VandenBos, & D. K. Freedheim (Eds.), *APA handbook of clinical psychology* (Vol. 2, pp. 79–115). Washington, DC: American Psychological Association.

Fishman, D. B., & Messer, S. B. (2013). Pragmatic case studies as a source of unity in applied psychology. *Review of General Psychology*, *17*, 156–161. http://dx.doi.org/10.1037/a0032927

Fishman, D. B., Messer, S. B., Edwards, D. J. A., & Dattilio, F. (Eds.). (2017). *Case studies within psychotherapy trials: Integrating qualitative and quantitative methods*. New York, NY: Oxford University Press. http://dx.doi.org/10.1093/med:psych/9780199344635.001.0001

Goldfried, M. R. (1980). Toward the delineation of therapeutic change principles. *American Psychologist*, *35*, 991–999. http://dx.doi.org/10.1037/0003-066X.35.11.991

Hersen, M. (2002). Rationale for clinical case studies: An editorial. *Clinical Case Studies*, *1*, 3–5. http://dx.doi.org/10.1177/1534650102001001001

Linehan, M. (1993). *Cognitive–behavioral treatment of borderline personality disorder*. New York, NY: Guilford Press.

Messer, S. B. (1986). Behavioral and psychoanalytic perspectives at therapeutic choice points. *American Psychologist*, *41*, 1261–1272. http://dx.doi.org/10.1037/0003-066X.41.11.1261

Messer, S. B. (2015a). Assimilative psychotherapy integration. In E. Neukrug (Ed.), *The Sage encyclopedia of theory in counseling and psychotherapy* (Vol. 1, pp. 63–66). Thousand Oaks, CA: Sage.

Messer, S. B. (2015b). Psychoanalytic and psychodynamic therapies: Long-term and short-term. In R. L. Cautin & S. O. Lilienfeld (Eds.), *The encyclopedia of clinical psychology* (pp. 1–9). Hoboken, NJ: Wiley-Blackwell. http://dx.doi.org/10.1002/9781118625392.wbecp260

Messer, S. B. (2017). Assimilative integration. In A. Wenzel (Ed.), *The sage encyclopedia of abnormal and clinical psychology* (p. 314). Thousand Oaks, CA: Sage.

Messer, S. B., & Winokur, M. (1981). Therapeutic change principles: Are commonalities more apparent than real? *American Psychologist, 36*, 1547–1548. http://dx.doi.org/10.1037/0003-066X.36.12.1547

Persons, J. B. (2008). *The case formulation approach to cognitive–behavior therapy*. New York, NY: Guilford Press.

14

CONCLUSIONS: THE TAPESTRY OF THE THERAPEUTIC RELATIONSHIP AND RECOMMENDATIONS FOR CLINICIANS AND RESEARCHERS

ORYA TISHBY AND HADAS WISEMAN

The ongoing search to better understand what makes therapy work has led clinicians and researchers to focus on the therapeutic relationship. The pan-theoretical concept of the alliance has taken center stage, beginning with the writings of Bordin (1979) and Luborsky, Crits-Christoph, Alexander, Margolis, and Cohen (1983), which prompted the development of a host of alliance measures. The availability of these measures led to a significant and impressive body of research that provided evidence for the impact of the alliance on therapy outcome. However, Horvath's question in Chapter 1, "Where Does the Alliance Fit?" points to the potential cost of blurring the distinction between the alliance and "the broader concept of the therapy relationship" (p. 22). He suggests that "our central task, core mission, as therapy researchers, is to better understand what makes therapy 'work.' To reach this goal we need to pull apart the fabric, make careful distinctions, to gain insights about what works with whom in which circumstances" (p. 22).

http://dx.doi.org/10.1037/0000093-015
Developing the Therapeutic Relationship: Integrating Case Studies, Research, and Practice, O. Tishby and H. Wiseman (Editors)

CONSTRUCTING A TAPESTRY OF INTERWOVEN RELATIONAL THEMES AND LAYERS

The other authors in this book follow Horvath's lead by either extending the use of the alliance concept or adding conceptualizations of new and rich perspectives on the relationship. Examples of such extensions are concurrent multiple alliances in family therapy that the therapist needs to monitor and balance (Chapter 11), the interface of alliance with professional ethics (Chapter 6), and alliance-focused interventions in cognitive therapy (Chapter 7). Other chapters introduce process aspects of the relationship, such as closeness and distance dynamics (Chapter 4), enactments of transference–countertransference dynamics (Chapter 3), feeling understood (Chapter 5), different patterns of rupture and repair in three consecutive treatments (Chapter 2), immediacy events (Chapter 12), positive regard (Chapter 9), and the use of empathic attunement and responsiveness (Chapter 10). We would like to suggest that another way of viewing the challenge "to pull apart the fabric" is to consider the chapters in this book as constructing a tapestry of interwoven relational themes and layers. Although each chapter puts forward a distinct relational dimension, it is our conviction that these relational processes are intertwined, with some being in the forefront and others in the background at various time points in therapy. The meaning and impact of these relational themes may change across the process of psychotherapy, depending on clients' needs and characteristics, therapists' contribution, and the interaction between them. Therapists are actually constantly making choices as to which relational dimension to attend to at any given moment and how to fit their interventions to best address these dimensions. The idea of keeping tabs on fluctuations in the relationship, be they minor misunderstandings or more dramatic breaches that may lead to dropout, appears to be present to some extent in almost all the chapters in the book. Through the clinical cases one can observe how therapists attempt to meet this challenge in different ways in order to create new possibilities of relating that would serve the goal of facilitating client change. These challenges are easier to recognize when a relational process is explicit, such as the patient confronting the therapist with her feeling that the cognitive–behavioral therapy (CBT) course of treatment she is receiving is not helping her (Chapter 2).[1] Other times, a relational process is implicit and not readily apparent, such as the therapist's countertransference regarding her refusal to make directive interventions that the client asked for (Chapter 3). Finally, implicit themes might become apparent at a later stage of therapy as a result of the therapist identifying the nature of the tension in the relationship. An example of this can be seen in the patient who experienced recurrence of skin-picking symptoms

[1]Details of case examples have been altered to protect confidentiality.

towards termination in CBT. This setback was unexpected and surprising, but when the relationship was explored (not a typical intervention in CBT), strong feelings of rejection surfaced that were previously implicit, and once addressed helped the client and therapist resume treatment.

On the moment-to-moment level, for example, in immediacy interventions (Chapter 12) therapists reflect on their strong emotions and approach the client with insight about what is happening in the here and now.

> The therapist then articulates what is going on between the two of them, owning his or her feelings and asking about the client's feelings (making the implicit explicit). By then exploring openly and dialoguing about what is going on between them, the therapist and client can emerge with a new understanding of their relationship and new ideas for how to approach the relationship differently. (pp. 290–291)

Connected to the concepts of explicit and implicit are the psychodynamic concepts of levels of consciousness, which view the relationship as operating simultaneously on conscious, preconscious, and unconscious levels. For example, in Shefler's first illustration, the conscious aspect of the relationship is the psychoanalyst not attending to the tall patient's physical discomfort while lying on a short psychoanalytic sofa, and the patient's irritation and attempts to communicate his discomfort. On the unconscious level, however, this discomfort may have stemmed from the deeper resistance to the psychoanalytic process. The therapist's and patient's struggle operated on both levels; almost metaphorically speaking they had to both "extend the physical sofa" and enlarge the space for deeper psychoanalytic work, with the conscious and unconscious processes mutually affecting each other. Given that the psychoanalytic treatment that Shefler writes about was undertaken many years ago, it refrains from metacommunicating about the sofa incident, as would probably be part of Safran and Muran's (2000) model. Using contemporary concepts that were illustrated in the cases in the book, communicating openly about the sofa incident could potentially be constituted as an "immediacy event" (Hill & Knox, 2009).

The 2 × 2 matrix that Messer and Fishman outline (Chapter 13, Table 13.1) maps the use of and focuses on the relationship in the different cases, and consists of two dimensions: The first is *the therapist's goal in establishing a relationship vis-à-vis therapeutic change*; the second is *how directly the therapists' actions address the therapeutic relationship*. Regarding the latter, they suggest that the various kinds of interventions therapists use to develop and maintain the therapeutic relationship can be considered as either *relationship-focused interventions* (RFIs) or *non–relationship-focused interventions*. We would like to add to this heuristic distinction the observation that within the array of RFIs, a specific intervention can serve purposes that correspond to the four threads outlined by Horvath (Chapter 1): focusing on transference, increasing safety, facilitating more collaboration, and experiencing something new in the here and now. For example, in the case of Dan presented by Zilcha-Mano and Barber (Chapter 5), the patient was reluctant to be the first to talk in the session, saying that in sales the first to talk loses. The therapist reacted empathically, explaining that she wanted to keep quiet in order to allow him sufficient space for deciding what he wanted to discuss in the session. This intervention can simultaneously serve to increase safety, facilitate collaboration, and allow the patient to experience something new (i.e., putting him first, which others in his life never did).

WHAT MORE CAN PRACTITIONERS LEARN ABOUT THE RELATIONSHIP?

Zooming in on how the authors of these chapters work with the relationship within different therapeutic frameworks provides clinicians with fresh insights that can be translated into practice within different therapy models. As we read various chapters in the book, they illuminate new ways of thinking about what clients need from their therapists in order to change, such as the centrality of empathic attunement (Chapter 10), the patient's need to feel understood (Chapter 5), finding the optimal closeness versus distance to feel safe (Chapter 4), and the salience of providing positive regard (Chapter 9). It seems to us that these ideas can be assimilated into different modalities of therapy (Chapter 7) without having to use the exact same interventions described in the chapters. In this sense the assimilation may take on different shapes and forms, because what guides the therapist is the *relational concept* rather than the specific technique. For example, working with clients with unexpressed anger (as described in Watson's case in Chapter 10) through empathic attunement and responsiveness highlights the clinical value of these concepts, whether or not the therapist chooses to employ the two-chair technique in emotion-focused therapy, interpretation in psychodynamic therapy, or anger management in CBT.

INTEGRATING THE CASES AND SYSTEMATIC RESEARCH ON THE RELATIONSHIP

Pluralism of research paradigms and multiple methods are needed to study such complex phenomena as human relationships and therapeutic change (Castonguay, 2011; Wiseman, 2017). This book provides, in our view, a convincing case for studying psychotherapy through reliance on methodological pluralism. Specifically, we advocate combining systematic case studies with quantitative data that can be used to describe the therapeutic relationship, processes, and outcomes. The chapters demonstrate a variety of methods for data collection and analysis: self-report questionnaires, observer coding systems of therapy sessions, semistructured interviews, and qualitative analysis. All of the cases combine the use of such measures with supplemental clinical information—watching the video recordings, reviewing process notes, and more. The use of these multiple methods allows for rigorous systematic studies that remain close to the clinical material (Wiseman & Tishby, 2017). Such a combination is in line with recommendations by Fishman (2013) as to the types of data needed for systematic cases studies. Moreover, Stiles, Hill, and Elliott (2015) advocate using mixed methodology in the systematic investigation of a small number of cases to learn about microlevel processes.

With regard to the use of measures of the therapeutic relationship (see Chapter 1), some of the authors extend and elaborate on an existing measure or research tool, finding creative ways to use it for analyzing data, whereas others developed new measures. For example, in Chapter 2, Kohberger, Safran, and Muran use their own measure of rupture and repair to track changes in the working alliance and identify ruptures in three consecutive treatments with the same client. They use a discovery-oriented approach to go beyond the data provided by their measure to conduct microanalyses of rupture episodes and add the client's perspective using interpersonal process recall. Wiseman and Atzil-Slonim (Chapter 4) conduct a qualitative analysis of the narratives collected in Relationship Anecdote Paradigm interviews to track the therapist's and client's experience of closeness and distance. These narratives are usually coded on Core Conflictual Relationship Theme categories of wishes, responses of other, and responses of self, and the authors expand the use of the narrative data (Wiseman & Tishby, 2017). Schattner and Tishby (Chapter 3), using the same database, select the most successful case, as defined by quantitative process and outcome measures. They apply qualitative analysis to the narratives told by therapist and client to study transference and countertransference phenomena in this treatment. Chapters 7 and 8 focus on the significance of the relationship at different stages of cognitive therapy and CBT, based on research findings. Both use the Working Alliance Inventory to track the relationship, and demonstrate in detail how a focus on the relationship can prevent pitfalls in therapy. Castonguay, Youn, Xiao, and McAleavey (Chapter 7), integrate work on rupture and repair, based on studies by Safran and Muran (2000), into cognitive therapy. Elizur and Huppert (Chapter 8) define and describe the therapist's role at different stages of treatment, such as attunement to the client, balancing between pushing for change and letting go, encouraging the client versus critiquing.

They point out that "these aspects of therapy are not usually specified in CBT manuals, because they are specific to the client and the therapist at different points in the process" (p. 205). Thus, they present a systematic framework for observing the therapeutic relationship in CBT.

Looking at new measures that were presented in the chapters, Heatherington, Escudero, and Friedlander (Chapter 11) developed the System for Observing Family Therapy Alliances (SOFTA), a multidimensional tool developed to capture the complexity of alliances in family therapy. The SOFTA has therapist and client self-report questionnaires, as well as an observer-rated measure based on video recordings of family therapy sessions. Watson (Chapter 10), describing the use of empathy in emotion-focused therapy, presents the Measure of Expressed Empathy that she developed. This measure attempts to capture therapists' nonverbal behaviors as well as the verbal content of their reflections and responses to clients in order to assess their level of empathy in the session. Like other observer measures, it is based on ratings of video-recorded sessions. A related measure is the Feeling Understood in Treatment coding system, developed by Zilcha-Mano and applied to therapy sessions, as described in Chapter 5. Hill and Gupta (Chapter 12), using Hill's concept of immediacy, developed a coding system to identify different types of immediacy events and their usefulness in supervision. Farber and Suzuki (Chapter 9), building on the Rogerian concept of positive regard, collected data from clients on affirming interventions and identify three factors that depict three dimensions of positive regard that can be applied to therapy transcripts: (a) supportive/caring interventions, (b) unique responsiveness, and (c) intimacy/disclosure.

Finally, Shefler's chapter offers a unique contribution, looking at a distinct therapy event—the clash between professional ethics and the alliance. Although this chapter does not include a standard research component, the selection of these events is based on research findings on the importance of the alliance, which is pitted against traditional psychoanalytic rules and ethics. Shefler suggests conducting qualitative research to collect data on these issues.

The use of various research tools and measures and the incorporation of research findings into existing treatments demonstrate the strong links between research and practice. Many, if not all, of these measures were developed on the basis of clinical theory, which is often rich but difficult to define accurately, and thus many concepts remain "fuzzy." The creation and application of research measures and coding systems helps us to clarify and "nail down" some of these concepts. The data collected helps clarify clinical process even further. Of course, the interpretation of research results often relies on clinical data, so that the two are interrelated and their integration creates a more complex and rich picture of the therapy process.

As for future research, we believe that readers of various psychotherapy schools, including those seeking assimilative integration, will find a wealth of ideas for new studies on the therapeutic relationship, or on integrating some of the concepts into existing treatments and testing their contribution to outcome (Castonguay, Eubanks, Goldfried, Muran, & Lutz, 2015; Romano, Orlinsky, Rønnestad, & Wiseman, 2016). Finally, we hope that this book will make research more accessible and more relevant to clinicians and to students of clinical psychology and of other professions training in psychotherapy. There is much to be learned from the continuous back-and-forth movement between research and practice, towards enhancing the fit of our treatments to our clients.

REFERENCES

Bordin, E. S. (1979). The generalizability of the psychoanalytic concept of the working alliance. *Psychotherapy*, *16*, 252–260. http://dx.doi.org/10.1037/h0085885

Castonguay, L. G. (2011). Psychotherapy, psychopathology, research and practice: Pathways of connections and integration. *Psychotherapy Research*, *21*, 125–140. http://dx.doi.org/10.1080/10503307.2011.563250

Castonguay, L. G., Eubanks, C. F., Goldfried, M. R., Muran, J. C., & Lutz, W. (2015). Research on psychotherapy integration: Building on the past, looking to the future. *Psychotherapy Research*, *25*, 365–382. http://dx.doi.org/10.1080/10503307.2015.1014010

Fishman, D. B. (2013). The pragmatic case study method for creating rigorous and systematic, practitioner-friendly research. *Pragmatic Case Studies in Psychotherapy*, 9, 403–425. http://dx.doi.org/10.14713/pcsp.v9i4.1833

Hill, C. E., & Knox, S. (2009). Processing the therapeutic relationship. *Psychotherapy Research*, *19*, 13–29. http://dx.doi.org/10.1080/10503300802621206

Luborsky, L., Crits-Christoph, P., Alexander, L., Margolis, M., & Cohen, M. (1983). Two helping alliance methods for predicting outcomes of psychotherapy: A counting signs vs. a global rating method. *Journal of Nervous and Mental Disease*, *171*, 480–491. http://dx.doi.org/10.1097/00005053-198308000-00005

Romano, V., Orlinsky, D. E., Rønnestad, M. H., & Wiseman, H. (2016, June). *Therapeutic orientation, theoretical breadth and development of early career therapists*. Paper presented at the 47th SPR International Annual Meeting, Jerusalem, Israel.

Safran, J. D., & Muran, J. C. (2000). *Negotiating the therapeutic alliance: A relational treatment guide*. New York, NY: Guilford Press.

Stiles, W. B., Hill, C. E., & Elliott, R. (2015). Looking both ways. *Psychotherapy Research*, *25*, 282–293. http://dx.doi.org/10.1080/10503307.2014.981681

Wiseman, H. (2017). The quest for connection in interpersonal and therapeutic relationships. *Psychotherapy Research, 27*, 469–487. http://dx.doi.org/10.1080/10503307.2015.1119327

Wiseman, H., & Tishby, O. (2017). Applying relationship anecdotes paradigm interviews to study client–therapist relationship narratives: Core conflictual relationship theme analyses. Special Section: Narrative measures in psychotherapy. *Psychotherapy Research, 27*, 283–299. http://dx.doi.org/10.1080/10503307.2016.1271958

INDEX

ABCT (Association for the Advancement of Behavior Therapy), 158
Acceptance, 174
Acceptance and commitment therapy, 162
Affect regulation
  and emotion-focused therapy, 236–238
  measurement of, 245–246
AFT (alliance-focused training), 98
Ainsworth, M. D. S., 82
Akhtar, S., 139
Alexander, L., 341
Alice's Adventures in Wonderland (Carroll), 18
Alliance-focused training (AFT), 98
Ally role (cognitive–behavioral therapy), 186, 187
American Psychological Association (APA), 4, 133
Anderson, T., 165
Anger, 166
Angus, L., 284
Antisocial tendency, 121
APA (American Psychological Association), 4, 133
Applied psychology, 167
Arnkoff, D. B., 162
Aron, L., 84
Assessment
  in case example, 263, 266–272
  of closeness and distance dynamics, 84–86, 97
  in cognitive–behavioral therapy, 188–192
Assimilative integration, 320, 327–328, 337
Association for the Advancement of Behavior Therapy (ABCT), 158
Attachment
  and affect regulation, 238
  anxious, 82
  avoidant, 82, 170, 172
  and closeness/distance dynamics, 81–83
  and cognitive–behavioral therapy, 167–168, 170, 172
  contributions of research on, 249
  dismissive, 173
  secondary strategies, 82
  and Therapeutic Relationship Matrix, 323–324
Attachment-based family therapy, 259
Atzil-Slonim, D., 322
Avoidance behaviors
  and cognitive–behavioral therapy, 184, 187
  and Therapeutic Relationship Matrix, 335

Barber, Jacques P., 158, 324, 344
Barnes, K. L., 294–295
Barrett-Lennard, 238
Barrett-Lennard Relationship Inventory (BLRI)
  overview, 250
  and positive regard, 215–216, 228–229
BDI. *See* Beck Depression Inventory
Beck, A. T., 159, 160, 182
Beck Depression Inventory (BDI)
  in emotion-focused therapy case example, 244, 247
  in research on feeling understood, 111, 120
Behavioral techniques, 160. *See also* Cognitive–behavioral therapy
Benjamin, J., 84
Bennett, D., 125
Bhatia, A., 293
Bion, W. R., 82, 223
Bleger, J., 140
BLRI. *See* Barrett-Lennard Relationship Inventory
Body language
  in case example, 219
  and research on feeling understood, 120

Borderline personality disorder, 163
Bordin, E. S.
and brief family therapy, 260
and cognitive–behavioral therapy, 182
and feeling understood, 109
and history of therapeutic alliance, 20, 21
writings of, 341
Boundaries
and ethical principles in psychoanalysis, 133, 136–139, 326
and immediacy in supervisory relationships, 293, 308–309
Boundary crossings, 136
Boundary violations, 136
Bowlby, J., 81–82
Brady, J. P., 319
Brief family therapy, 257–286
alliances with family members in, 258
case example, 262–283
change mechanisms in, 259–260, 283
in clinical work and supervision, 283–285
connections between practice and research on, 283–286
theoretical and conceptual background of, 258–261
Brief Psychotherapy Research Program (Beth Israel Medical Center)
therapeutic rupture research at, 33. *See also* Therapeutic rupture research
Brief relational therapy (BRT)
overview, 32
and Therapeutic Relationship Matrix, 320–322
in therapeutic rupture research, 35–43, 46–57
Buddhism, 335, 337
Burns, D. D., 163

Caring, expression of, 212, 293. *See also* Positive regard
Carkhuff, R. R., 290
Carroll, Lewis, 18
Castonguay, Louis G., 157–159, 164, 327, 345
CATS (Client Attachment to Therapist Scale), 85, 92–96
CBT. *See* Cognitive–behavioral therapy
CCRT method. *See* Core Conflictual Relationship Theme method
CEs. *See* Corrective experiences
Change mechanisms
in brief family therapy, 259–260, 283
and closeness/distance dynamics, 100
contexts of, 4
and empathy/responsiveness in emotion-focused therapy, 247–249
and feeling understood, 120–121
and implicit negotiations, 75–77
and positive regard, 225–227
in therapeutic rupture research, 55–56
Charcot, Jean-Martin, 15
Chetrit-Vatine, V., 139
Circumplex models of personality, 249
Clearing a Space task, 251
Client Attachment to Therapist Scale (CATS), 85, 92–96
Client-centered therapy
and emotion-focused therapy, 235
goals of, 166
and incorporation of techniques in CBT, 337
in Therapeutic Relationship Matrix, 320, 329–332
use of positive regard in, 212
Client Expressed Arousal Scale–III, 250
Client Task Specific Change, 240
Clinical Case Studies (journal), 339
Closeness and distance dynamics, 81–100
assessment of, 84–86, 97
and attachment, 81–83
case study, 86–97
and change mechanisms, 100
and conceptualizations of therapeutic relationship, 342
and contemporary relational psychotherapy, 83–84
in research and practice, 98–99
and supervision, 99
Coach role (cognitive–behavioral therapy), 186, 187, 193, 200

Cognitive–behavioral therapy (CBT), 157–175, 181–207
aspects of therapeutic relationship in, 183–190
and barriers, 335
case examples, 168–172, 190–205
and change mechanisms, 172–174
clinical and training recommendations for, 174–175, 206–207
different expressions of, 5
engagement stage in, 192–196
evaluation stage in, 188–192
implications of research on, 206
incorporation of other interventions in, 337
intervention stage in, 194, 197–202
overview, 9
role of relationship in, 319
supportive stance in, 214
termination and maintenance in, 203–206
and therapeutic alliance, 17
therapeutic contract in, 183
in Therapeutic Relationship Matrix, 320, 327–329
in therapeutic rupture research, 35–37, 43–46, 52–53, 56
warmth of relationship in, 159–168, 174, 182
Cognitive techniques, 160
Cognitive therapy
integrative, 164
interventions in, 342
overview, 9
research approaches to, 345–346
treating alliance ruptures in, 163–164
Cohen, M., 341
Cohesiveness, 108
Collaborative empiricism, 160, 327
Colli, A., 293
Commitment, 22
Common factors approach
awakening of interest in, 19
specific factors approach vs., 3
and therapeutic rupture research, 55
Compliments, 222–223
Comprehensive process analysis (CPA), 37
"Conditions of worth," 213
Confederate feedback, 206
Confidence, 17, 22
Congruence
and history of therapeutic alliance, 24
and positive regard, 213
and Therapeutic Relationship Matrix, 332
Conjoint family therapy, 260–261
Connection, 270, 274–276, 280–281
Consensual qualitative research (CQR) method, 123
Constructivist approaches, 263
"Containing" environments, 82
Core Conflictual Relationship Theme (CCRT) method
assessment of closeness/distance dynamics with, 85, 86, 88–91, 93–94, 96–97
and feeling understood, 109
and implicit negotiations, 64, 67, 69–70, 77
and research on feeling understood, 127
and systemic research, 345
Coresearcher role (cognitive–behavioral therapy), 193
Corrective emotional experiences, 83, 99, 324
Corrective experiences (CEs)
in case examples, 122, 303
in cognitive–behavioral therapy, 165–166
formation of, 109
and immediacy in supervisory relationships, 293
and interpersonal experiences, 107, 293
opportunities for, 322, 325
types of, 327
Couches, 134
Countertransference
and conceptualizations of therapeutic relationship, 342
and immediacy in supervisory relationships, 294
and implicit negotiations, 64–65
universality of, 136
uses of, 137

Couples therapy, 259
CPA (comprehensive process analysis), 37
CQR (consensual qualitative research) method, 123
Cristol, A. H., 160
Crits-Christoph, P., 341
Culture, 127, 311

Daly, K. D., 83
DBT (dialectical behavior therapy), 163, 335
Deference, 125
Demoralization, 327
Depression
  and anger, 166
  cognitive–behavioral therapy for, 158
Depressive Experiences Questionnaire (DEQ)
  in emotion-focused therapy case example, 244
  in research on feeling understood, 111, 112
DeRubeis, Robert, 5
Diagnostic and Statistical Manual of Mental Disorders (DSM)
  generalized anxiety disorder in, 87
  PTSD in, 112
  and therapeutic rupture research, 36
Dialectical behavior therapy (DBT), 163, 335
Disarming technique, 163
Distortions, 297, 301–302, 310
Distress tolerance, 184
Dodo Bird verdict, 18–19
Doolin, E. M., 227
DSM. *See Diagnostic and Statistical Manual of Mental Disorders*
Dupetit, S., 139
Dysfunctional Attitudes Scale, 245

ECRS (Experiences in Close Relationships Scale), 85, 86
EFT. *See* Emotion-focused therapy
Ego, 19
Egozi, S., 98
Elizur, Y., 328, 345
Elliott, R., 62, 345
Emery, G., 159
Emotional connection, 258, 261
Emotion-focused couples therapy, 259
Emotion-focused therapy (EFT), 9–10
  empathy and responsiveness in. *See* Empathy and responsiveness in emotion-focused therapy
  in Therapeutic Relationship Matrix, 320, 330–331
Empathy
  in cognitive–behavioral therapy, 159, 160, 202
  and conceptualizations of therapeutic relationship, 342, 344
  and feeling understood, 108
  and history of therapeutic alliance, 24
  and immediacy in supervisory relationships, 290, 294
  and positive regard, 212–214
  and Therapeutic Relationship Matrix, 332
Empathy and responsiveness in emotion-focused therapy, 235–252, 346
  case example, 239–247
  in clinical work and supervision, 251–252
  connections between practice and research on, 249–250
  and mechanisms of change, 247–249
  theoretical basis of, 236–239
Empowerment, 22
Enactments
  and implicit negotiations, 62–63
  in process of therapy, 322
Engagement
  in brief family therapy, 258, 261, 267
  in case example, 270–272, 275–276, 280–281
  in cognitive–behavioral therapy, 192–196
  as phase in treatment, 83
Erikson, E. H., 136
Escudero, V., 332, 346
Etchegoyen, R. H., 136, 138
Ethical misconduct, 136
Ethical principles in psychoanalysis, 133–154, 325–326, 346
  and future research, 152–153
  theoretical and conceptual factors in, 134–140
  and therapeutic setting, 133, 140–152

Ethics, 135–139, 342
  definitively ethical–professional choice, 138
European Psychoanalytic Federation, 153
Evaluation, 188–192
Evans, A. L., 294–295
Evidence-based treatments, 3
Evolutionary science, 167
Excoriation (skin-picking) disorder, 168–170
Existential therapy, 17
Experiences in Close Relationships Scale (ECRS), 85, 86
Experiential techniques, 160
Experiential therapy, 9–10
Experimental psychology, 161
Expert role (cognitive–behavioral therapy), 186
Exposure techniques, 194, 198–200, 206
Eye contact, 222

False alliances (pseudoalliances), 121, 125
False selves, 17
Family systems therapy
  and conceptualizations of therapeutic relationship, 342
  overview, 10
  in Therapeutic Relationship Matrix, 320, 332–333
Fantasy, 135
Farber, B. A., 98, 227, 329, 346
Fear hierarchy, 198
Feedback, 285, 294
"Feeling understood" (therapeutic construct), 105–128, 324–325
  case studies, 110–123
  and change mechanisms, 120–121
  conceptual background of, 106–110
  in research and practice, 123–127
Feeling Understood in Treatment (FUT) coding system
  development of, 123–124, 346
  overview, 110
  in research on feeling understood, 110, 112–120, 122
  and Therapeutic Relationship Matrix, 325
  uses of, 127
Ferenczi, S., 153
Fishman, Dan B., 5, 62, 343
Foa, E. B., 159–160
Following, 235
Frank, J. D., 18
Free association, 134
Free floating attention, 134
Frequency of sessions, 134
Freud, Sigmund
  and ethical principles in psychoanalysis, 134
  and history of therapeutic alliance, 19–20
  on importance of rapport, 158
  invention of talk therapy by, 15
  on transference, 17
Friedlander, M. L., 284, 332, 346
Functional family therapy, 259
FUT coding system. *See* Feeling Understood in Treatment coding system

Gabbard, G. O., 137, 152
Geller, J. D., 98
Gelso, C. J., 64, 293
Generalized anxiety disorder, 87, 158
Gentile, D., 293
Genuineness, 159, 160
Godley, W., 137, 152
Goldberg, Arnold, 136, 138–140
Goldfried, M. R.
  and cognitive–behavioral therapy, 162–163
  and history of therapeutic alliance, 21
Greenberg, Jay, 62
Greenson, R. R., 19
Gupta, S., 333, 346

Ham, J., 63
Hamilton Rating Scale for Depression (HRSD), 111, 120
Hayes, S. C., 162
Heatherington, L., 332, 346
Heckman, B. D., 165
Helping skills, 174
Hembree, E. A., 159–160
"Here and now"
  and attachment, 82
  in cognitive–behavioral therapy, 163
  and immediacy in supervisory relationships, 290
  and implicit negotiations, 63

Hierarchy of fears, 198
Hill, C. E.
and history of psychotherapy research, 62
and immediacy in therapy, 291, 293, 311–312, 333, 346
and research methods, 123, 345
"Holding" environments, 82
Hopelessness, 184
Horvath, A. O., 341, 342, 344
HRSD (Hamilton Rating Scale for Depression), 111, 120
Humanistic psychotherapy
overview, 9–10
self-psychology as bridge between psychoanalysis and, 214
use of positive regard in, 212
Huppert, J. D., 328, 345

ICT (integrative cognitive therapy), 164
Immediacy
and conceptualizations of therapeutic relationship, 342, 343
and implicit negotiations, 63–64
Immediacy in supervisory relationships, 289–312
case example, 295–309
clinical implications of research on, 309–311
and future research, 311–312
theoretical and conceptual bases of, 290–295
and Therapeutic Relationship Matrix, 333–334
Implicit negotiations, 61–78
case study, 66–75
and change mechanisms, 75–77
and links between research and practice, 77
theoretical and conceptual basis for, 62–65
and therapeutic relationship method, 65–66
training and practice implications of, 77–78
Implosive therapy, 158
Insight, 293
Insight-oriented therapy, 335
Integrative approaches, 259, 263
Integrative cognitive therapy (ICT), 164
Internalization of therapist, 166
Internal working models, 81
International Psychoanalytic Association, 133, 152
Interpersonal process recall, 34, 345
Interpersonal techniques, 160, 333–334
Inventory of Interpersonal Problems (IIP), 35, 36
in emotion-focused therapy case example, 245, 247
in research on feeling understood, 111
"Inverse tower of Babel" effect, 22
In vivo interventions, 163, 199
Involvement, 22, 154

Jacobson, N. S., 36
Jerusalem–Haifa psychodynamic psychotherapy study, 4
Joining (cognitive–behavioral therapy), 202
Joseph, Betty, 137, 138

Kasher, A., 135, 139, 140
Kivlighan, D. M., 293
Klimovsky, G., 139
Knox, S., 293
Kohberger, L., 321, 345
Kohut, Heinz, 214

Lazarus, A., 161
Leading
in cognitive–behavioral therapy, 202
in emotion-focused therapy, 235
Learning theory models, 17, 18, 161
LeMoult, J., 166
Lester, E., 137
Levinas, Emanuel, 139, 140
Levis, Donald, 158
Ligiéro, D. P., 64
Linehan, Marsha, 163, 327, 335
Lingiardi, V., 293
Listening skills, 163, 294
Loewald, H. W., 81
Loneliness, 164, 327
Luborsky, L., 20, 341

MacFarlane, P., 165
Maintenance, 203–206
Major depressive disorder, 111, 112

Mallinckrodt, B., 83, 98
Manualized treatment
in cognitive–behavioral therapy, 157
supportive stance in, 214
Margolis, M., 341
McAleavey, Andrew, 157, 327, 345
McNeill, B. W., 293–294
Meaning making, 322
Measure of Expressed Empathy, 250
Messer, S. B., 5, 337, 343
Metacommunication. *See also* Immediacy
in brief relational therapy, 32
in cognitive therapy, 163
paying attention to, 285
repair of ruptures with, 163, 165, 173
Metaperspectives, 259
Michels, R., 138
Microprocess research, 206
Mixed methodology, 345
Modeling, 310–311, 327
Morality, 136
Muran, J. C.
and conceptualizations of therapeutic relationship, 343
development of brief relational therapy by, 32
and feeling understood, 108
and implicit negotiations, 63
and measure of ruptures, 345
and negotiation of alliance ruptures, 56, 164
and stage process model of rupture resolution, 57
and Therapeutic Relationship Matrix, 321
Mutual affirmation, 22

Narrative approaches, 263
Nelson, M. L., 294–295, 301
Neuroception, 248
Non–relationship-focused interventions (N-RFIs)
barriers with, 335
classification of, 343–344
overview, 317–318
relationship between RFIs and, 319
in Therapeutic Relationship Matrix, 321

Object relations theory
and ethical principles in psychoanalysis, 134
and implicit negotiations, 68
Observer Measure of Affect Regulation (O–MAR), 245–246, 249–250
Ogles, B. M., 165
Openness, 22
Outcome Questionnaire (OQ), 67–68, 75, 97
Outcomes
in brief family therapy, 282–283
in closeness/distance dynamics research, 97
in cognitive–behavioral therapy, 164, 182
in emotion-focused therapy case example, 244–247
and feeling understood, 106, 120
and history of therapeutic alliance, 23
and positive regard, 214, 225
therapeutic alliance as predictor of, 184. *See also* Therapeutic alliance
in therapeutic rupture research, 54–56

Parallel process, 294, 296–297, 300–301, 310
Parry, G., 125
Personality, 64
Personality disorders, 162
not otherwise specified, 111
Personalized treatment, 126–127
Person-centered models, 18. *See also* Client-centered therapy
Persons, J. B., 182, 319
Phobia, 193
Pluralism, 337–338, 344–345
Porges, S. W., 247, 248
Positive introjects, 238–239
Positive regard, 211–230
case study, 216–227
and change mechanisms, 225–227
in clinical work and supervision, 229–230
connections between practice and research on, 227–229
data collected on, 346

Positive regard, *continued*
theoretical and conceptual basis of, 212–216
and Therapeutic Relationship Matrix, 329–330
Positivistic behaviorism, 335
Post Session Questionnaire (PSQ)
and implicit negotiations, 65–66
in therapeutic rupture research, 34, 38, 41, 42, 44–50
Posttraumatic stress disorder (PTSD), 112, 127
Power struggles, 294
Pragmatic Case Studies in Psychotherapy (journal), 284, 339
Pride, 223
Professional conduct, 135–136
Professional ethics, 135–139, 342. *See also* Ethical principles in psychoanalysis
Prophylactic immediacy, 298–300
Proximal zones of development, 238
Pseudoalliances (false alliance), 121, 125
PSQ. *See* Post Session Questionnaire
Psychodynamic and psychoanalytic therapies, 8–9
dialectics in, 335
ethical principles in. *See* Ethical principles in psychoanalysis
and implicit negotiations, 68
and incorporation of techniques in CBT, 337
internalization of therapist in, 166
self-psychology as bridge between humanistic therapy and, 214
and therapeutic alliance, 18
in Therapeutic Relationship Matrix, 320–326, 333–334
warmth of relationship in, 160
Psychoeducation, 192
Psychotherapy (journal), 24
Psychotherapy research, 3–4. *See also specific headings*
Psychotherapy Research, 5
PTSD (posttraumatic stress disorder), 112, 127
Purpose. *See* Shared sense of purpose
QLESQ (Quality of Life Enjoyment and Satisfaction Questionnaire), 111, 117
Qualitative analysis, 62, 345
Quality of Life Enjoyment and Satisfaction Questionnaire (QLESQ), 111, 117
Quantitative data analysis, 62

Randomized controlled trials (RCTs), 62, 110–111
RAP. *See* Relationship Anecdote Paradigm Interview
Rapport, 158
RasT (Relationship as Treatment) approach, 319, 320
Rauch, S. A. M., 159–160
RCIs (Reliable Change Indexes), 36
RCTs (randomized controlled trials), 62, 110–111
Reassurance, 293
Relational communication, 285
Relational concept, 344
Relational patterns. *See* Implicit negotiations
Relational psychoanalysis, 214
Relational psychotherapy
and closeness/distance dynamics, 83–84
and ethical principles in psychoanalysis, 134, 136
and implicit negotiations, 68
in Therapeutic Relationship Matrix, 322–325
Relationship Anecdote Paradigm Interview (RAP)
assessment of closeness/distance dynamics with, 85, 95–96
and implicit negotiations, 65–66, 68
Relationship as Necessary but Insufficient (RNBI) approach, 319, 320
Relationship as Treatment (RasT) approach, 319, 320
Relationship-focused interventions (RFIs)
classification of, 343–344
overview, 317–318

relationship between N-RFIs and, 319
in Therapeutic Relationship Matrix, 321
Reliable Change Indexes (RCIs), 36
Resistance, 206
Responsibility, 139–140
Responsiveness of therapist
and conceptualizations of therapeutic relationship, 344
in emotion-focused therapy. *See* Empathy and responsiveness in emotion-focused therapy
and positive regard, 212
Reverie, 134
RFIs. *See* Relationship-focused interventions
RNBI (Relationship as Necessary but Insufficient) approach, 319, 320
Rogers, C. R.
and positive regard, 211–215, 219, 224
support for ideas of, 250
and therapeutic alliance, 17
Rosenberg Self-Esteem Inventory, 245
Rosenzweig, S., 18
Rush, J. J., 159
Ryle, A., 125

Safety
and brief family therapy, 258, 261, 269–271, 279
and history of therapeutic alliance, 22
and Therapeutic Relationship Matrix, 332
Safran, J. D.
and closeness/distance dynamics, 83
and conceptualizations of therapeutic relationship, 343
development of brief relational therapy by, 32, 321
and feeling understood, 108
and implicit negotiations, 63
and measure of alliance rupture, 345
and negotiation of alliance ruptures, 56, 165
and stage process model of rupture resolution, 57
and treating alliance ruptures in cognitive therapy, 163–164
Salesperson role (cognitive–behavioral therapy), 186–187, 193
Sandler, A. M., 137, 152
Schattner, E., 322
Schemata, 162
SCL-90–R (Symptom Checklist-90–Revised), 35–37, 244
Secure base, 82
Segal, Hannah, 137
Segal, Z. V., 165
Self-efficacy, 244
Self-empathy, 238
Self-psychology, 134, 136, 214
Self-report questionnaires, 85–86
Semiotic dysphoria, 22
Shafran, N., 293
Sharabany, R., 98
Shared sense of purpose
in brief family therapy, 258, 261
in case example, 267, 276, 278–279, 281
Shaw, B. F., 159
Shefler, G, 325, 346
Siegel, Daniel, 247
Sloane, R. B., 160
Social anxiety disorder, 190–205
Social interactions, 247
Social phobia, 193
SOFTA. *See* System for Observing Family Therapy Alliances
Specific factors approach, 3
Staples, F. R., 160
State perspective on therapeutic alliance, 106–108, 120, 123–126
Sterba, R. F., 19
Stiles, W. B., 62, 345
Stoltenberg, C. D., 293–294
Strachey, J., 17
Strengths, client, 222–223
Structured Clinical Interviews for *Diagnostic and Statistical Manual of Mental Disorders*, 36
Strupp, Hans, 62
Subjectivity, 237
Suggestibility, 15
Supervision
and closeness/distance dynamics, 99
and cognitive–behavioral therapy, 174–175, 206–207

Supervision, *continued*
and empathy/responsiveness in emotion-focused therapy, 251–252
and positive regard, 229–230
use of Feeling Understood in Treatment measure in, 127
use of immediacy in. *See* Immediacy in supervisory relationships
Support, therapist, 212. *See also* Positive regard
Supportive expressive therapy, 110
Suzuki, J. Y., 329, 346
Symington, N., 152
Symptom Checklist-90–Revised (SCL-90–R), 35–37, 244
System for Observing Family Therapy Alliances (SOFTA)
in case example, 267, 269–272, 282. *See also specific headings*
overview, 258, 260–261, 346
student instruction in, 284
Systemic family therapy, 258–261, 263. *See also* Brief family therapy

Talk therapy, 15
Tanzilli, A., 293
Target Complaints Scale (TCS)
assessment of closeness/distance dynamics with, 85–86, 97
and implicit negotiations, 65–66
TDS (Therapeutic Distance Scale), 98–99
Team member (cognitive–behavioral therapy), 193
Technique
Cognitive–behavioral therapy's emphasis on, 160
in dialectical behavior therapy, 163
in integrative cognitive therapy, 164
intertwined nature of therapeutic relationship and, 4
relationships vs., 334–335
Termination, 203–206
Therapeutic alliance, 15–24. *See also specific headings*
definitions of, 21–22, 32
with family members in brief family therapy, 258, 260–261. *See also* Brief family therapy
frequently used measures of, 22
history of, 19–24
and implicit negotiations. *See* Implicit negotiations
measurement of, 341
relationship between therapy outcome and, 23
and relationships in therapy, 15–19
ruptures in. *See* Therapeutic rupture research
working, 135
Therapeutic contract, 183
Therapeutic distance, 83
Therapeutic Distance Scale (TDS), 98–99
Therapeutic immediacy. *See* Immediacy; Immediacy in supervisory relationships
Therapeutic relationship(s), 341–347. *See also specific headings*
and future directions for practitioners, 344
and history of psychotherapy research, 3–4
integration of cases and research on, 344–347
intertwined nature of technique and, 4
overview, 15–19
tapestry of themes and layers in, 342–344
unique properties of, 16
Therapeutic Relationship Matrix, 317–339, 343–344
and comparison of therapeutic models, 334–339
theory and case vignettes contributing to development of, 321–334
therapeutic models represented in, 319–321
Therapeutic relationship method, 65–66
Therapeutic rupture research, 31–57
approaches to, 345
courses of treatment in, 38–50
implications of, 56–57
and microprocess research, 206
multiple therapists and one client in, 33–38

nature of rupture and resolution events in, 50–54
repair of ruptures in, 32–33, 63
and Therapeutic Relationship Matrix, 321
treatment outcomes in, 54–56
Therapeutic ruptures
in cognitive–behavioral therapy case example, 170–172
in cognitive therapy, 163–164
and conceptualizations of therapeutic relationship, 342
and feeling understood, 107–108, 115–116, 126
and immediacy in supervisory relationships, 293, 297, 301–310
and implicit negotiations, 63
monitoring of, 174
use of metacommunication for repairing of, 163, 165, 173
Therapeutic setting, 133, 140–152
Therapist attitudes and behaviors, 250
Therapy outcomes. *See* Outcomes
Tishby, O., 64, 86, 98, 322
Tone of voice, 223–224
Training
and cognitive–behavioral therapy, 174–175, 206–207
and implicit negotiations, 77–78
use of Feeling Understood in Treatment measure in, 127
Trait perspective on therapeutic alliance, 106–108, 121–125, 127
Transference
and conceptualizations of therapeutic relationship, 342
and immediacy in supervisory relationships, 294, 297
interpretation of, 133–135
and therapeutic alliance, 16–17, 19
universality of, 136
and use of schemata in cognitive–behavioral therapy, 162
uses of, 137
Trauma, 239
Treatment outcomes. *See* Outcomes
Triggiano, P. J., 294–295
Tronick, E., 63
Truax, P., 36
Trust, 17, 160
Two-person psychology
and closeness/distance dynamics, 83
emergence of, 32–33

Unconditional positive regard, 213. *See also* Positive regard
Unconscious, 136–138
Understanding, 22. *See also* "Feeling understood"

Vagus nerve, 248
Validation, 174, 293, 327
Video feedback, 199, 206

Wachtel, Paul, 337
WAI. *See* Working Alliance Inventory
Warmth of relationship
in cognitive–behavioral therapy, 159–168, 174, 182
and positive regard, 212
Watson, J. C., 248, 330, 346
Weinberger, J., 182
Whipple, K., 160
Winnicott, D. W., 82, 108, 121, 140
Wiseman, H., 64, 86, 98, 322
Within alliance, 261
Wolfe, B. E., 21
Wolpe, J., 161
Working Alliance Inventory (WAI)
assessment of closeness/distance dynamics with, 85, 92–96
and empathy/responsiveness in emotion-focused therapy, 240
and implicit negotiations, 65–66, 72, 74
in research on feeling understood, 111, 115–117, 121
uses of, 345
Working capacity, 22
Working phase, 83

Xiao, H., 327, 345

Yalom, I. D., 226
Yorkston, N. J., 160
Youn, S. J., 327, 345
Young, J. E., 162

Zetzel, E. R., 19
Zilcha-Mano, S., 324, 344, 346
Zysman, S., 139

ABOUT THE EDITORS

Orya Tishby, PsyD, received her master's degree from Hebrew University and doctorate from Rutgers, where she received the 1991 Best Dissertation Award from the New Jersey Psychological Association. She is an associate professor in clinical psychology and clinical social work, Hebrew University of Jerusalem in Israel, and is the former director of the Hebrew University Psychological Services. She is head of the clinical psychology graduate program, and clinical faculty at the School of Social Work and Social Welfare, as well as the director of the Freud Center for Research in Psychoanalysis. Dr. Tishby practices and supervises long- and short-term psychodynamic psychotherapy, and her research focuses on the therapeutic relationship and countertransference. She is coeditor (with Hadas Wiseman) of *The Therapeutic Relationship: Innovative Investigations.*

Hadas Wiseman, PhD, completed her doctorate in clinical psychology at York University, Toronto, Ontario, Canada. She received clinical training at the Clark Institute of Psychiatry, Toronto, and at the Psychological Services at Hebrew University, where she also completed her postdoctorate. She is currently a professor in the Department of Counseling and Human Development, Faculty of Education, at the University of Haifa, Israel, and chair of the doctoral studies committee of the Department of Counseling and Human Development. Dr. Wiseman is also on faculty in the Weiss–Livnat International MA Program in Holocaust Studies, University of Haifa. Her scholarly work and research has focused on psychotherapy process, the therapeutic relationship, attachment and relationship patterns in psychotherapy, personal and professional development of psychotherapists, and intergenerational trauma and interpersonal relationships in families of Holocaust survivors. She served as president of the International Society for Psychotherapy Research. She coauthored (with Jacques P. Barber) *Echoes of the Trauma: Relational Themes and Emotions in Children of Holocaust Survivors* and coedited (with Orya Tishby) *The Therapeutic Relationship: Innovative Investigations*. Dr. Wiseman is a certified clinical psychologist in private practice in Kiryat Tivon, Israel.